BAR

Business Analysis & Reporting

CPA Exam Review

2025
Edition

Permissions

The following items are utilized in this program, and are copyright property of the American Institute of Certified Public Accountants, Inc. (AICPA), all rights reserved:

- Uniform CPA Examination and Questions and Unofficial Answers, Copyright © 1991 – 2025
- Audit and Accounting Guides, Auditing Procedure Studies, Risk Alerts, Statements of Position, and Code of Professional Conduct
- Statements on Auditing Standards
- Statements on Standards for Accounting and Review Services
- Statements on Quality Control Standards
- Statements on Standards for Attestation Engagements
- Accounting Research Bulletins, APB Opinions
- Uniform CPA Examination Blueprints
- Independence Standards Board (ISB) Standards

Portions of various FASB and GASB documents, copyright property of the Financial Accounting Foundation, 401 Merritt 7, PO Box 5116, Norwalk, CT 06856-5116, are utilized with permission. Complete copies of these documents are available from the Financial Accounting Foundation. These selections include the following:

Financial Accounting Standards Board (FASB)

- The FASB Accounting Standards Codification™
- Statements of Financial Accounting Concepts
- FASB Statements, Interpretations, and Technical Bulletins

Governmental Accounting Standards Board (GASB)

- GASB Codification of Governmental Accounting and Financial Reporting Standards and GASB Statements
- GASB Concepts Statements
- GASB Interpretations and Technical Bulletins

Published by UWorld
9111 Cypress Waters Blvd.
Suite 300
Dallas, TX 75019
accounting.uworld.com/cpa-review

Printed in English, in the United States of America.

Acknowledgments

Keeping the course materials updated and accurate would not be possible without the contribution of our team of content experts. Our team includes academics and professionals who have expertise and experience in their respective fields; several have had experience at the Big Four or have PhDs in areas related to the exam. All are passionate about helping candidates pass the exam and about UWorld's dedication to creating the highest quality materials.

Business Analysis & Reporting

Introduction

Introduction

Introduction

How to Best Use Your Course

Welcome to the UWorld CPA Review course! Our expert team is passionate about helping you succeed and has developed an award-winning program that is proven to yield results. Before you get started, please read through this guide on how to best use your course so that you can master all of the topics laid out for you in the AICPA Blueprints and ultimately pass the CPA Exam. At UWorld, our passion is to make the hard stuff easy to learn and understand.

Plan Your Studies

When preparing for the CPA Exam, half the battle is setting yourself up for success with a solid plan from the get go. This includes establishing short- and long-term goals to ensure you're staying on track.

To get started, use the Study Plan in your course. Start your plan by setting the beginning and ending dates for your schedule. Then select your pace (Fast Track vs Customize) and set the number of hours per day you will study. The system will create your plan based on your choices. It is important to follow your plan steadily so that you can ensure you hit your goals. If you miss a day, make it up!

Tip!

Download the app! This gives you access to everything your course offers while on the go.

Master the Concepts through Active Learning

With this program, you will build your foundational knowledge and mastery of core exam topics through **active learning**. This evidence-based learning methodology centers around the principle that students retain information best when they actively participate in answering questions.

- **Begin with the Representative Task.** Read through each representative task carefully. (The Representative Tasks are from the AICPA Blueprints and are presented in our books and videos to guide you through the materials.) Pay particular attention to the words at the beginning of the task; they provide guidance on level and focus
- **Scan the book chapter.** Do you feel confident with the material? If you do, you might want to move directly to the questions and begin to practice. If you find that you are hesitant about an area, read the book or watch the video to solidify your understanding before you practice on some questions
- **Watch the videos.** If you prefer to absorb material on video rather than by reading the book, you will notice that the videos are deliberately set up in small segments. Our team created these segments so you can review what you need, either as part of the whole topic or for specific review of a smaller area
- **Practice the questions.** In our question bank (our QBank) we have taken great care to provide you with very high-quality questions and explanations. Each explanation not only tells you why the concept tested is important to understand but also teaches you why the answer is correct and why the other answer choices are not correct. Images, tables, and links to definitions also help fill in gaps as you use the questions and explanations to learn by doing

Track Your Progress and Performance

As you complete each chapter, track your progress and performance using our signature **SmartPath Predictive Technology™**. SmartPath is a data-driven platform that provides recommended targets based on previous students who have passed the CPA Exam. This is an important tool to help you study efficiently and gauge whether you are *exam-ready*. Your goal is to hit both your progress target (Questions Attempted) and performance target (Score) for each chapter.

As you work through the material, don't worry about hitting your "Score" target right away and focus your efforts on hitting the "Questions Attempted" target first. This approach may feel uncomfortable, but trust that you are building your knowledge as you absorb the answer explanations.

Once you've completed all the topics in a chapter, you can go back and focus your efforts on hitting the "Score" target. If you are falling short, drill down in the Performance tab to see which topics need extra attention.

Tip!

Don't over-study. **SmartPath™** helps determine when you can move on to the next topic.

Solidify the Concepts

Need extra help mastering the concept? Take advantage of the additional learning tools that are integrated into your course. For example, you could be working through a difficult question and find you need further explanation. No problem! There's a link to the supporting lecture right there in the question. Want to remember something for later review? Easily transfer content directly from the question to a digital flashcard. These are just a few ways we make it easy to navigate to and access the right tools you need at the right time.

These additional tools are designed to enhance your studies—**you do not necessarily need to read or watch all of this material!** Rather, use these tools as a means to improve on weak areas:

- **Video Lectures** – From the Lectures tab or directly integrated in the link at the bottom of each practice question, you have access to the profession's most motivating and effective lecturers. Lectures break down difficult topics into simplified concepts and provide helpful memory aids. These are especially recommended for visual and auditory learners
- **Textbooks** – Digital eTextbooks are accessible side by side with the video lectures or in a printed format with some of our course packages. These can be used as a reference if you need further explanation of a concept. Many students also find it beneficial to follow along in the textbook while watching the lectures and either take notes directly in the physical books or by using the Notes feature and highlighting tool in the platform
- **Digital Flashcards** – Create custom flashcards directly from your practice questions by clicking on the lightning bolt symbol. Depending on your program package, your course may also be pre-loaded with an "Expert Deck" of flashcards covering the most heavily tested topics. You can review all your cards in Study Mode or using our **Spaced-Repetition Technology**. This is an evidence-based learning method that presents cards you've marked as *difficult* more frequently and cards you've marked as *easy* less frequently. The spacing of how and when the flashcards are introduced has been proven to increase retention and strengthen memory recall

Get Exam-Ready

The final days leading up to the exam are a critical time in which you're going to want to review your SmartPath data and ask, "Am I *exam-ready*?" If you have hit all the targets, you are in a really good spot. However, if any areas are still marked "Needs Improvement," now is the time to focus your efforts on meeting those targets.

Finally, we recommend you **take at least one full practice exam before exam day** (click on the "Exam Sim" tab in the QBank). This allows you to hone your test-taking skills in an exam-like environment that follows the same 5-testlet, 4-hour structure as the exam.

AICPA Blueprints

The UWorld CPA Review course is based on the AICPA Blueprints, which show candidates what skills and content topics will be tested on the CPA Exam. You don't have to make tough decisions about what concepts to focus on. If you follow our methodology, you will be well on your way to passing the exam.

Let's take a look at what we mean by starting with the AICPA Blueprints. The Blueprints have four levels:

- Area
- Group
- Topic
- Representative Task

Each Representative Task also has a Skill level.

- Remembering & Understanding
- Application
- Analysis
- Evaluation (used only in AUD)

Here is a snapshot of a Blueprint with the levels and skills marked.

Area I – Business Analysis (40–50%)

	Skill				
Content group/topic	**Remembering & Understanding**	**Application**	**Analysis**	**Evaluation**	**Representative Task**
A. Current period/historical analysis, including the use of data					
1. Financial statement analysis		✓			Determine attribute structures, format, and sources of data needed to prepare financial statement analysis.
			✓		Compare current period financial statement accounts to prior periods or budget and explain variances.
			✓		Interpret financial statement fluctuations and ratios (eg, profitability, liquidity, solvency, performance).
			✓		Use outputs (eg, reports, visualizations) from data analytic techniques to identify patterns, trends, and correlations to explain an entity's results.
			✓		Derive the impact of transactions on the financial statements and notes to the financial statements.

BAR
Area I: Business Analysis
Group A: Current Period/Historical Analysis
Topic 1: Financial Statement Analysis

The Table of Contents of the BAR book shows how each UWorld textbook is set up to follow the order of the AICPA Blueprints, with

- Area
- Group
- Topic

Business Analysis & Reporting

In the pages of each book, we provide the Representative Tasks from the AICPA Blueprints. We did that to make a direct connection between the exam and our content. Our team deliberately focused on what the Tasks say and wrote study materials that match with the Task. There is no closer connection between what will be tested and what you are studying.

1.01 Financial Statement Analysis

Overview

A company appraises the past, present, and future execution of goals and economic fitness by performing **financial statement analysis** on its results from operations in a given period. Refer to the financial ratios used in the FAR exam for this section.

The results are viewed in relation to prior periods, budgets, and key performance indicators (ie, benchmarks). Companies **make informed decisions** using this analysis. The analysis is often presented using summaries and visualizations that present the financial data in an easy-to-understand, meaningful report.

Attribute Structures, Format, and Sources of Data

Representative Task (Application): Determine attribute structures, format, and sources of data needed to prepare financial statement analysis.

Beyond connecting to the topics of the AICPA Blueprints, our team also differentiated the textbook content to match the skill levels of the Tasks.

- **Remembering & Understanding** tasks require you to understand the definitions and fundamentals of the topic. We have presented the information in these areas with an eye to creating clear explanations of the topics
- **Application** tasks are more about using your knowledge in scenarios to indicate that you understand the concepts. Our authors have therefore provided examples that show you how to apply your knowledge in specific situations. Many of these examples are similar to questions that you will find on the exam
- **Analysis** tasks require a higher level of thinking, many times leading you to choose one outcome over another or to make a decision. On the exam, these tasks will always be addressed in Task-Based Simulations, or TBSs. The AICPA intentionally makes these more challenging to determine if you really know the material and can work with it as a professional. In our materials, our authors often guide you through the critical thinking required to work with TBSs
- **Evaluation** tasks are only in the AUD section of the exam and are at the highest level of thinking. They go a step further than the Analysis level and require you to evaluate or judge different approaches or outcomes

The CPA Exam

Within the AICPA Blueprints, there is information about how much time candidates have for each section and how many questions by question type each section contains. Question types include Multiple-Choice Questions (MCQs) and Task-Based Simulations (TBSs).

Section	Section Time	Multiple-Choice Questions (MCQs)	Task-Based Simulations (TBSs)
AUD – Core	4 hours	78	7
FAR – Core	4 hours	50	7
REG – Core	4 hours	72	8
BAR – Discipline	4 hours	50	7
ISC – Discipline	4 hours	82	6
TCP – Discipline	4 hours	68	7

Scoring Weight by Exam Section

The AICPA also shows candidates how the question types for each section are weighted and account for their overall score.

	Score Weighting	
Section	**Multiple-Choice Questions (MCQs)**	**Task-Based Simulations (TBSs)**
AUD – Core	50%	50%
FAR – Core	50%	50%
REG – Core	50%	50%
BAR – Discipline	50%	50%
ISC – Discipline	60%	40%
TCP – Discipline	50%	50%

Skill Allocations

As mentioned earlier, each Representative Task is tested at a specific Skill Level, and each part of the exam has its own weighting of the Skill Levels, as seen here.

Section	Remembering & Understanding	Application	Analysis	Evaluation
AUD – Core	30–40%	30–40%	15–25%	5–15%
FAR – Core	5–15%	45–55%	35–45%	–
REG – Core	25–35%	35–45%	25–35%	–
BAR – Discipline	10–20%	45–55%	30–40%	–
ISC – Discipline	55–65%	20–30%	10–20%	–
TCP – Discipline	5–15%	55–65%	25–35%	–

Content Allocations

The AICPA Blueprints address how coverage of the various content areas is allocated in each exam. Using the UWorld system that ties directly to the Blueprint structure, it is easy to see which topics are covered to what extent.

AUD

Content Area		Allocation
Area I	Ethics, Professional Responsibilities, and General Principles	15–25%
Area II	Assessing Risk and Developing a Planned Response	25–35%
Area III	Performing Further Procedures and Obtaining Evidence	30–40%
Area IV	Forming Conclusions and Reporting	10–20%

FAR

Content Area		Allocation
Area I	Financial Reporting	30–40%
Area II	Select Balance Sheet Accounts	30–40%
Area III	Select Transactions	25–35%

REG

Content Area		Allocation
Area I	Ethics, Professional Responsibilities, and Federal Tax Procedures	10–20%
Area II	Business Law	15–25%
Area III	Federal Taxation of Property Transactions	5–15%
Area IV	Federal Taxation of Individuals	22–32%
Area V	Federal Taxation of Entities (including tax preparation)	23–33%

BAR

Content Area		Allocation
Area I	Business Analysis	40–50%
Area II	Technical Accounting and Reporting	35–45%
Area III	State and Local Governments	10–20%

ISC

Content Area		Allocation
Area I	Information Systems and Data Management	35–45%
Area II	Security, Confidentiality, and Privacy	35–45%
Area III	Considerations for System and Organization Controls (SOC) Engagements	15–25%

TCP

Content Area		Allocation
Area I	Tax Compliance and Planning for Individuals and Personal Financial Planning	30–40%
Area II	Entity Tax Compliance	30–40%
Area III	Entity Tax Planning	10–20%
Area IV	Property Transactions (disposition of assets)	10–20%

Exam Testlets

Each section of the exam is divided into five testlets. Two testlets cover MCQs, and three testlets cover TBSs. Not all sections have an equal number of MCQs and TBSs, as the following chart shows.

	Testlet					Total	
	1	2	3	4	5		
Section	MCQ	MCQ	TBS	TBS	TBS	MCQ	TBS
AUD - Core	39	39	2	3	2	78	7
FAR - Core	25	25	2	3	2	50	7
REG - Core	36	36	2	3	3	72	8
BAR - Discipline	25	25	2	3	2	50	7
ISC - Discipline	41	41	1	3	2	82	6
TCP - Discipline	34	34	2	3	2	68	7

Finally, to manage your time effectively in the exam, we recommend that you:

- Use 75 seconds per multiple-choice question as a benchmark,
- Allocate 15-20 minutes per task-based simulation, depending on complexity, and
- Take the standard 15-minute break after the third testlet; it doesn't count against your time.

To see the full AICPA Blueprints, visit https://www.aicpa.org/becomeacpa/cpaexam/examinationcontent

Above all, start the study process with confidence! As Roger always says, "You do not have to be a genius to pass the CPA Exam. If you study, you will pass!" You've got this.

BAR

Area I: Business Analysis

BAR 1

Current Period/Historical Analysis, Including the Use of Data

BAR 1: Current Period/Historical Analysis, Including the Use of Data

1.01 Financial Statement Analysis

Overview

A company appraises the past, present, and future execution of goals and economic fitness by performing **financial statement analysis** on its results from operations in a given period. Refer to the financial ratios used in the FAR exam for this section.

The results are viewed in relation to prior periods, budgets, and key performance indicators (ie, benchmarks). Companies **make informed decisions** using this analysis. The analysis is often presented using summaries and visualizations that present the financial data in an easy-to-understand, meaningful report.

Attribute Structures, Format, and Sources of Data

Representative Task (Application): Determine attribute structures, format, and sources of data needed to prepare financial statement analysis.

Entities generate large volumes of data due to enterprise resource planning (ERP) systems, customer relationship management (CRM) systems, social media use, website-tracking data, and e-commerce transactions. Instead of merely storing information for contractual, operational, reporting, and compliance purposes, this **data can be mined** and analyzed to **identify trends**, enhance insight, and support decision-making.

Not all data and data sources are the same. Depending on the method of extraction and compatibility of different software applications, data may be extracted and loaded in a readily useable format. Structured data that comes from relational databases can normally be transferred between applications by CSV file. However, other types of data, such as unstructured and semi-structured, may need to be transformed prior to analysis.

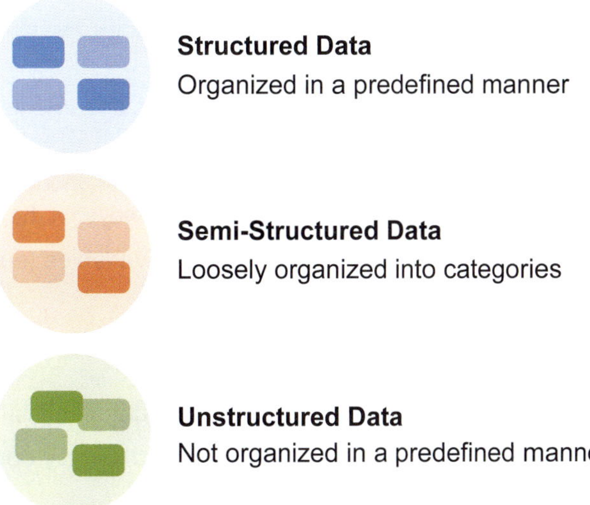

Structured: Data contained in fields within records or files (eg, databases and spreadsheets)

Semi-structured: Data that has information associated (ie, metadata or tags) that makes it easier to process than unstructured data (eg, HTML-tagged text)

Unstructured: Raw data not contained within a database/spreadsheet (eg, text, video, audio, photos, etc.)

Financial data is used to perform financial statement analysis. It is important to understand the data attributes (ie, data characteristics or features) in order to perform the analysis. Data attributes can be qualitative or quantitative.

Qualitative data attributes	Quantitative data attributes
Nominal: names of data	Numeric: measurable quantity
Binary: only two values (Yes/No)	Discrete: finite values (numeric or categorical)
Ordinal: data with a meaningful sequence	Continuous: infinite values

Generally, the data used to perform financial statement analysis comes from an entity's accounting system. The entity's results of operations and financial position are represented with numeric data. Other types of data can be combined with the financial results to generate a meaningful analysis. Examples include the following:

- **Nominal data:** regions, product descriptions, macroeconomic data (eg, GDP, inflation)
- **Binary data:** yes/no fields on information like open invoices, debt covenants met, etc.
- **Ordinal data:** top 10 clients
- **Discrete data:** average sales price for products

Techniques used to extract, transform, and load data in the context of prospective analysis are covered later in BAR. The focus of this section is the analysis of current and historical financial data.

Data Analysis Techniques

The following techniques are used to perform data analysis:

- **Sorting:** A simple categorizing of data in ascending/descending order (eg, largest A/R balance by customer) to identify outliers
- **Cluster analysis:** Grouping data by similarities in a way that shows the structure/relationships between the data
- **Matching:** Comparing data from various sources (eg, electronic documents) to identify unexpected differences
- **Process mining:** Identifying the specific activities to create a process model for achieving a defined goal so that deviations from the model (eg, bottlenecks) can be corrected, with the goal of optimizing processes
- **Comparative analysis:** Comparing the relationships between variables (eg, financial statement items) over two or more periods
- **Trend analysis:** Analyzing changes in data (eg, account balances) over time to look for trends (a type of comparative analysis).
- **Ratio analysis:** Calculating ratios to discover relationships among financial and nonfinancial data
- **Predictive modeling:** Comparing expectations to actual data to identify deviations (eg, reasonableness test).

- **Regression analysis:** Using a statistical analysis to examine the relationship between one or more independent variables (eg, predictors) and a dependent variable
- **Time-series regression analysis:** A regression analysis that uses data from *more than one past period* to make predictions for future periods
- **Cross-sectional regression analysis:** A regression analysis that uses data from *one period of time or a point in time* to make predictions

There are many different software applications (eg, Microsoft Excel, Tableau, Power BI) that perform data analytics. These programs can be used in conjunction with accounting software (eg, QuickBooks, Sage Intacct) to report the financial results of a company using visualizations showing relationships between financial and nonfinancial data.

Comparison of Current Period Results to Prior Periods or Budget

Representative Task (Analysis): Compare current period financial statement accounts to prior periods or budget and explain variances.

A company compares current-period financial statement accounts to prior-period or budgeted amounts as a way to provide context for current-period performance. **Variances** are used to identify and investigate areas where the actual results were over or under the amounts being compared. Variances are either **favorable** (ie, positive) or **unfavorable** (ie, negative).

A favorable variance is the result of **actual performance being better** than the amounts compared. This type of analysis can be performed monthly, quarterly, annually, or even for longer periods of time.

Once the variance is determined, the reasons for the **difference are investigated**. Understanding budget variances can also improve **forecasting** results. For example, a company might have seasonal fluctuations in sales. By comparing current results to prior periods, the company can confirm this pattern and adjust staffing and expenses accordingly.

A toy company is comparing monthly revenue for the past three years. Sales tend to increase in the last quarter of the year for holiday shopping. The company launched a marketing campaign in August of Year 3 in an attempt to increase sales.

By comparing the monthly revenue results, the company can easily see the seasonality of its sales as well as the effectiveness of the marketing campaign.

Monthly Revenue Comparison

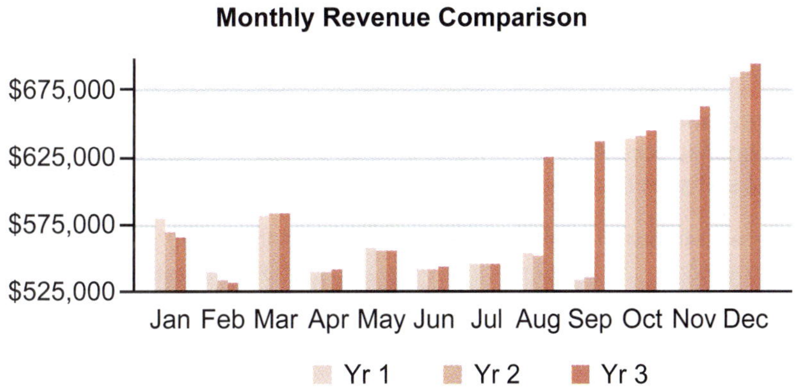

A service company compares budgeted expenses to actual results each period. The variances are identified, and significant variances are investigated. Positive variances (ie, actual expense is less than budget) are flagged with green, and negative variances (ie, actual expense is greater than budget) are flagged with red.

In this example, overall expenses were $6,011 more than budgeted. However, that only shows part of the picture. A comparison of each expense line shows the following:

- Marketing and personnel costs were higher than expected
- Legal and other general and administrative expenses were lower than expected

These differences should be investigated.

Expenses:	Budget	Actual	Variance
Personnel			
Contract	$ 17,843	17,402 •	(441)
In-house	67, 435	71,094 •	3,569
Benefits	6,329	8,985 •	2,656
Sales & marketing			
Services	5,900	12,565 •	6,665
Marketing collateral	500	1,963 •	1,463
Technology	8,000	9,035 •	1,035
Legal & professional	12,000	6,587 •	(5,413)
Occupancy	3,000	2,490 •	(510)
Other office G&A	2,500	83 •	(2,417)
Interest expense	5,000	4,305 •	(695)
Amortization	1,600	1,609 •	9
Total expenses	$ 130,107	136,118 •	6,011

Financial Statement Fluctuations and Ratios

Representative Task (Analysis): Interpret financial statement fluctuations and ratios.

Ratio Analysis

Ratio analysis entails reviewing a company's liquidity, activity, leverage, profitability, and coverage ratios. Detecting important economic connections between different ratios is crucial in making economic decisions; the ratios alone are just statistics regarding a company's performance.

A company can compare its financial ratios internally over different time periods, with competitor ratios, or in relation to industry averages to benchmark performance. This comparison provides insight that management can use to determine the company's strategy going forward. The ratios are also used by investors and lenders in assessing the company's health.

Ratio Analysis Limitations

Companies use ratios to analyze and assess financial performance or position. Although ratio analysis may provide useful insight, it also comes with limitations:

- **Heterogeneity in operation:** If the company's divisions individually operate in distinct industries, then combining performance may oversimplify data at an aggregate level and not provide insight into divisional performance
- **Inconsistent interpretation of results:** Different ratios may provide conflicting interpretations of performance for the same company. For example, one ratio can suggest improving liquidity, whereas another ratio can suggest worsening liquidity
- **Need for judgment:** Companies must determine whether ratios are reliable in the context of industry and company history. Ratios are statistical measures with no inherent value and alone are incomplete; it is the company's interpretation that creates insight
- **Different accounting standards:** Differences in accounting methods or standards limit the comparability of ratios across companies. For example, one company may use FIFO inventory reporting, whereas another company uses LIFO inventory reporting

Effects of Changes on Ratios

It's important to understand how changes to financial statement accounts can impact ratios.

- The **numerator** has a **direct relationship** with the ratio; increases to the numerator result in an increased ratio
- The **denominator** has an **inverse relationship** with the ratio; increases to the denominator result in a decreased ratio
- If the numerator and the denominator are both impacted by a change, the impact to the ratio may not be easy to determine; substitute numbers into the ratio to see the impact of the change in this instance

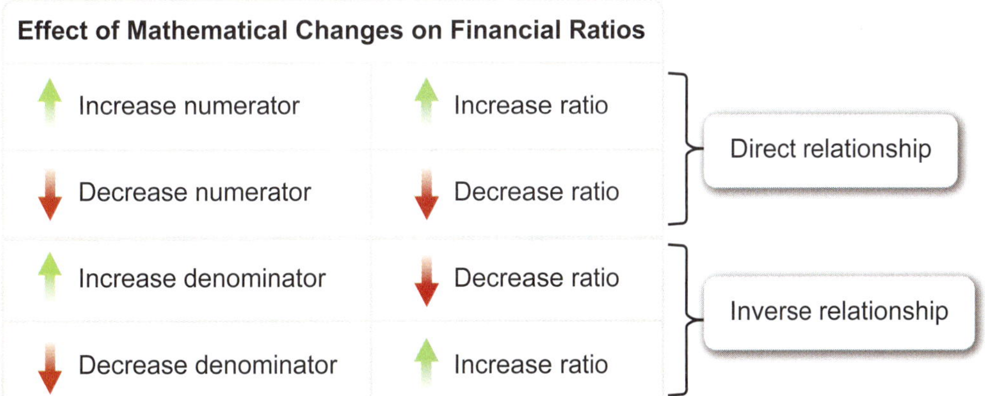

The following information pertains to Ali Corp. as of and for the year ended December 31, Year 1:

Liabilities	$60,000
Stockholders' equity	$500,000
Net income	$30,000
Shares of common stock issued and outstanding	10,000

During Year 1, Ali's officers exercised stock options for 1,000 shares of stock at an option price of $8 per share. This transaction is reflected in the above balances. Determine the effect of exercising the stock options on the following ratios:

- Debt to equity
- Asset turnover
- Earnings per share

Remember, when stock options are exercised, additional shares of stock are issued. The original equity related to the options is reclassified to common stock at par value and APIC. Assets (cash) and common shares outstanding increase.

For the following ratios, the denominator increases from exercising stock options, causing the ratios to decrease.

- **Debt to equity** (Total debt / Stockholders' equity): Debt of $60,000 (numerator) is unchanged, but equity (denominator) increases to $500,000. This results in a decreased ratio
- **Asset turnover ratio** (Net sales / Average total assets): Net sales (numerator) is unchanged, but average total assets (denominator) increase by the cash received. Therefore, the ratio decreases
- **Earnings per share** ([Net income − Preferred dividends] / Weighted shares outstanding): Net income is decreased when compensation expense is recognized, not when the options are exercised. The weighted number of shares outstanding (denominator) increases from 9,000 to 10,000 shares. EPS therefore decreases

Analyzing Company Results

Let's look at the financial results of a company to perform financial statement analysis and **interpret the results**.

StickU is a health care company that provides specialized medical equipment to hospitals and health care facilities. StickU's Year 2 and Year 3 balance sheet, income statement, and condensed statement of cash flows are used for all ratio calculations. Here is some additional information:

- StickU began operations on January 2, Year 1, as a corporation by issuing 10,000, $1 par value shares of common stock. There is no preferred stock. No dividends have been declared or paid
- All sales are on credit
- StickU uses the LIFO inventory method
- In Year 2, StickU recognized other income from the government Paycheck Protection Program loan forgiveness
- StickU is a small company that has elected to amortize goodwill over 10 years
- StickU's largest supply vendor has 60-day payment terms and does not offer incentives for early payments
- For the purposes of average calculations used in certain ratios, assume the following Year 1 ending balances: A/R $652,786, Inventory $172,359, Total assets $1,784,358, Current liabilities $872,634, Total equity (Common stock + APIC + Retained earnings + Net income) ($607,397)
- StickU uses 365 days for all relevant calculations

StickU
Balance Sheet

	Year 2	Year 3	Initial Observations
Current assets:			
Cash and cash equivalents	404,359	175,736	
Accounts receivable, net	788,972	865,936	Current assets decreased. Decline in cash is the main driver.
Inventory	199,703	252,118	
Prepaid expenses	26,751	46,618	
Other receivables	101,642	129,149	
Total current assets	1,521,409	1,469,557	
Fixed assets:			Fixed assets and intangible assets increased. StickU is making investments into the business.
Property, plant, and equipment	902,173	1,304,361	
Less: Accumulated depreciation	(782,457)	(956,102)	
Total fixed assets	119,715	348,259	
Intangible assets:			
Goodwill	339,548	339,548	
ROU asset for office space lease	–	44,243	New office space lease in Year 3.
Internally developed software	15,000	85,815	
Less: Accumulated amortization	(30,563)	(49,867)	
Total intangible assets	323,985	419,739	
Total assets	**1,965,109**	**2,237,556**	
Current liabilities:			
Accounts payable	615,294	848,733	Current liabilities increased slightly. Large increase in A/P offset by decreases in accrued liabilities.
Notes payable	52,798	19,357	
Accrued and other liabilities	263,573	84,558	
Total current liabilities	931,665	952,647	
Long-term liabilities:			
Notes payable	1,173,815	1,049,201	
Total liabilities	2,105,480	2,001,849	
Stockholders' equity:			
Common stock ($10,000 shares at $1 par)	10,000	10,000	Retained earnings deficit decreased due to Year 2 net income. Therefore, the overall equity position improved from Year 2 to Year 3.
Additional paid-in capital	40,000	40,000	
Retained earnings	(657,397)	(190,371)	
Net income	467,026	376,079	
Total liabilities and equity	**1,965,109**	**2,237,556**	

StickU

Income statement for year ended	Year 2	Year 3	Initial Observations
Sales	5,847,407	7,280,893	Sales and COGS increased, but gross profit decreased. Costs are increasing at a higher rate than sales.
Costs of goods sold	3,915,498	5,408,988	
Gross profit	1,931,909	1,871,905	
Operating expenses	1,207,545	1,144,049	
Interest expense	101,532	64,549	
Depreciation and amortization	287,228	287,228	
Total expenses	1,596,305	1,495,826	
Operating income	335,605	376,079	Year over year operating income increased.
Other income	131,421	-	
Net income before taxes	**467,026**	**376,079**	

StickU
Condensed Statement of cash flows

	Year 2	Year 3	Initial Observations
Operating activities			
Net income	467,026	376,079	
Net adjustments to reconcile net income	(195,228)	(155,790)	Use of cash for investing activities increased.
Cash provided by Operating activities	271,798	220,289	
Investing activities	(115,412)	(324,289)	
Financing activities	223,491	(124,614)	Repayments of debt impacted financing activities. This corresponds with the decrease in notes payable on the balance sheet.
Net cash increase for period	379,877	(228,623)	
Cash balance, beginning	24,482	404,359	
Cash balance, ending	**404,359**	**175,736**	

Using StickU's financial ratios provides more insight into business operations. Without the ratio analysis, a quick review shows that StickU's total assets and equity increased. StickU is making investments into the business in PP&E and internally developed software.

Let's look deeper into StickU's financial picture by calculating the common financial ratios and interpreting the results.

Liquidity: What is StickU's short-term ability to pay its obligations?

Ratio	Formula	Year 2		Year 3	
Working capital	Current assets – Current liabilities	$1,521,409 – $931,665 = $589,744		$1,469,557 – $952,647 = $516,910	
Current ratio	Current assets / Current liabilities	$1,521,409 / $931,665	= 1.63	$1,469,557 / $952,647	= 1.54
Quick ratio	(Cash + Marketable Securities + Net receivables) / = Current liabilities	($404,359 + $788,972) / $931,665	= 1.28	($175,736 + $865,936) / $952,647	= 1.09

Current and quick ratios are greater than 1.0, indicating that StickU *can meet* short-term obligations. Working capital is positive in both years.

However, all liquidity measures declined in Year 3. A/P increased, and cash decreased significantly. Because StickU is a young company, the decrease in cash is probably due to reinvesting resources into the business. However, the decline in liquidity ratios leads to questions such as the following:

- How much leverage is StickU using to grow business?
- What happens if sales decline? Can the company keep up with borrowing costs?

Activity: How effectively is StickU using assets?

Ratio	Formula	Year 2		Year 3	
Receivables turnover	Net credit sales / Average net receivables	$5,847,407 / (($652,786 + $788,972) / 2)	= 8.11	$7,280,893 / (($788,972 + $865,936) / 2)	= 8.80
# Days' sales in receivables	365 days / Receivables turnover	365 days / 8.11	= 45.00 days	365 days / 8.80	= 41.48 days
Inventory turnover	Cost of goods sold / Average inventory	$3,915,498 / (($172,359 + $199,703) / 2)	= 21.05	$5,408,988 / (($199,703 + $252,118) / 2)	= 23.94
# Days' supply in inventory	365 days / Inventory turnover	365 days / 21.05	= 17.34 days	365 days / 23.94	= 15.24 days
Asset turnover	Net sales / Average total assets	$5,847,407 / (($1,784,358 + 1,965,109) / 2)	= 3.12	$7,280,893 / (($1,965,109 + $2,237,556) / 2)	= 3.46
Operating cycle	# Days' sales in receivables + # Days' supply in inventory	45.00 + 17.34	= 62.34 days	41.48 + 15.24	= 56.73 days
Days payables outstanding	Ending A/P / (COGS / 365)	$615,294 / ($3,915,498 / 365)	= 57.36 days	$848,733 / ($5,408,988 / 365)	= 57.27 days
Cash conversion cycle	Operating cycle – Days payables outstanding	62.34 – 57.36	= 4.98 days	56.73 – 57.27 days	= (0.55) days

For both years, the number of days that payables are outstanding is slightly less than 60 days. This correlates with StickU's largest supplies vendor's 60-day payment terms. Receivable collection days have improved (ie, decreased), and inventory turnover has increased, resulting in shortened operating and cash-conversion cycles from Year 2 to Year 3.

This shows that StickU is becoming more efficient with cash and inventory to manage operations.

Coverage: How protected are StickU's creditors?

Ratio	Formula	Year 2		Year 3	
Debt to equity	Total debt / Total equity	$2,105,480 / ($140,371)	= (15.00)	$2,001,849 / $235,707	= 8.49
Debt to total assets	Total debt / Total assets	$2,105,480 / $1,965,109	= 1.07	$2,001,849 / $2,237,556	= 0.89
Times interest earned*	Income before interest and taxes / Interest expense	$467,026 + 101,532 / $101,532	= 5.60	$376,079 + $64,549 / $64,549	= 6.83
Current cash debt coverage ratio	Cash provided by operating activities / Average current liabilities	$271,798 / ($872,634 + 931,665)/2	= 0.30	$220,289 / ($931,665 + $952,647)/2	= 0.23

** Note: Interest expense is added back to net income for this ratio, because net income includes a reduction for interest expense.*

StickU's debt to total assets is high. In Year 3, this ratio was 0.89, down from 1.07 in Year 2, indicating that most of the assets are financed by creditors. This confirms that StickU uses leverage in the business.

Equity has improved from Year 2 to Year 3. While StickU's debt is concerning, the business seems to be operationally improving.

Profitability: How successful are StickU's operations?

Ratio	Formula	Year 2		Year 3	
Profit margin	Net income / Net sales	$467,026 / $5,847,407	= 7.99%	$376,079 / $7,280,893	= 5.17%
Gross profit percentage	Gross profit / Net sales	$1,931,909 / $5,847,407	= 33.04%	$1,871,905 / $7,280,893	= 25.71%
Return on assets	Net income / Average total assets	$467,026 / ($1,784,358 + $1,965,109) / 2	= 24.91%	$376,079 / ($1,965,109 + $2,237,556) / 2	= 17.90%
Return on total assets	Net income + Interest expense / Average total assets	$467,026 + $101,532 / ($1,784,358 + $1,965,109) / 2	= 30.33%	$376,079 + $64,549 / ($1,965,109 + $2,237,556) / 2	= 20.97%

Gross profit, profit margin, and return on assets are all down in Year 3. In Year 3, COGS increased more than the increase in sales, leading to reduced profitability. StickU uses LIFO to account for inventory. When prices increase, this reduces profitability, because COGS is higher (ie, most recent units purchased and sold are the most expensive) than with other inventory methods. The balance in inventory increased in Year 3. The cost of inventory may be rising with StickU's main supplier, or health care costs in general are rising.

Management should investigate how overall health care costs are impacting the business. As sales and related inventory increase, StickU should explore options to diversify suppliers or renegotiate volume discounts with the current supplier to reduce costs.

If the $131,421 in other income reported in Year 2 is removed from net income, the resulting profit margin is 5.74%, which is similar to the profit margin in Year 3.

StickU's financial ratios provide a more complete picture of its financial results. As a young business, it makes sense that StickU is using debt to grow the business. StickU could compare its financial results to industry or competitor information, if available, to provide more context.

Data Reports and Visualizations to Explain an Entity's Results

Representative Task (Analysis): Use outputs (e.g., reports, visualizations) from data analytic techniques to identify patterns, trends, and correlations to explain an entity's results.

An entity's financial results can be represented in many ways to generate meaningful insights and make business decisions. As discussed earlier in the chapter, there are several different types of data analytic techniques that StickU can use to interpret its financial results and attempt to learn more about the drivers of the business. Let's look at how StickU uses these techniques to improve decision-making.

Sorting: StickU divides the business into four segments, North, South, East, and West. Sorting can be used to report StickU's Year 3 revenues in descending order by segment:

Year 3 Revenue by Segment

North	$3,208,593
South	2,257,077
West	1,310,561
East	509,662
Total	$7,280,893

Revenue by Segment

18%
7%
44%
31%
North
South
East
West

Another way to view StickU's Year 3 sorted revenue by segment is using a data visualization. The donut chart represents the same data but is much easier to understand quickly.

Cluster analysis: StickU wants to understand its customer base and target its marketing strategy for the sales team. Hospitals are StickU's typical customer. However, there are several different kinds of hospitals (eg, long-term care facilities, emergency and outpatient hospitals, and surgical hospitals).

StickU performed a **cluster analysis** for revenue over the past year to see how **specific types** of hospitals **made up its sales**. StickU looked at the number of transactions and the revenue per transaction grouped by long-term care facilities, emergency and outpatient facilities, and surgical hospitals.

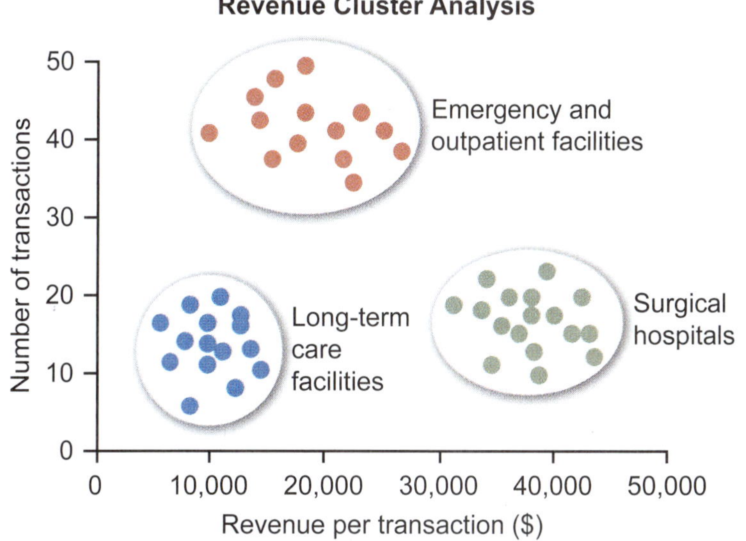

The cluster analysis shows that surgical hospitals have a low volume of transactions that yield a higher amount of revenue per transaction.

The results help the sales team focus sales efforts on surgical hospitals (low volume and high revenue) and away from long-term care facilities (low volume and low revenue).

Matching: StickU is concerned that it might have duplicate customer records in its database. New customers are added by the call center. The accounting department sends out invoices based on those records but has found instances when customer information entered with a slightly different name creates a new customer record. The accounts receivable reports show each customer's balance separately.

StickU has the following customer balances reported on the accounts receivable aging report at the end of Year 2:

Customer	1-30 days	31-60 days
Capetown Hospital	23,720	
Cape Town Hospital		12,327

StickU uses data matching to identify duplicate records and merge customer data. The analysis results in several customer records requiring corrections.

In this instance, the only difference between the two customers is the spacing in the name. StickU will confirm the correct name and merge the two customer records. After the data is corrected, StickU puts a process in place that requires the call center to check existing customer records before adding a new customer.

Process mining: StickU's management has noticed that it takes approximately two weeks for a customer to be invoiced for orders. StickU would like to reduce this time by at least one week as a way to speed up customer payments and improve cash flow.

StickU uses process mining to **identify all the activities** involved from when the customer places an order until the invoice is generated, on the basis of the **activity logs** from each step of the process. From there, StickU creates a **process model** for optimized results.

When implementing the new process, StickU discovered there was a bottleneck in the accounting department. The orders are manually matched to shipping confirmations before an invoice is generated. The analysis allowed StickU to adjust its process, resulting in faster invoicing and increased cash flow.

Comparative and trend analysis: A simple report from the accounting system can be used to show balances, changes from period to period, and trends. The financial data can also be reported using horizontal and vertical analysis.

- **Horizontal analysis** measures the dollar and percentage **change over a period of time**. This is useful in discovering trends and material changes in the business
- **Vertical analysis** (ie, common sizing) reports financial **data** expressed as a **percentage of a common number** (eg, income statement items as a percentage of revenue, balance sheet items as a percentage of total assets). Vertical analysis helps with comparisons with other companies using percentages instead of actual dollar amounts

StickU's balance sheet can be reported using horizontal and vertical analysis to provide more insight into the results.

The *vertical analysis* displays StickU's results as a percentage of total assets each year. This quickly shows the composition of assets and liabilities as well as how they changed from year to year.

The *horizontal analysis* reports StickU's dollar and percentage change of financial results from Year 2 to Year 3. This analysis quickly shows increases in total assets, PP&E, and A/P as well as decreases in cash and net income, reinforcing the ratio analysis done previously.

StickU Balance Sheet					Horizontal Analysis	
	Year 2	Year 2% of total assets	Year 3	Year 3% of total assets	Dollar change	Percentage change
Current assets:						
Cash and cash equivalents	404,359	21%	175,736	8%	(228,623)	-57%
Accounts receivable, net	788,972	40%	865,936	39%	76,963	10%
Inventory	199,703	10%	252,118	11%	52,415	26%
Prepaid expenses	26,751	1%	46,618	2%	19,868	74%
Other receivables	101,642	5%	129,149	6%	27,525	27%
Total current assets	1,521,409	77%	1,469,557	66%	(51,851)	-3%
Fixed assets:						
Property, plant, and equipment	902,173	46%	1,304,361	58%	402,189	45%
Less: Accumulated depreciation	(782,457)	-40%	(956,102)	-43%	(173,645)	22%
Total fixed assets	119,715	6%	348,259	16%	228,544	191%
Intangible assets:						
Goodwill	339,548	17%	339,548	15%	–	0%
ROU asset for office space lease	–	0%	44,243	2%	44,243	100%
Internally developed software	15,000	1%	85,815	4%	70,815	472%
Less: Accumulated amortization	(30,563)	-2%	(49,867)	21%	(19,303)	21%
Total intangible assets	323,985	14%	369,739	17%	95,754	35%
Total assets	**1,965,109**	**100%**	**2,237,556**	**100%**	**272,447**	**14%**
Current liabilities:						
Accounts payable	615,294	31%	848,733	38%	233,439	38%
Notes payable	52,798	3%	19,357	1%	(33,441)	-63%
Accrued and other liabilities	263,573	13%	84,558	4%	(179,016)	-68%
Total current liabilities	931,665	47%	952,647	43%	20,982	2%
Long-term liabilities:						
Notes payable	1,173,815	60%	1,049,201	47%	(124,614)	-11%
Total liabilities	2,105,480	107%	2,001,849	89%	(103,632)	21%
Stockholders' equity:						
Common stock ($10,000 shares at $1 par)	10,000	1%	10,000	0%	–	0%
Additional paid-in capital	40,000	2%	40,000	2%	–	0%
Retained earnings	(657,397)	-33%	(190,371)	-9%	467,026	-71%
Net income	467,026	24%	376,079	17%	(90,947)	21%
Total liabilities and equity	1,965,109	100%	2,237,556	100%	272,447	14%

Data visualizations can be used to show trends and relationships in financial data. StickU reports some of its *semiannual* key balances and ratios using charts next to the current-period results to graphically show prior-period balances as *monthly data trends.*

The "Key Balances" image shows the dollar amount and the monthly trend (in the bar chart) for certain accounts. "Cash & Working Capital" shows the dollar amount or ratio and a trend line. Insights provided by these images include the following:

- The changes in the cash balance over time appear to be directly related to the changes in the receivables balances
- When cash balances in a period are lower, payables and credit card balances are higher

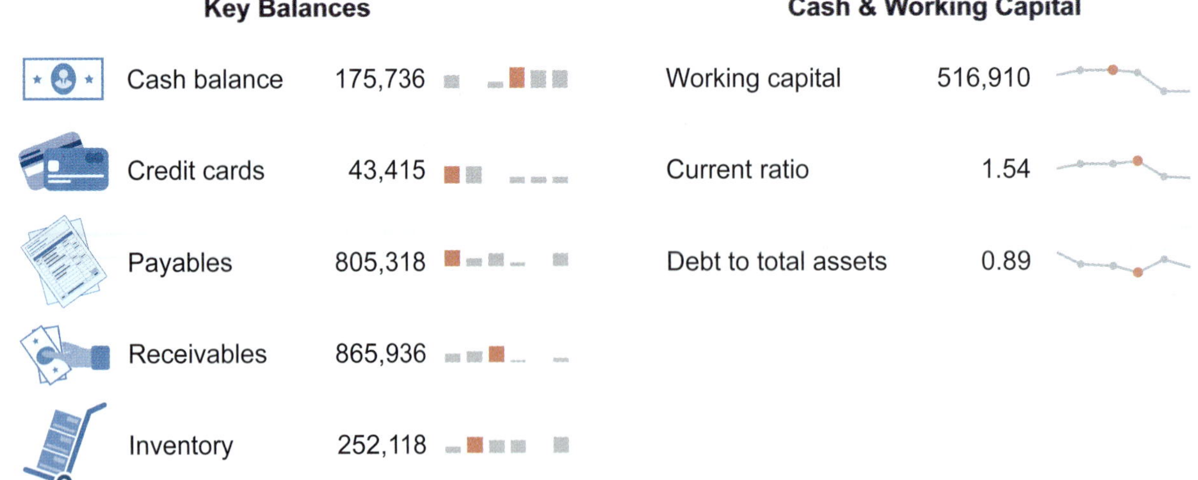

Regression analysis: Data visualizations can also be used to combine financial and nonfinancial results to help identify connections between financial results and economic factors. StickU is a health care company, and activity levels appear to be impacted by COVID-19 hospitalizations.

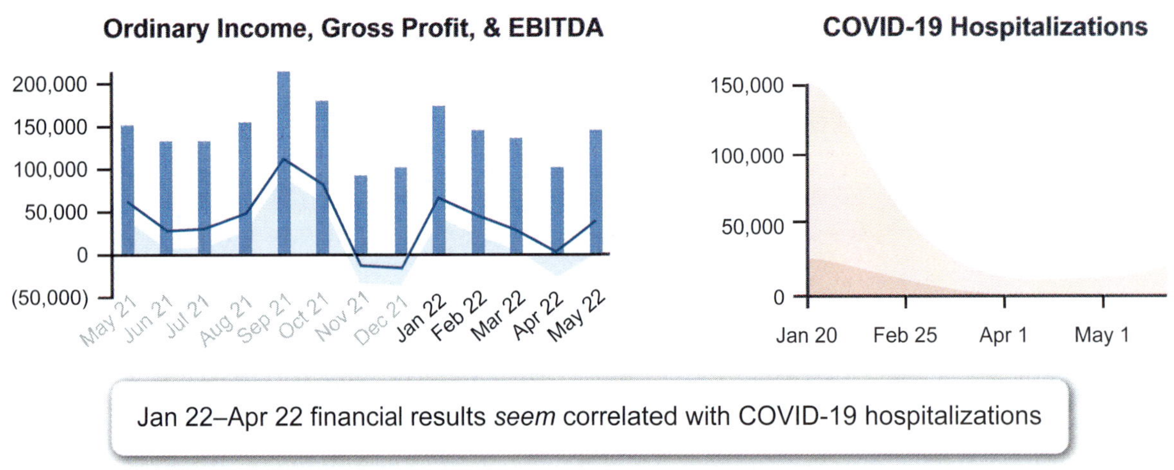

The financial results showing ordinary income, gross profit, and EBITA compared with US hospitalizations from COVID-19 (the chart on the right from an external source) indicate that there may be correlation between the two. StickU would like to analyze the data to determine if COVID-19 hospitalizations were a driver of its sales activity.

Regression analysis is used to estimate the relationship between a set of variables. In this case, StickU's sales are the **dependent variable** (ie, the outcome StickU wants to predict), and COVID-19 hospitalizations are the **independent variable** (ie, the factor that has an impact on the dependent variable). Regression analysis produces the following outputs:

- **Goodness of fit:** How well does the linear regression equation fit the data? For a basic linear regression, these outputs are the most important

Regression analysis: goodness of fit outputs	
Multiple R	**Correlation coefficient** that measures the direction and strength of the linear relationship between two variables; it can range from −1 (perfectly negative correlation) to 1 (perfectly positive correlation)
R squared	Measures the proportion of the change in the **dependent variable** (Y) **explained** by changes in the **independent variable**; it is a relative measure that ranges from 0 to 1, and the closer to 1, the better the regression explains Y
Adjusted R squared	Adjusts for the number of terms in a model and should be used if there is *more than one independent variable* (X)
Standard error	Refers to the **precision** of the regression coefficient (ie, how spread out the Y variables are around the mean)
Observations	Number of observations in the sample

- **ANOVA (Analysis of variance):** These outputs split the sum of squares used in the analysis into individual components
- **Regression coefficients:** These outputs provide specific information about the inputs of the analysis:
  - T-statistic: A higher value is evidence that the results are significantly different from the average results and vice versa
  - P-value: A higher value (ie, greater than 5%) indicates that the results are probably happening by chance
  - Generates the following linear regression equation:

Dependent variable (Y) = [slope × Independent variable (X)] + Intercept

StickU performed a regression analysis to determine the relationship between the average monthly COVID-19 hospitalizations and monthly sales data from January 2020 through May 2022. The summary output from the analysis shows the following results:

Summary Output

Regression Statistics	
Multiple R	0.382657845
R Square	0.146427027
Adjusted R Square	0.114813213
Standard Error	81500.36434
Observations	29

Anova

	df	SS	MS	F	Significance F
Regression	1	30765462819	30765462819	4.631741918	0.040486442
Residual	27	1.79342E+11	6642309387		
Total	28	2.10108E+11			

	Coefficients	Standard Error	t Stat	P-value	Lower 95%	Upper 95%	Lower 95.0%	Upper 95.0%
Intercept	489134.0243	25991.99214	18.81864313	4.74031E-17	435802.8616	542465.1869	435802.8616	542465.1869
COVID-19 rates	4364.1764	2027.823353	2.15214821	0.040486442	203.4265616	8524.926238	203.4265616	8524.926238

Based on the results of the regression analysis, there doesn't appear to be a strong relationship between average monthly COVID-19 hospitalizations and sales.

- Multiple R = 0.382 (rounded) indicates a slightly positive correlation
- R Square = 0.146 (rounded) is not close to 1, indicating that the change in sales is not explained by the change in COVID-19 hospitalizations
- Linear regression equation generated from the analysis: Sales = 4364.2X + 489134

Another way to show the regression analysis is graphically:

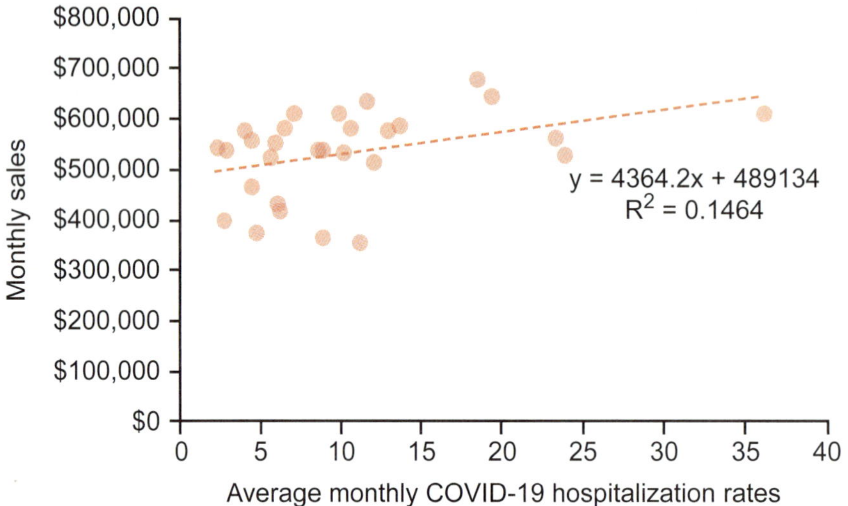

On the basis of the results of the regression analysis, StickU's monthly sales do not appear to be driven by average monthly COVID-19 hospitalization rates.

Derive the Impact of Transactions on Financial Statements

Representative Task (Analysis): Derive the impact of transactions on the financial statements and notes to the financial statements.

Let's continue using StickU's Year 3 financial results to understand the impact of the following transactions on the financial statements and notes to the financial statements.

Assume that StickU signs a contract in Year 3 to be the exclusive supplier for the region's largest hospital system. The contract guarantees a minimum purchase of 100,000 units annually for the next three years at $25 per unit.

- StickU's additional annual revenue is $2,500,000 (100,000 units × $25 per unit)
- StickU contracts with its main supplier to purchase the additional units for $17 each, resulting in annual COGS of $1,700,000 (100,000 units × $17 per unit)
- Operating expenses increased 20%, resulting from the increased sales
- With the additional net income from the contract, in Year 3, StickU makes $300,000 payment on the long-term note payable at the end of the year, increases inventory on hand from $252,118 to $350,000, and reduces accounts payable from $848,733 to $675,425

What is the impact of the new contract and related transactions on StickU's Year 3 results? We can use the analysis toolbox and apply it to our company data.

The toolbox helps to focus the analysis on these four questions:

What are you trying to find out?

First, we need to include the new contract and related transactions in StickU's Year 3 results. Then we need to update the appropriate financial ratios to determine the impact of the transactions on StickU's financial condition.

What data do you have?

Impact on income statement:

- Sales increased by $2,500,000
- COGS increased by $1,700,000
- Operating expenses increased by 20% to $1,372,859 ($1,144,049 × 1.20); total increase in operating expenses is $228,810 ($1,372,859 – $1,144,049)
- Resulting increase to net income is $571,190 ($2,500,000 – $1,700,000 – $228,810)

StickU

Income statement for the year ended	Year 3 original results	Year 3 results including new contract	Change
Sales	7,280,893	9,780,893	2,500,000
Cost of goods sold	5,408,988	7,108,988	1,700,000
Gross profit	1,871,905	2,671,905	800,000
Operating expenses	1,144,049	1,372,859	22,810
Interest expense	64,549	64,549	–
Depreciation and amortization	287,228	287,228	–
Total expenses	1,495,826	1,724,636	228,810
Other income	–	–	–
Net income before taxes	**376,079**	**947,269**	**571,190**

Impact on balance sheet:

- Current assets and total assets: Inventory balance increased to $350,000; change = $97,882 ($350,000 − $252,118)
- Current liabilities: Accounts payable balance decreased to $675,425; change = $173,308 ($848,733 − $675,425)
- Long-term liabilities: Payment on long-term note payable of $300,000 reduces balance to $749,201 ($1,049,201 − $300,000); because the additional payment is made at the end of the year, Year 3 interest expense does not change
- Equity: Net income increased by $571,190 to $947,269

StickU
Balance Sheet

	Year 3 original results	Year 3 results including new contract	Change
Current assets:			
Cash and cash equivalents	175,736	175,736	–
Accounts receivable, net	865,936	865,936	–
Inventory	252,118	350,000	97,882
Prepaid expenses	46,618	46,618	–
Other receivables	129,149	129,149	–
Total current assets	1,469,557	1,567,439	97,882
Fixed assets:			
Property, plant, and equipment	1,305,361	1,304,361	–
Less: Accumulated depreciation	(956,102)	(956,102)	–
Total fixed assets	348,259	348,259	–
Intangible assets:			
Goodwill	339,548	339,548	–
ROU assets for office space lease	44,243	44,243	–
Internally developed software	85,815	85,815	–
Less: Accumulated amortization	49,867	49,867	–
Total intangible assets	419,739	419,739	–
Total assets	**2,237,556**	**2,335,438**	**97,882**
Current liabilities:			
Accounts payable	848,733	675,425	(173,308)
Notes payable	19,357	19,357	–
Accrued and other liabilities	84,558	848,558	–
Total current liabilities	952,647	779,339	(173,308)
Long-term liabilities:			
Notes payable	1,049,201	749,201	(300,000)
Total liabilities:	2,001,849	1,528,541	(473,308)

StickU
Balance Sheet

	Year 3 original results	Year 3 results including new contract	Change
Stockholders' equity:			
Common stock (10,000 shares at $1 par)	10,000	10,000	–
Additional paid-in capital	40,000	40,000	–
Retained earnings	(190,371)	(190,371)	–
Net income	376,079	947,269	376,079
Total liabilities and equity	**2,237,556**	**2,335,438**	**97,882**

Impact on statement of cash flows:

- Operating activities: Cash provided by operating activities increased by $300,000
  - Net income *increased* by $571,190
  - *Cash used* for operating activities increased by $271,190 ($97,882 inventory increase + $173,308 accounts payable decrease)
- Financing activities: *Cash used* for financing activities *increased* by $300,000 payment on long-termnote payable

StickU
Condensed Statement of cash flows

	Year 3 original results	Year 3 results including new contract	Change
Operating activities			
Net income	376,079	947,269	571,190
Net adjustments to reconcile net income	(155,790)	(426,980)	(271,190)
Cash provided by operating activities	220,289	520,289	300,000
Investing activities	(324,298)	(324,289)	–
Financing activities	(124,614)	(424,614)	(300,000)
Net cash increase for period	(228,623)	(228,623)	–
Cash balance, beginning	404,359	404,359	–
Cash balance, ending	**175,736**	**175,736**	**(0)**

What data do you need?

Determine the ratios impacted by the changes.

Liquidity:

Ratio	Formula	Original Year 3		Updated Year 3	
Working capital	Current assets – Current liabilities	$1,469,557 – $952,647	=$516,910	$1,567,439 – $779,339	=$788,100
Current ratio	Current assets / Current liabilities	$1,469,557 / $952,647	=1.54	$1,567,439 / $779,339	=2.01
Quick ratio	(Cash + Marketable Securities + Net receivables) / = Current liabilities	$175,736 + $865,936 / $952,647	=1.09	$175,736 + $865,936 / $779,339	=1.34

Activity:

Ratio	Formula	Original Year 3		Updated Year 3	
Receivables turnover	Net credit sales / Average net receivables	$7,280,893 / ($788,972 + $865,936) / 2	=8.80	$9,780,893 / ($788,972 + $865,936) / 2	=11.82
# Days' sales in receivables	365 days / Receivables turnover	365 days / 8.80	=41.48 days	365 days / 11.82	=30.88 days
Inventory turnover	Cost of goods sold / Average inventory	$5,408,988 / ($199,703 + $252,118) / 2	=23.94	$7,108,988 / ($199,703 + $350,000) / 2	=25.86
# Days' supply in inventory	365 days / Inventory turnover	365 days / 23.94	=15.24 days	365 days / 25.86	=14.11 days
Asset turnover	Net sales / Average total assets	$7,280,893 / ($1,965,109 + $2,237,556) / 2	=3.46	$9,780,893 / ($1,965,109 + $2,335,438) / 2	=4.55
Operating cycle	# Days' sales in receivables + # Days' supply in inventory	41.48 + 15.24	=56.73 days	30.88 + 14.11	=44.99 days
Days payables outstanding	Ending A/P / (COGS / 365)	$848,733 / ($5,408,988 / 365)	=57.27 days	$675,425 / ($7,108,988 / 365)	=34.68 days
Cash conversion cycle	Operating cycle – Days payables outstanding	56.73 – 57.27	=(0.55) days	44.99 – 34.68	=10.31 days

Coverage:

Ratio	Formula	Original Year 3		Updated Year 3	
Debt to equity	Total debt / Total equity	$2,001,849 / $235,707	=8.49	$1,528,541 / $806,897	=1.89
Debt to total assets	Total debt / Total assets	$2,001,849 / $2,237,556	=0.89	$1,528,541 / $2,335,438	=0.6
Times interest earned	Income before interest and taxes / Interest expense	$376,079 + $64,549 / $64,549	=6.83	$947,269 + $64,549 / $64,549	=15.68
Current cash debt coverage ratio	Cash provided by operating activities / Average current liabilities	$220,289 / ($931,665 + $952,647)/2	=0.23	$520,289 / ($931,665 + $779,339)/2	=0.61

Profitability:

Ratio	Formula	Original Year 3		Updated Year 3	
Profit margin	Net income / Net sales	$376,079 / $7,280,893	=5.17%	$947,269 / $9,780,893	=9.68%
Gross profit percentage	Gross profit / Net sales	$1,871,905 / $7,280,893	=25.71%	$2,671,905 / $9,780,893	=27.32%
Return on assets	Net income / Average total assets	$376,079 / ($1,965,109 + $2,237,556) / 2	=17.90%	$947,269 / ($1,965,109 + $2,335,438) / 2	=44.05%
Return on total assets	Net income + interest expense / Average total assets	$376,079 + $64,549 / ($1,965,109 + $2,237,556) / 2	=20.97%	$947,269 + $64,549 / ($1,965,109 + $2,335,438) / 2	=47.06%

What do the results indicate?

Obviously, the new contract will have a *positive impact* for StickU. The $2,500,000 revenue generated from the contract is almost a third of the $7,280,893 original Year 3 revenue. This should result in more net income. It is also important to understand the impact of StickU's decision to take the additional income generated to increase inventory and pay down debt.

Liquidity: All liquidity ratios increased. StickU is in a much stronger position to pay its short-term obligations.

Activity: All activity ratios improved, resulting in a shorter operating cycle and an increased cash-conversion cycle. By reducing accounts payable, StickU significantly improved its days payables outstanding.

Coverage: StickU's decision to pay down debt with the additional income generated has improved its coverage ratios considerably. Because StickU made the debt payment at the end of Year 3, current interest expense did not decrease. However, with the reduced principal amount outstanding, there will be a significant reduction in interest expense going forward, which will help profitability.

Profitability: All profitability ratios improved. The gross profit percentage improved only slightly, indicating that the cost per unit sold was relatively constant, even with the new contract for supplies. StickU uses LIFO to account for inventory; consistently high unit costs result in high COGS and lower net income.

Notes to the financial statements: StickU will need to add a revenue recognition note to the financial statements regarding the new contract. The note should include information about disaggregated revenues, contracts balances, and performance obligations. StickU should also include information about the debt repayment in the note about its long-term note payable.

1.02 Nonfinancial and NonGAAP Measures of Performance

Performance Measures

Representative Task (Remembering & Understanding): Identify relevant nonfinancial and nonGAAP measures used to analyze an entity's performance.

Representative Task (Analysis): Interpret nonfinancial (eg, customer retention rate, employee turnover, labor productivity rate, ticket response time) and nonGAAP (eg, EBITDA, free cash flow, core earnings, adjusted net income for nonrecurring expenses) measures and analyze specific aspects of an entity's performance and risk profile.

Nonfinancial Performance Measures

Nonfinancial performance techniques are based on measures other than money, such as time, quality, or quantity of a business process. These techniques are often better at identifying strengths and weaknesses than financial measures are.

Units of Measurement

(Time, length, weight, temperature)

Nonfinancial measures are often used to improve employees' motivation and/or performance and may be connected to a balanced scorecard. Common examples are listed below.

Customer retention rate summarizes the number or percentage of customers who continue to use an entity's products or services for a specified time. To maintain or improve this rate, businesses typically need to improve product offerings and value. Customer loyalty programs and/or multiyear contracts are two effective methods for retaining customers.

Employee turnover represents the number or percentage of workers/employees who voluntarily or involuntarily (or both) leave the business within a certain time frame (usually one year) and are replaced by new employees. High turnover rates may be indicative of culture and morale problems. Hiring and training new employees is costly and has a direct impact on productivity.

Labor productivity rate indicates the number of units of work completed by a worker in a defined period of time (ie, man-hours or man-days). Total value of output for the specified period of time is divided by the total number of labor hours. The rate is used to measure worker efficiency. Increased productivity leads to lower average costs and higher profits.

Ticket response time identifies how long it takes customer service to first respond to the ticket (not necessarily to resolve the issue). A ticket is generated for internal or external action items (eg, a product is not working correctly). Response time is an important metric to assess customer satisfaction and retention.

NonGAAP Performance Measures

Management often presents **pro forma** (nonGAAP) **financial** measures, alongside US GAAP measures, to convey its own interpretation of the company's performance. A nonGAAP technique is an alternative method for measuring the earnings of an entity (see examples below).

Adjustments are often made to GAAP financial information to determine "normal" operating income. NonGAAP reports may exclude certain items outside the core business earnings, such as goodwill impairment and gains/losses from the sale of a segment. Common nonGAAP techniques include EBITDA (earnings before interest, taxes, depreciation, and amortization), free cash flows, and core earnings.

EBITDA is considered a rough proxy for **operating cash flow** (ie, the entity's ability to pay interest, dividends, and taxes). Adjusted EBITDA varies across companies and often excludes the impact of equity-based compensation, acquisition-related charges, impairment, lawsuits, and gain or loss on disposal of assets or extinguishment of debt. These management adjustments (ie, addbacks) are meant to normalize reported earnings (eg, net income) by eliminating the impact of nonrecurring items.

Adjusted EBITDA reconciliation

	(USD millions)	
	Net Income	100
	Interest	10
	Taxes	42
	Depreciation & amortization	5
Management adjustments (ie, addbacks)	Litigation charges	3
	Stock-based compensation	4
	Acquisition-related charges	3
	Impairment	1
	Loss on sale of assets	2
	Adjusted EBITDA (Non-GAAP)	170

EBITDA can be misleading if users do not understand the computation. Entities do have to pay interest and taxes; thus, these items negatively affect cash flow. By "adjusting" for items such as depreciation and/or interest expense, high-cost fixed-asset acquisitions and/or high-cost debt can be "hidden" from users.

Free cash flows (FCF) represent the after-tax cash available to capital providers (ie, investors) after accounting for operating expenses and investments in fixed and working capital; thus, this is a nonGAAP technique. FCF exclude noncash items like depreciation and amortization. FCF are commonly used to value securities, capital projects, and firms.

Typically, the higher the free cash flow, the stronger the entity is financially, measured in its ability to pay down debt, distribute cash dividends, and contribute to growth (ie, purchase new equipment, upgrade technology).

Calculation of and Uses of Free Cash Flow

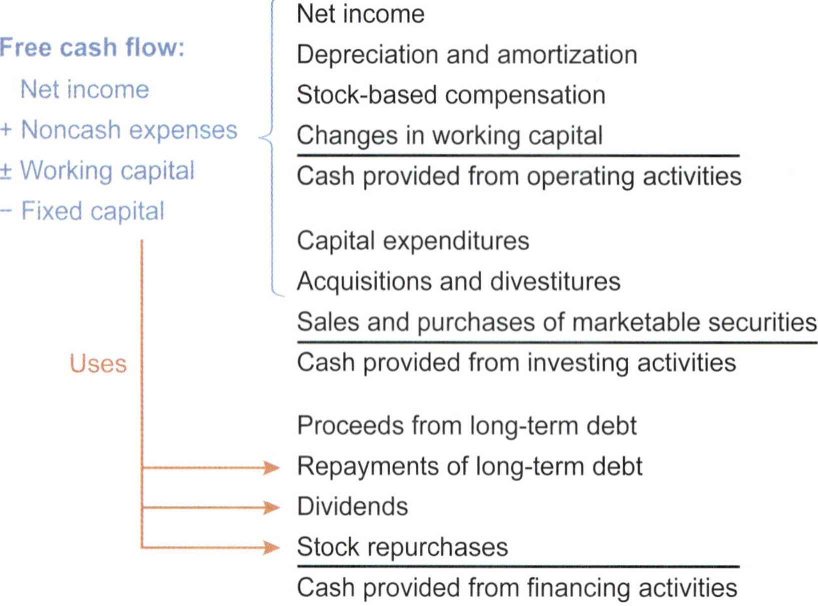

Core earnings is a concept that was developed by Standard & Poor's to identify the "business-as-usual" income generated by normal, recurring business operations. Core earnings are not recognized as a GAAP concept but are used by management and investors to assess the profitability of the underlying business. Core earnings excludes items such as noncore gains/losses (eg, pension gains), gains/losses from sale of capital assets, and nonoperating items (eg, goodwill impairment).

Calculation of core earnings	
Pretax earnings	$3,200
(−) Nonrecurring income	(400)
(−) Pension gains	(300)
(+) Loss on asset sales	150
Core earnings	**$2,650**

Adjusted net income for nonrecurring expenses is calculated by removing nonrecurring items from net income to arrive at an amount that represents typical (ie, recurring) net income.

A nonrecurring item is unusual/infrequent in nature (eg, loss from fire) and does not result from normal operations. Nonrecurring items are generally grouped into one of the following categories:

- **Discontinued operations:** Gain/loss from the disposal of a component (ie, segment) of an entity that has a significant effect on the entity's operations and financial results
- **Unusual/infrequent items:** Items that are either unusual in nature or infrequent in occurrence (eg, restructuring charges)
- **Change in estimate:** A gain or loss resulting from a voluntary change in an entity's estimation policies, such as a change in depreciation methods (eg, straight-line to double declining)

Cost of quality is a philosophy with three core tenets: that *failures have causes*, that **preventing failures is cheaper** than remediating subsequent failures, and that measuring a firm's performance regarding cost of quality helps the firm.

Quality costs are grouped into one of the following four types of cost:

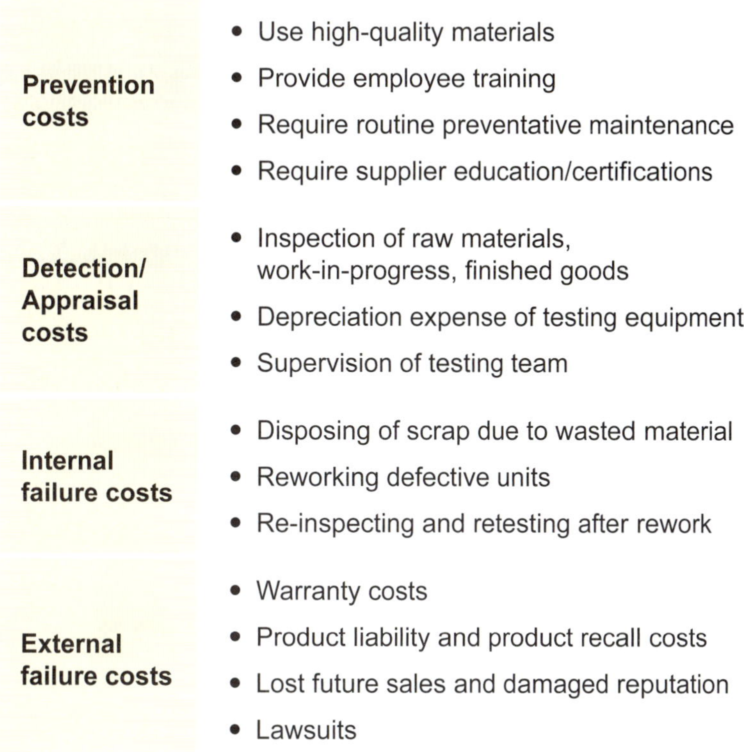

The later in a process that a firm addresses quality issues, the more costly (ie, expensive) the remediation.

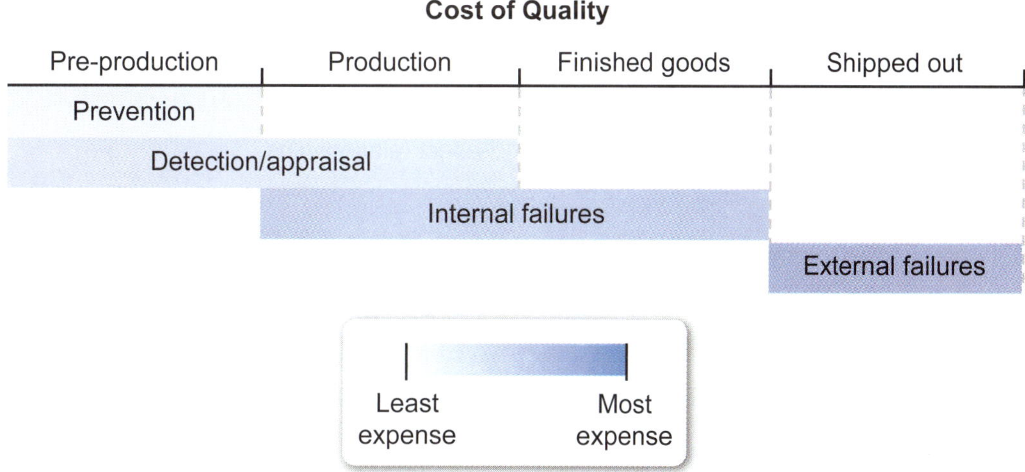

Costs of conforming to quality-control standards are called **conformance costs** (ie, prevention + detection/ appraisal costs). Costs of quality-control failures are called **nonconformance costs** (ie, internal + external failure costs).

Six-sigma quality is a statistical measure of the percentage of products that are in acceptable form (ie, reflect the firm's quality goals), based on standard deviation measures (hence the name "sigma"). To achieve one sigma, 68% of products must be acceptable. To achieve six sigma, 99.999997% of products must be acceptable. Six-sigma constitutes the practical hypothetical goal of perfection in manufacturing: 3.4 defects per million units.

Less-Common Performance Measures

Total quality management (TQM) is an entity-wide effort to continuously improve the ability to deliver high-quality products and services through systematic analysis; thus, it includes insights from suppliers as well as employees.

Theory of constraints (TOC) is used to maximize operating income and overcome bottlenecks in operations. Under TOC, if demand exceeds capacity for a resource, then the resource is defined as a **bottleneck resource**. If capacity exceeds demand, then the resource is defined as a nonbottleneck resource.

Bottleneck vs. Nonbottleneck Processes

Only an improvement here will improve production (minimize the bottleneck)

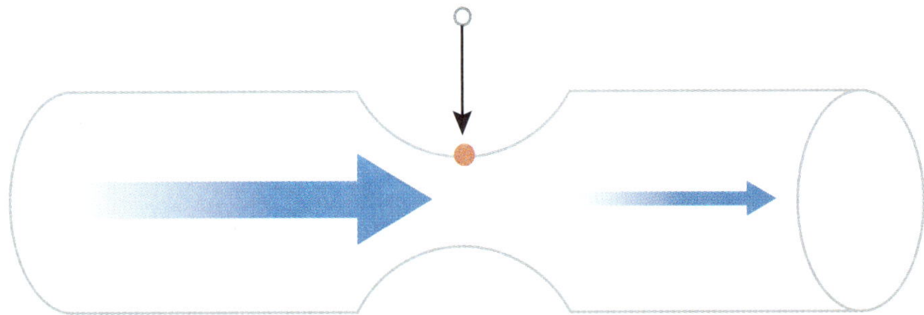

TOC seeks to simultaneously maximize throughput contribution and minimize investment and operating costs.

- Throughput contribution equals revenues minus the direct materials cost of goods sold (COGS)
- Investment equals the cost of materials, work-in-process, and inventories; research and development expenses; and (up-front) expenses for equipment and buildings
- Operating costs equal employee compensation, rents, utilities (eg, electricity, sanitation), and depreciation (eg, of equipment and buildings)

Strategy maps (ie, diagrams) help to identify cause-and-effect relationships:

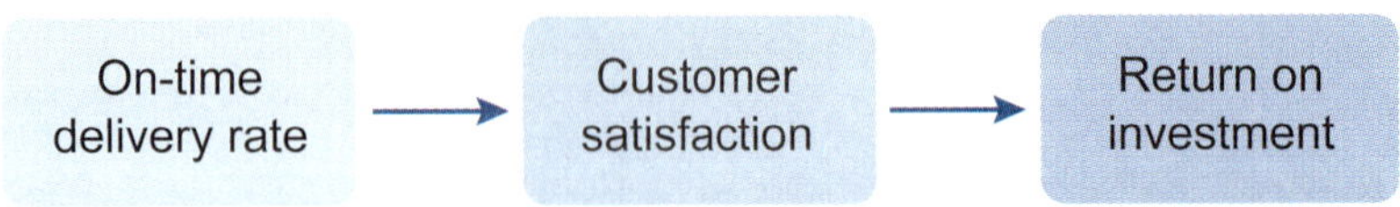

Decision trees: Managers constantly face decisions for which they cannot have all relevant information initially. As any project evolves, conditions evolve, requiring new decisions (eg, a change in prices or availability of labor and material, project modifications). Managers may use decision trees as graphical aids to highlight the chains of decisions that will or will not happen under various scenarios (eg, if X happens, then the choices about Y are...).

Value-based management (VBM): VBM seeks to determine each activity's financial value (or contribution) to the firm. In other words, VBM identifies an activity's economic value added (EVA), which is defined as net operating profit after taxes minus the cost of capital. If misapplied, VBM may fail to reflect activities where value is created; however, the links from cost to value creation are less easy to identify.

For instance, cost cutting may yield value in the short term but not in the long term. Similarly, research expenditures may yield value in the long term or erratically or through improvements that are shared with other departments but with enhancements in revenues that are never clearly credited to the research expenditures.

Value chain: Most companies have a strategy to produce high-quality products as efficiently as possible to maintain a competitive edge. A value chain is a sequence of processes that creates a product or service and then identifies production areas that can be redesigned to improve productivity or quality or can be eliminated altogether. By making these adjustments, a business can, in theory, increase profit margins.

Value proposition: This is a measure of the value added for customers by the firm's competitive advantages. This includes value created within the supply chain (eg, convenient delivery) and other areas, such as the following:

- Product differentiation
- Sales processes
- Customer service and support
- Pricing

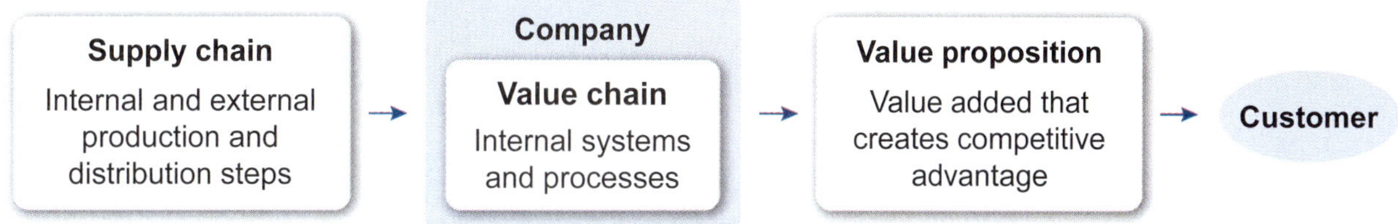

Representative Task (Application): Identify and apply internal and external benchmarking (eg, competitor analysis) techniques to measure an entity's performance

Benchmarking

Benchmarking involves **evaluating performance** of an entity's products, services, and/or processes on an ongoing basis (ie, continuous improvement), relative to the performance *within and outside the organization*. Most frequently, the comparison is external in nature and focuses on examining **competitors' operations**.

Organizations also engage in benchmarking to identify **best practices** that may then be adopted more widely across the entity. There are many types of benchmarking, including the following:

- **Internal:** Compares *relative performance* of divisions, stores, product lines, etc.
- **Technical:** Compares against competitors, often using a SWOT analysis to identify threats and opportunities
- **Customer and competitive:** Focuses on intangibles, such as adding value, ESG attributes, etc.
- **Industry:** Focuses on a higher level, often assessing financial and/or process performance
- **Strategic:** Compares an entity's strategy to competitors', similar to comparing processes

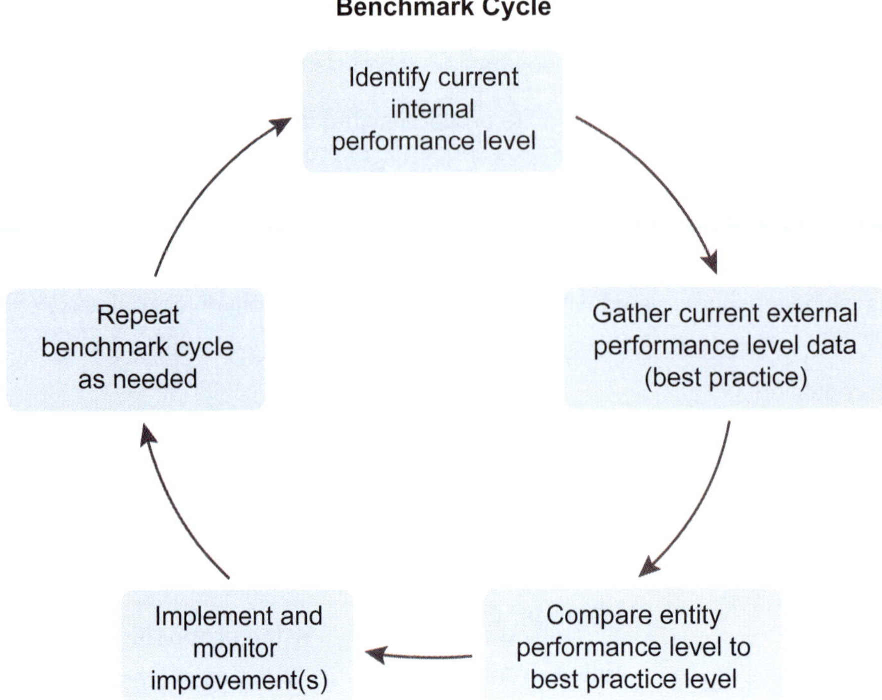

Advantages of benchmarking include the following:

- Improvement of competitive edge
- Enhancement in employee morale by creating an atmosphere where everyone is working toward a defined goal
- Identification of strengths and weaknesses in the entity as a whole or individual products and services
- Creation of new, improved products/services to differentiate the entity from competitors

Representative Task (Application): Use a balanced scorecard approach to measure an entity's performance.

Balanced Scorecards

The balanced scorecard is a strategic management framework that translates an organization's mission and strategy into a set of performance targets. It recognizes that organizations are made up of different stakeholders with different needs; therefore, performance should be measured across four perspectives:

- **Financial:** How do our shareholders perceive us?
- **Customer:** How do our customers perceive us?
- **Internal Business Process:** How well are we running our operations?
- **Learning & Growth (Innovation):** How do our employees perceive us?

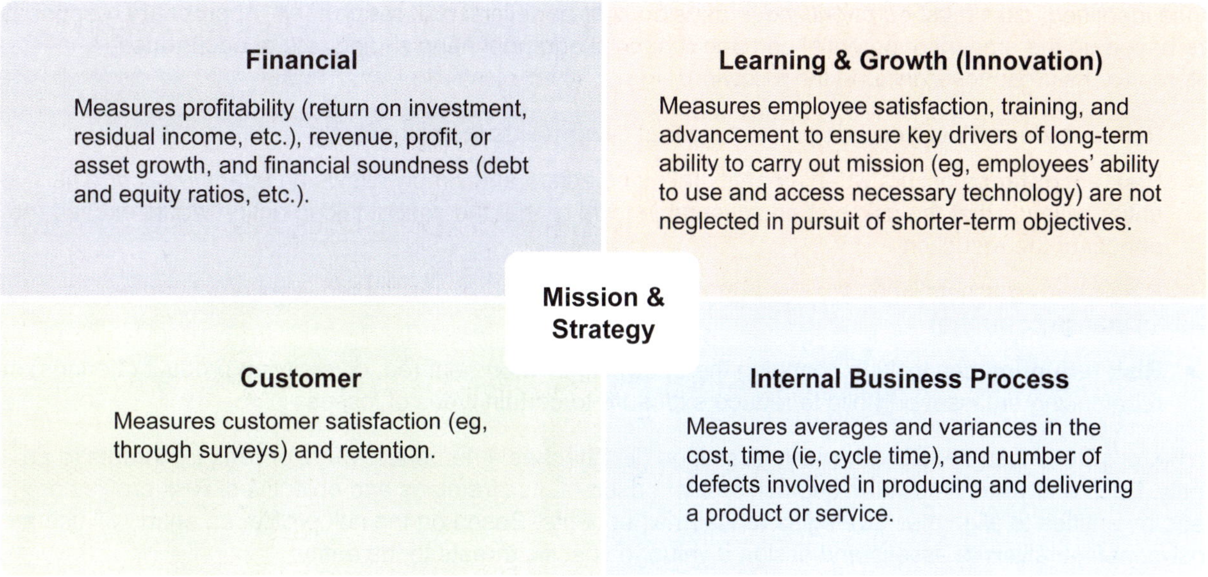

Financial

Measures profitability (return on investment, residual income, etc.), revenue, profit, or asset growth, and financial soundness (debt and equity ratios, etc.).

Learning & Growth (Innovation)

Measures employee satisfaction, training, and advancement to ensure key drivers of long-term ability to carry out mission (eg, employees' ability to use and access necessary technology) are not neglected in pursuit of shorter-term objectives.

Mission & Strategy

Customer

Measures customer satisfaction (eg, through surveys) and retention.

Internal Business Process

Measures averages and variances in the cost, time (ie, cycle time), and number of defects involved in producing and delivering a product or service.

In addition to the four perspectives, balanced scorecards may also include:

- **Strategic objectives:** A statement of the firm's goals and what is needed to achieve them
- **Performance measures:** The quantitative methods to be used to determine how much of the strategic objectives are being reached (yardstick)
- **Baseline performance:** How well the firm is currently doing under each performance measure
- **Targets:** The amount of improvement being sought for each performance measure
- **Strategic initiatives:** What specific changes the firm will undertake to achieve its objectives and targets

Risk Profile

Companies face **business risks** that include the following:

- **External factors** such as macroeconomic or industry risks that affect overall industry demand or profitability
- **Internal (ie, company) factors** that affect an individual company and that are typically related to competitive positioning or management actions

Business Risks

Industry-specific cyclicality

Market concentration

Value chain dynamics

Lack of competitive advantage

Overestimating product market opportunity

Management execution

Capital misallocation

Environmental/social/governance

Operating leverage

Growth outlook

Competitive intensity

Regulatory

= Industry-specific risks = Company-specific risks

Once identified, risks must be *prioritized* to develop cost-beneficial **risk responses**. Appropriate responses are based on the amount of potential damage (financial and nonfinancial) and rate of occurrence. Alternative risk responses include the following:

- **Risk avoidance** involves using a strategy that circumvents the risk entirely
- **Risk acceptance** occurs when an entity takes no action and simply allows an event to occur. The entity believes that the risk is at an acceptable level or that the cost of taking action would exceed the benefit of the reduction
- **Risk sharing** occurs when the risk burden is partially or wholly distributed to external parties (eg, insurance coverage)
- **Risk reduction** can include changing the operating environment (eg, diversifying product offerings) or rebalancing an asset portfolio to reduce exposure to certain types of losses

A **risk profile** is then developed, which quantifies (ie, attaches a numerical value or rank to) threats to an entity. Each entity has its own unique risk profile, based on its strategies and objectives. Risk profiles are used by entities to align their strategies to their risk appetite. Based on the risk profile, an entity will use a cost-benefit analysis to assess and assign a value to specific threats to the entity.

A threat to an information system with a total potential dollar loss impact of $7 million has been discovered. The risk of loss from the identified threat is currently 10%. The following four proposed controls are under consideration to mitigate the risk of loss:

Control	Risk of loss	Implementation cost
W	8%	$100,000
X	6%	250,000
Y	4%	350,000
Z	2%	500,000

The original **risk of loss (ROL)** is given as $700,000 ($7 million × 10%). This amount is multiplied by the ROL percentage for each control option to determine the dollar amount of the ROL (eg, $280,000 ROL if Control Y is implemented).

Savings derived from implementation of the control are then calculated by deducting the revised ROL from the original ROL (ie, Column B − Column D). The cost of the new control is then deducted from the savings amount to determine the net benefit (Column E − Column F).

Control Y provides the greatest net benefit of **$70,000**, as determined below:

	A	B	C	D	E	F	G
1	**Control**	**Original risk of loss (ROL) ($7,000,000 × 10%)**	**ROL percent**	**ROL with new control ($7,000,000 x C)**	**Savings from new control (B − D)**	**Cost of new control**	**Net benefit (E − F)**
2	W	$700,000	8%	$560,000	$140,000	$100,000	$40,000
3	X	700,000	6%	420,000	280,000	250,000	30,000
4	Y	700,000	4%	280,000	420,000	350,000	70,000
5	Z	700,000	2%	140,000	560,000	500,000	60,000

1.03 Managerial and Cost Accounting

Types of Costs (Fixed, Variable, Mixed)

Representative Task (Application): Calculate fixed, variable, and mixed costs

Cost Characteristics

A primary purpose of cost measurement is to allocate the costs of production (direct materials, direct manufacturing labor, and manufacturing overhead) to the units produced. It also provides important information for management decisions, such as product pricing decisions.

y = A + Bx [TC = Fixed + Var (X)]

The variables in this formula are defined as follows:

- The **y** is equal to **total cost** and is referred to as the *dependent variable* since its amount is dependent on the other factors
- The **x** is equal to **volume** and is referred to as the *independent variable* since it can be increased or decreased at the company's discretion. This is also often referred to as the **cost driver** as the amount of costs incurred will be largely dependent on the volume of this variable
- The **A** is equal to **fixed costs** and remains constant at any volume as long as the company is operating within a given range of volume
- The **B** is equal to the **variable cost** per unit

Effect of Change in Production Volume on Fixed and Variable Costs

Total Variable Cost

Variable Cost per Unit

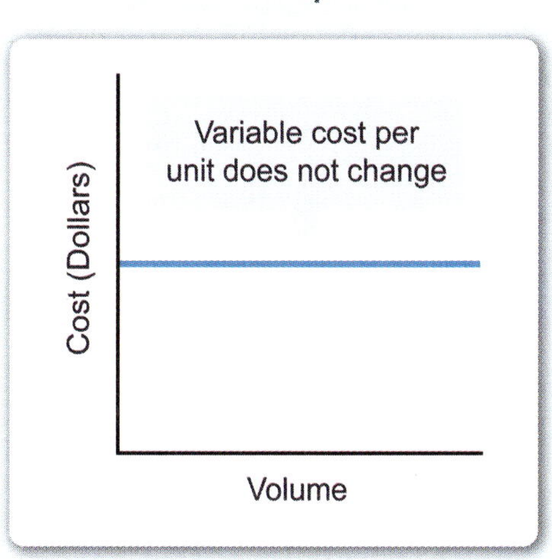

Total Fixed Costs

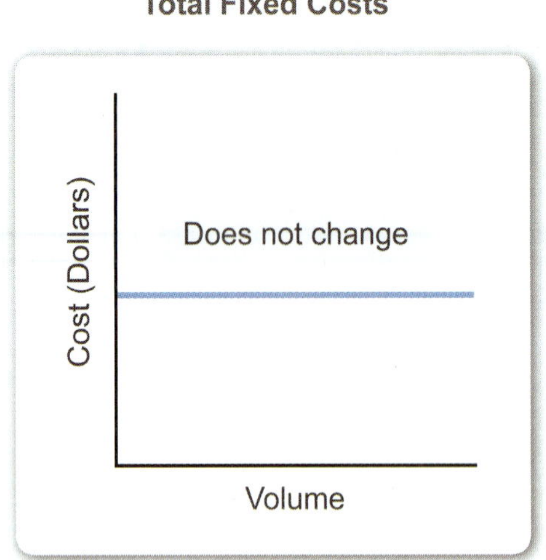

Fixed Cost per Unit

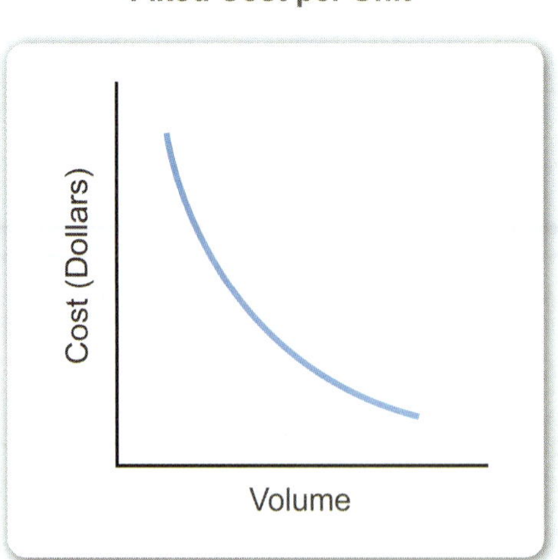

Note: These cost assumptions only remain valid within the **relevant range** *(ie, the normal range of operations).*

Mixed cost (ie, total cost) is a combination of fixed and variable cost. For example, an electric bill has a set monthly charge, regardless of usage, and then an additional charge, based on usage. A short-cut method to split a mixed cost apart is the High-Low method. This method computes the slope for the variable rate from the highest and lowest observations. The difference in cost is divided by the difference in activity to obtain the variable cost.

$$\text{Variable cost per unit} = \frac{\text{Highest activity cost} - \text{Lowest activity cost}}{\text{Highest activity units} - \text{Lowest activity units}}$$

$$\text{Fixed cost} = \text{Highest activity cost} - (\text{Variable cost per unit} \times \text{Highest activity units})$$

Alternatively, we know that fixed cost is constant. Therefore, any change in total cost from one period to the other must, by definition, be variable cost. Once variable cost is known, fixed cost can be deduced, as follows:

High-Low method	
Total cost	**Hours**
$110,000	30,000
$80,000	20,000
$30,000	**/10,000 = $3hr**

Total Cost/Hours = $3 per hour
TC = F + V(X)
110 = F + 3(30,000)
F = 20
TC = 20 + 3(X)

Cost Allocation Methods

Representative Task (Application): Describe and use the different costing methods including absorption, variable, activity-based, process, and job order costing.

Cost Classifications

Cost accounting refers to the calculation of the cost of manufactured inventory. There are three types of *product costs*:

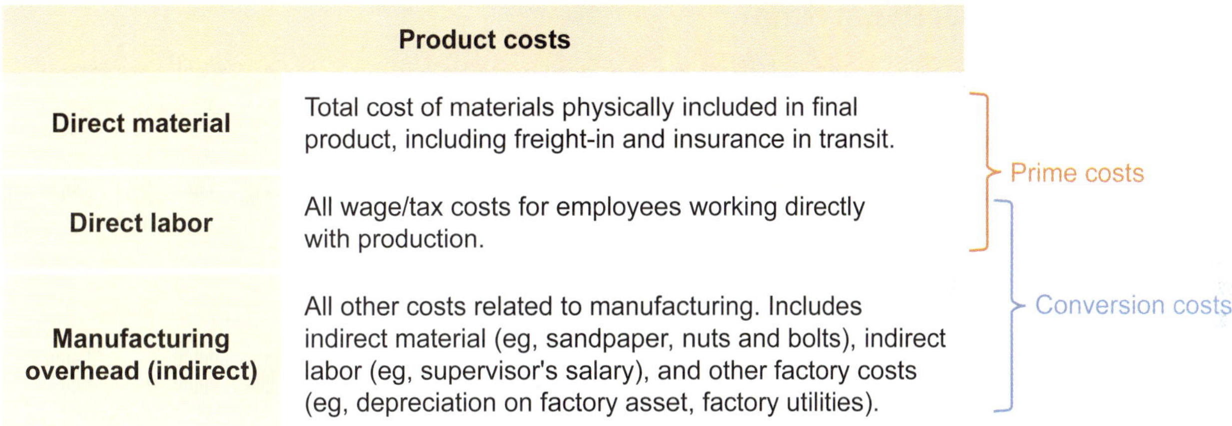

Product costs	
Direct material	Total cost of materials physically included in final product, including freight-in and insurance in transit.
Direct labor	All wage/tax costs for employees working directly with production.
Manufacturing overhead (indirect)	All other costs related to manufacturing. Includes indirect material (eg, sandpaper, nuts and bolts), indirect labor (eg, supervisor's salary), and other factory costs (eg, depreciation on factory asset, factory utilities).

Prime costs
Conversion costs

Direct materials and direct labor are known as the **prime costs** of manufacturing. Direct labor and overhead are known as the **conversion costs** of production.

Manufacturing costs are often called **product costs** since they are matched to the product and not expensed until the product is sold. Costs that are not associated with manufacturing, such as selling, general, and administrative expenses, are often described as **period costs**, as they are *expensed* in the period incurred.

Nonmanufacturing costs: Period costs

- Selling, general, and administrative costs (SG&A)
- Marketing costs, freight out, rehandling costs
- Abnormal spoilage
- An expense in the period

Other cost classifications:

- Relevant costs: an anticipated future cost that differs among alternative plans
- Avoidable costs: costs that will not be incurred if a planned activity is changed or discontinued
- Marginal costs: additional costs incurred owing to one more output unit

Spoilage in a manufacturing process is treated as follows:

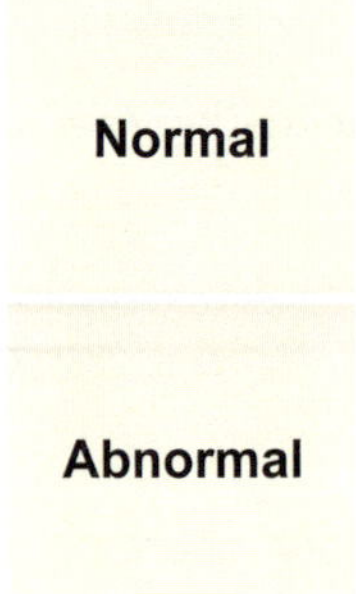

Normal	• Occurs under normal operating conditions • Inherent to the production process • Charged to product cost
Abnormal	• Should not occur under normal operating conditions • Avoidable and controllable • Expense as period cost to separate loss account

Predetermined Overhead Rate

Accounting for manufacturing overhead (OH) is an important part of a costing system. The distinguishing feature of manufacturing overhead is that while it must be incurred to produce goods, it cannot be directly traced to the final product, as can direct material and direct manufacturing labor.

Because the matching principle requires a systematic and rational approach to cost allocation, OH costs are typically applied to jobs during production using a predetermined OH rate. The OH rate is usually based on budgeted (or estimated) machine hours or direct labor hours because actual costs are not yet known.

At the end of the period, applied OH is compared to actual OH (which is now known). The difference is underapplied or overapplied OH and is usually closed to COGS. If actual OH is less than applied OH (as shown in the T-accounts below), the variance is positive and will result in a decrease to COGS, and vice versa.

In the T-account example below, assume that the predetermined overhead rate is $24 per direct labor hour. The estimated OH is applied to work-in-process (WIP), using actual direct labor hours of 215,000. At the end of the accounting period, actual overhead incurred will be charged to the Overhead account, offsetting the applied overhead.

Applied and actual overhead

	Work in process			Overhead			Cost of goods sold	
Beginning balance	XXX		actual**	4,730,000	5,160,000	applied		
Direct material	XXX		variance***	430,000				430,000
Direct labor	XXX							
Applied overhead*	5,160,000							
Ending balance	X,XXX			0				

**based on predetermined rate $24 x 215,000 hours*

***credit cash for actual payments*

****variance closed to COGS*

Flow of a Cost System

Merchandising Company

For a **merchandising** company, the cost of goods sold calculation is the following:

Beginning inventory
+ Purchases
Costs of goods available for sale
− Ending inventory
Cost of goods sold (COGS)

Manufacturing Company

For a **manufacturing** company, the **flow of a cost system** is a bit more complicated due to applied OH, as follows:

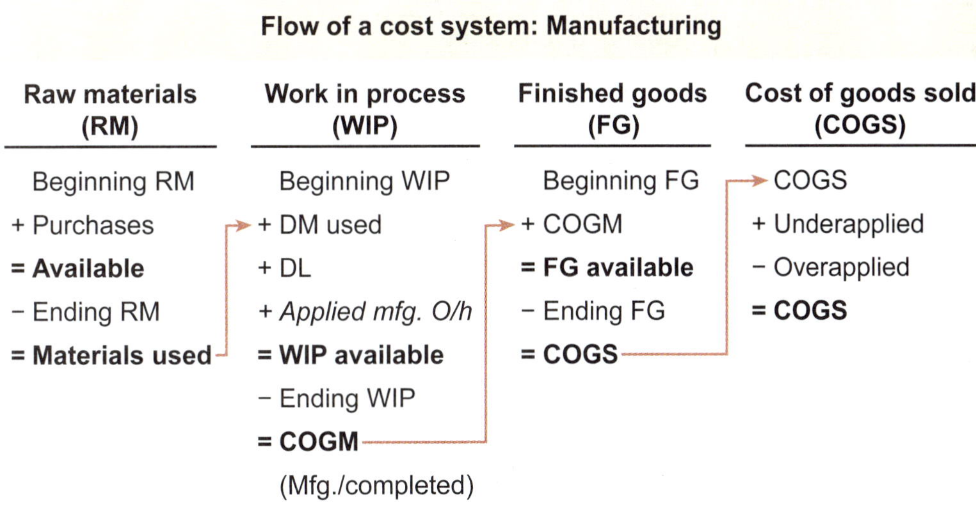

To determine **direct materials used**, the calculation is as follows:

Beginning direct materials inventory
+ Direct materials purchased
− Ending direct materials inventory
Direct materials used

To determine **cost of goods manufactured**, the calculation is as follows:

Direct materials used
+ Direct labor incurred
+ Overhead applied
Costs added to production
+ Beginning work-in-process inventory
− Ending work-in-process inventory
Cost of goods manufactured

To determine **cost of goods sold**, the calculation is as follows:

Beginning finished goods inventory
+ Cost of goods manufactured
Costs of goods available for sale
− Ending finished goods inventory
Cost of goods sold

Overhead cost drivers (ie, how the OH is applied to WIP) are generally based on direct labor hours/dollars or machine hours for highly automated entities.

For example, assume the company is paying $2,000 of rent on factory equipment and expects to produce 1,000 units during the year. The company also estimates that it requires approximately two hours for each unit to be produced and expects wage rates to average $10 per hour. If the company applies overhead based on direct labor hours, then it will use the following:

$2,000 / 2,000 hours = $1 per direct labor hour

If the company chooses *direct labor dollars*, the result is the following:

$2,000 / $20,000 = 10% of direct labor cost

Absorption and Variable Costing

There are two methods for **accounting for fixed overhead (FOH)**: absorption and variable costing. Variable costing may also be referred to as direct costing.

- Under absorption costing, FOH is a **product cost** that is inventoried and then expensed as COGS when the product is sold
- Under variable costing, **FOH is expensed** in the period incurred

The treatment of FOH often results in **different levels of net income** between the absorption and variable costing methods. The differences are timing differences, which result from recognizing FOH in different time periods.

Income Statement Formats

Absorption costing (external use)	Variable costing (internal use)
Sales	Sales
(Variable COGS)	(Variable COGS)
(Fixed COGS)	(Variable SG&A)
Gross margin	**Contribution margin**
(Variable SG&A)	(Fixed COGS)
(Fixed SG&A)	(Fixed SG&A)
Operating income	Operating income

COGS = Cost of goods sold (ie, manufacturing costs)
SG&A = Selling, general, and administrative costs

Absorption costing groups all **manufacturing costs** together (ie, these costs are absorbed as product cost). Product cost (and eventually COGS) includes *variable manufacturing costs* (ie, direct material, direct labor, and variable overhead) and fixed manufacturing costs (ie, fixed overhead). When deducted from sales, gross margin is computed.

Under **variable** (ie, **direct**) costing, variable manufacturing costs and variable selling, general, and administrative costs are grouped together. When deducted from sales, contribution margin (CM) is determined.

Remember that *variable selling expenses* are not included in inventory but are included in the computation of CM. All fixed costs are "below" the line.

Inventoriable/Product costs

	Absorption costing	Variable costing
Direct material	Yes	Yes
Direct labor	Yes	Yes
Variable overhead	Yes	Yes
Fixed overhead	Yes	No
Variable selling, general, and administrative	No	No
Fixed selling, general, and administrative	No	No

The direct costing statement differs in two ways:

1. Variable selling expenses are matched to sales along with the variable manufacturing costs
2. Fixed overhead costs are expensed as incurred along with the fixed selling and administrative expenses

The first difference doesn't affect total operating income, since selling expenses are the result of sales and will be the same amount in either statement. The second difference does affect total operating income, however, and is the reason direct costing statements *violate GAAP* and may only be used internally.

Assume that a company incurred $100 of fixed overhead (FOH) during the year and produced 100 units, applying FOH at the rate of $1 per unit produced*. If the company sells 90 of the 100 units produced, then only $90 of FOH will be in COGS, and the remaining $10 will be absorbed into ending inventory on the balance sheet when using *absorption costing*.

Under *variable costing*, however, the entire $100 is expensed as a period cost, causing operating income to be understated by $10. Variable costing normally understates income as inventory levels rise and overstates income as inventory levels fall, due to the different treatment of FOH.

**For simplicity, we're assuming that overhead is applied based on units and not direct labor, but the results are effectively the same either way.*

The difference in operating income will be equal to the FOH per unit multiplied by the increase/decrease in units in inventory.

- When ending inventory *equals* beginning inventory, both methods will result in the same operating income
- When ending inventory is *greater than* beginning inventory, absorption costing will result in higher operating income
- When ending inventory is *lower than* beginning inventory, variable costing will result in higher operating income

Assume the following:

Beginning inventory in units	30,000
Plus: production in units	50,000
Less: units sold	(70,000)
Ending inventory in units	10,000

Because sales of 70,000 exceeded production of 50,000, units from both beginning inventory and current production were sold. If FOH was $100,000, then FOH per unit was $2 ($100,000 / 50,000 units produced). A net decrease in inventory of 20,000 units (30,000 beginning − 10,000 ending) indicates that an additional $40,000 (20,000 × $2) of FOH was charged to COGS under absorption costing. Therefore, absorption COGS exceeds variable COGS

Determine how much lower Roxy Manufacturing's net income would be if it used variable costing (V/C) instead of absorption costing (A/C) during its first full year of operations. Assume that Roxy had the following costs for production of 120,000 units and sales of 90,000 units:

Manufacturing costs:	Fixed	$180,000
	Variable	160,000
Selling & administrative costs:	Fixed	90,000
	Variable	40,000

With production of 120,000 units and FOH of $180,000, fixed overhead is $1.50 per unit. A net increase in inventory of 30,000 units (120,000 − 90,000) indicates that $45,000 ($1.50 × 30,000) of FOH was allocated to ending inventory under A/C, making net income under A/C $45,000 higher. In other words, V/C income was $45,000 lower than under A/C.

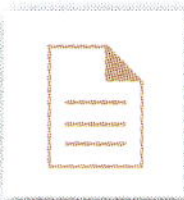

Jako Manufacturing Co. prepares income statements using both standard absorption and standard variable costing methods. For Year 2, unit standard costs were unchanged from Year 1. In Year 2, the only beginning and ending inventories were finished goods of 5,000 units. How would Jako's current ratio and return on stockholders' equity ratio be affected using absorption costing compared with those using variable costing?

Ending inventory (EI) will be greater under A/C by the amount of FOH. Therefore, current assets and the current ratio (Current assets / Current liabilities) will both be greater under A/C than under V/C. The return on stockholders' equity (Net income / Average stockholders' equity) will be smaller under A/C than under V/C. Net income will be same under either method because an equal amount of FOH will be either expensed as a period cost under V/C or included in COGS as a product cost under A/C. However, the denominator will be larger under A/C, generating a smaller return. (Remember, if assets increase with no change in liabilities, then equity must also increase.)

Activity-Based Costing (ABC)

Overhead consists of *many assorted, diverse costs* that have different recognition patterns. Therefore, some organizations choose not to apply overhead with a single, unit-based driver because there is not a one-to-one correlation of cost to activity.

Under the activity-based costing (ABC) method, companies segregate manufacturing overhead into numerous **overhead cost pools**. Each pool will include costs that have common elements, usually the particular activity that will result in an increase in the costs included in that pool (ie, same cause-and-effect relationship). The activity is the **cost driver** or allocation base.

For example, depreciation, repairs, and maintenance might be grouped together as activities affected by machine hours (ie, the usage of machines). In contrast, payroll taxes, employee wages, and benefits might be grouped together as activities affected by direct labor hours.

Management should consider the following when selecting a cost driver:

- **Behavioral effects on employees:** For example, basing a cost driver on the amount of preventive maintenance performed might discourage employees from performing that maintenance at the risk of incurring additional expense
- **Cost of measurement:** If the cost of measuring a driver is excessive, it is generally better to select another cost driver
- **Degree of correlation:** ABC uses drivers with a high correlation to the cost-producing activity; low correlation drivers will not result in accurate cost allocations

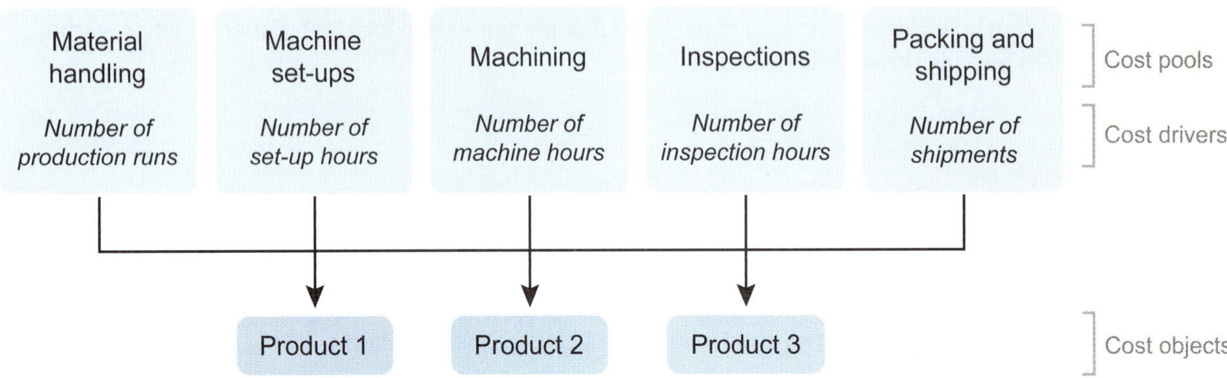

ABC **manages production cost** by providing detailed cost analyses based on cause-and-effect relationships. It can also reduce production cost by identifying and eliminating nonvalue-added (ie, waste, such as storage) activities.

There are several common assumptions related to the ABC method:

- Products or services require the performance of activities
- Activities consume resources that can be identified and measured (ie, cost pools)
- Cost pools are homogeneous and include variable costs and fixed costs

The Perk Co. is considering using the ABC method (with two cost pools) for allocating overhead to its two products: regular and premium coffee beans. Machine hours (MH) would be used as a cost driver for separating and roasting beans, and pounds (lb.) of coffee would be used as a cost driver for packing and shipping.

MH for the current month are 700 hours, direct labor cost per pound of coffee is $1.25, and direct materials cost per pound of coffee is $1.50. There are 1,000 pounds of coffee packed and shipped for the current month. The following data is also available:

		Regular	Premium
Overhead for the current month	$5,000		
Cost pool for separating and roasting beans	$3,500	150 MH	550 MH
Cost pool for packing and shipping	$1,500	500 pounds	500 pounds

Determine the total cost per pound for both types of coffee using activity-based costing.

Total cost per pound for each type of coffee is calculated as follows:

	Regular	Premium
Direct material ($1.50/lb. × 500 lbs.)	$ 750	$ 750
Direct labor ($1.25/lb. × 500 lbs.)	625	625
Overhead (indirect):		
Separating and roasting (700 total MH)	$ 750*	$2,750*
Packing and shipping (1,000 total lbs.)	750	750
Total cost	$2,875	$4,875
Total lbs.	÷ 500	÷ 500
Cost/lbs.	**$ 5.75**	**$ 9.75**

**Usage ratios are unique to each cost pool. For example, the $3,500 cost pool "separating and roasting beans" uses the number of machine hours (MH) as a cost driver. Regular coffee requires 150 MH out of a total of 700 MH, so it is allocated $750 in cost [(150 MH / 700 MH) × $3,500]. Premium coffee requires 550 MH, so it is allocated $2,750 in cost [(550 MH / 700 MH) × $3,500].*

ABC systems are often more reliable than other allocation systems due to the focus on identifying cause-and-effect relationships. However, one of the limitations of an ABC system is that data analysis can be **quite expensive** and gathering the data can be time-consuming.

One advantage of segregating costs in this manner is that it enhances the usefulness of multiple regression analysis, because it will both yield a greater number of potential cost drivers (which commonly enhances regression's ability to yield relevant results) and ensure that the boundaries across costs drivers are more sensible.

Value-Adding and Nonvalue-Adding Costs

Costs may also be classified as either **value-adding** or **nonvalue-adding**. Value-adding costs are those that make the product itself or make it better for customers (such as engineering activity, direct manufacturing costs, the operation of production machinery, modifying products to better meet customers' specifications, or expenses that improve the product's endurance or performance, such as research & development).

Costs are ultimately value-adding if they result in specific outcomes that customers perceive as increasing the worth of a product or service, for which they would pay more. Nonvalue-adding costs (such as moving, handling, and storing raw materials, factory utilities, or depreciation of manufacturing equipment) are costs that increase the cost of a product but that customers do not specifically value.

Nonvalue-Added vs. Value-Added

Nonvalue-add: Pure waste	**Nonvalue-add: Business required**	**Value-added**
Activities that the customer would not pay for	Activities that must be performed for legal or regulatory/ compliance reasons	Activity that a customer is willing to pay for that contributes to the end product they expect

Eliminate

Minimize

Optimize

Production Cost Allocation

There are two methods of allocating production costs to inventory and cost of goods sold accounts:

- **Job order costing** allocates manufacturing costs directly to unique products (eg, custom-built furniture) and is generally used when costs can be directly traced to specific units
- **Process costing (PC)** is used for a continuous production process of the same or similar goods (eg, cans of red paint) and is generally used when it is difficult to trace costs directly to specific units

Job order versus process costing systems

	Job order system	Process costing system
Balance sheet account(s)	Multiple work-in-process accounts	One work-in-process account
Level of cost allocation	Directly to each job (WIP account)	Indirectly allocated to the group
Calculation of retail cost	Total cost / total units	Total cost / equivalent units*
Documentation	Job cost sheets	Production cost reports

**A theoretical number that represents the total number of units that could have been completed, given the amount of production costs incurred.*

Job Order Costing

Job order costing is a system for allocating costs to groups of **unique products**. Each job becomes a cost center for which costs are accumulated. Job order costing is generally used when units are relatively expensive and when costs can be identified to specific units or batches of units (eg, custom-built homes).

Because costs are traced to specific jobs, certain items that might otherwise be classified as manufacturing overhead (overtime premiums paid to accommodate a customer change order, for instance) are classified as direct costs.

Job Order Cost Flow

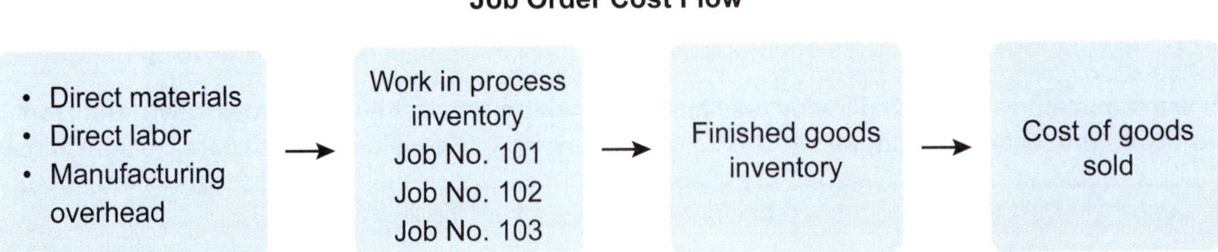

Process Costing

Process costing, in contrast to job order costing, is applicable to a **continuous process** of production of the same or similar goods (eg, cans of red paint). Since the product is uniform, there is no need to determine the costs of different groups of products, and each processing department becomes a cost center.

Process costing is generally used when units are relatively inexpensive and when it is difficult to trace costs to specific units being produced, such as when units are mass-produced in large quantities.

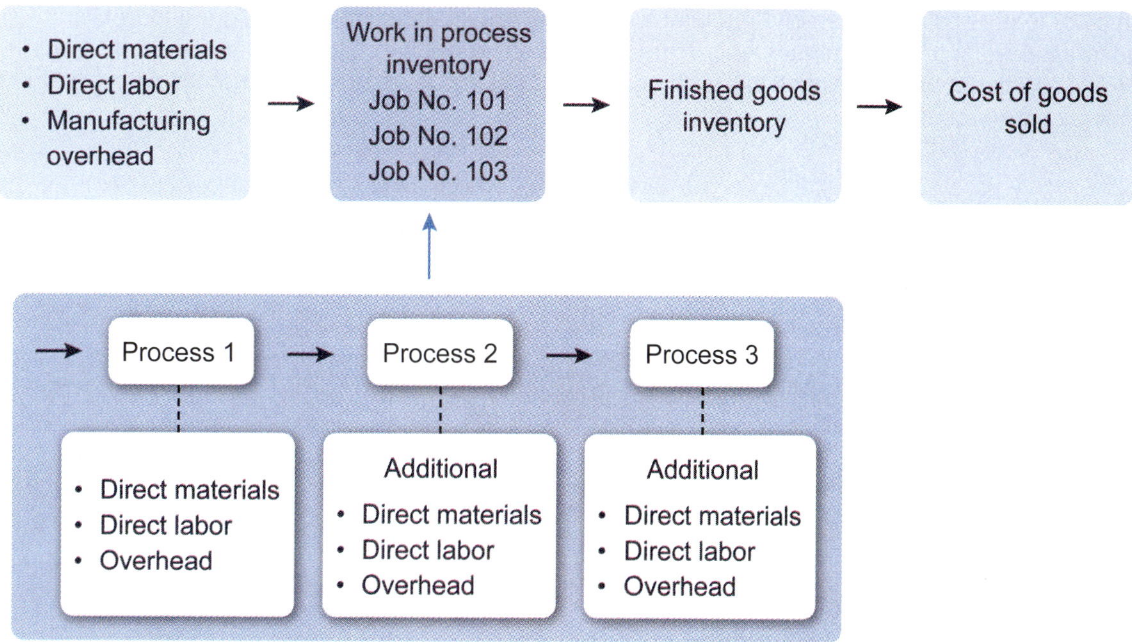

One significant aspect of process costing is the computation of **equivalent units**. The objective is to analyze the period's production, including units completed and units partially completed, and **determine the number of whole units** that the production is equivalent to.

Equivalent Units of Production

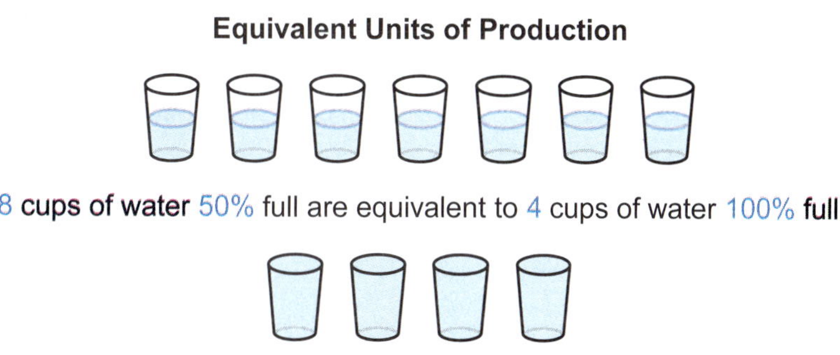

The calculation of equivalent production will depend on the point in time at which costs are incurred. The weighted average method allocates cost to all units in production; **FIFO excludes any units from beginning WIP in the cost allocation**.

- When costs are incurred at the beginning of the process, partially completed units will be considered equivalent to whole units as soon as they are started
- When costs are incurred at a specific time during the process, such as when units are 40% complete, partially completed units will be considered equivalent to nothing until they reach that point and equivalent to whole units when that point is reached
- When costs are incurred at the end of the process, partially completed units will be considered equivalent to nothing until completed, at which time they will be equivalent to whole units
- When costs are incurred evenly throughout the process, the percentage of completion will be multiplied by the number of units in process to determine the number of equivalent whole units

When a company has more than one manufacturing department, the costs are assigned to WIP and to goods transferred to the next department. In the subsequent department, the units transferred from a previous department are considered similar to a raw material that is added to the production cycle at the beginning of the process.

The Alexes Co. is the first of a two-stage production process. The following information concerns the conversion costs in May of Year 3:

	Units	Conversion costs (CC)
Beginning work-in-process (60% complete)	30	$68
Units started	60	96
Units completed and transferred	50	
Ending work-in-process (80% complete)	40	

Using the weighted average and the FIFO methods, calculate equivalent units, the cost of goods completed, and ending inventory.

Weighted Average (Total Costs/Total Equivalent Whole Units)

		Units	% complete CC		Equivalent units (EU)			Costs
	Beginning units	30	60%					$ 68
	Started	60						$ 96
	Units to account for	90						$164
Same under both	Completed	50	100%	=	50 × $2*	=	$100	
	End	40	80%	=	(50 × 80%) × $2*	=	64	
	Units to account for	90			82 EU			$164

Equivalent units	82 EU
Cost of goods completed	**$100**
Ending inventory	$ 64

**$164 / 82 equivalent units = $2 per unit*

FIFO (Costs incurred this period / Units actually worked on this period)

	Units	% complete CC	EU	Costs
Beginning units	30	60%		$ 68
Started	60	0%		96
Units to account for	90			$164
Completed	50	30 × 40% = 12	12 × $1.50* = $ 18	
		20 × 100% = 20	20 × $1.50* = 30	
			$ 48	
			+ started 68	
			completed $116	
Same under both → End	40	80% complete =	32 × $1.5 = $ 48	
			$164	
Units to account for	90		64 EU	$164
Equivalent units			64 EU	
Cost of goods completed			**$116**	
Ending inventory			$ 48	

**$96 / 64 equivalent units = $1.50 (remember the cost of beginning units is excluded under FIFO)*

When a company produces large quantities of identical goods, it will often use **process costing** to determine the average cost per unit of products. When using this approach, costs are accumulated in WIP until the end of the period, and then a calculation is made of the cost per equivalent unit of products completed and incomplete at the end of the period.

Assume that a company had work-in-process (WIP) at the beginning of the month of $30, associated with 2 units that were 50% complete at the time. During the month, it spent $150 and started an additional 8 units. At the end of the month, WIP consisted of 4 units that were 75% complete. Assume that there was no spoilage in the production process.

The total cost in WIP before allocating is $30 + $150 = $180. With 2 units at the start and 8 more begun during the month, there were 10 units to account for at the end of the month. Since 4 were in process, 6 must have been completed.

The **equivalent units (EU)** include the 6 that were completed and 4 × 75% = 3 equivalent units for the ending WIP, for a total of 9 equivalent units. The costs of $180 are allocated over 9 equivalent units at $20 per equivalent unit. Ending WIP is $20 × 3 equivalent units, or $60, and the remaining $120 must represent the costs associated with the 6 units completed and transferred to finished goods.

	Units	Costs	Cost / EU
Beginning WIP (50%)	2	$ 30	
Added	8	150	
To account for	10	$180	$180

	Units	Units	EU	Allocation @ $20
Ending WIP (75%)	4	3		$ 60
Completed	6	6		120
Accounted for	10	9	9	$180
Cost / EU			$20	

For costs added at the beginning of a process, EU are the same for WIP as they are for completed units. For example, if raw materials are added at the *beginning* of the process, the 4 units in process at the end of the month *already have* all the raw materials and are assigned 4 EU instead of 3.

The EU include the 6 that were completed and 4 × 75% = 3 EU for the ending WIP, for a total of **9 EUs**. The costs of **$180** are allocated over 9 EU at **$20 per EU**. Ending WIP is $20 × 3 EU, or $60, and the remaining $120 must represent the costs associated with the 6 units completed and transferred to finished goods.

Under the **weighted average approach**, equivalent production for a period will include units that are **completed** during the period, considered whole units as to all costs, and units in process at the end of the period. The ending WIP will be converted into EU on the basis of the level of completion.

Total equivalent production will be divided into costs for the period to determine an average cost per EU. The costs included will be the costs associated with beginning inventory and the costs incurred during the period.

Under the **FIFO approach**, equivalent production for a period will include the units that are **started and completed** during the period, considered whole units as to all costs. Both beginning and ending WIP inventory will be converted into equivalent whole units.

- For beginning inventory, the portion of the work that needed to be completed during the period will be multiplied by the number of units to determine equivalent production
- For ending inventory, the percentage of completion will be multiplied by the number of units to determine equivalent production

Total equivalent production will be divided into costs for the period to determine an average cost per equivalent unit. The costs included, however, will only be those costs that were incurred during the period.

The difference between weighted average and FIFO is the handling of beginning WIP inventory. When there is no beginning inventory, both will have the same result. When there is a beginning WIP inventory, the weighted average approach will yield a number of equivalent units that will be equal to or greater than equivalent production under FIFO.

- When costs are incurred at the end of the process or at some point in the process that the beginning inventory had not yet reached, equivalent production will be the same under both approaches
- When costs are incurred uniformly during the process, at the beginning of the process, or at some point in the process that the beginning inventory had already reached, equivalent production under weighted average would be greater than FIFO

Equivalent units

	Units in beginning WIP (EU % varies)	Units started and still in WIP (EU % varies)	Units started and completed (EU % varies)
Weighted average	✔	✔	✔
FIFO		✔	✔

Joint Product Costing

Joint products are two or more products **produced together** up to a **split-off point**, where they become separately identifiable. They cannot be produced by themselves. When more than one product is being produced, certain costs are associated with the production of more than one product and are known as joint product costs.

These costs are allocated to the different products using one of three acceptable methods:

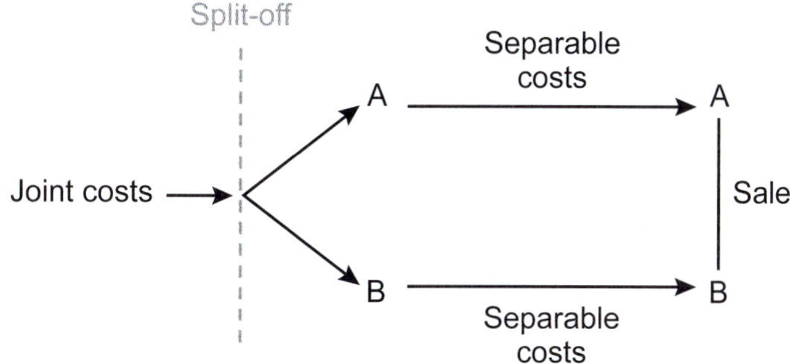

- **Relative sales value (RSV) at split-off:** The total sales value is reduced by the separable manufacturing costs incurred for each product after the split-off point. Use the RSV of each product to allocate the joint costs.
- **Physical quantity allocation:** This method requires two steps: first determine the ratio of each product's quantity produced to the total quantity produced at the split-off point; then use these ratios to allocate joint costs
- **Net realizable value (NRV):** This method also requires two steps: first determine each product's total sales revenue less its separable costs; then use the post-split NRV to allocate the joint costs.

The most popular method is the relative sales value at split-off approach. The total sales value of the products involved is determined and is reduced by separate costs incurred in the manufacture of each product after the split from the joint process. The result is the approximate sales value of each product at the point the joint process ended. This is referred to as the "sales value at split-off" or the "synthetic sales value" and is used to allocate the joint costs.

Under the relative sales value method:

- The **sales value** of each joint product is determined by multiplying the amount produced by the sales price per unit
- The sales value is reduced by **separable costs**. Separable costs are the costs incurred after the mutual manufacturing process is complete. They are the costs necessary to prepare a joint product to be sold. Not all joint products will have separable costs
- The resulting reduced amount is considered the **relative sales value** of the joint product at the **split-off point**. The split-off point is that point, at the conclusion of the joint manufacturing process, when individual joint products can be identified
- The relative sales values for each of the joint products are combined to obtain a total amount

The joint product costs to be allocated to a specific joint product will be determined by the relative sales value method using the following formula:

$$\text{Relative sales value at split-off} = (\text{Price per unit} \times \text{Units produced}) - \text{Separable costs}$$

$$\text{Joint cost allocation} = \text{Joint cost} \times \frac{\text{Relative sales value for one product}}{\text{Total production relative sales value}}$$

Sometimes, in addition to joint products, companies may have **by-products** that result from a process. By-products are output from the joint process that do not contribute significantly to the firm's revenue and are not products that the company is manufacturing by intent. For example, oil refining involves the removal of impurities from crude oil. The impurities are useful in the manufacture of glue, so oil companies sell them and subtract the net proceeds (sales price less costs of disposal) from the cost of refining oil.

Joint costs may be allocated to **by-products** in a variety of ways:

- The net proceeds from the sale of the by-product reduces the costs incurred by the main products after split-off
- Joint costs may be allocated to by-products in the same manner as to joint products using the relative sales value method, as if it were an additional joint product
- No costs may be allocated to the by-product

A company has joint product costs of $54,000 at split-off. There are 2 main products, A and B, and one by-product, Z. Division A has $30,000 of additional costs after split-off in order to sell all output for $80,000. Division B has $20,000 of additional costs after split-off in order to sell all output for $60,000. By-product Z has $1,000 of additional costs in order to sell for $5,000.

Determine how much of the joint product costs should be allocated to products A and B and by-product Z assuming that the net by-product revenue is used to reduce joint product cost.

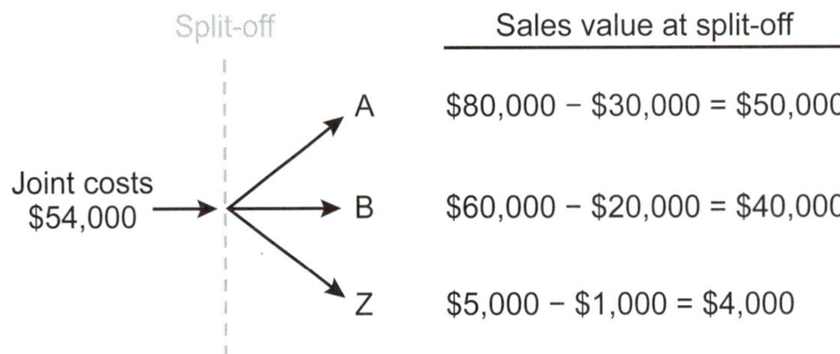

The $4,000 net contribution from by-product Z is used to offset the joint product costs of $54,000. Therefore, by-product Z would show zero revenue. A net $50,000 is allocated to the main products, as follows:

Product A would be allocated $50,000 × 50/90	=	$27,778
Product B would be allocated $50,000 × 40/90	=	22,222
		$50,000

Determine how much of the joint product costs should be allocated to products A and B and by-product Z, assuming that the $54,000 joint product cost is allocated to by-products in the same manner as to the joint products.

Product A would be allocated $54,000 × 50/94	=	$28,723
Product B would be allocated $54,000 × 40/94	=	22,979
By-product Z would be allocated $54,000 × 4/94	=	2,298
		$54,000

Variance Analysis

Representative Task (Analysis): Derive the appropriate variance analysis method to measure the key cost drivers by analyzing business scenarios.

Standard Costing

Standard costs are **predetermined target costs** that should be attainable under efficient conditions. Standard costs are used to aid in the budget process, pinpoint trouble areas, and evaluate performance. The industry (and, hence, the CPA exam) commonly uses more than one name for some variances.

Standard cost characteristics

- They are predetermined amounts that represent expected amounts
- They aid in developing price and quantity amounts for flexible budgets
- They are compared to actual amounts; differences create variances
- They are included in both process and job order costing systems
- They represent a benchmark for performance measurement

In setting internal goals for the efficient production of inventory, companies establish standards for the components that comprise direct materials, direct labor, and overhead. At the end of the period, these standards are compared with actual results to determine variances. The standards include the following:

- **Standard cost:** The unit purchase price of direct materials. Differences between standard cost and actual cost produce **direct materials price variances**
- **Standard quantity:** The number of units of direct materials used to produce each unit of inventory. Differences between standard quantity allowed and actual quantity used produce **direct materials usage variances**
- **Standard rate:** The hourly rate of pay for direct labor. Differences between standard rate of pay and actual rate of pay produce **direct labor rate variances**
- **Standard hours:** The number of hours of direct labor used to produce each unit of inventory. Differences between standard hours allowed and actual hours used produce **direct labor efficiency variances**
- **Predetermined overhead rate:** The amount of overhead applied (usually based on direct labor hours or machine hours). Differences between applied overhead and actual overhead produce overhead variances

Selling Price Variance

The **selling price variance** is the difference between the actual sales price per unit and the estimated sales price per unit multiplied by the actual total unit sales. Remember that this is a sales variance, not a cost variance.

If the **actual sales price** is **less than** the **estimated amount**, the variance will be **unfavorable** because less revenue was collected than anticipated. A significant selling price variance should be investigated. Candidates for investigation of a selling price variance include the sales, marketing and advertising departments.

Selling Price Variance

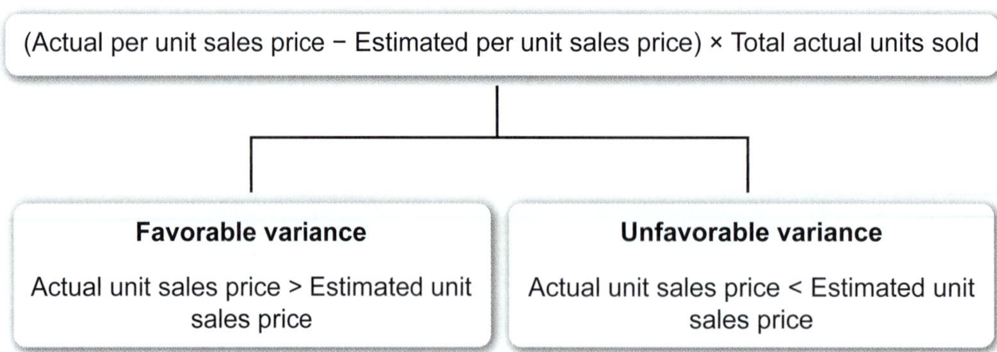

Direct Material (DM) and Direct Labor (DL) Variances

The chart below provides one set of formulas for direct material and direct labor variances. Since these variance calculations are based on algebra, the components of the formulas can be presented in arrangements. This chart is one way to remember the math, but if a different arrangement makes more sense, practice using that arrangement.

Variance analysis formulas

	Variance	Formula	While in the factory, I can
DM	DM Price	(AP − SP) AQ	Control the quantity (of material) used? YES–use actual quantity
	DM Quantity (usage)	(AQ − SQ) SP	Control the price (of material)? NO–use the standard price
DL	DL Price (rate)	(AP − SP) AQ	Control the quantity (of hours) used? YES–use actual quantity
	DL Quantity (efficiency)	(AQ − SQ) SP	Control the price (of labor)? NO–use the standard price

Tips:

1. *P = price; Q = quantity; A = actual; S =standard.*
2. *Start with the name of the variance, and set up the difference (eg, price variance is AP − SP).*
3. *If you started with the difference in price, then outside the brackets will be the quantity, and vice versa [eg, (AP − SP) AQ].*
4. *Treat the difference as an absolute value: cost variances are unfavorable if A > S, and favorable if A < S.*

Additional hints and suggestions:

- Every direct material, direct labor, and variable OH variance will have both a **price** variance and a **quantity** variance (remember by "mind your Ps and Qs")
- Price components are always "per" unit, and quantity components are always the "whole" amount (think of the "Q" as circling the "whole" amount)
- The price variance is always the amount purchased; the quantity variance is always the whole amount used
- The standard amount is the amount that "should" be paid or used (ie, it is the amount that is expected to be incurred, based on past experience and projections)
- When the actual is less than the standard, the variance is favorable (less was paid/used than expected/allowed, which is a good thing), and vice versa

Use this information for the following material and labor variances.

Assume that a company manufactures collectible life-size figurines, which are sold for $1,000 each. Typically, a single figurine is completed in a day, and the standard costs involved in the manufacture of each figurine are the following:

- Direct materials: 20 pounds of clay at $5 per pound
- Direct labor: 5 hours of labor at $10 per hour
- Overhead: Applied at $19 per direct labor hour

The estimated cost of manufacturing on a normal day (one figurine) is as follows:

	Normal
Direct materials	$100
Direct labor	50
Overhead	95
Total cost	$245

Assume that, on a particular day, the company manufactures **two** figurines and incurs the following **actual** costs:

- Direct materials: 36 pounds of clay at $4 per pound
- Direct labor: 12 hours of labor at $11 per hour
- Overhead: $255

It is not appropriate to compare the normal costs with the actual costs because the **normal costs are based on expected production** (one figurine). Instead, the actual costs are compared with **standard costs allowed based on actual production** (two figurines), as follows:

	Normal	Standard	Actual	Variance
Direct materials	100	200	144	56 F
Direct labor	50	100	132	32 U
Overhead	95	190	255	65 U
Total cost	245	490	531	41 U

Direct Material Price Variance (DMPV)

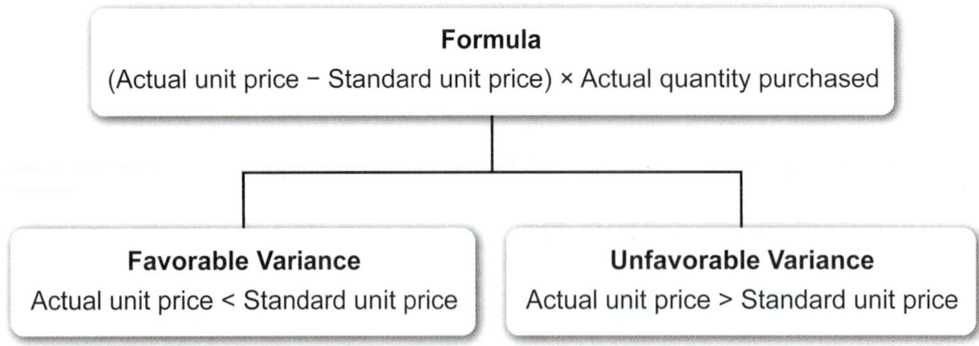

The DMPV is the difference between the actual price paid per unit (AC) of $4 and the standard cost (SC) per unit of $5, multiplied by the total actual quantity (AQ) purchased of 36. Remember, it is the price paid by the manufacturer, which is typically referred to as a cost, but the variance calls it a price. It is important not to confuse this amount with the sales price, which is what the manufacturer would charge a customer. The DMPV is generally considered the responsibility of the Purchasing department.

Assuming that the company maintains no inventories, it needs to purchase 36 units. Since the AP paid per unit was less than the SP per unit, the variance is favorable.

$$\text{DMPV} = (\text{AP} - \text{SP}) \times \text{AQ} = (\$4 - \$5) \times 36 = \$36\ \text{F}$$

Direct Material Quantity Variance (DMQV)

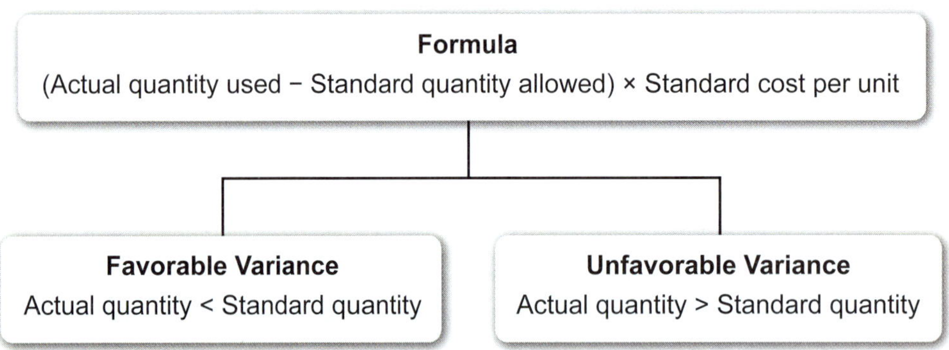

The DMQV is the difference between the total AQ used of 36 pounds and the total standard quantity allowed (SQ) based on total production (40 pounds expected to be used). Standard price is the per unit amount of $5. Since the total AQ used was less than the total SQ, the variance is favorable.

$$\text{DMQV} = (\text{AQ} - \text{SQ}) \times \text{SP} = (36 - 40) \times \$5 = \$20\ \text{F}$$

Direct Labor Price Variance (DLPV)

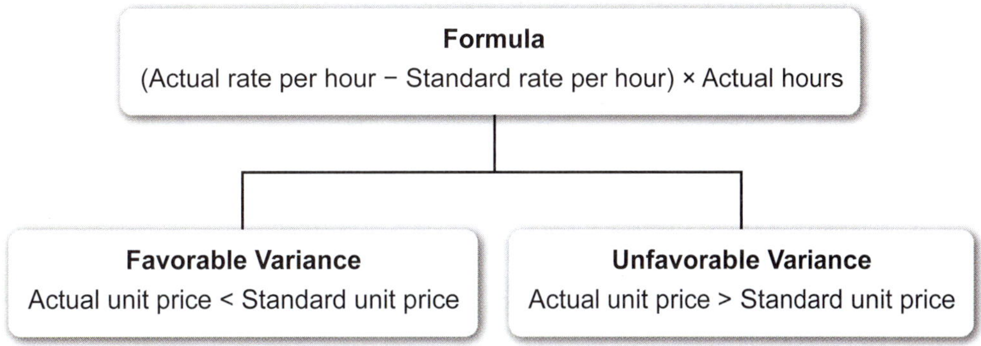

The DLPV is the difference between the actual price (AP) paid (ie, hourly rate) per hour of $11 and the standard pay per hour of $10. The difference is multiplied by the total actual number of hours (AH) of 12. Since the AP paid per hour was more than the SP per hour, the variance is unfavorable.

$$\text{DLPV} = (\text{AP} - \text{SP}) \times \text{AQ} = (\$11 - \$10) \times 12 = \$12\text{ U}$$

Direct Labor Quantity Variance (DLQV)

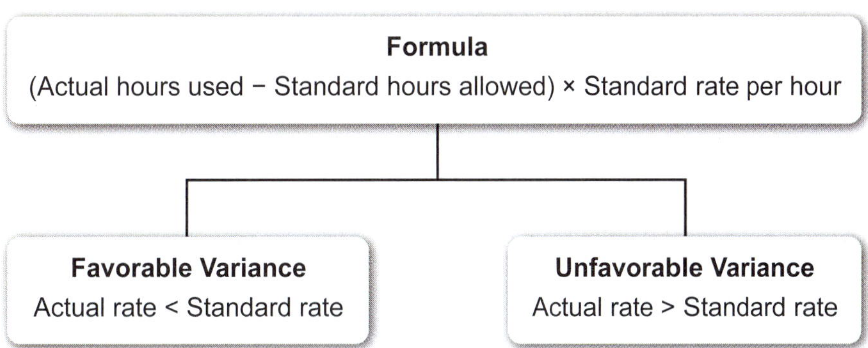

The DLQV is the difference between the total actual quantity (AQ) of 12 hours worked and the total standard quantity (SQ) of 10 hours allowed (based on actual production of two figurines). The total difference is multiplied by the standard price (SP) per hour of labor. Since the total AQ of hours is more than the SQ of hours allowed, the variance in unfavorable. The DLQV is generally considered the responsibility of the Production Department.

$$\text{DLQV} = (\text{AQ} - \text{SQ}) \times \text{SP} = (12 - 10) \times \$2 = \$20\text{ U}$$

Total Variances

The **total variance** for both material and labor consists of the price variance (PV) and the quantity variance (QV).

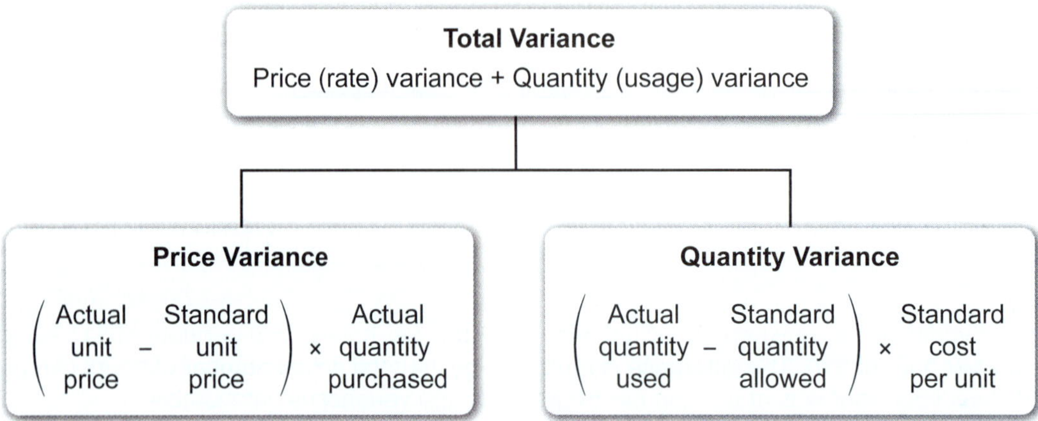

Using the above information, total variances are as follows:

Direct Material PV + QV = \$36F + \$20F = \$56F

Direct Labor PV + QV = \$12U + \$20U = \$32U

Variable Overhead Variances

Variable overhead (VOH) consists of various manufacturing expenses (other than direct material and direct labor) that vary with production volume (eg, factory electricity). Total VOH variance consists of the VOH price (spending) variance and the VOH quantity (efficiency) variance. Rather than analyzing each cost in VOH, it is assessed at the aggregate level generally using direct labor hours or machine hours as the cost driver.

Formulas similar to those used for direct material and direct labor variances can be used for VOH.

Use the following information to calculate the variable overhead variances.

Actual variable overhead cost per hour	\$8.00
Standard variable overhead cost per hour	\$7.50
Actual direct labor hours	4,500
Standard direct labor hours	5,000

VOH Price (Spending) Variance (VOHPV)

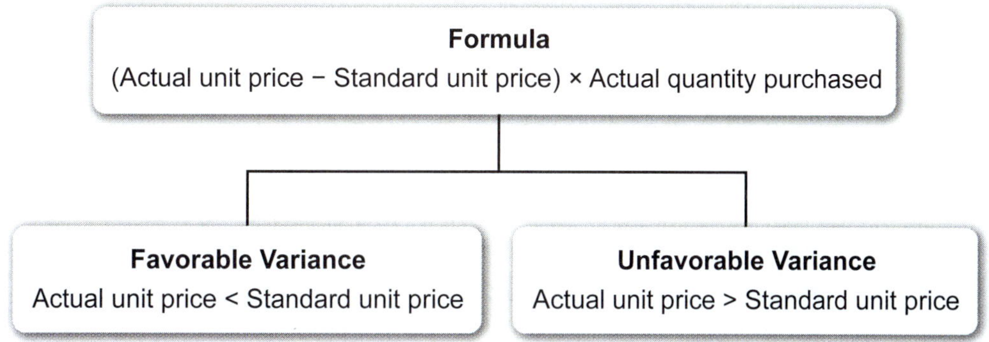

Here, VOH is based on direct labor hours. The VOHPV is the difference between the actual cost per hour of overhead of $8 and the standard cost per hour of overhead of $7.50, multiplied by the total actual quantity of direct labor hours used of 4,500. Since the actual cost was more than the standard cost, the variance will be unfavorable.

VOHPV = (AP − SP) × AQ = ($8.00 − $7.50) × 4,500 = **$2,250 U**

VOH Quantity (Efficiency) Variance (VOHQV)

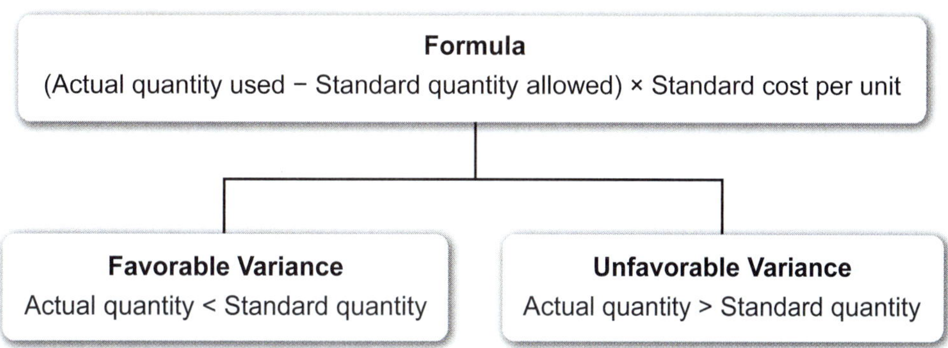

The VOHQV is the difference between the total actual quantity of VOH hours of 4,500 and the total standard quantity of hours of 5,000, multiplied by the standard price per hour of $7.50. Since the total actual quantity of hours is less than the standard, the variance will be favorable.

VOHQV = (AQ − SQ) × SP = (4,500 − 5,000) × $7.50 = **$3,750 F**

VOH Total Variance

The price and quantity VOH variances are netted to determine the total VOH variance:

VOHPV + VOHQV = $2,250 U + $3,750 F = **$1,500 F**

VOH Alternative Presentation

If both variances need to be calculated, or the net amount of both, an alternative setup can be used to solve, as follows:

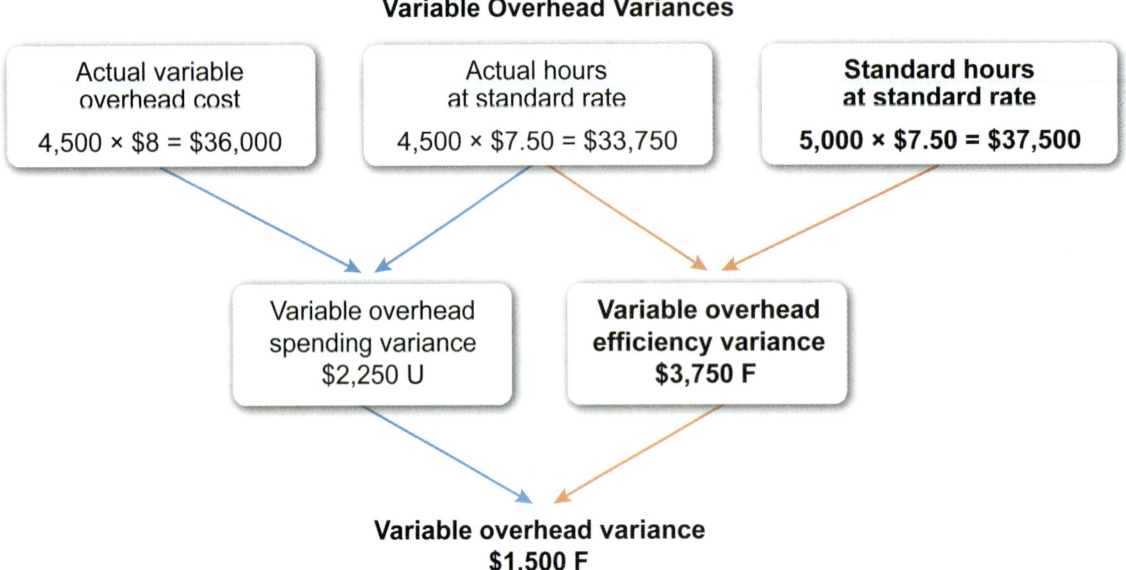

Fixed Overhead (FOH) Variances

Fixed overhead (FOH) consists of indirect manufacturing costs (eg, factory supervisor's salary) that do not vary with production volume. FOH variances include both a price (spending) variance and a production volume (ie, efficiency) variance. When actual FOH costs exceed budgeted FOH costs, the price/spending variance is unfavorable, and vice versa.

Similar to VOH, FOH variances generally use direct labor hours or machine hours as the cost driver.

Use the following information to calculate the fixed overhead variances.

	Actual	Budgeted
Number of frames produced	19,000	20,000
Fixed overhead costs	$22,000	$20,000; $1 per unit
Direct labor hours	2,100 hours	0.1 per frame

FOH Price (Spending) Variance (FOHPV)

Remember that FOH does not vary with changes in production. It is a given amount. Therefore, the actual versus standard quantity is irrelevant. The FOHPV is the difference between the actual FOH cost and the standard FOH cost. Since actual cost exceeds the standard amount, the variance is unfavorable.

FOHPV = (AP − SP) $22,000 − $20,000 = **$2,000 U**

FOH Production Volume Variance (PVV)

FOH does not have a quantity variance since quantity is irrelevant. The production volume variance (PVV) compares actual production to budgeted production. The price (ie, cost) amount is the budgeted amount, not the actual amount. Remember that FOH is applied as units are produced. Therefore, only the budgeted cost is known; the actual cost will not be computed until all production is completed for the period.

Higher production levels (ie, greater volume) result in the application of FOH cost to more units, which reduces the per-unit cost and results in a favorable variance. Lower production levels result in the application of FOH to fewer units, which increases the per-unit cost and results in an unfavorable variance.

Because the actual production volume of 19,000 frames was less than the budgeted volume of 20,000, production was less than anticipated, resulting in an increased cost per unit. The PVV is therefore unfavorable.

FOH PVV = (Actual hours − Budgeted hours) × Standard OH rate per hour
= [2,100 − (20,000 × 0.1 hour per frame)] × ($20,000 / 2,000)
= (2,100 − 2,000) × $10
= $1,000 unfavorable

FOH Total Variance

The total variance is the net amount of the FOH price/spending variance and the FOH PVV:

FOHPV + FOH PVV = $2,000 U + $1,000 U = **$3,000 U**

FOH Alternative Presentation

If both variances need to be calculated, or the net amount of both, an alternative setup can be used to solve, as follows:

Fixed Overhead Variances

Actual fixed overhead **= $22,000**

Budgeted fixed overhead (20,000 frames × $1/frame) **= $20,000**

Applied fixed overhead (19,000 frames × $1/frame) = $19,000

Fixed overhead spending variance **= $2,000 U**

Fixed overhead production volume variance = $1,000

Total fixed overhead variance = $3,000 U

Cost-Volume-Profit (CVP) Analysis

Representative Task (Analysis): Interpret sales results by performing price, volume, and mix analysis.

Cost-volume-profit (CVP) analysis, also used for breakeven analysis, provides management with profitability estimates at all levels of production in the relevant range (the normal operating range). In making decisions about offering new products or services, companies often rely on cost-volume-profit analysis.

CVP for number of units	CVP for sales dollars
$\dfrac{\text{Fixed cost + Desired profit}}{\text{Unit price − Unit variable cost}}$	$\dfrac{\text{Fixed cost + Desired profit}}{\text{Contribution margin ratio}}$

CVP can be computed for the number of units needed or for the amount of sales dollars that must be achieved for a given level of profit.

Assume that the following budget information has been provided to the Marketing Department for a product, based on estimated sales of 100 units per period, selling price of $10 per unit, variable costs of $6 per unit, and fixed costs of $300 per period.

Sales price per unit	$ 10
Variable cost per unit	6
Fixed cost in total	$300

If the company budgets $200 in operating profit, how many *sales in units* must be generated?

The formula for the **sales in units** is as follows:

(Fixed costs + Desired profit) / Contribution margin per unit

($300 + $200) / ($10 − $6) = $500 / $4 = 125 units

If the company budgets $200 in operating profit, how many *sales in dollars* must be generated?

The formula for the **sales in dollars** is as follows:

(Fixed costs + Desired profit) / Contribution margin percentage*

($300 + $200) / ($4 / $10) = $500 / 40% = $1,250

**Contribution margin percentage is contribution margin divided by sales.*

Using the same information above, assume that variable cost per unit decreases to $5.

How many *sales in units* must be generated?

The formula for the **sales in units** is as follows:

(Fixed costs + Desired profit) / Contribution margin per unit

($300 + $200) / ($10 − $5) = $500 / $5 = 100 units

Since variable cost decreased by $1 per unit, fewer units need to be sold to reach an operating profit of $200.

How many *sales in dollars* must be generated?

The formula for the **sales in dollars** is as follows:

(Fixed costs + Desired profit) / Contribution margin percentage*

($300 + $200) / ($5 / $10) = $500 / 50% = $1,000

**Contribution margin percentage is contribution margin divided by sales.*

Brewster Co. has the following financial information:

Fixed costs	$ 20,000
Variable costs	60%
Sales price	$ 50

What amount of sales is required for Brewster to achieve a 15% return on sales?

Here, unknown profit equals 15% of sales. If unknown sales = X, then profit = .15X.

If variable cost percentage is 60%, contribution margin percentage (CMP) must be 40%.

Brewster Co. needs **$80,000** in sales to achieve a 15% return, calculated as follows:

Required sales	=	(Fixed cost + desired profit) / CMP
X	=	($20,000 + .15X) / 40%
.40X	=	$20,000 + .15X
.40X – .15X	=	$20,000
.25X	=	$20,000
X	**=**	**$80,000**

Weighted average contribution margin (WACM) is the average amount that a certain group or combination of products (ie, **sales mix**) contributes toward fixed costs and eventually profit. Customers often buy related products at the same time, and these products' sales are affected by each other. For example, people often buy coffee and cream together.

WACM can be used to determine breakeven, sales in dollars, or sales in units for a given sales mix. The number of units computed is the number of batches that must be sold (ie, the sales mix bundle). The batch amount can then be broken down to individual products using the sales mix information.

Beach Basics Inc. has the following sales mix:

Product	Unit sales price	Unit variable cost	Sales mix
Flip-flops	$40	$25	40%
Sunglasses	80	45	30%
Hats	15	5	30%

What is Beach Basics' weighted average contribution margin (CM) per unit?

Product	Unit sales price	Unit variable cost	CM	Sales mix	WACM
Flip-flops	$40	$25	$15	40%	$ 6.00
Sunglasses	80	45	35	30%	10.50
Hats	15	5	10	30%	3.00
					$19.50

How many units does Beach Basics have to sell to break even, assuming fixed costs of $23,400?

The formula for the **sales in units** is as follows:

(Fixed costs + Desired profit) / WACM

($23,400 + $0) / $19.50 = 1,200 batches

Individual product breakeven units for a **batch of 1,200** are determined as follows:

Product	Batch Amount	Sales mix	Units
Flip-flops	1,200	40%	480
Sunglasses	1,200	30%	360
Hats	1,200	30%	360
			1,200

What if the sales mix changed to 40%/50%/10%? What effect would this have on breakeven assuming that fixed costs remained constant?

Product	Unit sales price	Unit variable cost	CM	Sales mix	WACM
Flip-flops	$40	$25	$15	40%	$ 6.00
Sunglasses	80	45	35	50%	17.50
Hats	15	5	10	10%	1.00
					$24.50

The formula for the **sales in units** is as follows:

($23,400 + $0) / $24.50 = 956 batches *(must round up the batch to next full amount)*

Individual product breakeven units for a total **batch of 956** are as follows:

Product	Batch Amount	Sales mix	Units
Flip-flops	956	40%	382
Sunglasses	956	30%	478
Hats	956	30%	96
			956

Because the new sales mix increases the weighting for sunglasses, which has the highest CM per unit of $35, fewer batches are required to break even.

Margin of Safety

The **margin of safety** is the *excess of sales over the breakeven* volume of sales. It calculates the amount by which *sales can drop* before losses begin to be incurred in an organization. If, for example, a company had sales of $3,500,000 and a breakeven volume of $3,200,000, the margin of safety would be $300,000.

Cost-Volume-Profit (CVP) Graph

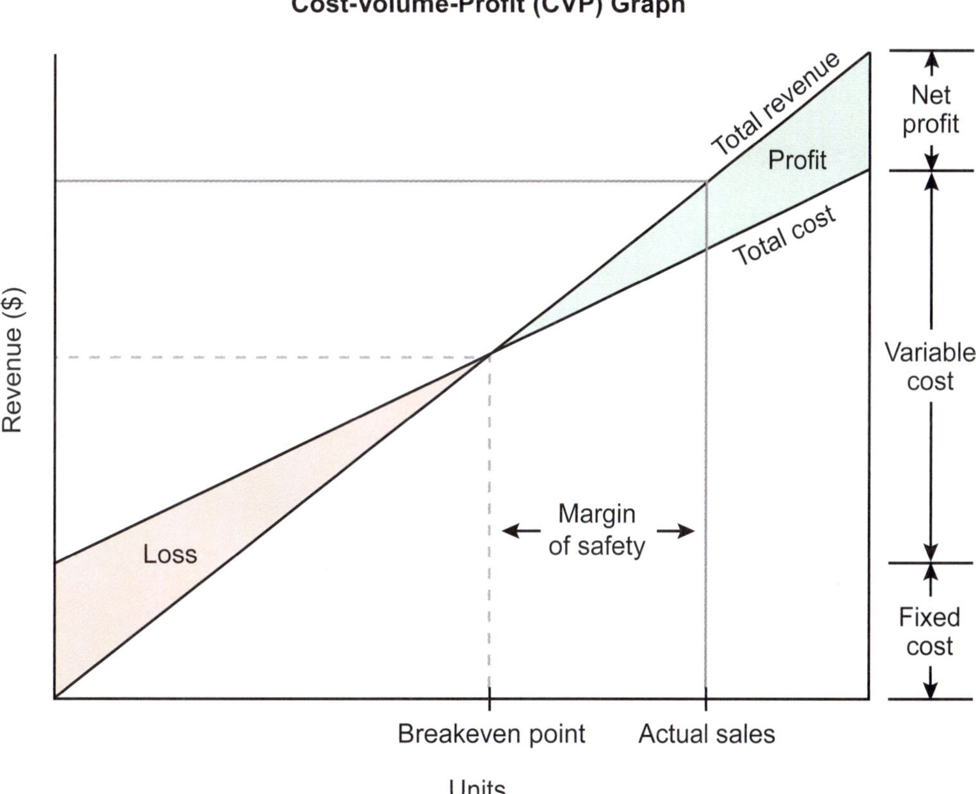

Effect of Change in Fixed Cost

CVP analysis can be used to determine the effect of a change in one of the formula inputs, such as fixed cost. Profit occurs after the breakeven point, which is when total revenue equals total cost. Total cost consists of total variable cost and total fixed cost (TFC). As TFC increases, the related breakeven point is also increased, requiring greater sales before profits can be achieved.

For example, an entity with TFC of $2,000 will have a much more difficult time realizing a profit at the same level of sales revenue than a competitor with TFC of only $500. Profit, as a percentage of revenue (ie, sales) increases from 16.7% to 66.7% for the competitor.

Effect of Increased Fixed Cost on Breakeven and Profit

High Fixed Cost		**Low Fixed Cost**	
Revenue:	$3,000	Revenue:	$3,000
Total cost:	2,500	Total cost:	1,000
Profit:	500	Profit:	2,000
Fixed cost:	$2,000	Fixed cost:	$500
Variable cost:	500	Variable cost:	500
Profit:	**$500 = 16.7%**	**Profit:**	**$2,000 = 66.7%**

BAR 2
Prospective Analysis, Including the Use of Data

BAR 2: Prospective Analysis, Including the Use of Data

2.01 Budgeting, Forecasting, and Projection

Sources and Types of Data

Representative Task (Application): Determine methods to transform (eg, preparing, cleaning, scrubbing) structured and unstructured data to make it useful for decision-making.

Companies today generate large volumes of data due to enterprise resource planning (ERP) systems, customer relationship management (CRM) systems, social media use, website-tracking data, and e-commerce transactions. Instead of merely being stored for contractual, operational, reporting, and compliance purposes, this data can be mined and analyzed to identify trends, enhance insight, and support decision-making.

Data is extracted and loaded into a readily usable format. *Structured data* can normally be transferred between applications by comma-separated value (CSV) file. Other types of data, such as unstructured and semi-structured, may need to be transformed prior to analysis.

Examples of data sources and data characteristics include the following:

Examples of Data Sources			
Internal*		**External***	
• Accounting data • Customer data • Employee data	• Marketing data • Supplier data • Shipping data	• Industry data • Government data	• Census data • Social media

**Consideration should be given to whether internal data is obtained from within the financial accounting reporting system or outside that system (ie, not controlled by the accounting department).*

Examples of Data Characteristics			
Nature			
• Financial • Non-financial • Descriptive	• Process-related • Control-related • Regulatory	• Demographic • Economic • Geographic	• Historical • Prospective • Time-sensitivity

Extract-Transform-Load (ETL)

Imagine that a retailer wants to analyze sales trends across its entire business. The sales data for its online and brick-and-mortar storefronts is stored in separate systems in different formats. The retailer also wants to incorporate data from social media and online weather sources to determine if these data affect sales trends.

To accomplish this task, the retailer first performs a three-step process called **Extract-Transform-Load (ETL)**.

- **Extract:** This involves gathering data from various sources. This data could reside in internal or external systems that are developed and supported by different vendors, hosted on different computer hardware, and managed by different employees. In our example, we begin by collecting sales data from different internal systems, as well as social media and weather data from online sources.
- **Transform:** This involves converting the raw data gathered from the extract phase into a consistent, useful format for loading the data into the target database.
- **Load:** This involves inserting the transformed data into the target database for analysis. The target database could be a data mart, data warehouse, data lake, or other form of data repository. The data is now ready to be analyzed.

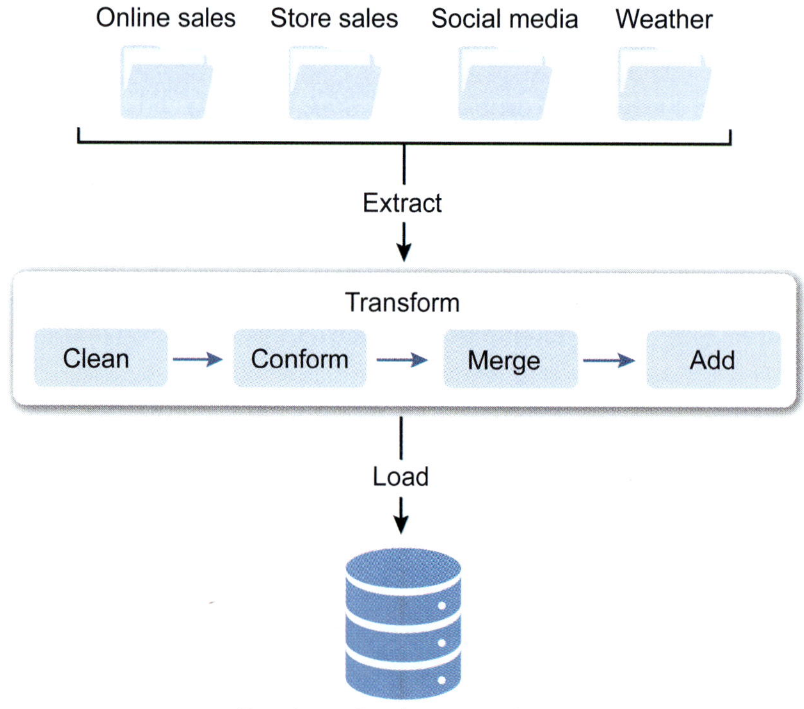

The phases in ETL may be completed *sequentially* or in *parallel*. For example, while the data is extracted, another process that runs in parallel transforms the extracted data. Then, a separate data-loading process may begin without waiting for the completion of the extract and transformation phases.

Alternatively, the transform and load phases may be reversed, resulting in **ELT**. This sequence is sometimes used to achieve faster loading times with respect to unstructured big data due to its size and variety of formats. ETL, however, is more commonly used than ELT; thus, we will focus our attention on ETL.

A retailer has multiple stores in the North, South, East, and West regions of the U.S. The retailer wants to use weather data from publicly available online sources and internal sales data to determine the impact of weather patterns on sales at each store.

In order to use the weather data, the retailer extracts sales data by store number, region, and date; extracts weather data by region and date; and joins the weather data to the sales data by region and date.

Data sets often need to be combined during the transform phase of ETL, usually **joined on fields common between them**. In this scenario, because the retailer wants to analyze the effect of weather on each store's daily sales, extracting sales by store, date, and zip code and then joining the data to weather data extracted by date and zip code is appropriate. These steps would allow the retailer to determine the daily **effects of weather on sales at each store**.

Sales data

Store ID	Zip Code	Date	Sales
1	22405	06042011	$50,000
2	22406	06042011	$75,000

+

Weather data

Zip code	Date	Temperature
22406	06042011	74
22406	06042011	55

=

Analysis set

Store ID	Zip Code	Date	Sales	Temperature
1	22405	06042011	$50,000	74
2	22406	06042011	$75,000	55

Transforming Data

Data extracted from sources is often not usable for analysis due to inconsistencies like formatting issues. At a high level, the **objectives** of the transformation phase are the following:

- Remove inconsistencies in the extracted data
- Correct mismatches and ensure that columns are in the same order
- Ensure that the data across sources is standardized to the same format
- Enrich data sets by including additional information

Various steps can be taken to prepare/cleanse data. These techniques can be grouped into the following categories:

Data Transformation Techniques

Technique	Purpose
Aggregating	Involves summarizing or grouping data (eg, summarizing total sales by store or region)
Constructing	Creating a new set of attributes from an existing set
Generalizing	Using hierarchies to create layers of summary data
Integrating	Combining records from multiple tables and data sets
Manipulating	Creating new values by pivoting, summarizing, scaling, sorting, etc.; can also be used to convert unstructured data to structured data
Revising	Reformatting data through cleaning, deduplication, validation, etc. to create data that is usable as intended
Smoothing	Cleaning data by removing leading and trailing zeros and non-printable characters (eg, white spaces, page breaks, line breaks, tabs)

Data Integrity

After each ETL phase, data validation should be performed to ensure that the data has integrity. **Data integrity** (ie, validation) refers to ensuring that data accurately reflects the business events underlying it and that any anomalies are rectified. It is important to ensure that data contains all relevant records needed from the source (ie, completeness), that the transformed data is consistent with the source data, and that the data loaded into the target source properly. Incorrect or invalid data can skew analysis and lead to inaccurate conclusions.

Data Validation Techniques

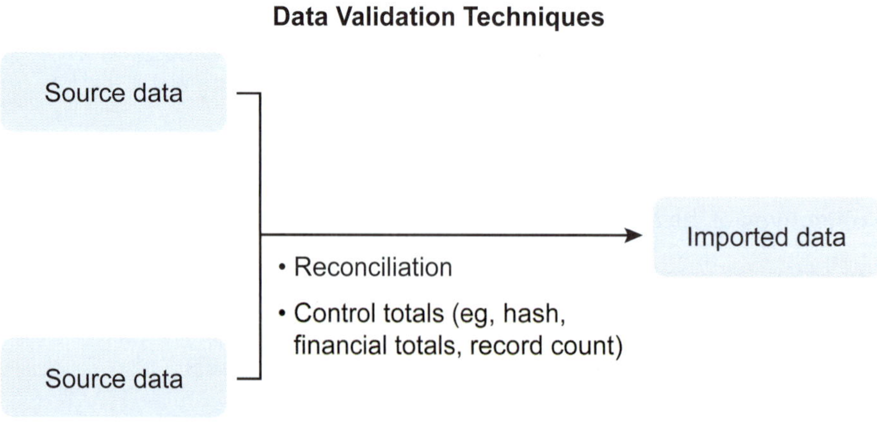

Note that **data quality** is a subset of data integrity. Quality data is accurate, complete, consistent, valid, and timely. Data integrity includes those characteristics in addition to relevance. That is, data that has integrity is relevant and useful in addition to being complete, accurate, consistent, valid, and timely.

Budgeting

Representative Task (Application): Prepare a budget using supportable assumptions.

Budgeting a company's financials (eg, revenue, working capital) requires a thorough understanding of which factors drive each metric. There are three general approaches to developing a budget forecast (for both revenues and expenses).

Financial Modeling Approaches

A **top-down approach** starts with assumptions about the overall economy, sector, or industry and then incorporates these assumptions into financial forecasts.

A **bottom-up approach** starts with the company itself, a business unit of the company (eg, product, geographic), or a specific company metric (eg, average price, revenue per square foot) and uses historical growth rates or ratios to construct forecasts that assume the continuation of a trend.

A **hybrid approach** uses elements of both the top-down and bottom-up approaches and may be useful for uncovering the types of biases or errors that might arise from either approach.

Assumptions

Any budget approach requires that *assumptions* be made (eg, revenue growth, cost of labor, utility cost, inflation rate). Assumptions are generally applied to existing data to develop a future, projected amount. Assumptions should be *supportable*, based on existing knowledge and past experiences, and not just randomly proposed.

Inflation Adjustments

When creating a budgeted income statement, the **impact of inflation**, economic conditions, and industry changes must be considered. Inflation would impact revenue and expense budget estimates that are based on last year's amounts (eg, total salaries expense, health-care costs). Inflation would not impact budgeted revenues or expenses associated with contractual obligations (eg, interest on the 10-year fixed note) or items based on historical information (eg, depreciation).

Effect of Inflation on Budgets

Diamond Co. uses a material that cost \$195 per ton at the beginning of the year and \$200 per ton at the end of the year. The industry experienced 4% inflation during the year. Determine the change in the real cost of Diamond's material.

Adjusting Nominal Value to Real Value

$$\text{Percentage change in nominal value} = \frac{\text{New value} - \text{Initial value}}{\text{Initial value}} \times 100$$

$$\text{Percentage change in real value} = \text{Percentage change in nominal value} - \text{inflation rate}$$

The cost of a product or service can be defined in either nominal or real value. *Nominal value* refers to the current price in dollars. *Real value* is the nominal value adjusted for inflation. **Inflation** is measured as the percentage change in overall prices over a period of time.

Here, the nominal value of materials increased by \$5 (\$200 − \$195). In percentage terms, nominal value increased by **2.56%** {[(200 − 195) / 195] × 100}.

The change in a real value equals the difference between the change in the nominal value and the inflation rate (given as **4.00%**), calculated as follows:

$$\begin{aligned}\%\text{ Change in real value} &= \%\text{ Change in nominal value} - \text{Inflation rate}\\ &= 2.56\% - 4.00\% = -1.44\% \text{ or } (.0144)\end{aligned}$$

The material's cost in real terms is a **\$2.81** [\$195 × (.0144)] per ton decrease.

Participative Budgeting

Participative budgeting is a process by which a budget is prepared with the involvement of managers and employees at all levels of the organization (ie, a **bottom-up approach**). Preliminary budgets are developed by departments or divisions and move up through the corporate structure for review and approval. Individual budgets are then combined into a corporate budget.

Inclusion of more layers of employees increases employee acceptance of the budget and can result in increased motivation to adhere to, or surpass, budget expectations. It can also improve the accuracy of the budget because lower-level managers are more familiar with costs and revenues at the department level than are higher-level supervisors.

Note that with any form of budgeting, there is always the risk of budgetary slack, in which the expense amounts are "padded" or increased to provide a bit of a cushion to cover unbudgeted costs. Conversely, revenue accounts may be underestimated.

The primary disadvantage to participative budgeting is the amount of time required to contact and gain feedback from the multiple layers of employees and management.

Participative Budgeting	
Advantages	• Creates company-wide goal congruence • Increases employee motivation and acceptance • Improves budget accuracy
Disadvantages	• Requires significant time • Creates budgetary slack (ie, excess cushion) • Overlooks high-level strategic objectives

Static vs. Flexible Budgets

Budgets used for internal planning and control purposes can be **static** or **flexible**. Both types of budgets include revenues, variable costs, contribution margins (CMs), and fixed costs.

Static vs. Flexible Budget Formulas	
Static	**Flexible**
Budget unit price × Budgeted units	Budgeted unit price × Actual units
Budgeted unit variable cost × Budgeted total units	Budgeted unit variable cost × Actual units
Less: budgeted total fixed costs	Less: budgeted total fixed costs
Projected operating income	Revised projected operating income

Static budgets estimate amounts for a specific level of activity (eg, 10,000 units of production). Static budgets do not change (or recalculate) each time activity levels change. For static budgets, amounts on an income statement may be budgeted as a percentage of sales.

When budgeted sales do not equal actual sales, a **variance** is generated, which must be investigated. A variance is the difference between the budgeted amount and the actual amount and is either favorable or unfavorable.

Flexible budgets can be adjusted for changes in volumes. Flexible budgets hold total fixed costs constant (within a relevant range) and adjust (ie, "flex") total revenues and variable costs for changes in activity levels.

Assume the current budget is as follows:

Sales (in dollars, not number of units)	$1,000
− Variable costs	600
Contribution margin	400
− Fixed costs	300
Operating profit	$ 100

If sales for a period turn out to be $1,500, one can readily modify the above budget. Sales increased from $1,000 to $1,500, or by 50%, and would be expected to also increase variable costs by 50%. One would not expect fixed costs to be affected. Thus,

Sales (in dollars, not number of units)	$1,000	× 1.5	=	$1,500
− Variable costs	600	× 1.5	=	900
Contribution margin	400			600
− Fixed costs	300		=	300
Operating profit	$ 100			$ 300

Alternatively, the mathematics underlying a **flexible budget** can be most readily expressed using a linear function: Y = a + (b × X)

- The "Y" is referred to as the **dependent variable**, or the item whose value is being estimated—in our example, expected total costs
- The "a" is referred to as "the constant" (or the intercept) and in our example stands for **fixed costs**
- The "X" is referred to as the **independent variable**, or the item whose changes may have an impact on the value of the dependent variable (Y). In linear functions applied to flexible budgeting, the independent variable is often called the **cost driver**. In our example, the cost driver is sales. In other settings, the independent variables are often called "predictors" or "determinants"
- The "b" is referred to as "the slope" and in our example stands for a **variable rate**, or the multiplier that reflects the effect of change in one unit of X on Y

In our example, when sales were $1,000, variable costs were $600, implying a variable rate (b) of 0.6 (ie, variable costs / sales = $600 / $1,000, or 60% of sales). Fixed costs (a) are $300. Thus,

Y = 300 + (0.6 * X)

When sales are $1,000: Expected total costs = $300 + (0.6 * $1,000) = $300 + $600 = $900

When sales are $1,500: Expected total costs = $300 + (0.6 * $1,500) = $300 + $900 = $1,200

Advantages of flexible budgets include the following:

- They can adapt readily to changes in variable costs that result from changes in the driver levels. For instance, it is reasonable to expect variable costs to double when sales volume doubles. A static budget masks true performance unless sales are at the budgeted level
- They promote management by exception. The insight gained by a clear understanding of cost drivers can assist in rewarding high performers and analyzing situations to improve future performance

Disadvantages include the following:

- Determining cost drivers and developing the appropriate rates can be challenging and time-consuming. It could require disruption in established routines to develop cost drivers and rates
- Depending on how sophisticated the system becomes, the cost of record keeping can also be a disadvantage. The cost-benefit of implementing a flexible budgeting system should be carefully considered
- The impact on morale could be detrimental. Various groups within the company might be concerned that their performance will be measured against a new, unfamiliar yardstick. Aside from the common resistance to any change, employees also might have concerns that the drivers or driver rates might be set inappropriately

Master Budget

Companies often use several specialized budgets to assist in their management. Companies use a **master budget** (a static budget for the company as a whole) to summarize various individual budgets. The two major categories of budgets that the master budget summarizes are the following:

- Operating budgets: a projected (or budgeted or future) income statement with its various supporting schedules
- Financial budgets: includes a projected (or budgeted or future) capital budget, cash budget, balance sheet, and statement of cash flows. This budget is usually for one year but could be a rolling budget as well

The order in which sub-budgets are completed is important because items from an earlier sub-budget are used as inputs for sub-budgets prepared later in the process. For example, net income from the budgeted income statement is required before the equity section of the budgeted balance sheet can be completed.

Sales Budget

Marketing generally provides expected sales volume (by product line and in the aggregate) and pricing information for each budgeted period of time. This information is the starting point for developing the sales budget, from which all other budgets are extrapolated.

Scooters R Us has the following projections for the current year. Note that scooter sales peak in the third quarter (mid- to late summer) and decline thereafter.

Quarter	First	Second	Third	Fourth	Total
Units	3,000	4,000	4,500	2,900	14,400

Scooter prices increase by 5% for the second and third quarters and then are decreased by 7% to clear out any remaining stock by year end. For the first quarter, scooter prices were $45 each. Amounts are rounded to the nearest dollar.

Quarter	First	Second	Third	Fourth	Total
Units	3,000	4,000	4,500	2,900	14,400
Per unit price	$ 45	$ 47	$ 50	$ 46	n/a
Projected sales	$135,000	$188,000	$225,000	$133,400	$681,400

Production Budget

Production budgets for each quarter are generally linked. For example, beginning inventory either is given or is the prior quarter's ending inventory. Estimated ending inventory is typically a percentage of the next quarter's sales projections.

Finished scooter inventory at the beginning of the year was budgeted to be 2,000. The quantity of finished goods inventory at the end of each quarter is equal to 30% of the next quarter's budgeted sales of units. Determine the units to be produced for the second quarter.

For this scenario, first calculate ending inventory and plug in the given units sold.

	First	Second	Third
Budgeted sales	3,000	4,000	4,500
Beginning inventory	2,000		
+ Units produced			
= Total units needed			
− Units sold	3,000	4,000	4,500
= Ending inventory	30% × 4,000	30% × 4,500	

Next, back into total units needed (units sold plus ending inventory). Fill in beginning inventory, which was the prior quarter's ending inventory.

	First	Second	Third
Beginning inventory	2,000	1,200	1,350
+ Units produced			
= Total units needed	4,200	5,350	
− Units sold	3,000	4,000	
= Ending inventory	1,200	1,350	

Finally, back into units to be produced (total units needed − beginning inventory). Production for the second quarter is 4,150 units.

	First	Second	Third
Beginning inventory	2,000	1,200	
+ Units produced	2,200	4,150	
= Total units needed	4,200	5,350	
− Units sold	3,000	4,000	
= Ending inventory	1,200	1,350	

Direct Material Budget(s)

Multiple direct material budgets may need to be created. Here, each scooter built requires two wheels, as well as all the other materials required to assemble a finished unit. Wheels are purchased from a vendor, not built internally. Below is the purchase budget for the wheels only. Note that first the *number* of units to purchase is determined then the *cost* of that purchase is calculated.

Scooter World's beginning wheel inventory was 1,000, while beginning scooter inventory was 1,500. First-quarter production of scooters is estimated to be 2,200, while second-quarter production is estimated to be 2,500. The quantity of finished goods wheel inventory at the end of each quarter is equal to 30% of the next quarter's estimated wheel requirements for scooter production. Cost per wheel is $2.

Determine the number of wheels that need to be purchased for the first quarter.

Wheels estimated for quarter 1 production (2,200 × 2)	4,400
Plus desired quarter 1 ending wheel inventory (2,500 × 2 × 30%)	1,500
Less beginning wheel inventory	1,000
Wheels to be purchased	4,900
Cost per wheel	$ 2.00
Total wheel cost	**$9,800**

Direct Labor Budget

Labor budgets are based on the number of hours needed for each completed unit. Obviously, there is no beginning or ending inventory, so the budget focuses on current production needs. Assume that it takes two and a half hours to assemble each scooter. Labor cost is $18 an hour. Determine the total estimated cost of labor for the first quarter.

First determine the total number of scooters to be produced, total labor hours, and then total labor cost.

Estimated units produced (given)	2,200
Labor hours per scooter	2.5
Total labor hours required	5,500
Labor cost per hour	$ 18
Total labor cost	**$99,000**

Overhead Budget

Overhead budgets consist of variable and fixed overhead costs. Variable costs are typically tied to a cost driver, such as direct labor hours or machine hours. The budget may be based on one level of production or provide alternate scenarios for "worst case" and "best case" production levels, as shown:

Prepare an overhead (OH) budget assuming three levels of production: 10,000, 13,000, and 17,000 units. Variable costs are driven by machine hours, which are estimated to be 2.5 hours for each unit of production.

Units of production	10,000	13,000	17,000
Total machine hours (2.5 per unit)	25,000	32,500	42,500
Variable OH costs:			
Indirect materials ($.75 per hour)	$ 18,750	$ 24,375	$ 31,875
Indirect labor ($3.50 per hour)	87,500	113,750	148,750
Utilities ($2.10 per hour)	52,500	68,250	89,250
Total variable OH costs	$158,750	$206,375	$269,875
Fixed OH costs:			
Factory supervisor salary	$ 75,000	$ 75,000	$ 75,000
Depreciation	110,000	110,000	110,000
Property taxes and insurance	37,600	37,600	37,600
Total fixed OH costs	$222,600	$222,600	$222,600
Total OH costs	**$381,350**	**$428,975**	**$492,475**

Cash Collections

Cash collections consist of money collected from **cash sales** and **accounts receivable** (ie, credit sales). Credit sale collections may be spread over several months, and a portion of the receivables balance may be *uncollectible* (ie, credit losses). Estimated collection rates are typically based on the company's historical experience.

A company forecast first-quarter sales of 10,000 units, second-quarter sales of 15,000 units, and third-quarter sales of 20,000 units at $5 per unit. Cash sales are 30% of total sales, and uncollectible sales are estimated to be 2%. Net credit sales are collected 80% in the month of sale and 20% in the following month. Determine total cash collections for the second quarter. (Note: all third-quarter information can be ignored as it is irrelevant).

Second-quarter cash collections are **$70,100**, as calculated below. The amount consists of cash sales from the current quarter ($22,500), a portion of credit sale collection from the prior quarter ($6,800), and a portion of credit sale collection from the current quarter ($40,800).

	1st Quarter	**2nd Quarter**	**3rd Quarter**
Units of production	10,000	15,000	20,000
Total quarter sales ($5 per unit)	$50,000	$75,000	$100,000
Cash sales (30%)	$15,000	**$22,500**	$ 30,000
Net credit sales (68%)*	$34,000	$51,000	$ 68,000
	20%	80%	
Collections in 2nd quarter:			
Current quarter cash sales (30%)	$15,000	**$22,500**	$ 30,000
Current quarter net credit sales (80%)		40,800	
Prior quarter net credit sales (20%)**		6,800	
Total estimated cash collections:		**$70,100**	

**100% − 30% cash = 70% credit − 2% uncollectible = 68% net credit*

***Net credit is collected 80% in month of sale and 20% in the following month.*

Ideally, once you are comfortable with the overall setup, you can go directly to the second step and compute each amount in a linear equation, as follows:

Current quarter cash collections	$75,000 × 30%	$22,500
Current quarter credit collections	($75,000 × 68%) × 80%	40,800
Prior quarter credit collections	($50,000 × 68%) × 20%	6,800
Total estimated cash collections:		**$70,100**

Master Budget Components

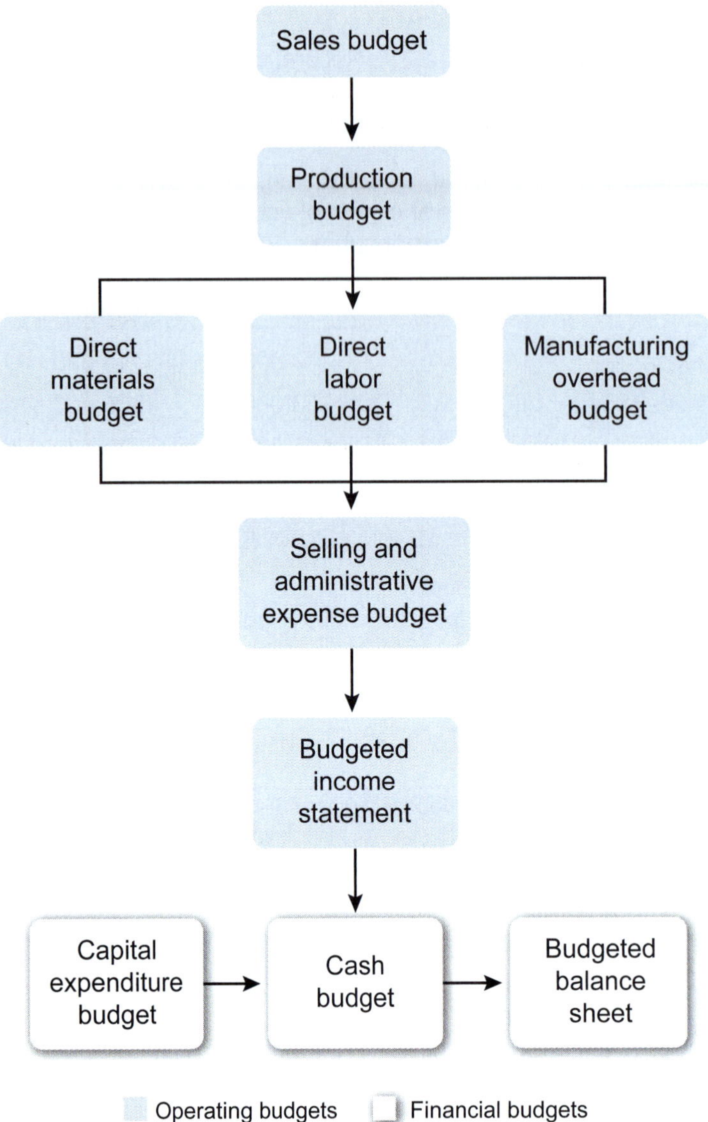

Forecasting and Projections

Representative Task (Application): Use forecasting and projection techniques to model financial results including revenue growth, cost and expense characteristics, and profitability.

Representative Task (Analysis): Analyze results of forecasts and projections using ratio analysis and explanations of correlations to, or variations from, key financial indices.

Overview

Financial forecasting incorporates the processes used by an entity to predict and prepare for the future. *Expectations* (ie, assumptions) are developed for future performance and operating results, which then become the basis for budgets and projections.

Financial modeling uses the forecasted expectations to calculate future financial statements. In other words, a *predictive model* is built from the forecast.

While forecasting techniques may be more or less computationally sophisticated, ultimately they involve determining past relationships among various variables and making projections based on:

- The assumption that past relationships (ie, **trends**) will continue, and/or
- Specific judgments about how some particular variables might behave in the future.

Prospective F/S include both forecasts and projections.

Prospective Financial Information		
Forecast	• Shows where business is expected to go based on expected **general** conditions and the entity's expected course of action • Example: forecasting future sales based on sales trends	For **general** or limited use
Projection	• Shows what management believes will occur given *specific* **hypothetical** assumptions (ie, "what if" scenarios) • Example: projecting *what* would happen *if* an entity lost a major customer	For **limited** use **only**

In developing **forecasts and projections**, analysts relate inputs to outputs, including the following:

Inputs	• Economic data (eg, GDP growth) • Industry data (eg, market share) • Company data (eg, common-sized financial statements, ratio analyses)
Outputs	• Earnings model • Earnings per share forecast used to make an equity valuation • Management presentations to secure external financing

Analysts may vary the inputs to determine a **range of possibilities**, not just a single-point estimate. For example, there might be a 10% probability of inflation below 0%, a 20% probability of inflation between 0% and 1%, a 40% probability of inflation between 1% and 3%, a 20% probability of inflation between 3% and 10%, and a 10% probability of inflation higher than 10%.

In addition, analysts may conduct sensitivity (ie, "what if") or scenario analysis to determine how the forecast reacts under different assumptions. Using simulations and sound judgment, analysts can ascertain whether the forecast is robust enough to make investment decisions (eg, buy a stock).

Analyzing Fluctuations and Patterns

When fluctuations and/or patterns are detected in data, the results should be analyzed to determine the driver(s) of the change. Future forecasts and budgets would then incorporate the identified driver, thus improving the accuracy of future projections.

For example, Emerald Corp. looked at the following revenue information to budget for Year 4.

Year	1st Qtr.	2nd Qtr.	3rd Qtr.	4th Qtr.
Year 1	500	500	550	750
Year 2	525	550	600	800
Year 3	550	525	625	850

During Years 1–3, there were no major changes to Emerald's selling strategies and total capital investment. To visualize the information, the data was assembled into the following graph:

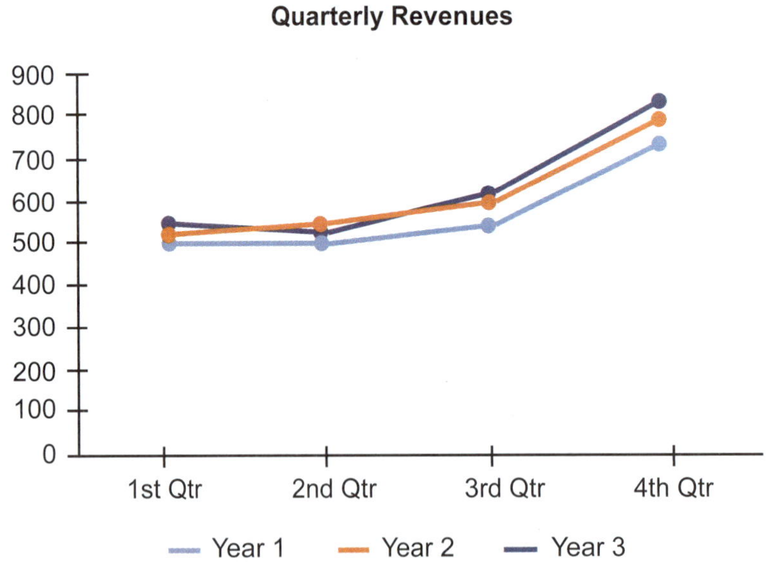

For each of the three years presented, there was a significant spike in sales for the fourth quarter. In the next year, revenues for the first quarter consistently return to lower levels. This indicates a seasonal demand pattern rather than changes in the economy.

Seasonal demand can have a significant impact on the management of inventory and cash flow. In this case, to cover sales demand changes, inventory purchases will need to increase in the third quarter, with significant increases in the fourth quarter. Enhanced cash flow will be needed to pay off the larger purchase invoices from retailers (or the increased material and labor costs from manufacturing entities).

Analyzing Variances

Another factor to be aware of is that a *favorable* variance is not always a "good thing." For example, even though sales would have an unfavorable variance when actual sales are less than budgeted, sales commissions (an expense) would be favorable because the actual expense would be less than budgeted. It is important to recognize that a favorable variance might indicate a negative operating situation; sales were under budget, so the entity may not meet its revenue goals.

Analyzing Capital Budgeting Decisions

Assume that a company is evaluating four projects as possible investments. All of the projects are for the same activity. The company will select only one project. The company's discount rate for such projects is 10%.

Additional information about the projects is as follows:

Project	Internal Rate of Return	Net Present Value
A	11%	$210,000
B	12%	195,000
C	13%	175,000
D	14%	200,000

When multiple projected criteria are presented, the data must be interpreted appropriately, and interrelationships between the data must be understood. Here, both net present value (NPV) and the internal rate of return (IRR) are provided.

NPV equals the excess of the present value (PV) of cash inflows over the PV of cash outflows (typically the initial project's cost). **NPV estimates an investment's profitability** in terms of today's dollars and can be used to **compare investments**.

The **IRR** is used by management to **allocate limited resources** to the **most profitable** projects. The IRR is the discount rate that sets cash inflows equal to cash outflows (ie, NPV equals $0, or essentially break-even).

The 10% discount rate is the minimum rate (also called the hurdle rate) at which the entity would find a project acceptable. Because all the IRRs exceed the minimum, all would be considered acceptable.

Remember that percentage information can be misleading. The most advantageous project for the company is the project that **returns the greatest NPV** (ie, net cash), which is Project A. Even though Project D has a greater IRR, it returns less cash and is therefore deemed to be less profitable.

Forecasting Limitations

Businesses use forecasting techniques to develop projections of the environment in which they will operate in the future. However, businesses need to be aware of **limitations** of certain forecasting techniques. In general, forecasts take into account the following:

- Economy-wide conditions such as inflation, economic growth, and retail sales
- Sector-specific issues, including sales demand and pricing decisions
- Business-specific concerns such as cash flows for inventory purchases

Forecasting and Projection Techniques

Delphi Method

The **Delphi Method** consists of a group of experts on a particular topic who are *questioned individually* about the topic. Their individual judgments are then examined and combined as applicable. The combined input is then returned individually to the panel, and the process is repeated until a consensus is determined.

The Delphi technique avoids experts meeting, to minimize the possibility of **group-think**. Group-think is the tendency of people at meetings to come to a consensus because of the pressures of conformity and fear of embarrassment, such that the consensus may fail to actually represent the best judgment of these same people individually.

Delphi Forecasting Method

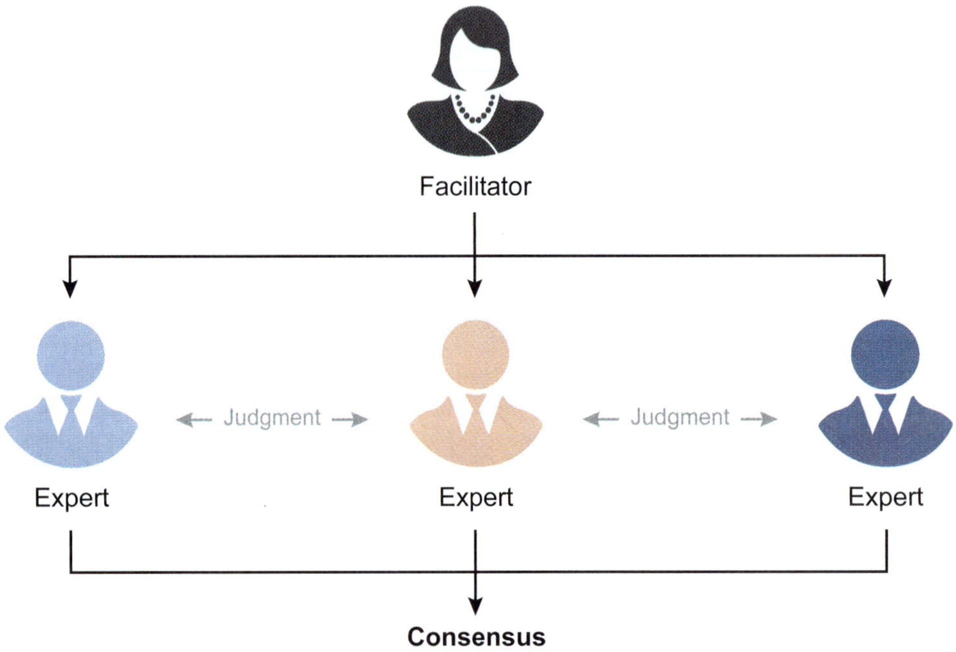

Facilitator

Expert ← Judgment → Expert ← Judgment → Expert

Consensus

Expected Value

Expected value is a process whereby possible (mutually exclusive) outcomes are multiplied by their likelihood (ie, probability of occurrence) and the amounts are summed into a **single weighted expected value.** The expected value is *compared to the eventual actual value*, and the estimation process is modified as appropriate, based on the difference between the two amounts.

Expected value can be used for budgets, projections, and cost-benefit analysis.

For example, if the decision to market a product is believed to have a 10% probability (chance) of resulting in sales of $100, a 40% probability of $200, a 30% probability of $300, and a 20% probability of $400, the calculation of expected value is as follows:

Revenue	Probability	Weighted value
$100	10%	$ 10
200	40%	80
300	30%	90
400	20%	80
Expected value	**100%**	**$ 260**

Correlation Analysis

To develop more relevant flexible budgets, companies may seek to identify **which predictors to use** as the Xs for which Ys in their linear functions. For instance, sales might be the best predictor for a company's total costs. In contrast, direct labor hours might be the best predictor for manufacturing overhead costs.

Correlation is a measure of the degree of **linear relationship** between two variables. The value of the **correlation coefficient (p)** ranges from negative one to one ($-1 \leq \rho \leq 1$): negative one indicates that two variables have a perfect inverse linear relationship. Positive one means the variables have a perfect linear relationship. Zero indicates no linear relationship.

A scatter-plot illustrates the relationship between the variables. The strength of the correlation (ie, how close ρ is to −1 or 1) is indicated by how close the points are to being in a straight line. If the slope of the indicated line is negative and the points are still somewhat dispersed, then there is a weak inverse (negative) correlation. If the slope of the line is positive, then the correlation is positive.

Scatterplots for Different Values of Correlation Coefficient (ρ)

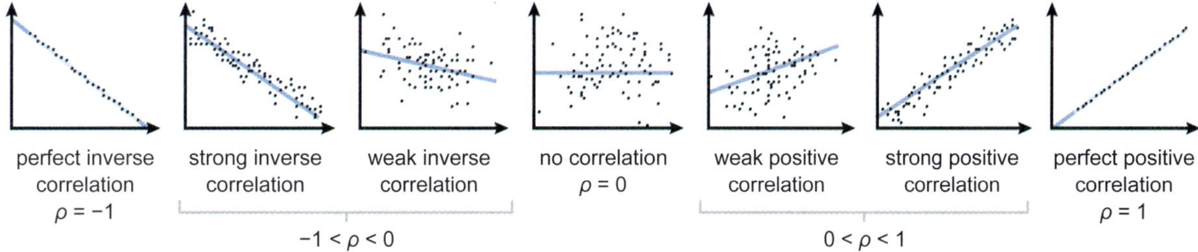

Planning Techniques

Representative Task (Analysis): Prepare and interpret the results of planning techniques including cost-benefit analysis, sensitivity analysis, "what if" scenarios, break-even analysis, and predictive analytics.

Probability Analysis

Most planning techniques require estimates of the revenues and costs that will result from various decisions. In the real world, many decisions may lead to many different possible outcomes. Managers may use **probability theory** to develop the most sensible possible single estimates from the range of possibilities. A *probability distribution* describes the possible outcomes relating to a single action and the likelihood of occurrence of each possible outcome. To turn a probability distribution into a single expected value, one would multiply each of the possible outcomes by its likelihood (or probability, weight, or percentage) and sum the amounts.

Cost-Benefit Analysis

Various factors should be considered in determining whether an entity implements a potential change (eg, moving headquarters to a newer, larger building). The analysis basically involves **comparing the costs to the benefits**. Items to consider can be both tangible and intangible (ie, happier employees).

Costs to consider include the following:

- Direct and indirect business costs (eg, increased delivery cost for raw material)
- Costs associated with a potential disruption in operations
- Training personnel (eg, new, more complicated equipment)
- Costs of potential mistakes (eg, scrapped production due to processing flaw)
- Opportunity cost (ie, cost of alternative use of funds)

Benefits to consider include the following:

- Greater accuracy for short-to-intermediate-length projects
- Data-driven approach, which results in more rational and less emotional decisions
- Decision-making simplified to two variables (cost, benefit)
- Hidden costs potentially identified (eg, opportunity cost)

Sensitivity Analysis

Sensitivity analysis refers to assessing how target variables (eg, risk-adjusted bond yields) respond (ie, their "sensitivity") to changes in input variables (eg, bond coupon rate). By conducting **"what if" scenarios**, investment managers gain a greater understanding of the potential risk and return profile of an investment strategy.

For example, sensitivity analysis can be used to determine bond pricing for various coupon and market interest rates. Assume that interest is paid twice a year and the bond has total par value of $100,000 with a maturity of five years. Using Excel, a data table is created with coupon rates of 6%, 7%, and 8%, while market rates are predicted to be 5%, 6%, and 7%. The "what if" results would be as follows:

	A	B	C	D
1	**Yield to Maturity**			
2	**Coupon rate**			
3		**5.00%**	**6.00%**	**7.00%**
4	6%	104,376	100,000	95,842
5	7%	108,752	104,265	100,000
6	8%	113,128	108,530	104,158

So the bond selling price would be $104,265 if the coupon rate were 7% with a market rate of 6%.

Break-even Analysis

Break-even uses cost-volume-profit (CVP) analysis but is only that one point at which all costs are covered by sales revenue (ie, profit is zero). The formula is [(fixed cost + desired net income) / contribution margin]. Remember that net income is $0 at break-even, so net income is typically not shown in the numerator.

Break-even analysis assumptions include the following:

- Fixed and variable costs can be easily identified
- Total variable costs vary directly with output; unit cost remains constant
- Total fixed costs remain constant over the relevant range
- Selling price per unit remains constant for all levels of output
- Sales mix of products remains constant
- All production is sold

Assume that a budget has been prepared for a product on the basis of estimated sales of 100 units per period, selling price of $10 per unit, variable costs of $6 per unit, and fixed costs of $300 per period. A direct costing statement based on this information follows:

Units	100
Sales ($10)	$1,000
– Variable costs ($6)	600
Contribution margin ($4)	$ 400
– Fixed costs	300
Operating profit	**$ 100**

The **break-even point** occurs when the **operating profit is $0**. Since fixed costs are $300, contribution margin at break-even must be at least $300 (ie, profit = $0). (Remember, the income statement above shows an operating profit, not break-even, so contribution margin is $400 rather than $300.)

To calculate the **number of units** that must be sold for contribution margin to equal fixed costs, the following formula is used:

Fixed costs / Contribution margin per unit = $300 / $4 = 75 units

To determine the **number of sales dollars** needed, contribution margin can be expressed as a percentage of sales (or contribution margin per dollar of sales). In this scenario, the contribution margin is 40% (either $4 / $10 or $400 / $1,000), so the formula is:

Fixed costs / Contribution margin percentage = $300 / 40% = $750

Of course, these are related, since 75 units at a $10 selling price equals $750 in sales. Let's look at the break-even statement next to the original budget:

Units	**100**	**75**
Sales ($10)	$1,000	$750
– Variable costs ($6)	600	450
Contribution margin ($4)	$ 400	$300
– Fixed costs	300	300
Operating profit	$ 100	$ 0

Predictive Analytics

Predictive analytics is an umbrella term for analytical/modeling techniques used to determine the probability of or to predict the outcome of a given value. Prediction can be for variables at the same point in time (eg, model expected sales as a function of inventory at a point in time) or at a future time (eg, predict future sales as a function of sales and customer trends).

Predictive models can use both historical and forward-looking data for prediction. They can use statistics, calculus, and often machine learning. Examples of predictive analytics' applications include the impact of business promotions or online advertising, employee turnover, and probability of financial downturn.

These models can be valuable to businesses looking to anticipate future trends and gauge the probability of different outcomes. Although the CPA exam does not expect candidates to develop predictive models, it can test knowledge of foundational theory and the ability to infer insights from a model's results.

There is a variety of predictive analytics methods that can be used. Each method is better suited for certain prediction exercises than others. Suitability depends, along with other factors, on the type of variable to be predicted. Variables can be quantitative or qualitative.

Quantitative variables have the following characteristics:

- **Discrete variables** are finitely countable and can only take certain values (eg, the number of completed inventory items can be definitively counted and can only be a whole number)
- **Continuous variables** are impossible to definitively count and can take any value (eg, square footage or average wait time). There is no "break" between two consecutive values
- Quantitative variables can also be classified into **ratio or interval scales**
  - **Interval scales** are similar to ordinal scales in that they provide a meaningful order but differ because the distance between values is equal. For example, contingent liabilities being classified as remote, possible, or probable is ordinal because the distance between values may be unequal. That is, moving from possible to probable may be more extreme than moving from remote to possible. On the other hand, temperature is an example of an interval scale; 40°F is five degrees colder than 45°F, and the temperature difference is the same as the difference between 50°F and 55°F.
  - **Ratio scales** are similar to interval scales in that they provide a meaningful order and the distance between values in the scale is equal. Ratio scales are more informative than interval scales because they have an absolute zero point. For example, consider monetary values (eg, dollars), which is an example of a ratio scale. An individual with zero dollars has no money. On the other hand, a temperature of zero (ie, interval scale) does not mean that there is no temperature; that is, temperature does not have an absolute zero point

Qualitative/categorical variables have the following characteristics:

- **Nominal variables** are categorical in nature with no order between them (eg, cash flows can be categorized as operating, financing, or investing activities). Nominal variables are sometimes denoted with numbers but do not signify a quantitative value (eg, groups 1 and 2)
- **Ordinal variables** are categorical with a meaningful order (eg, under US GAAP, a contingent liability can be classified as either remote, possible, or probable). Each category denotes a higher chance of occurrence than the former

Predictive Analytic Methods

Regression analysis estimates the relationship between a dependent variable and one or more independent variables. It is widely used in practice to predict values for continuous dependent variables. Regression can be linear or logistic in nature.

Linear regression models the dependent variable as a *linear* (straight line) function of the independent variable(s).

- The **intercept** in a regression equation is the point at which the regression line crosses the y-axis; it can be interpreted as the mean for the dependent variable when all of the independent variables have a value of zero
- The **regression coefficients** describe the mathematical relationship between each independent variable and the dependent variable. Regression coefficients can be interpreted as the influence of each independent variable on the dependent variable. Regression coefficients can be negative or positive
  - A **negative coefficient** implies that the independent variable has an inverse relationship with the dependent variable, whereas a **positive coefficient** implies a positive relationship
  - For example, a remote work policy may have a positive regression coefficient when predicting employee retention, whereas commute time may have a negative regression coefficient when predicting employee retention

Regression Analysis Components

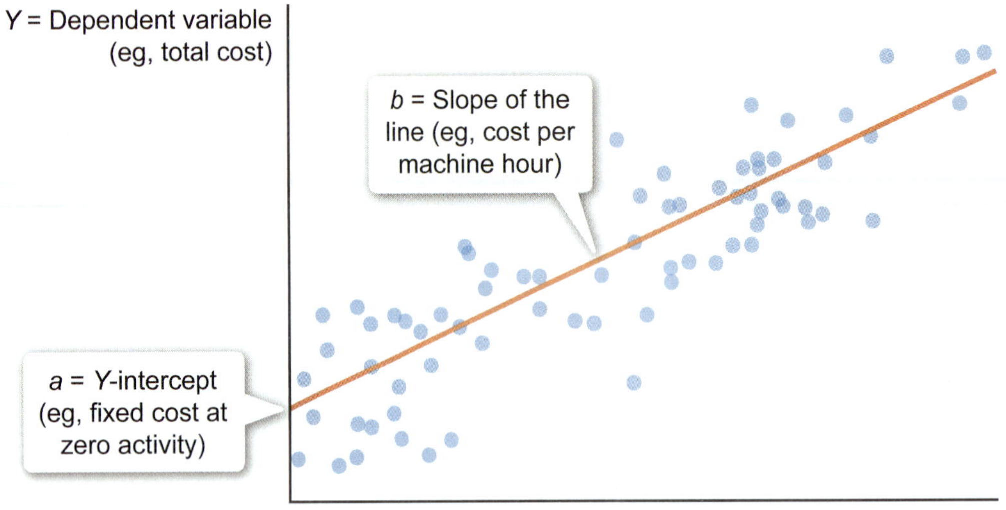

- The **p-value** tests the statistical significance of the regression coefficients as well as the significance of the overall regression
- The **f-test** is used to determine the significance of the overall regression
- The **t-statistic** is used to determine the significance of each regression coefficient
- Both the f-statistic and the t-statistic are associated with a p-value, which determines statistical significance
  - If the p-value associated with the f-test is statistically significant (typically $p < .05$), then the regression model is more predictive than simply using the mean of the response
  - If the p-value associated with the t-statistic is statistically significant ($p < .05$), then the correlation between the independent variable and dependent variable is not zero. As such, changes in the independent variable are associated with changes in the dependent variable; thus, this independent variable is a meaningful addition to the model
  - On the other hand, if the p-value for the regression coefficient is not statistically significant ($p > .05$), then the correlation between the independent variable and the dependent variable is not significantly different from zero. Therefore, changes in the independent variable may not be associated with changes in the dependent variable
  - Typically, regression coefficients with significant p-values should be retained and considered, whereas those with non-significant p-values could be removed or ignored. Keep in mind that statistical significance, as indicated by the p-value, is different from practical significance. That is, although an independent variable may be statistically significant, its significance may not significantly matter for business decisions
- The **coefficient of determination** (ie, **r-squared**) is the variance in the dependent variable explained by the independent variables. It is a measure of the accuracy and efficacy of the regression model. The coefficient of determination ranges from 0 to 1 and is expressed as a percentage (eg, .7 as 70%)
  - Regression models with high coefficients of determination better explain and predict the dependent variable than do regression models with low coefficients of determination
- The **error term** in the regression model represents the difference between the estimated values per the regression and the actual values. An error term essentially means that the model is not completely accurate and leads to differing results during real-world applications

US GAAP requires entities to estimate and recognize the amount of credit loss expense in a reporting period. To develop a well-supported estimate of the allowance for credit losses, an entity develops a series of regression models and finalizes the model below.

Here, cl_t is the monthly credit loss expense, cs_t is the monthly credit sales, be_t is the number of monthly billing errors, and cr_t is the average credit rating of the entity's customers, all at time *t*.

Dependent Variable			cl_t
Model Statistics:			
Coefficient of Determination (R^2)			.78
F-Statistic			116.15
P-Value (Model-Level)			.0000
Intercept			350
Variable Statistics:	cs_t	be_t	cr_t
Coefficient Estimates	4.00	1.75	−50.17
T-Statistic	2.56	0.14	−14.40
P-Value (For T-Statistic)	<.01	.89	.000

In equation form, the regression is written as

$$cl_t = 350 + 4\,(cs_t) + 1.75(be_t) - 50.17(cr_t) + \varepsilon$$

At any point of time *t*, the entity's estimated bad debts are

$350 + (4 × credit sales) + (1.75 × billing errors) − (50.17 × the credit rating).

The unknown error *e* denotes the difference between the actual and estimated value of bad debts.

- Credit rating cr_t is the *most significant variable*, with a p-value smaller than .000, meaning that there is very small probability that the impact of cr_t on cl_t occurred by chance.
- Monthly billing errors be_t is *not significant* because the p-value is greater than .05
- Monthly credit sales cs_t is *significant* at $p < .01$

Estimated bad debt expense would equal $350 (the intercept) when all independent variables are equal to 0. All independent variables combined explain 78% of the variation in bad debts, as denoted by the R^2.

Logistic regression models are similar to linear regression models in construct but are used for classification when the dependent variable is categorical, rather than continuous. Since the dependent variable is categorical, logistic regression predictions always lie between 0 and 1 and represent the probability of a data point belonging to a particular class.

Using a maximum likelihood approach, the data point is assigned to the class with the highest probability. Popular use cases for logistic regression include fraud detection, loan defaults, and whether a customer will respond to a targeted advertisement. For example, logistic regression could be used to determine whether a car insurance claim is fraudulent (ie, the dependent variable). The independent variables for predicting whether the claim is fraudulent may include number of years an insured has been with the company, total number of claims filed by the insured, and whether the claim was reported to the police.

Classification algorithms are applicable when data is discrete, nominal, or ordinal and can be divided into a finite number of classes. The algorithms **predict the classification of a given observation**. Classification problems may be binary (two groups) or multi-class (> two groups).

Several classification algorithms exist, and one may be better suited to a particular type of data set than others:

- **Naïve Bayes** classifier uses a foundational statistical formula called the Bayes theorem. It uses a probabilistic approach to calculate the respective likelihood of a data point belonging to each of the available classes. The data point is assigned to the class with the highest probability
- **Decision trees** can handle both regression and classification problems, although they are more frequently used for the latter. The algorithm creates a tree-like structure by splitting data on the basis of different variable values. Decision trees can be highly accurate and involve minimal preprocessing of data
- **K-Nearest Neighbors** is one of the most straightforward classification algorithms. All data points are plotted on a graph. For each data point to be classified, the majority class among the k nearest data points is assigned to the data point. For example, assume k = 5. Of the five closest data points to an unclassified point, three belong to class A and two belong to class B. The data point is assigned class A.

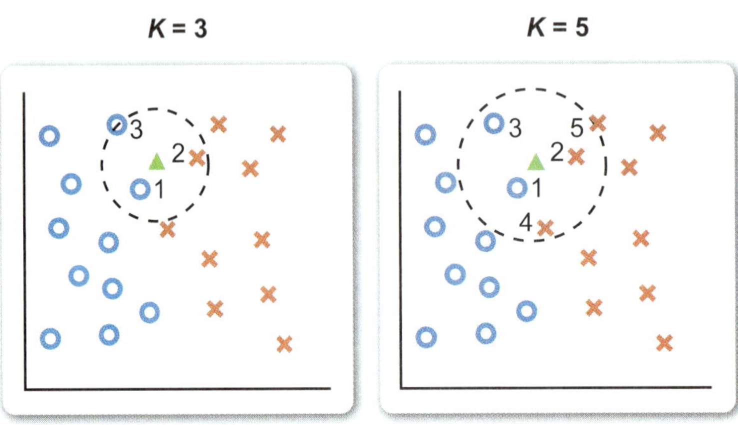

Assume that a lessee entity holds thousands of lease contracts, making it cumbersome for the auditor to evaluate each contract's classification. The auditor decides to classify documents on the basis of number of pages and lease amount.

Given the greater complexity of finance leases, contracts for finance leases may be more in-depth and therefore may have a greater number of pages. Furthermore, finance leases typically have larger dollar amounts than operating leases do. Given these potential differences between finance and operating leases, number of pages and dollar amount can be used to classify a lease as finance or operating.

The following past data is available:

# Of Pages	Lease Amount	Lease Classification
5	$ 7,787	Operating
50	$ 39,480	Finance
34	$ 25,591	Finance
5	$ 24,723	Operating
19	$ 42,536	Finance
20	$ 33,233	Finance
55	$ 8,245	Operating
49	$ 16,548	Operating
27	$ 22,726	Operating
16	$ 41,973	Finance

The auditor wants to classify a new lease with 40 pages worth $35,000. It develops a scatter-plot of available data:

Lease Classification

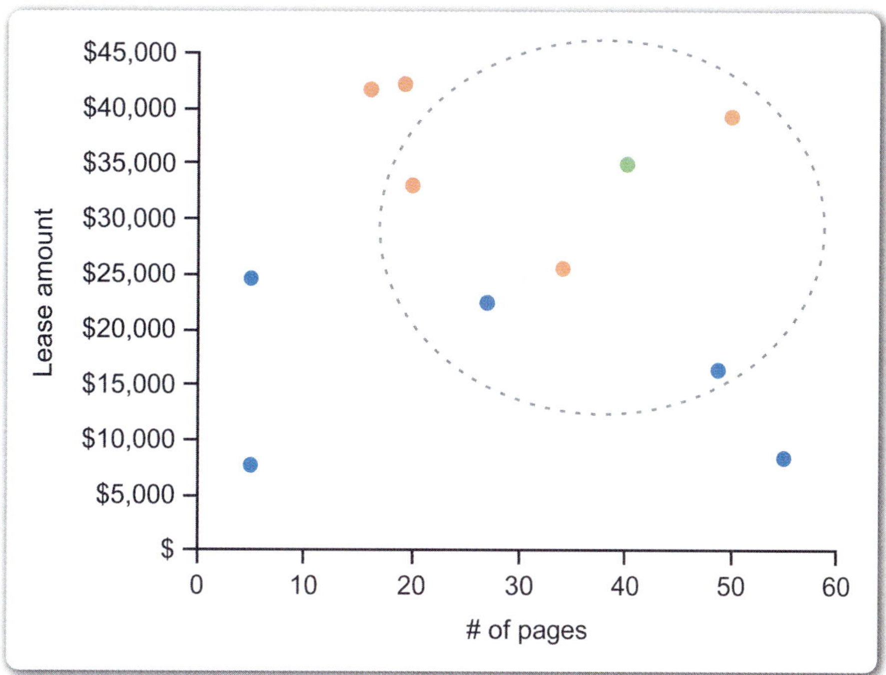

The orange points denote finance leases, while the blue points denote operating leases. The green point needs to be classified. Using k-nearest neighbors with k = 5, the auditor identifies the five nearest data points to the green point (the dotted oval). Three of the nearest points are finance leases, and two are operating leases. By majority, the auditor classifies the new lease document as a finance lease

Neural networks are predictive models inspired by the structure of the human brain. They can be for either classification or regression. Although they have existed since the twentieth century, they have gained considerable traction since modern technologies of the twenty-first century have made large amounts of data available.

- Neural networks fall under a branch of machine learning called **deep learning** because of their ability to model extremely intricate nuances from the training data. Today, neural networks are used in face-detection programs, self-driving cars, and fraud analytics

Clustering techniques are used to group data with similar characteristics together and are useful in finding patterns. In the absence of relevant past values for the dependent variable, clustering algorithms assign data points to bins independent of prior knowledge.

A data point is assigned to a cluster using statistical techniques and similarity scores. Because of clustering techniques' dual ability to (a) group data with similarities and (b) separate data with distinctions, they are often used to create a representative sample of a larger population, which can then be used as training data for other predictive algorithms.

Clustering techniques can also be used to detect *outliers and anomalies*. Each clustering algorithm has a grouping criterion and a stopping criterion. The former defines how points will be grouped together, and the latter defines when clustering will terminate and clusters will be final.

Monte Carlo simulation can be used to solve complex financial problems (eg, planning, risk management, valuation) by randomly generating large sets of data over repeated trials. In simple terms, a Monte Carlo simulation projects a set of random values for several independent variables to approximate the value for a dependent variable, over repeated trials. Each trial generates one set of data. At the end of the simulation, the probability of different outcomes for the dependent variable can be approximated.

- A strength of the Monte Carlo model is that it provides sensitivity ("what if") analysis by allowing users flexibility to adjust the parameters of the simulation (ie, probability distributions of the data, as well as mean and standard deviation of the distribution). A limitation is that it provides statistical estimates rather than exact results. Furthermore, these estimates do not establish causal relationships

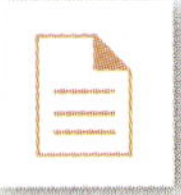

A CFO uses Monte Carlo simulations to assess the risk of not meeting the interest coverage ratio required by its lender. The ratio is equal to EBIT divided by interest expense.

Based on prior years' data and projections for key variables, the simulation model computes different ratio outcomes using variables for customer growth, sales mix, variable cost percentage of sales, and economic conditions. Other statistical techniques like regression and descriptive analysis of prior-year data could also be used to estimate relationships and the variation of these variables.

After running the model over 10,000 iterations, the CFO estimates the probability of outcomes in which the interest coverage ratio is not met.

2.02 Capital Structure

Cost of Capital

Representative Task (Application): Calculate the cost of capital for a given financial scenario.

Capital Structure

There are three general sources of funds companies use to finance operations:

- Issuing common or preferred stock
- Borrowing (eg, loans, bonds)
- Generating cash from operations

Ultimately, these amounts are reflected on balance sheets as debt or equity. The proportional split between the amounts of debt and equities is a company's **capital structure**.

Capital Structure and Sources of Capital

Cost of Capital

A business's cost of capital is the average of the costs of its debt and equity (including preferred stock, common stock, and retained earnings), each weighted by its market value. These costs are expressed as percentages per annum.

The word "capital" can have different meanings in different contexts. In some contexts (eg, bank regulation), capital is roughly equivalent to "equity" and excludes most liabilities (eg, deposits and senior bonds). In the context of calculations of the cost of capital, project selection, etc., capital means all sources of funds, including both debt and equity.

The **cost of debt financing** is the after-tax cost of interest payments as measured by yields to maturity. It can be calculated in *two ways*:

- Yield to maturity × (1 − effective tax rate)
- (Interest expense − Tax deduction for interest) / Carrying value of debt

The **cost of preferred stock** financing is the stipulated dividend divided by the net issue price of the stock.

- Cost of Preferred stock = *Dividend/Net* issue price

$$\frac{\text{Next expected dividend}}{\text{(Current stock price - Flotation costs)}} + \text{Expected growth in earnings} = \text{Cost of new common stock}$$

The **cost of new common stock** is a little higher than that of existing stock since the business must recover the cost of issuing the new shares (selling or flotation costs).

Weighted Average Cost of Capital (WACC)

The weighted average cost of capital (WACC) is a calculation of a firm's effective cost of capital, taking into account the portion of its capital that was obtained as debt, preferred stock, and common stock.

Businesses with capital structures that result in low WACCs have lower required rates of return, or hurdle rates, and are more likely to find projects that add to shareholder wealth. Therefore, businesses seek capital structures that minimize their WACC.

Changes to Capital Structure

Representative Task: Determine the impact of changes in an entity's capital structure on cost of capital, loan covenants, liquidity, and leverage.

Effect of Raising Capital on COC

Assume that a company has the following marginal cost of capital schedule (MCCS) for issuing new debt and equity:

New Debt (in $ billions)	After-Tax Cost of Debt	New Equity (in $ billions)	Cost of Equity
New debt ≤ 10	7.0%	New equity ≤ 50	11.5%
10 ≤ New debt ≤ 15	7.5%	50 ≤ New equity ≤ 75	12.0%
15 ≤ New debt	8.0%	75 ≤ New equity	12.5%

If the company wants to issue $70 billion in new capital and plans to maintain its current capital structure of 20% debt and 80% equity, then its marginal cost of capital will be 11.1%.

	Capital Structure	New Capital ($)	After-Tax Cost of Debt	Cost of Capital
Debt	20%	$70 billion × 20% = $14 billion	7.5%	20% × 7.5% = 1.5%
Equity	80%	$70 billion × 80% = $56 billion	12.0%	80% × 12% = 9.6%
				11.1%

As a company raises additional capital, the costs of different sources of capital may increase, as depicted by the MCCS below, resulting in a higher WACC. The rising cost structure stems from default risk and potential deviations from the company's target capital structure.

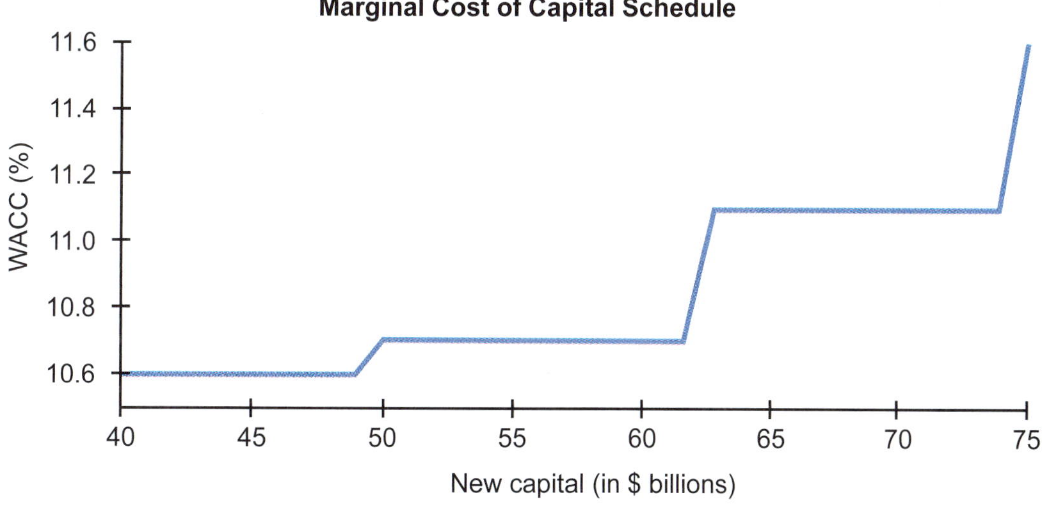

Effect on Loan Covenants

Covenants are **legally enforceable promises** made by a bond issuer (ie, borrower) to its bondholders (ie, lender). These promises are set forth in the bond indenture, which is the legal contract that establishes all rights and obligations of the issuer and bondholders.

There are two main types of covenants: affirmative covenants and negative covenants. **Affirmative covenants** tend to be administrative in nature. They cover issues such as timely payment of interest and principal, maintenance of existing lines of business, and payment of obligations such as taxes and payroll. Affirmative covenants do not materially affect the issuer's discretion over how to conduct its business.

Negative covenants protect bondholders by restricting actions by the issuer that would impair the issuer's ability to pay interest and/or repay principal. For example, a negative covenant may **restrict** the issuance of **new debt** that would be senior to debt already outstanding.

Examples of Affirmative And Negative Covenants	
Affirmative	**Negative**
• Pay interest and principle on time • Keep collateral in good working order • Pay taxes and other expenses on time • Comply with legal and regulatory requirements	• Restriction on paying dividends • Cannot take on additional debt above a certain level • Assets cannot be sold until debt is repaid • Collateral cannot be pledged as security or additional debt

Collateral consists of **assets** that the issuer pledges as security for the bonds. Generally, the bond indenture gives the bondholders the right to *sell the collateral* to satisfy their claims under the bond if the issuer defaults. Collateral can consist of the asset purchased with the bond proceeds or other assets (including securities and other bonds).

Loan covenants can impact how an entity makes changes to its capital structure. Consider the effects of the following negative covenants on an entity's decisions:

Negative Covenant	Effect on Business
Restriction on paying dividends	Reduce or eliminate dividends paid to shareholders, which could lead to decreased stock valuation
Cannot take on additional debt above a certain level	Issue equity instead of debt, which may cost more to business that needs additional capital
Assets cannot be sold until debt is repaid	No asset sales, resulting in missed opportunities to maximize value or inability to raise capital from asset sales to pay creditors
Collateral cannot be pledged as security for additional debt.	Reduces assets available to pledge for collateral, resulting in reduced amount of debt available to entity

Effect on Liquidity

Liquidity ratios measure an entity's ability to repay short-term obligations (ie, current liabilities). Generally, liquidity ratios should be greater than 1. However, an excessively high ratio could be an indication that the entity is holding too much cash and not using its resources effectively.

There are three common liquidity ratios:

Liquidity Ratios	
Current Ratio	$\frac{\text{Current assets}}{\text{Current liabilities}}$
Quick Ratio*	$\frac{\text{Cash + Marketable securities + Accounts receivable}}{\text{Current liabilities}}$
Cash Ratio	$\frac{\text{Cash + Marketable securities}}{\text{Current liabilities}}$

**Also called the acid-test ratio*

Increases or decreases in any of the ratio components that are included in the entity's capital structure affect liquidity as follows:

	Current Ratio	**Quick Ratio**	**Cash Ratio**
Increase Debt:			
Increase Cash (CA)	↑	↑	↑
Interest Payable (CL)	↓	↓	↓
Bonds Payable (LTL)	N/A	N/A	N/A
Increase Equity:			
Increase Cash (CA)	↑	↑	↑
Dividends Payable (CL)	↓	↓	↓
Common Stock (Equity)	N/A	N/A	N/A

Effect on Leverage

Leverage involves the use of debt or borrowed funds to finance assets. Because using borrowed funds expands the amount of assets in a business, leverage has the potential of amplifying returns on those assets. Likewise, the use of leverage can amplify losses in cases of negative returns.

Capital Structure and Leverage

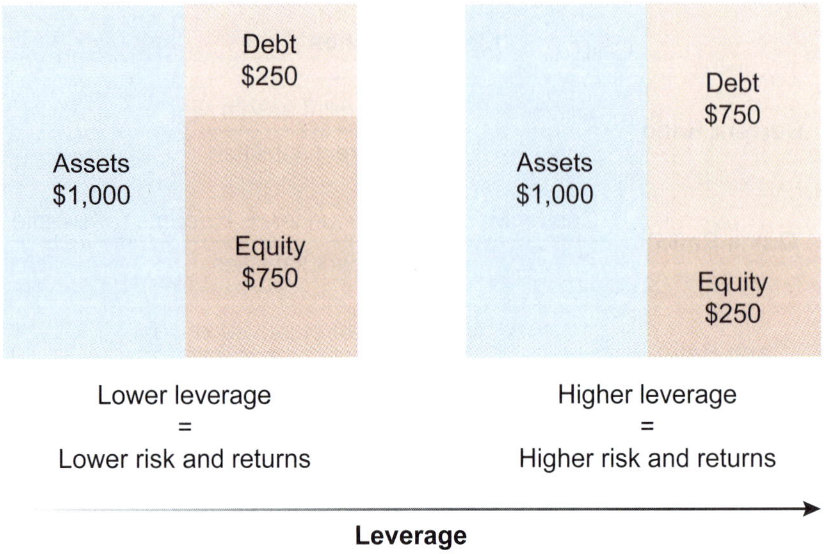

Assets	Debt / Equity
Assets $1,000	Debt $250
	Equity $750

Lower leverage = Lower risk and returns

Assets	Debt / Equity
Assets $1,000	Debt $750
	Equity $250

Higher leverage = Higher risk and returns

Leverage →

The degree of **operating leverage (DOL)** measures how the size of a business's *fixed costs* affects its performance when revenues change.

$$\text{DOL} = \frac{\text{\% Change in EBIT (Earnings before interest and taxes)}}{\text{\% Change in sales volume}}$$

- Higher fixed costs (relative to total costs) mean there is greater risk of low (or negative) earnings should revenues (sales volumes) fall below expectations. The risk that profits may be lower than anticipated is commonly known as **business risk** and is measured by the DOL
- Increases in revenues for businesses with high fixed costs (ie, a high DOL) result in proportionately larger increases in return on equity. Having lower variable costs with increases in revenue results in proportionately larger increases in profit

The degree of **financial leverage (DFL)** measures how much a business relies on *debt financing*. Using more debt can increase returns on equity but also increases risks for stockholders. Because debt is generally cheaper than equity, businesses have an incentive to increase their reliance on debt. However, ever-larger increases in debt increase leverage, risk, and ultimately the interest rate demanded by subsequent lenders. Of course, financial leverage is an extension of operating leverage that purely focuses on one type of fixed cost: the interest costs resulting from debt financing.

- Higher debt means higher interest and principal obligations for repayment, increasing risk if performance is not up to expectations
- Debt financing costs less than equity financing and doesn't increase with greater performance, so overall profit potential and asset growth potential are greater

The **degree of total leverage (DTL)** measures the **sensitivity of net income** to a change in the quantity of units sold. When units are sold, revenue is offset by fixed operating and **fixed financing costs** (ie, total leverage). Therefore, incremental net income is significantly impacted by the presence of fixed costs. All else equal, **higher fixed costs lead to higher DTL**, which leads to greater volatility in net income relative to various levels of sales.

Measures of Leverage Calculations

Revenue	75
− Variable costs	45
Contribution margin	30
− Fixed operating costs	15
Operating income	15
− Interest expense	1
Net income	14

$$\text{DOL} = \frac{\text{Contribution margin}}{\text{Operating income}} = \frac{30}{15} = 2.00$$

$$\text{DFL} = \frac{\text{Operating income}}{\text{Net income}} = \frac{15}{14} = 1.07$$

$$\text{DTL} = \frac{\text{Contribution margin}}{\text{Net income}} = \frac{30}{14} = \mathbf{2.14}$$

DTL can be expressed as the ratio of the total contribution margin to net income. In the image above, DTL of 2.14 is the ratio of 30 (contribution margin) to 14 (net income). Alternatively, DTL can be calculated as the product of the DOL and the DFL. In this case, 1.07 × 2.00 = 2.14.

Financial Leverage Ratio

The financial leverage ratio (ie, total assets to total equity) is one of several solvency ratios used to measure a company's ability to meet its long-term obligations and understand its financial risk. The **greater the ratio**, the more the **company uses debt** to finance its assets. Therefore, a lower financial ratio implies greater solvency, and vice versa.

$$\text{Financial leverage ratio} = \frac{\text{Total assets}}{\text{Total equity}} = \frac{\text{Total assets}}{\text{(Common stock + additional paid-in capital + retained earnings - Treasury stock)}}$$

Using the following information, calculate the financial leverage ratio for each company.

	Company X	Company Y	Company Z
Total assets	6,340	3,460	7,030
Common stock	2,800	1,890	3,900
Additional paid-in capital	750	140	470
Retained earnings	900	310	110
Treasury stock	50	100	110

Results: Company X has the lowest financial leverage ratio and therefore the greatest ability to meet long-term obligations.

	Company X	Company Y	Company Z
Financial Leverage Ratio	$\frac{6{,}340}{2{,}800 + 750 + 900 - 50} \approx 1.44$	$\frac{3{,}460}{1{,}890 + 140 + 310 - 100} \approx 1.54$	$\frac{7{,}030}{3{,}900 + 470 + 110 - 110} \approx 1.61$

Strategies for Financing Business Initiatives

Representative Task (Analysis): Compare the strategies for financing new business initiatives and operations within the context of an optimal capital structure.

Optimal Capital Structure

A firm's stated capital structure (ie, mix of debt and equity) policy is often based on **how much debt** the firm can assume. Mature companies typically prefer to issue debt since debt is cheaper than equity and its market value is more predictable. Debt such as tax shields (from interest deductions) can enhance a firm's value, but debt may also reduce the value by increasing the risk of financial distress and bankruptcy.

In theory, an optimal (ie, target) capital structure results in the **lowest WACC** and the **highest firm valuation**. At this optimal ratio of debt to equity, the difference between the expected benefits and costs of debt is maximized.

Optimal Capital Structure

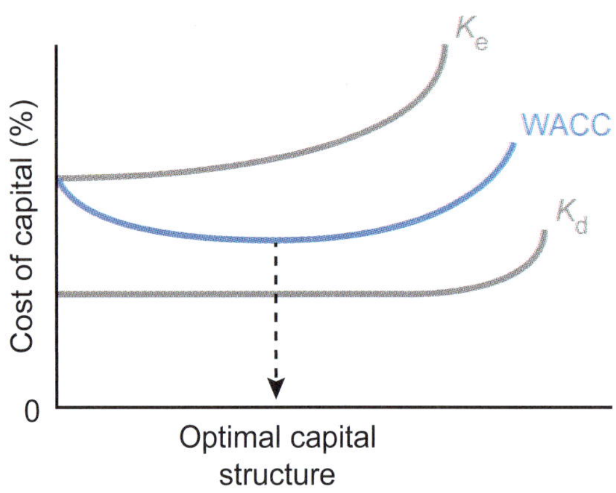

K_e = Cost of equity K_d = Cost of debt WACC = Weighted average cost of capital

In reality, capital structures often deviate from their optimal targets. For example, investors may desire an increase in a company's market cap to satisfy index listing requirements. In response, the company may issue more public equity, which can cause the actual capital structure to deviate from the target.

Reasons for Deviations from Target Capital Structure

- Additional debt may cause deterioration in debt ratings
- Type of capital may depend on investment cash flows
- Actual market conditions may vary from target market
- Aspirations to list stock on an index may influence the mix of debt and equity
- Existing debt covenants may contain restrictions that differ from target assumptions

While conditions change, in general, determining the optimal capital structure for a business involves finding the debt-to-assets ratio that minimizes WACC.

For example, if 40% of capital was obtained through long-term debt at an effective cost of 6%, 10% of capital was obtained by issuing preferred stock with an effective cost of 8%, and 50% of capital was obtained by issuing common stock expected to return 11% to shareholders, the WACC is as follows:

= (Debt % × Cost of debt) + (Preferred stock % × Cost of preferred stock) + (Common stock % × Cost of common stock)

= (40% × 6%) + (10% × 8%) + (50% × 11%)

= 2.4% + 0.8% + 5.5%

= 8.7%

Debt

Determining the ideal set of maturities (short-term versus long-term) and loan types (eg, fixed versus variable rates) for a firm to use is inherently difficult.

- A borrower using mostly short-term (and thus effectively variable rate) debt will experience more liquidity risk, may suffer more earnings volatility, and may, thus, be charged higher rates by lenders
- A borrower using mostly long-term, fixed-rate debt would forgo the benefits of falling interest rates, should interest rates fall

Prudent financial policy would thus call for **diversifying a firm's debt maturities and types.**

Bank loans are the primary source of debt financing for small- and medium-size companies. A **syndicated loan** is made by a group (ie, syndicate) of financial institutions (eg, banks, insurance companies, and other lenders) to a single borrower. A syndicated loan is appropriate when no single lender wishes to make a bilateral loan (ie, single lender to single borrower) and take on all the credit risk of the loan.

Sources of Company Debt

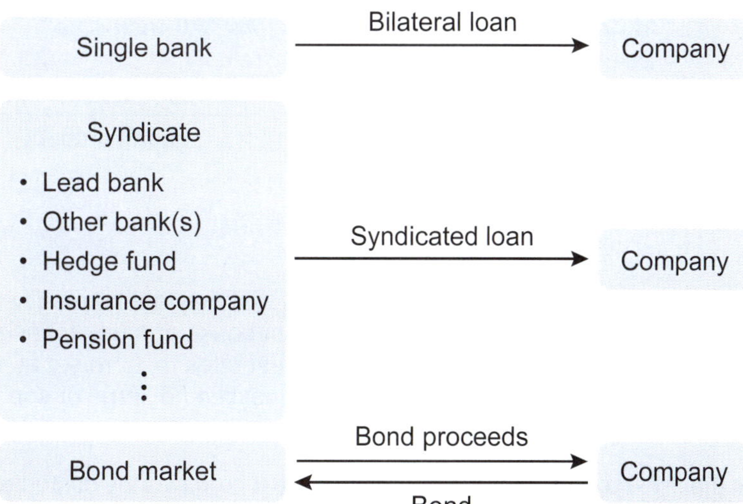

Short-Term Debt

A major objective of an effective short-term borrowing strategy is to ensure that funds are obtained in a cost-effective manner (ie, lowest cost of borrowing) by evaluating different sources of short-term funding. Line of credit, commercial paper, and banker's acceptance are common forms of short-term borrowing.

Type of Investment	Maturity	Description
Banker's acceptance	30 to 180 days	Bank obligations for trade transactions, issued at a discount
Commercial paper	1 to 270 days	Unsecured obligations of corporate and financial institutions, issued at a discount
Line of credit	Varies	Secured or unsecured sources of bank funding

A **compensating balance** is a percentage of the loan that the borrower must keep on deposit with the lender. In effect, it forces the borrower to pay more than the stated rate since the borrower pays interest on a portion of the loan that cannot be used. An all-inclusive interest rate means that the lender deducts the interest from the loan amount, so the borrower receives less than the entire loan but repays the full loan amount when the loan matures. As demonstrated in the banker's acceptance cost calculation, this also increases the borrower's costs.

Borrowers incur various costs in the borrowing process. When calculating total costs as a percentage, all borrowing costs (eg, interest, commitment fees, commissions, backup costs) are divided by the net proceeds. The net proceeds are the loan amount minus upfront fees.

Calculating Short-Term Borrowing Costs

Interest Rate Stated As "All-Inclusive"	Interest Rate *Not* Stated As "All-Inclusive"
$\text{Cost} = \dfrac{\text{Interest + additional costs}}{\text{Loan amount - Interest}}$	$\text{Cost} = \dfrac{\text{Interest + additional costs}}{\text{Loan amount}}$

Long-Term Debt

Private debt (variable interest) includes business obligations that may not be readily resold to (ie, traded with) the general public. Private debt largely includes loans from banks or other financial institutions or from syndicates of lenders. Most business loans have variable interest rates that are set at a premium over some base rate or **index**. Some businesses may also sell bonds to qualified (ie, large or sophisticated) investors in "private placements" that may not be readily traded to other parties.

- The **prime rate** is the rate that each lender charges its most creditworthy customers. Since the mid-1990s, most banks have set their prime rates 3% above the federal funds rate. Other business customers may obtain loans at some premium above the prime rate (eg, prime plus 2%)
- The **Secured Overnight Financing Rate** is a broad measure of the cost of borrowing cash overnight collateralized by U.S. Treasury securities in the repurchase agreement market. This is becoming the benchmark rate for dollar-denominated derivatives and loans

Public debt (fixed interest) includes business obligations that may be readily resold (ie, traded with) the general public in markets (eg, exchanges) that the Securities and Exchange Commission (SEC) regulates. Public debt largely includes bonds that (typically large) corporations may issue directly to retail and institutional investors.

Issuing bonds permits corporations to borrow from sources other than banks, paying interest rates that may be fixed and, depending on their credit history, may actually be lower than those that banks would charge.

- **Eurobonds** are bonds denominated in U.S. dollars that are sold abroad (ie, despite their name, not only in Europe). Some countries have less stringent registration and disclosure requirements than those of the SEC

Bonds (Secured and Unsecured)

A **bond** is a debt security **issued to investors** willing to lend money to the issuer for a certain period of time. In return, the issuer promises to pay interest over the life of the bond and repay the principal (ie, par value) when the bond matures. Bonds are classified by characteristics including maturity pattern, debt securitization, ownership, and redemption terms.

Bond Classifications	
Maturity Pattern	Term bond: single maturity date at end of term Serial bond: matures in stated amounts at regular intervals
Secured vs. Unsecured	Debentures: backed by borrower's general credit Collateralized: backed by specific assets
Ownership	Registered: issued to specific owner Bearer (coupon bonds): not registered
Redemption	Callable: bonds can be repurchased by issuer before maturity Convertible: bonds can be converted into equity securities at the option of the buyer Sinking: bonds can be repurchased in limited quantities periodically at specified prices

To calculate the present value (PV) of the proceeds for a bond, two amounts need to be determined:

- **PV of the face value** of the bonds (Face value × PV of a lump sum using the effective interest rate)
- **PV of the interest payments** as an annuity (Face value × stated rate × time = interest × PV of an ordinary annuity at the effective interest rate)
  - The sum of these two amounts represents the PV of the bond
  - If semiannual interest is being paid, take the years × 2 and the interest rate/2
- Example: five-year bonds at 10% semiannual; use the PV table for 10 periods @ 5%

Debt obligations may be **secured by certain collateral** or may specifically be placed behind other forms of debt in the priority of repayment. For instance, larger firms sometimes float public debt offerings collateralized by the firms' accounts receivable. The creation of such asset-backed securities is sometimes called *securitization of assets*.

Bond interest rates are generally fixed, calculated from the face value of the bond. The interest rate is known as the **coupon rate**, **face rate**, **stated rate**, or **nominal rate**.

- **Current yield:** The fixed interest payment divided by the current selling price of the bond. When the bond is trading at a discount, the current yield will be higher than the stated rate, and when the bond is trading at a premium, the current yield will be lower than the stated rate. The current yield should be interpreted with some caution, since it reports the interest payment as a percentage of the current price, not taking into account the fact that the principal repayment of the bond will not be the current selling price but the face value.

$$\frac{\text{Annual interest paid}}{\text{Bond market price}} = \text{Current Yield}$$

- **Yield to maturity:** The interest rate at which the present value of the cash flows of interest and principal will equal the current selling price of a bond. For a bond selling at a discount, yield to maturity will be higher than the current yield, since it accounts for the "bonus" interest payments reflected in the discount. For a bond selling at a premium, yield to maturity will be lower than the current yield since it reflects the loss of the premium when the face value is repaid. Yield to maturity is also known as the **effective rate** or **market rate**. The formula for calculating the **effective annual interest rate** (**EAR**) is as follows:

$$EAR = (1 + r/m)m - 1$$

r = Stated interest rate

m = Compounding frequency

Yield Curve

The yield curve presents U.S. Treasury interest rates (yields) in the y-axis (vertical) and terms (or maturities, usually three months to 30 years) in the x-axis (horizontal). Most non-government bonds and loans are more or less loosely priced in reference to the yield curve, such that changes in the yield curve affect interest rates in almost all markets throughout the U.S. economy.

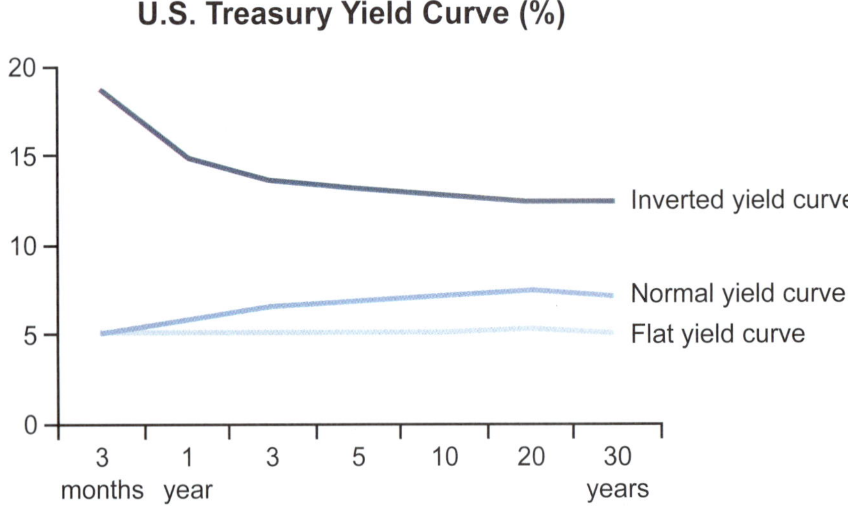

- **Normal yield curve:** Interest rates are higher for longer terms
  - According to the **liquidity preference theory**, interest rates would normally be higher for longer terms than for shorter terms since investors demand more compensation for long-term investments that are more subject to various risks (such as inflation or interest rate risk)

- **Inverted yield curve:** Interest rates are lower for longer terms
  - According to the **expectations theory**, long-term interest rates reflect future expected short-term interest rates. An inverted yield curve usually reflects investors' expectations of upcoming declines in economy-wide interest rates, usually because investors expect falling inflation rates and/or worsening economy-wide conditions (eg, a recession)
- **Flat yield curve:** Interest rates are similar across terms. Of course, normal yield curves typically flatten before becoming inverted, and inverted yield curves typically flatten before returning to normal

In practice, yield curves may not always be "straight lines." **Changing expectations** about the future and the **relative liquidity** of bond (and loan) markets at various terms may even cause the yield curve to become temporarily "**humped**," with higher rates for intermediate terms than for short or long terms.

Advantages and Disadvantages of Debt Financing

Some of the **advantages** of using debt to finance a business are the following:

- Interest is tax-deductible
- With certain caveats, the obligation (ie, interest and principal payments) is generally fixed (eg, assuming that the debt was fixed rate, considering only nominal interest rates are considered, and considering only the period until the maturity date of the debt)
- If current owners issue debt instead of new shares of stock, the current owners avoid giving up control to the new shareholders
- If the business has excess earnings, those earnings will accrue to owners, not to debt holders
- Debt is less costly than equity, so the cost of capital will be lower
- During inflationary periods, the debt is paid back with less valuable dollars

Some of the **disadvantages** of using debt to finance a business are the following:

- The business must make predetermined interest and principal payments independently of its performance
- While debt holders do not gain any formal control of the business (like new shareholders), by agreeing to the terms of loan and bond covenants, businesses effectively forgo some control (ie, flexibility)
- High debt levels increase the risk that the business may fail, wipe out owners' claims, and thus (despite their sometimes-positive effects on returns on equity), high debt levels may reduce stock prices

Equity (Stock)

Businesses are ultimately owned by their common shareholders (or stockholders). They control the business (ie, they may appoint and remove management through elections to a board of directors) and have a claim to the residual (or leftover) assets and income after the claims by all creditors and preferred shareholders are satisfied.

While most companies have only one class of common stock (class A), companies may have a second class of common stock (class B) with different rights to vote or to receive dividends. Common stock is generally issued at par value, unless there is no par value, in which case stated value is used.

Existing Common Stock

The cost of *existing* common stock financing represents the expected returns of common shareholders and is difficult to estimate. Some techniques include the following:

The **Capital Asset Pricing Model (CAPM)** assumes that the expected return of a particular stock depends on its **volatility** relative to the overall stock market (beta). CAPM determines the rate of return (ROR) required for a stock to **compensate for market risk**. The greater the risk, the higher the required ROR.

To calculate CAPM, the risk-free rate, beta coefficient, and equity risk premium are used. Beta measures how much an individual stock's price moves in relation to the overall stock market. For example, if the stock's price goes up 10% and the market goes up 5%, the stock's beta is 2.0 (10/5). The resulting CAPM is then compared to the company's required rate of return on its stock.

CAPM Equation for Cost of Equity

$$E(R_i) = R_f + \beta_i\,[E(R_m) - R_f]$$

Market return ($E(R_m)$); Risk-free rate (R_f); Beta (β_i)

The Arbitrage Pricing Model is a more detailed version of CAPM that uses separate excess returns and betas for various factors contributing to a stock performance.

The **Bond Yield Plus** method is based on the historical relationship between equities and debt and, thus, simply adds 3% to 5% to the interest rate on the business's long-term debt.

The **Dividend Yield Plus Growth Rate** method adds the current dividend (as a percentage of the stock price) and the expected growth rate in earnings.

$$\frac{\text{Next expected dividend}}{\text{Current stock price}} + \text{Expected growth in earnings} = \textbf{Dividend Yield Plus Growth Rate}$$

New Common Stock

The cost of new common stock is a little higher than that of existing stock since the business must recover the cost of issuing the new shares (selling or flotation costs).

$$\frac{\text{Next expected dividend}}{(\text{Current stock price} - \text{Flotation costs})} + \text{Expected growth in earnings} = \textbf{Cost of new common stock}$$

Some **advantages** of common stock to the business are the following:

- Businesses have the flexibility that dividend payments to common shareholders are not fixed (ie, they may be increased or decreased depending on performance)
- Businesses with more equity pose less risk to lenders, thus reducing businesses' borrowing costs
- Many investors find common stock to be very attractive since it entitles them to businesses' future profit growth

Some **disadvantages** of common stock to the business are the following:

- The costs of issuing common stock are larger than those for debt
- Current owners dilute their ownership and control with each new issuance of stock
- While tax law considers interest a tax-deductible cost, common dividends are not tax deductible (out of retained earnings)
- Shareholders ultimately receive a much higher return than lenders if the business is successful, so relying more on common stock results in a higher cost of capital for the business

Common stock trades in different markets:

- **Primary market:** New issues market (initial price offerings, IPOs)
- **Secondary market:** Where already outstanding shares are resold
- **Over-the-counter:** Market for unlisted securities

Preferred Stock

Preferred (preference) share ownership represents a form of equity investment in a company. Preference shares may grant certain benefits to **preferred** shareholders such as high dividend payments and in some cases conversion rights (to common stock).

Dividend payments to preferred shareholders take **precedence over** dividend payments to **common** shareholders. Preferred dividends can be cumulative or noncumulative. In a liquidation, preferred stockholders must be paid in full before any payments are made to common stockholders; that is, preferred have priority (or are "preferred") over common stockholders.

Unlike common shareholders, preferred shareholders normally **do not participate** directly in a company's operating performance since the preferred dividend (and thus share value) is fixed at issuance.

Types of preferred shares include the following:

Types of Preferred Shares	Description
Cumulative	Accrues for past dividends that are unpaid
Noncumulative	Does not accrue dividends that are undeclared and unpaid in past periods
Participating	Allows for additional dividend payments if company profits exceed a certain threshold
Nonparticipating	Fixed dividend; no additional payments based on company performance
Convertible	Can convert into a specified number of common shares
Callable	Allows issuer to buy back shares from investors for a specified price
Putable	Allows investors to sell shares back to issuer for a specified price

Some **advantages** of preferred stock are the following:

- The business has the flexibility of being able to skip preferred dividends (even if those dividends may have to be paid later when the business wants to pay common dividends)
- Businesses with more equity pose less risk to lenders, thus reducing businesses' borrowing costs
- Issuing more preferred stock does not entail common stockholders giving up control over the business's decision-making
- If the business has more earnings, preferred stockholders rarely receive any of them

Some **disadvantages** of preferred stock are the following:

- The costs of issuing preferred stock are larger than those for debt, and the dividend rates paid on preferred stock are higher than the interest rates paid on debt
- While tax law considers interest a tax-deductible cost, preferred dividends are not tax deductible
- A business that has accumulated skipped dividends (arrears) over extended periods of time may encounter difficulties reducing that backlog and/or finding new sources of funding

To make appropriate financing decisions, businesses take into account leverage and the cost of capital.

Lease Versus Buy Decisions

A company can either lease or buy assets for business use. Although leasing can be more expensive than buying in the long term, it tends to have lower up-front costs. Common types of leases include the following:

Lease Type	Description
Net Lease	Tenant is responsible for paying operating expenses
Gross Lease	Property owner is responsible for paying operating expenses
Triple-Net Lease	Each tenant pays a share of the following: • Common-area maintenance • Property taxes • Building insurance costs
Sale Leaseback	Owner sells property to another but leases property back from new owner
Percentage Lease	Tenant pays additional rent once sales reach a certain level

Lease payments include recurring lease components (eg, rent), non-lease components (eg, maintenance), and non-components (eg, taxes, insurance). If there is a purchase option that is likely to be exercised, the total lease payments include the recurring payments and the purchase option amount.

Lease Payments

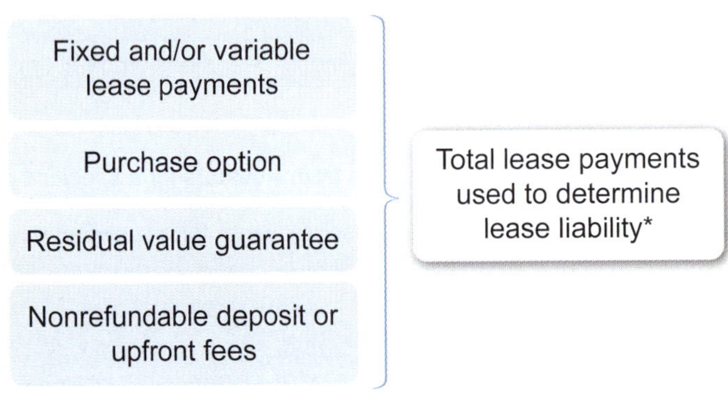

**Lease liability = present value of lease payments*

The decision to lease or buy an asset can be complex. The following is a comparison of features between the two options:

Feature	Lease	Buy (assumes financing)
Payment Amount	Generally lower	Generally higher
Down Payment	Generally low or no down payment	Potentially 10%–20% of selling price
Ownership of Asset	• Finance lease: lessee or lessor • Operating lease: lessor	Buyer

Feature	Lease	Buy (assumes financing)
Tax Impact	• Amortization of right-of-use asset has similar impact as depreciation in creating a tax shield • Interest expense is tax deductible	• Bonus or Section 179 depreciation can be taken on assets purchased for business use • Interest expense is tax deductible
Disposition of Asset	If title does not transfer to lessee, asset returns to lessor at end of lease	Asset sold to a new buyer or completely depreciated over useful life
Balance Sheet	Right-of-use asset and lease liability at present value of payments	Fixed asset at cost and long-term liability at financed amount
Income Statement	Interest expense and amortization expense of right-of-use asset	Interest expense and depreciation expense of asset, gain or loss on asset disposition

As a result of ASC 842, **finance and operating leases are capitalized** and recorded on the balance sheet. (Note: short-term leases less than one year are *not* required to be capitalized.) The costs and benefits associated with each option should be analyzed before making the decision to lease or buy an asset.

For example, Foster Co. is a software company that needs new servers to expand operations. Foster is very concerned with obsolescence, as technology is always improving. Foster's lease versus buy options are as follows:

Lease: No money is required as a down payment. The lease term is three years. Foster has the option to purchase the servers at the end of the lease term at FV or trade them in for a 10% discount on new servers. Foster is unlikely to exercise the purchase option. Monthly lease payments are $4,000, and the implicit borrowing rate in the lease is 6%. The present value of lease payments is $132,141.

Buy: Foster can purchase the servers for $120,000. They are required to put 10% (ie, $12,000) down and can finance the rest at 5% over three years, resulting in a monthly payment of $3,223. Foster anticipates the servers to be worthless after three years.

The comparison between leasing and buying is below (advantages are in green):

	Lease	Buy
Payment	$4,000	$3,223
Down Payment	$0	$12,000
Overall Cost	$132,141	$120,000
Interest Rate	6%	5%
Term	3 years	3 years
Ownership	No	Yes
End of Term	Purchase option at FV or return to lessor for 10% discount on new servers	Worthless

Buying is less expensive overall; but a down payment is required, and the servers have no value at the end of three years. Because obsolescence is a primary concern for Foster, the lease is a better option. Foster also gets the benefit of no down payment.

Advantages of Leasing versus Buying

Some **advantages** of leasing versus buying include the following:

- Capital that could be used to acquire an asset could be put to another use
- Businesses unable to obtain credit to purchase an asset may be able to lease it instead
- Leases often do not involve down payments
- A lease provides an additional source of capital with level payments, sometimes over a longer term
- Leases are generally less expensive in that the lessee is not paying the entire amount of the asset's cost; thus, payments are generally lower than a loan, meaning lease payments may fit the cash flow budget better than loan payments to purchase the same asset
- Terms in lease agreements are often less strict than in bond indentures
- In bankruptcy, creditors have weaker rights over some assets financed by leases (eg, real estate)
- Leases may transfer the tax benefits of debt financing to lessors, prompting lessors to reduce the cost of leases to lessees
- Some leases provide maintenance services, making management of the asset easier and possibly less expensive
- Leasing an asset versus buying it provides a hedge against obsolescence; that is, a lease provides more flexibility, thus reducing risk to the lessee
- Disposal of the asset at the end of its useful life remains with the lessor

Disadvantages of Leasing versus Buying

Some **disadvantages** of leasing versus buying include the following:

- In some leases, ownership of the asset does not transfer to the lessor
- Overall, the cost of the lease may be higher than purchasing the asset with financing
- ASC 842 requires operating leases to be capitalized. The liability will impact leverage ratios and potential debt covenants
- Assets purchased for business use may be eligible for bonus tax depreciation. If the lessor retains title to the asset, the lessee will not be able to utilize the additional tax benefit
- Assets purchased can be customized without potentially violating lease terms

Impact of Capital Structures

Representative Task (Analysis): Interpret the impact of various capital structures on financial statements and key performance measures.

Let's look at an example to see the impact of a change in capital structure on a company. We can use the analysis toolbox and apply it to our company data.

The toolbox helps to focus the analysis on these four questions:

Company information: Rounders, Inc. manufactures and sells playing cards. It is going to add a new poker chip division and needs $1 million of capital to fund the expansion. It is considering either issuing bonds or issuing common stock. The board of directors uses WACC (ie, average cost of capital) as a key measure in the company's valuation. The board has indicated that it will not approve of an option resulting in a WACC of more than 8% and has requested that Rounders provide an analysis of the current cost of capital and the new cost of capital for issuing bonds versus issuing stock.

Rounders' current condensed balance sheet for Year 3 is below:

Rounders, Inc.
Balance Sheet

	Year 3
Current assets	1,468,250
Fixed assets	1,400,000
Intangible assets	420,000
Total assets	**3,288,250**
Current liabilities	955,000
Long-term liabilities (8% bonds payable)	1,050,000
Stockholders' equity:	
Common stock (100,000 shares at $10 par)	1,000,000
Additional paid-in capital	100,000
Retained earnings	108,250
Net income	75,000
Total liabilities and equity	**3,288,250**

Additional information:

- Rounders' tax rate is 30%
- The bond payable on the balance sheet has an 8% stated rate and a 5% effective rate
- Rounders has a 5% cash dividend on common stock. The stock's current market value is $5.75 per share
- If Rounders issues $1 million in new bonds, the effective rate on the bonds is 8%. After the impact from tax savings, the new total cost of debt would be 4.6%
- If Rounders issues $1 million in new common stock, the estimated new cost of equity would be 12.5%

What are you trying to find out?

First, we need to determine the current cost of capital (ie, WACC). Then we need to calculate the impact of adding $1 million as debt or equity to the cost of capital. Finally, we need to determine the most cost-effective option and compare that with the board of directors' directive of keeping the new cost of capital at 8% or lower.

What information do you have?

Financial statements: The financial statements show Rounders' current capital structure.

- Total debt = $2,005,000 ($955,000 Current liabilities + $1,050,000 Long-term liabilities)
- Total equity = $1,283,250 ($1,000,000 stock + $100,000 APIC + $108,250 retained earnings + $75,000 net income)
- Total assets = $3,288,250
- Total debt to total assets = 61% ($2,005,000 / $3,288,250)
- Total equity to total assets = 39% ($1,283,250 / $3,288,250)

Tax rate: 30% *(used for cost of debt)*

Debt: Effective rate = 5% *(used for cost of debt)*

Equity: Cash dividend = 5%, Market value = $5.75 per share *(used for cost of equity)*

Capital needed: $1 million

Maximum cost of capital (WACC): 8% *(instruction from board of directors)*

What information do you need?

Current WACC: (Cost of debt × Percentage of total debt to total assets) + (Cost of equity × Percentage of total equity to total assets)

- **Debt** = (Debt effective rate × [1 – Tax rate]) × Percentage of total debt to total assets
  Cost of debt = 2.1% = (5% effective rate × [1 – 30% tax rate]) × 61% total debt to total assets)
- **Equity** = ([Stock par value × Cash dividend] / Market value per share) × Percentage of total equity to total assets
  - Cost of equity = 3.4% = ([$10 par × 5% dividend] / $5.75 per share) × 39% total equity to total assets)
- **Current WACC** = 5.5% (2.1% cost of debt + 3.4% cost of equity)

New WACC if $1 million in debt is issued:

- New cost of debt given as 4.6%
- New total debt = $3,005,000 ($2,005,000 original + $1,000,000)
- New total assets = $4,288,250 ($3,288,250 original + $1,000,000)
- Updated percentage of total debt to total assets: 70% ($3,005,000 / $4,288,250)
- **New WACC = 5.83%** = (4.6% new cost of debt × 70%) + (8.7% original cost of equity × [1 – 70%])

New WACC if $1 million in equity is issued:

- New cost of equity given as 12.5%
- New total equity = $2,283,250 ($1,283,250 original + $1,000,000)
- New total assets = $4,288,250 ($3,288,250 original + $1,000,000)
- Updated percentage of total equity to total assets: 53% ($2,283,250 / $4,288,250)
- **New WACC = 8.27%** = (3.5% original cost of debt × [1 – 53%]) + (12.5% new cost of equity × 53%)

What do the results indicate?

Rounders should compare the WACCs calculated for issuing debt versus issuing equity and determine which is most cost-effective. Further, the new WACCs should be compared with the maximum 8% WACC requirement from the board of directors.

New WACC	Most Cost-effective	Meets Board Requirements?
Issue bonds: 5.83%	Yes	Yes
Issue stock: 8.27%	No	No

The results from the analysis indicate that Rounders should issue $1 million in bonds instead of stock to raise capital to fund the new poker chip division. In doing so, it would also comply with the board of directors' requirements.

2.03 Investment Alternatives Using Financial Valuation Decision Models

Fair Value Measurement

Representative Task (Application): Use assumptions (eg, highest and best use, market participant assumptions, unit of account) and approaches (cost, income, market) to measure fair value.

Fair Value (FV) Definition

ASC 820 defines FV as "the price that would be received to sell an asset or paid to transfer a liability in an orderly transaction between market participants at the measurement date." For a transaction to be orderly, it cannot be a forced transaction. Instead, the asset or liability is assumed to be exposed to the market for a time period that is customary for that type of asset or liability.

Market Participants

Market participants are parties that are the following:

Fair Value: Market Participants

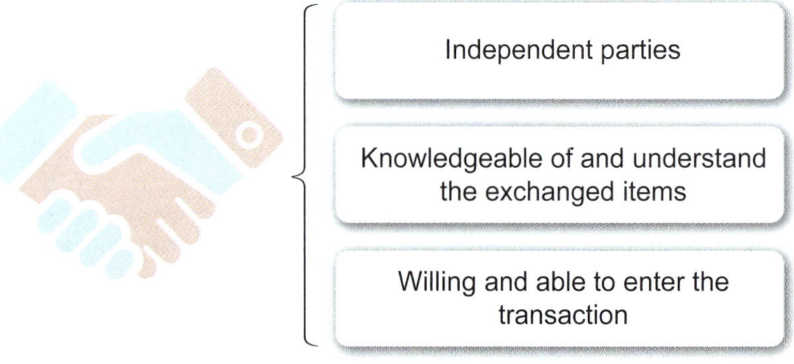

Items Required to Be Reported at FV

An entity is required to recognize various items at FV, including the following:

- Investments in **marketable debt securities:** Securities that are classified as either trading securities or available-for-sale (AFS) securities are reported at FV (ie, *marked to market*) as of each balance sheet date
- Investments in **equity securities** (except those accounted for under the equity method)
- Investments required to be consolidated
- Investments for which the market value is not readily determinable (assuming the appropriate election has been made)

- With very few exceptions, **assets acquired** and **liabilities assumed** in a **business combination** are initially recognized at FV but are not adjusted to FV in subsequent periods for presentation on the balance sheet unless that asset/liability is being reported at FV for some other reason
- **Impairment losses** result in the reduction of an asset's carrying value to its FV in the period of the impairment
- All **derivatives**, which are reported at FV, except for interest rate swaps that are hedges when the alternative accounting approach available to nonpublic entities is elected

Determining FV

Assets, other than financial assets, are measured on the basis of their "highest and best use." Some assets are more valuable **in exchange** and are measured at what would be received upon their sale. Others are more valuable in use and are measured at the value represented in the form of some combination of potential revenues earned and cost savings that result from their use.

- It is assumed that a transaction will occur in the **principal market** in which the asset or liability would most frequently be traded
- When there is no principal market, values are based on the assumption that a transaction would occur in the **most advantageous** market

This is intended as a measure of an asset's or liability's FV without assuming that the asset will actually be disposed of or the liability transferred. As a result, the value is determined without taking into consideration costs of the transaction, such as costs to transfer the asset or liability. If an asset (eg, a commodity) needs to be transported to its principal market, however, the cost of doing so is considered when measuring the asset's FV.

FV measurement techniques include the following:

Fair Value Measurement Technique (MIC)		
Approach	**Definition**	**Example**
Market	Information generated by market transactions for identical or similar items	Quoted price from stock exchange
Income	Estimated future amounts discounted to a single, current amount	Discounted cash flow analysis
Cost	Amount currently required to replace benefit derived from an asset	Current replacement cost (adjusted for obsolescence)

Three Levels of Input

- **Level 1**, the most reliable, involves the use of observable data from actual market transactions, occurring in an active market, for identical assets or liabilities
- **Level 2** also involves the use of observable data from actual market transactions, but with *either* of the following conditions:
  - The transactions did not occur in an active market
  - The transactions relate to similar, but not identical, assets or liabilities
- **Level 3** involves the use of unobservable data and is largely based on management's judgment

Practical Expedient for Certain Equity Interests

In some cases, an entity will have an equity interest in an entity that reports its net asset value (NAV) per share. As a practical expedient, such an investment may be reported as the published NAV per share.

- Since the FV is not determined using a technique designated by standards for doing so, the FV measurement does not fit into the hierarchy
- As a result, an entity applying the practical expedient is not required to disclose the level of inputs that were used to determine FV
- Entities using the practical expedient are required to provide a reconciliation of the FV hierarchy disclosure to the balance sheet by disclosing the FV of investments measured at NAV per share

An investor has a $100,000 investment in a hedge fund on October 1, Year 1. The investor's initial investment was recorded by the hedge fund company by issuing the 571.429 shares at the NAV per share of $175. These shares are the basis for investor subscription (ie, purchase) and redemption (ie, sale) transactions in the fund.

The fund is not traded on an exchange with a published unit price per share. Therefore, the fund does not have a readily determinable FV. The hedge fund manager issues a quarterly report to all investors with the NAV per share of the fund based on the values of the fund holdings.

On December 31, Year 1, the hedge fund manager reported the NAV per share of the fund as $187.25. The investor would use the NAV per share as a practical expedient for FV and report the investment at $107,000.00 (571.429 shares × $187.25 NAV per share).

Steps to FV Measurement

FV measurement may be applied using the following approach:

1. Identify the asset or liability to be measured
2. Determine the principal or most advantageous market *(highest and best use)*
3. Determine the valuation premise *(in-use or in-exchange)*
4. Determine the appropriate valuation technique *(market, income, or cost approach)*
5. Obtain inputs for valuation *(Level 1, Level 2, or Level 3)*
    a. **FV hierarchy** must be used to prioritize the inputs to valuation techniques
6. Calculate the FV of the asset

Fair Value Hierarchy for Eligible Assets and Liabilities

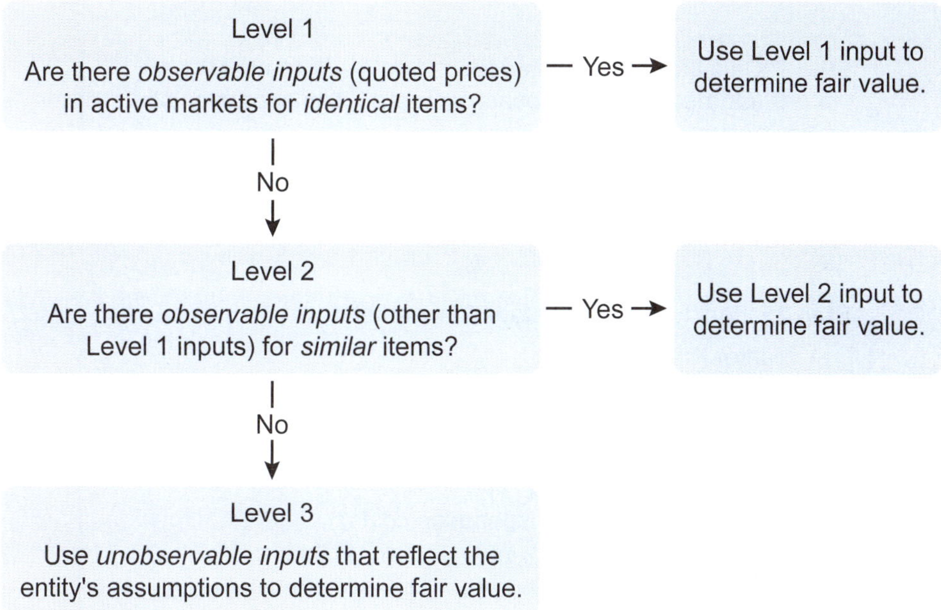

FV Using Principal Market

A company has an equity investment with a historical cost of $500,000 that is traded in an active market. At December 31, the quoted price for an *identical* investment was $400,000, and the quoted price for a *similar* investment was $430,000. Using the company's internal present value of cash flows model, the company arrived at a value of $410,000. What amount is the value of the investment on December 31?

The equity investment should be measured at $400,000, the price sold for an identical asset traded in an active market (ie, market approach). This price represents the asset's FV and uses a Level 1 (most reliable) input.

FV Using Most Advantageous Market (ie, No Principal Market)

Determine the FV of the financial asset for which there is no principal market. The asset is actively traded on two different exchanges: Market X and Market Y. The information on the two exchanges is as follows:

	Quoted Asset Price	Transaction Costs	Transportation Costs
Market X	$100	$10	$ 7
Market Y	105	5	20

The financial asset's FV is $93, calculated as follows:

Step 1: Calculate net sales proceeds from each market
(Quoted price − Transaction costs − Transportation costs)

- Market X: $100 − $10 − $7 = $83
- Market Y: $105 − $5 − $20 = $80

↓

Step 2: Identify most advantageous market

- Market X: $83

↓

Step 3: Determine fair value
(Quoted price − Transportation costs)

- Market X: $100 − $7 = **$93**

FV of Non-financial Asset

The **FV** of a **non-financial asset** should reflect that asset's **highest and best use** because sellers will transact wherever they will receive the most consideration. That use must be physically possible, legally permissible, and financially feasible. If the highest and best use for an asset differs from the current use, the former equals FV.

Assume that a company owns land and a building that houses its manufacturing operations. When the company purchased the manufacturing facility, the purchase price allocated to the land account was $100,000.

The manufacturing facility is located in an area that was once the site of many factories. The owners of several of the neighboring factories have recently sold their facilities to residential real estate developers. The company's land is also suitable for residential development.

The estimated current value of the land as part of the manufacturing facility is $150,000. The estimated current value of the land as an undeveloped investment is $160,000, and the current value of the land as part of a residential development would be $200,000.

The highest and best use of the land reflects a FV of $200,000. Because neighboring factories have sold their land to be used for residential development, this use is physically possible, legally permissible, and financially feasible.

F/S Disclosures

Disclosures about the use of FV to measure assets and liabilities should provide F/S users with information about the following:

- The valuation techniques applied (market, income, or cost), including judgments and assumptions
- The level of inputs that were applied in measuring FV
- The uncertainty in the FV measurements as of the reporting date
- The disposition of changes in FV (income or comprehensive income)

FV Option

In addition to those items that are required to be measured at FV, ASC 825 allows an entity to **elect** to report some or all of its financial instruments (ie, financial assets and liabilities) at their FV. A **financial instrument** is defined as *cash*, evidence of an *ownership interest* in an entity, or a *contract* that does *both* of the following:

- Imposes on one entity a contractual **obligation** either:
  - To deliver cash or another financial instrument to a second entity; or
  - To exchange other financial instruments on potentially unfavorable terms with the second entity.
- Conveys to that second entity a contractual right either:
  - To receive cash or another financial instrument from the first entity; or
  - To exchange other financial instruments on potentially favorable terms with the first entity.

Examples of financial assets and liabilities that would qualify for the FV option include the following:

- Most investments that do not already require FV measurement, such as investments accounted for under the equity method
- Firm commitments involving financial instruments, such as forward exchange contracts to purchase or sell a foreign currency

Certain items have their own established accounting principles, which are required to be followed. These items may involve measurements at FV, but they **do not qualify** for the "FV option" election:

- Pension plan, post-retirement, and other post-employment benefits (ASC 712 and 715)
- Leases (ASC 842)
- Financial instruments that are components of equity (ASC 505)
- Share-based payments and stock options (ASC 718)

If an entity decides to elect the FV option, it may apply it to any qualifying financial instrument, without being required to apply it to others, including those that are similar. An election may be made only when a financial asset or liability is acquired or in other limited circumstances, referred to as election dates. Likewise, once elected, the FV option is permanent and may be discontinued only on a subsequent election date.

When the FV option is elected, **unrealized gains and losses are reported in income.**

Impact of Assumption Changes to Asset Value

Representative Task (Application): Determine the impact of changes to assumptions used to value an asset.

Entities select valuation techniques that attempt to incorporate as much relevant observable market data that is available and minimize the use of unobservable data based on judgment. These inputs can change over time, and the impact of these changes is reflected in the valuation reported on the F/S. As discussed earlier, inputs are categorized as Level 1 (quoted prices in active markets), Level 2 (based on observable market data for similar investments), or Level 3 (unobservable data).

A company has the following investments:

Investment	Cost	FV	Category
Equity ownership in private company	$100,000	$87,000	Level 3: No observable inputs, value based on discounted cash flow (DCF) analysis
5,000 shares stock, publicly traded	$ 45,000	$50,000	Level 1: Shares traded on public exchange
1,000 shares restricted stock (same company as 5,000 share position)	$ 1,000	$ 7,500	Level 2: Unrestricted shares traded on public exchange; discount on valuation for restriction
Hedge fund (100 shares)	$ 70,000	$75,000	Practical expedient: NAV per share provided quarterly

Let's look at how changing the input assumptions impacts the FV for each security.

Equity ownership in a private company: The company uses a DCF analysis to determine the value for this investment. In the model, the discount rate used is 5%.

- Conditions can change, resulting in an updated discount rate of 8%. The impact of the change in assumption results in a decrease in the value based on an updated DCF analysis.

Shares of publicly traded stock: The 5,000 shares are traded on a public exchange. The FV is based on the published closing price.

- If the public company suffers from a natural disaster after the market closed, the company can reduce the value based on how it assumes the event will impact the stock's FV.

Restricted shares of stock: The FV of the 1,000 shares of stock is based on the FV of the unrestricted shares with a discount applied for the restriction.

- The restriction on the stock is removed by the public company. The discount would no longer be applicable, and the FV would be the stock's published closing price.

Hedge fund: The FV is based on a practical expedient of NAV per share.

- If the hedge fund decides to limit investor redemptions, this will have an impact on the FV of the shares. The company would assume that the shares would not be as valuable and apply a discount to the NAV per share.

Investment Alternatives

Representative Task (Analysis): Compare investment alternatives (eg, system replacement, make, lease, or buy decisions) using financial metrics and modeling (eg, payback period, net-present value, economic value added, cash flow analysis, internal rate of return).

Special decisions require management to choose **between two options**. The general rule is to consider only the **relevant revenues and costs** (ie, future revenues and costs that differ between the alternatives). Relevant items are *future* amounts that change between choices (ie, they make a difference). For example, maintenance on keeping an old machine would be $20,000 a year, while maintenance on a new machine would only be $5,000 a year.

Relevant vs. Non-Relevant	
Relevant	Future costs that differ between alternatives: • Opportunity costs • Old asset sales price • New asset purchase price
Non-Relevant	Historical information that does not differ: • Old asset purchase price • Accumulated depreciation on existing asset • Sunk costs

Retain (Keep) or Eliminate (System Replacement)

The Retain or Eliminate type of question typically involves an unprofitable product line or division. One must consider whether the at-risk line or division helps the other, more profitable divisions cover the fixed costs—generally allocated from corporate or administrative sources—that do not cease with the product line or division elimination. In other words, in some cases, the reason the product line or division is not profitable is due to costs allocated to that product line or division that will continue to be incurred after the product line is discontinued or the division is closed.

If, for example, the CEO's salary is allocated among all four products that an entity manufactures, and one of the four products is discontinued, the CEO's salary will not be reduced proportionately; it will be allocated among the remaining products. As a result, when performing such an analysis, only those revenues and costs that will change should be considered.

Roving Epicure Company (REC) has four product lines: quality fruits, game meats, fine wines, and fine cheeses. For the past three years, the fruit line has seen dwindling profits; this trend seems unlikely to reverse. Additional information (in 1,000s) is as follows:

Product line	Fruit	Meat	Wine	Cheese
Revenue	$4,000	$2,000	$6,000	$2,000
Variable costs	3,000	1,000	2,000	1,000
Contribution margin	1,000	1,000	4,000	1,000
Avoidable fixed costs	200	400	2,000	300
Unavoidable fixed costs	1,000	200	400	100
Net income	$ (200)	$ 400	$1,600	$ 600

While the $200,000 of net loss from the fruit line can be eliminated, the $1,000,000 unavoidable fixed costs borne by the fruit line cannot be eliminated. These fixed costs remain to be allocated to the remaining product lines. In other words, even though the fruit product line appears to be unprofitable, it should be retained.

If the fruit line is eliminated, revenues will be reduced by $4,000,000. Variable costs will be reduced by $3,000,000, and avoidable fixed costs of $200,000 will no longer be incurred. The unavoidable fixed costs will continue to be incurred and will be allocated to the other product lines.

As a result, the reduction in revenues ($4,000,000) exceeds the reduction in costs ($3,200,000) by $800,000, thus reducing company profitability if the fruit product line is eliminated.

The following chart is expressed in 1,000s:

Product line	With	Without	Reduction
Revenue	$14,000	$10,000	$4,000
Variable costs	7,000	4,000	3,000
Contribution margin	7,000	6,000	1,000
Avoidable fixed costs	2,900	2,700	200
Unavoidable fixed costs	1,700	1,700	0
Net income	$ 2,400	$ 1,600	$ 800

Make or Buy

The Make or Buy type of question typically involves a component that can be produced in-house or by a subcontractor.

Miller & Baker Company (MBC) uses 13,000 units of Part 1322 monthly. The per unit costs are $4 for direct material, $2 for direct labor, $2 for variable overhead, and $4 for fixed overhead (FOH). If MBC buys the parts, they will cost $13 apiece, but the company will eliminate $3 of FOH costs per unit.

The remaining FOH of $1 ($4 − $3) cannot be eliminated, regardless of whether MBC purchases or makes the part. Since the remaining $1 of FOH is part of both scenarios, it is considered irrelevant and not reflected in the math below (remember, only *relevant costs* are included).

The facilities used to manufacture Part 1322 alternatively could be used to manufacture Part 668 at a monthly profit of $50,000.

An analysis of revenues and costs that differ between the two options indicates that it is more profitable to buy the part and use the facilities to manufacture Part 668:

	Make	**Buy**
Direct material	$ 4	
Direct labor	2	
Variable overhead	2	
Fixed overhead subject to elimination*	3	
Relevant unit costs	$ 11	$ 13
Units	13,000	13,000
Relevant costs for 13,000 units	$143,000	$169,000
Opportunity cost of making Part 1322	50,000	0
Total relevant costs	$193,000	$169,000

**Note: The remaining $1 of FOH that cannot be eliminated is irrelevant to this decision.*

If the alternative equipment use for Part 668 were not an option ($50,000 opportunity cost), it would be $26,000 ($169,000 − $143,000) more profitable to make the part in-house; however, because of the $50,000 opportunity cost, it is $24,000 ($193,000 − $169,000) more profitable to buy the part and use the equipment to make Part 668.

Special Orders

The Special Order type of question typically involves an order at a **lower than usual price**, sometimes reducing regular sales. Assuming the facility has *excess capacity*, accepting a special order might make sense, as long as the variable costs are covered. Remember that total fixed costs are generally constant and would not increase due to a special order. If fixed costs did increase, that would be factored into the minimum acceptable price to cover all costs

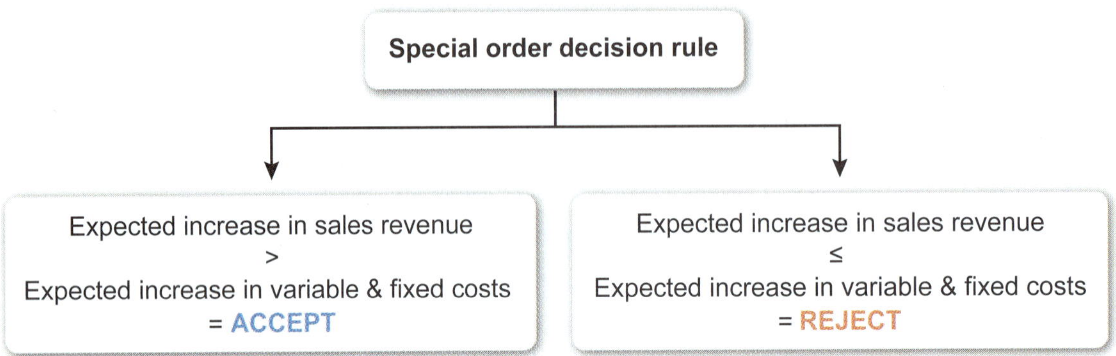

Flexco originally prepared an annual budget for a product on the basis of estimated sales of 100,000 units with a per unit sales price of $100, variable manufacturing costs of $35, fixed manufacturing costs of $15, variable selling and administrative (S&A) costs of $20, and fixed S&A costs of $10, resulting in per-unit operating income of $20. This budget does not use Flexco's full annual capacity of 105,000 units and neither increases nor decreases year-end inventory counts.

Big Mart offers to buy 10,000 units at $80 per unit. Filling this order will not affect regular sale prices or change fixed manufacturing costs and fixed and variable selling and administrative expenses; however, it will eliminate 5,000 units of regular sales since Flexco has insufficient capacity for them. An analysis of revenues and costs that change shows that Flexco will increase its operating income by accepting the order.

Revenues due to special order ($80/unit × 10,000 units)	$800,000
Less: special order manufacturing costs ($35/unit × 10,000)	(350,000)
Less: reduction in revenues from regular sales ($100/unit × 5,000 units)	(500,000)
Plus: reduction in variable manufacturing costs ($35/unit × 5,000 units)	175,000
Plus: reduction in variable S&A costs ($20/unit × 5,000 units)	100,000
Increase in operating income	**$225,000**

The fact that fixed manufacturing costs amount to $15 per unit and fixed S&A expenses amount to $10 per unit at a volume of 100,000 units indicates that fixed manufacturing costs are $1,500,000 per period, and fixed S&A expenses are $1,000,000 per period, regardless of the number of units produced and sold and regardless of whether a special order is accepted.

Revenue (100,000 units × $100/unit)	$10,000,000
Variable manufacturing costs (100,000 units × $35/unit)	3,500,000
Variable S&A expenses (100,000 units × $20/unit)	2,000,000
Contribution margin	4,500,000
Fixed manufacturing costs ($1,500,000)	1,500,000
Fixed S&A expenses ($1,000,000)	1,000,000
Operating Income	**$2,000,0000**

If Flexco does accept the order, the volume will consist of 10,000 units included in the special order and 95,000 units to be sold through normal channels, for a total of 105,000 units. Revenues, costs, and expenses will be as follows:

Revenue regular (95,000 units × $100/unit)	$9,500,000
Revenue special (10,000 units × $80/unit)	80,000
Variable manufacturing costs (105,000 units × $35/unit)	3,675,000
Variable S&A expenses (95,000 units × $35/unit)	1,900,000
Contribution margin	4,725,000
Fixed manufacturing costs ($1,500,000)	1,500,000
Fixed S&A expenses ($1,000,000)	1,000,000
Operating Income	**$2,225,000**

Fixed costs, including both fixed manufacturing costs and fixed S&A expense, remain the same regardless of the number of units produced or sold as long as the volume falls within the entity's normal range of operations, referred to as the relevant range.

Sell or Process Further

The Sell or Process Further type of question typically involves a component that can be sold in an early stage or processed further (with additional cost) before being sold.

Assume Sailor & Pirate Company makes products X, Y, and Z jointly. Each product may be processed further or sold at the split-off point. Joint production costs of $100,000 are allocated using the relative-sales-value at split-off method. Additional per-unit information is as follows:

	X	Y	Z
Sales value at spilt-off	$ 25	$50	$10
Additional processing cost	20	10	15
Final sales value	$100	$60	$20

An analysis of revenues and costs that change for the two alternatives for each product indicates that it is most profitable to process product X further and sell product Z. For product Y, there is no difference.

	X	Y	Z
Final sales value	$100	$60	$20
Less: Sales value at spilt-off	25	50	10
Incremental revenue	75	10	10
Less: Incremental costs	20	10	15
Additional profit (loss)	$ 55	$ 0	$ (5)

By processing product X further at a cost of $20, revenue will increase by $75 ($100 − $25), resulting in a net benefit of $55 ($75 revenue increase − $20 cost increase), making it more profitable to process product X further before sale.

By processing product Y further at a price of $10, revenue will increase by $10 per unit ($60 – $50), resulting in no net difference between processing product Y further and selling it at the split-off point ($10 revenue increase – $10 cost increase).

By processing product Z further at a cost of $15, revenue will increase by $10 per unit ($20 – $10), resulting in a net reduction in income of $5 per unit ($10 revenue increase – $15 cost increase). Product Z will not be processed further.

The joint production costs are irrelevant to this decision, as they will remain the same regardless of whether any of the products are processed further or not.

Scrap or Rework

The Scrap or Rework type of question typically involves defective parts that could be either reworked and sold or merely sold for scrap.

Sneak & Rogue Company has 20,000 defective units of product Loot with a total cost of $18,000. As scrap, they can be sold for $1,500. If they are reworked for $10,000, they may be sold for $12,000. The rework option is the more profitable alternative, contributing more to net income than the scrap option.

	Scrap	Rework
Incremental revenue	$1,500	$12,000
Less: Incremental costs	0	10,000
Additional profit (loss)	**$1,500**	**$ 2,000**

The total cost of the defective units before rework is irrelevant; this sunk cost is the same between the two alternatives.

Financial Modeling

A financial model is designed to forecast an entity's financial performance into the future. Generally, a spreadsheet such as Excel is used to build the formulas, based on key assumptions such as the following:

- A growth rate to forecast sales
- Cost or profit margin as a percentage of sales to forecast cost or margin in currency terms
- Working capital investments
- Fixed capital investments
- Financing from external sources (eg, issuing debt or equity)

The models can then be used for decision-making, including decisions about the following:

- Raising capital or modifying the capital structure of the entity
- Making acquisitions or divestitures (businesses and/or assets)
- Expanding the business (eg, opening new stores, entering new markets)
- Valuing a business or segment
- Financial statement analysis/ratio analysis
- Management accounting

Businesses use **capital budgeting techniques** to make long-term capital investment decisions. Although all the financial models are based on **uncertain predictions** of future income or cash flows, capital budgeting is still a useful approach to selecting the best investment option based on available information.

Characteristics of Capital Budgeting Techniques

	Time value of money	Trial and error calculations	Calculates length of time	Uses accounting income
Payback			✓	
Discounted Payback	✓		✓	
Net Present Value (NPV)	✓			
Internal Rate of Return (IRR)	✓	✓		
Accounting Rate of Return (ARR)				✓

Payback Period

The payback period is the length of time it takes for an initial cash outlay for the investment to be recovered in cash. Net cash flows are not the same as income since depreciation is not subtracted in the determination of net cash flows. If the net cash flows are the same each year, then the payback period equals the initial investment divided by the annual net cash inflow.

Payback period = Initial investment / After tax net cash inflows

For **uneven cash flow**, the cumulative cash flow for each year must be determined.

A company is investing in a machine costing $365,000. The following table shows selected financial data for the company for the next five years. Calculate the payback period.

Year	Annual Cash Flow	Cumulative Cash Flow
1	$ 50,000	$ 50,000
2	125,000	175,000
3	150,000	**325,000**
4	50,000	375,000
5	30,000	n/a

The cumulative cash inflows from the first three years total $325,000. Therefore, only an additional $40,000 is needed from Year 4 to recover the $365,000 cost, or 80% ($40,000 / $50,000) of Year 4. Payback is 3.8 years. Note that Year 5 cash inflows are not included in the calculation because payback was reached in Year 4.

The **discounted payback method** uses the present value of each individual annual net cash flow.

A company purchases an item for $43,000. The cost of capital is 8%. Pertinent information related to this purchase is as follows:

Year	Annual Cash Flow	Present Value Factor of 8%
1	$10,000	0.926
2	15,000	0.857
3	20,000	**0.794**
4	27,000	0.735

The payback period is the first three years plus 25% of Year 4—a total of **3.25 years**, as shown below:

Year	Annual Cash Flow	Present Value Factor of 8%	Present Value Cash Flows	Cumulative PV Cash Flows
1	$10,000	0.926	$ 9,260	$ 9,260
2	15,000	0.857	12,855	22,115
3	20,000	0.794	15,880	37,995
4	27,000	0.735	19,845	57,840

The cumulative cash inflows from the first three years total **$37,995**. Therefore, only an additional $5,005 is needed from Year 4 to recover the $43,000 cost, or 25% ($5,005 / $19,845) of Year 4. **Payback is 3.25 years.**

Present Value: Time Value of Money

Money that is received at a future date is *less valuable* than money received immediately, and present value concepts measure future cash flows in terms of the equivalent present dollars. Present value is defined as the current measure of an estimated future cash inflow or outflow, discounted at an interest rate for the number of periods between today and the date of the estimated cash flow. Many decisions require adjustments related to the time value of money:

- The **present value of an amount (lump sum)** is used to examine a single cash flow that will occur at a future date and determine its equivalent value today. Alternatively, it is the amount you need to invest today, for a certain number of years, at a specific interest rate, to get some amount back in the future
- The **present value of an ordinary annuity** refers to the value today of repeated cash flows on a systematic basis, with amounts being paid at the *end* of each period (it may also be known as an **annuity in arrears**). Bond interest payments are commonly made at the end of each period and use these factors
- The **present value of an annuity due** refers to the value today of repeated cash flows on a systematic basis, with amounts being paid at the *beginning* of each period (it may also be known as an **annuity in advance** or special annuity). Rent payments are commonly made at the beginning of each period and use these factors
- **Future values** look at cash flows and project them to a given future date. Future values can be computed using the three variations applicable to present values. The future value factor is the amount that would accumulate at a future point in time if $1 were invested now. As a result, the future value factor is equal to 1 divided by the present value factor

For example, an investment of $10,000 in two years at 10% would result in the principal multiplied by the future value factor. In this case the $10,000 × 1/0.8265 = $12,100.

Depreciation Tax Shield

When determining the net cash amount for financial analysis, the effect of depreciation expense on cash flows must be considered if the given information starts with *net income*, rather than cash inflows and outflows. While depreciation is not a cash expense, it affects the cash paid for taxes (ie, it produces tax savings). Depreciation expense reduces taxable income and therefore reduces taxes due and payable.

In other words, the noncash expense shields what would otherwise be taxable income, resulting in a reduced cash outflow for taxes. The depreciation tax shield can be simply calculated as the **tax rate × depreciation**.

Assume that estimated annual net income before taxes from a project is $100,000; the estimated annual depreciation expense is $30,000; and the estimated marginal tax rate is 40%. The estimated annual taxes are 0.40 × $100,000 NI = $40,000. Thus, the estimated annual cash inflow is equal to net income before taxes with the noncash expense of depreciation added back, less taxes: $100,000 NI + $30,000 dep. − $40,000 taxes = $90,000 inflow.

Without the depreciation deduction, annual taxes would be 0.40 × ($100,000 + $30,000) = $52,000 taxes; thus, the cash inflow would be $100,000 NI + $30,000 dep. − $52,000 taxes = $78,000 inflow.

The depreciation tax shield is the $12,000 difference ($52,000 − $40,000) between the tax amounts with and without the depreciation deduction. It can also be calculated as 40% × $30,000 dep. = $12,000.

Net Present Value (NPV)

Net Present Value (NPV), also referred to as the discounted cash flow model, is the excess of the present value of the cash inflows over the present value of the outflows (typically the cost of the investment).

Discounted Cash Flow Model

Key points about NPV include the following:

- Present value (PV) calculations adjust future amount(s) to present amounts with a discount factor.
- The discount factor is based on given rate of return and the number of compounding periods
- Multiple payments use a PV *annuity table* rather than a PV single sum table
- NPV is the PV of net cash inflows less the undiscounted cost
- Generally, only projects where NPV > $0 are acceptable

NPVs are the most accepted approach to compare projects financially. Some **advantages** of NPVs are the following:

- NPVs consider the time value of money
- NPVs may take into account risk, using higher discount rates for riskier projects
- NPVs take into account total profitability
- NPVs yield results in dollars, which may be readily interpreted as the changes in owners' wealth if a project is carried out

Some **disadvantages** of NPVs are the following:

- NPVs require more involved computations (not simple and intuitive)
- Some audiences may understand NPVs less readily
- NPVs do not take into account that managers may not actually follow the originally scheduled investments (or expenses)

Economic Value Added

One way in which the performance of an investment center is evaluated is based on its **economic value added** (EVA). The EVA is equal to the earnings of the investment center in excess of its cost of capital.

EVA is calculated by first multiplying the cost of the investment center by the entity's weighted average cost of capital to determine the cost of capital, which is generally the minimum return that the investment center is expected to yield. Subtracting that amount from the investment center's operating profit determines the amount by which profits exceed the cost of capital and by which the investment center adds economic value to the entity.

$$\text{EVA} = \text{NOPAT} - (\text{C\%} \times \text{TC})$$

NOPAT = Net operating profit after tax *C% = Cost of capital* *TC = Total capital*

Ideally, a manager should not be held responsible for costs that the manager cannot affect, such as costs that have somehow been allocated to that department but that are directed by and incurred on behalf of either the corporate level or other divisions. Similarly, if the manager's own salary is determined by someone other than the manager, the manager should not be held responsible for that cost.

Cash Flow Analysis

One of the key components to financial modeling is the cash projection. Assumptions generally include projected sales, net profit to sales ratio, working capital to sales, and sales growth rate.

An entrepreneur starts a company by investing $300,000 of equity to fund working capital. The entrepreneur makes the following forecast assumptions:

- First-year sales of $500,000
- Net profit margin of 30% of sales
- Annual sales growth at 8%
- Working capital is 80% of projected sales

The company's projected cash balance at the end of the second year is as follows:

Projected Working Capital (WC) Schedule

	YR 0	YR 1	YR 2	Comments
Projected WC	$300,000	$400,000	$432,000	80% of sales

Projected Cash Schedule

	YR 1	YR 2	Comments
Sales	$500,000	$540,000	8% of growth
Net income	150,000	162,000	30% of sales
Change in WC*	(100,000)	(32,000)	
Change in cash	$ 50,000	$130,000	

Note that Year 1 working capital is projected to be **$400,000 ($500,000 sales × 80%). The **$100,000** ($400,000 − $300,000) increase in working capital reduces available cash and is a "plug" in the above projected cash schedule.*

Internal Rate of Return (IRR)

The **internal rate of return (IRR)** is the discount rate at which the **net present value (NPV) is zero**.

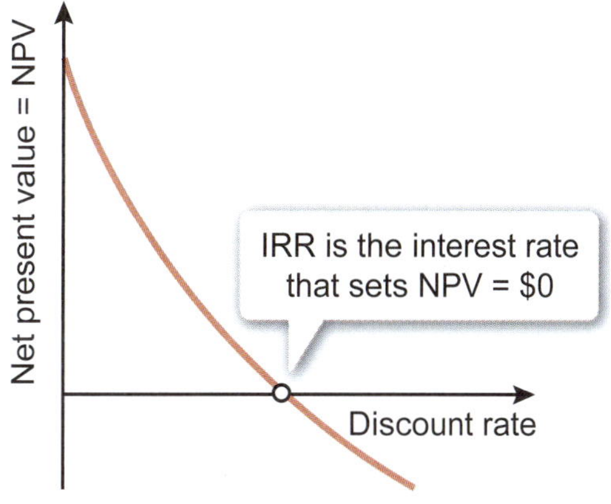

If the NPV decreases, the IRR, represented by the red line in the image, will also decrease, and vice versa. This would occur when net cash inflows decrease or the investment cost rises.

Alternatively, the IRR is the rate of interest that equates the present value of cash outflows and the present value of cash inflows (ie, essentially the breakeven point). Businesses may set several hurdle rates based on market rates of return for projects with similar risk. They would accept projects only if the IRR is greater than the hurdle rate.

Businesses commonly use the weighted average cost of capital (WACC) as the hurdle rate against which they compare projects' IRRs to decide whether to undertake those projects.

Assume that a business is considering buying a machine and has the following information:

Cost	$900
Useful life	5 years
Salvage value	None
Annual net cash flow	$250
Hurdle rate of return	10%

In addition, present value information is available for a five-year ordinary annuity:

Rate	10%	11%	12%	13%
Factor	3.79	3.70	3.60	3.52

The **internal rate of return** is the rate at which the present value of the annual cash inflows of $250 equals the investment of $900. This occurs when the present value factor for the annuity is $900 / $250 = 3.60, or 12%. To double check this, verify that the net present value at 12% is zero:

	Cash	**PV Factor**	**Present Value**
Inflows	250	3.60	$900
Outflows	900	1.00	900
Net			$ 0

Some **advantages** of using IRRs are the following:

- They take into account the time value of money
- Hurdle rates may take into account rates of return on investments with similar risk
- Many practitioners and audiences find IRRs to be more readily understandable than net present values

Some **disadvantages** of IRRs are the following:

- Under different assumptions, some cash-flow patterns may actually yield multiple IRRs
- Some cash-flow patterns may not have an IRR for which the project's NPV equates to zero

Accounting Rate of Return (ARR)

The accounting rate of return (ARR) is generally used as a **comparison tool** between multiple projects. ARR calculates the anticipated rate of return for a given project and is the average annual profit (also called accounting income) divided by the average investment cost. The numerator is calculated as the project's average annual income less the project's depreciation expense (if given) and any other related expenses.

ARR = Accounting income / Average (or initial) investment

The ARR is simple to calculate and understand. For example, an ARR of 9% means that the project will generate an average of 9% annual accounting profit over the life of the investment. However, the ARR ignores the time value of money and does not focus on actual cash flows.

Springs Co. is considering the purchase of equipment that would cost $100,000 and would save an estimated $25,000 per year in after-tax cash costs. The equipment's estimated useful life is five years, with no residual value, and would be depreciated by the straight-line method. Spring's predetermined minimum desired rate of return is 8%.

The annual depreciation expense is $20,000 (ie, $100,000 / 5 years), reducing the average annual profit (ie, the numerator) from $25,000 to $5,000. Because there is no information indicating that the denominator should be the *average* investment, the average annual profit of $5,000 is divided by the initial cost of $100,000 for an **ARR of 5%**. Since the ARR is below the minimum rate of return of 8%, the project should be rejected.

Some *disadvantages* of ARRs are the following:

- ARRs do not take into account the time value of money
- ARRs do not take into account differences in risk across investments (no project risk)
- Using different depreciation methods yields different ARRs

Profitability Index

The profitability index (PI) is the ratio of the present value of cash inflows to the initial cost of a project. When businesses are faced with several potential projects with positive NPVs but do not have the funds to carry out all of them, they may use this index to choose which projects to carry out first.

If PI is > 1.0, then the NPV is positive and the project is considered acceptable. To calculate the PI, divide the present value of the annual after-tax cash flows by the original cash invested in the project. Note that the PI does not consider the size of the project (ie, total dollars). Questions on the exam related to PI tend to be conceptual rather than numerical; therefore, no example is provided here.

2.04 Risk Management

COSO ERM Framework

Representative Task (Remembering & Understanding): Recall the purpose and objectives of the COSO ERM Framework.

Representative Task (Application): Apply the COSO ERM Framework to identify risk/opportunity scenarios in an entity.

Purpose

The business and economic environment is often unpredictable, with significant technology evolution, rapidly shifting customer behavior, global influences, and fierce competition—all factors that stress strategic planning and the need to maximize operational capabilities to survive and thrive.

This uncertainty **provides both risk and opportunity**, and management must determine how to balance those risks and opportunities in alignment with the objectives of the entity. To respond to the need for an organized approach, COSO developed the Enterprise Risk Management (ERM) Framework in 2004.

The framework was updated in 2017 due to the increasing complexity of business risks, the accelerated rate of emerging new risks, and the demand for better risk reporting.

COSO's ERM Framework is designed to be applied by all types and sizes of entities to *strategically identify events that may affect the entity and to manage those risks in accordance with the entity's risk appetite in order to provide reasonable assurance of achieving the entity's objectives.*

Risk Profile

The updated framework, retitled *Enterprise Risk Management—Integrating with Strategy and Performance*, dives deeper to **redefine risk** in relation to **strategy and performance** and focuses on the need to embed ERM proactively throughout the entity. The goal is to increase the probability that the entity will achieve its goals and objectives.

Once identified, risks must be *prioritized* to develop cost-beneficial **risk responses**. Appropriate responses are based on the amount of potential damage (financial and nonfinancial) and rate of occurrence.

A **risk profile** is then developed, which quantifies (ie, attaches a numerical value or rank to) threats to an entity.

Each entity has its own unique risk profile, based on its strategies and objectives. Risk profiles are used by entities to align their strategies to their risk appetite. Factors that an entity should consider in developing their risk profile include the following:

- **External factors**, such as macroeconomic or industry risks that affect overall industry demand or profitability
- **Internal (ie, company) factors** that affect an individual company and that are typically related to competitive positioning or management actions

Enterprise Risk Management: Risk Principles

- Identify risk
- Assess the severity of each risk
- Prioritize each risk
- Implement risk responses
- Develop a portfolio view of risk

ERM Components and Principles

COSO's new ERM Framework has *five components* and *20* different associated *principles*, as outlined below. COSO touts several **benefits** to implementing its ERM Framework:

- Promotes identification and management of entity-wide risks
- Increases identification of opportunities by examining the pros and cons of possibilities
- Reduces costs of negative surprises and maximizes positive outcomes
- Manages performance risks to reduce disruption and increase opportunity
- Prioritizes and maximizes allocation of resources

Governance and Culture Component

- Exercises board risk oversight
- Establishes operating structures
- Demonstrates commitment to core values
- Designs desired culture
- Attracts, develops, and retains capable employees

The first of the five components of the COSO ERM Framework is *Governance and Culture*. It sets the overall tone for the organization, addressing such issues as mission, vision, and core values. Governance encompasses the establishment of oversight responsibilities for ERM and the entity's tone. Culture refers to the ethical mindset, standards of acceptable behavior, and understanding the entity's risk.

Principle 1: Exercises Board Risk Oversight

"The board of directors provides oversight of the strategy and carries out governance responsibilities to support management in achieving strategy and business objectives."

The board's oversight role supports the creation of value in an entity and prevents its decline. The framework catalogs risk oversight responsibilities for boards. These responsibilities include overseeing governance and culture; strategy and objective setting; performance; information, communication, and reporting; and the reevaluation and improvement of practices to enrich entity performance.

The board's risk oversight role includes the following:

- Cultivating investor and stakeholder relations
- Authorizing management pay and incentives
- Reevaluating, questioning, and agreeing with management on:
  - Suggested strategy and target risk appetite;
  - Coordination of strategy and business objectives with the entity's mission, vision, and values;
  - Major decisions including mergers, acquisitions, capital allocations, funding, and dividend-related decisions;
  - Reactions to substantial fluctuations in entity performance or the risk portfolio; and
  - Treatment of instances of deviation from values.

Principle 2: Establishes Operating Structures

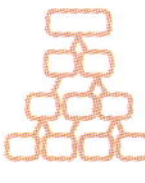

"The organization establishes operating structures in the pursuit of strategy and business objectives."

Principle 3: Defines Desired Culture

"The organization defines the desired behaviors that characterize the entity's desired culture."

Principle 4: Demonstrates Commitment to Core Values

"The organization demonstrates a commitment to the entity's core values."

Principle 5: Attracts, Develops, and Retains Capable Individuals

"The organization is committed to building human capital in alignment with the strategy and business objectives."

Principles 2 through 5 represent the **internal environment**, which **sets the tone** for the organization. It establishes a basis for the analysis of risk, incorporating management's philosophy, the entity's risk appetite, and the values that are important to the entity, such as *integrity and ethical values*. The internal environment is exhibited in a variety of ways, both formal and informal. Some of the more **formal components** include the entity's mission statement and its code of conduct.

These should be evident in all aspects of the entity and should be incorporated into the entity's culture. A well-designed **mission statement** may address some or all of the following:

- The moral or ethical position of the entity and its desired public image
- The key strategic influence for the entity's operations
- A description of the entity's products or services, target market, and geographical domain
- Expectations in relation to growth and profitability

The **informal aspect** of the internal environment is probably the *most important*. It is composed of the actual behavior of members of management and others who might be seen as influential within the organization.

Whenever the behavior of such individuals conflicts with the entity's mission statement or core values or its formal policies and procedures, individuals both inside the organization and outside of it will assign more significance to the behavior.

Strategy and Objective-Setting Component

- Analyzes business context
- Defines risk appetite
- Evaluates alternative strategies
- Formulates business objectives

The second component of the COSO ERM Framework is *Strategy and Objective Setting*. It represents the entity's process for **strategic planning**. The entity determines its risk appetite, aligns it with its strategy, and develops business objectives to execute the strategy. This process serves as a basis for recognizing, evaluating, and responding to risk.

Principle 6: Analyzes Business Context

"The organization considers potential effects of business context on risk profile."

"Business context" refers to the environment in which the business operates. ERM involves considering a full range of potential events, enabling management to identify and take advantage of opportunities. Also see principle 10.

Principle 7: Defines Risk Appetite

"The organization defines risk appetite in the context of creating, preserving, and realizing value."

It is important for management to consider what level of risk is acceptable when evaluating alternatives, establishing goals, and developing policies, procedures, and other mechanisms to manage risks.

For example, an entity should consider its risk appetite when determining its policy regarding the amount of information that must be obtained about a potential customer and how much must be verified independently before extending credit to avoid selling to someone who is not likely to pay.

Principle 8: Evaluates Alternative Strategies

"The organization evaluates alternative strategies and potential impact on risk profile."

Strategy is about developing a plan of action to achieve the entity's objectives. In evaluating alternative strategies, the entity must first align potential business strategies with the entity's mission, vision, and core values and then determine the impact of those strategies with respect to the entity's risk profile (ie, risk appetite).

COSO's ERM Framework provides three types of risks to consider in this process:

- **Risks to a chosen strategy** and the performance of that strategy. These are factors that an entity should address when choosing a strategy, such as customer demand, supply, competition, and technology infrastructure
- **Risks that the strategy chosen will not align** with the mission, vision, and values. Even if a strategy is successful, a misaligned strategy increases the risk that the entity will not achieve its mission and vision or that its values will be compromised. While some entities have been reluctant to truly embrace their mission, vision, and values, these objectives have been shown to be extremely important to risk management and resilience in times of change
- **Risks of, or from, the chosen strategy**. Every choice has some downsides. The risks of the strategy that is chosen should be considered and aligned with the risk appetite of the entity. The board and management should determine how the strategy will steer the entity in setting objectives and whether resources will be allocated efficiently

Note: It's important to realize that ERM is as much about *understanding* all the risks as it is about managing them to enhance the performance of the entity.

Principle 9: Formulates Business Objectives

"The organization considers risk while establishing the business objectives at various levels that align and support strategy."

While an entity's mission describes what it would like to accomplish, it does not set out a specific plan for accomplishing the mission. Management translates the mission into goals or objectives that support the mission and reflect the entity's risk appetite.

There are four types of **business objectives:**

- **Strategic objectives** are the beginning point. They establish a unifying theme for the entity and direct actions and decisions. While strategic objectives set the direction for the entity, objectives related to *operations*, *reporting*, *and compliance* provide the mechanisms for meeting those objectives. To be most effective, objectives should be set at each operating division and, when appropriate, in each of the three categories
- **Operational objectives**, as a result, may be set to address the acquisition of raw materials, the screening and assignment of employees, the acquisition and maintenance of equipment and support, and the process for completing the outputs
- **Reporting objectives** would be established to determine how the division is progressing toward meeting the operational objectives and, ultimately, the strategic objectives. The most effective information is often limited in scope to one or very few parameters, does not require a great deal of effort to accumulate and report on a timely basis, and can be simply understood
- **Compliance objectives** make certain that each division operates within appropriate guidelines, including both regulatory requirements and internal company policies. This includes making certain that employees are not working against the better interests of the employing entity. At the same time, the compliance objectives must be designed so that an employee does not violate externally imposed requirements in a misguided attempt to help the entity

Performance Component

- Identifies risk
- Assesses severity of risk
- Implements risk responses
- Prioritizes risks
- Develops portfolio view

The third component of COSO's ERM Framework is *Performance*. It represents the process of actually identifying, evaluating, and responding to **risks**. The risks should be prioritized by severity with regard to the entity's risk appetite. The entity then chooses the appropriate responses, while keeping an overall view of the amount of risk assumed. Results are reported to the appropriate stakeholders.

Principle 10: Identifies Risks

"The organization identifies risk that impacts the performance of strategy and business objectives."

The occurrence or nonoccurrence of certain events (ie, risks) will determine whether the entity will achieve its objectives. Thus, **risk identification** involves determining what those events may be and how to distinguish between those events that represent **opportunities**, which should be encouraged and exploited, and those that represent threats, which should be dealt with in accordance with the entity's risk appetite.

- **Opportunities must be exploited** to gain a competitive advantage, to sustain one, or to prevent a competitor from obtaining one. As such, opportunities should be considered in developing the strategic and other objectives of the entity. A plan might be established, and resources might be set aside, to take advantage of an opportunity in case it arises
- **Risks must be prepared for** so that the entity does not lose a competitive advantage or allow a competitor to gain one. As a result, adverse events are considered in the entity's risk management process. In determining an appropriate response to an event, the entity will consider the likelihood that it will occur, the magnitude of its effect, and the amount that the effect will be influenced by actions of the entity

Event identification is primarily the identification and monitoring of the *sources of information* that pertain to areas of risk for the entity. Since resources are limited, the entity must be prudent in deciding which sources of information will be monitored.

Principle 11: Assesses Severity of Risks

"The organization assesses the severity of risks."

Management must evaluate the effect(s) of identified events on the ability of the entity to *achieve its objectives*. The likelihood of the occurrence of each risk is *measured*, using an appropriate approach, including the following:

- **Benchmarking**, which compares expected outcomes to common measures
- **Probabilistic models**, which develop expected values using probabilities of possible outcomes (quantifying risk)
- **Nonprobabilistic models**, which use subjective assumptions to measure possible outcomes (qualitative, not quantitative)

Principles 12: Prioritizes Risks

"The organization prioritizes risks as a basis for selecting responses to risks."

Once management has identified and assessed the severity of the risks that may affect the entity's ability to achieve its objectives, it can decide how to prioritize the risks so that management can effectively assess capital needs and allocate capital where it is most needed or will be most productive.

Principle 13: Risk Responses

"The organization identifies and selects risk responses."

When deciding on an appropriate risk response, the entity must consider inherent risk and residual risk.

- **Inherent risk:** the risk to the entity if no action is taken
- **Residual risk:** the risk to the entity that would remain if action were taken and controls are taken into account

The *reduction in risk*—basically the difference between an event's inherent risk and its residual risk—*can be compared to the cost of taking action to determine if action is appropriate*. This type of analysis is also useful in deciding among alternative actions when more than one risk response is available.

Among the **alternative responses to risks** are the decisions to *avoid* the risk, *mitigate* the risk, *share* the risk, or simply *accept* the risk.

Risk Responses

Risk responses include the following:

- **Risk avoidance** involves using a strategy that circumvents the risk entirely
- **Risk acceptance** occurs when an entity takes *no action* and simply allows an event to occur. The entity believes that risk is at an acceptable level or that the cost of taking action would exceed the benefit of the reduction
- **Risk sharing** occurs when the risk burden is partially or wholly distributed to external parties (eg, insurance coverage)
- **Risk reduction** can include changing the operating environment (eg, diversifying product offerings) or rebalancing an asset portfolio to reduce exposure to certain types of losses

Principle 14: Risk Portfolio

"The organization develops and evaluates a portfolio view of risk."

ERM is designed to help management evaluate the interrelated impacts of decisions and deal with multiple risks. One risk may combine with other risks or offset other risks. Management must be careful when developing policies and procedures that are designed to affect one issue as, due to the integrated nature of business, it increases a different risk.

Review and Revision Component

- Assesses substantial change
- Reviews risk and performance
- Pursues improvement in enterprise risk management

The fourth component of the COSO ERM Framework is *Review and Revision*, which represents the process of evaluating how well ERM components perform over time and refining the components as conditions change, as necessary.

Principle 15: Assesses Substantial Change

"The organization identifies and assesses changes that may substantially affect strategy and business objectives."

Principle 16: Reviews Risk and Performance

"The organization reviews entity performance and considers risk."

Principle 17: Pursues Improvement in ERM

"The organization pursues improvement of enterprise risk management."

Risk assessment is an ongoing process, not a "one-time" activity. The entire ERM system must be monitored so that changes can be made on a timely basis. Monitoring may be through ongoing management activities or as part of a separate evaluation of the entity's ERM process.

Information, Communication, and Reporting Component

- Leverages information and technology
- Communicates risk information
- Reports on risk, culture, and performance

The last of the five COSO ERM Framework components is *Information, Communication, and Reporting*, which represents the ongoing exchange of internal and external information up and down as well as across the entity.

Principle 18: Leverages Information and Technology

"The organization leverages the entity's information and technology systems to support enterprise risk management."

Principle 19: Communicates Risk Information

"The organization uses communication channels to support enterprise risk management."

Principle 20: Reports on Risk, Culture, and Performance

"The organization reports on risk, culture, and performance at multiple levels and across the entity."

People must have relevant information to carry out their responsibilities. As a result, the entity must have a means of identifying what information is pertinent from all of its internal and external sources.

Relevant information may be financial or nonfinancial and may be quantitative or qualitative in nature. It may also be formal or informal, such as that derived from conversations with customers or suppliers. It can potentially come from such a wide range of sources that it becomes very important for an entity to determine what sources are reliable as well as what information is relevant.

Once identified, relevant information must be captured, processed, and communicated to those who can benefit from it. It must be put into a form that is usable and must be provided on a timely basis so that decisions can be made to prevent losses.

Communication must include parties to whom it is relevant. It is most effective when lines of communication move in all directions within and around an organization. There should be communication at all levels, including upward and downward communication. Likewise, relevant information should be communicated with customers or suppliers to enhance the entity's ability to meet the needs of customers and have its needs met by suppliers.

ERM and Environmental, Social, and Governance (ESG) Risks

Representative Task (Remembering & Understanding): Recall how the COSO ERM Framework can be applied to identify, respond to, and report environmental, social, and governance (ESG) related risks.

Management and auditors will increasingly need to address how **environmental, social, and governance (ESG)** matters affect the entity's *operating environment* and determine whether there are any *material* effects on the F/S.

Common ESG-Related Financial Adjustments	
Income Statement	• Projected revenue • Projected operating costs • Gross and operating margins
Balance Sheet	• Impaired assets
Cash Flow Statement	• Capital expenditures • Capital structure • Shareholder returns

Actions by authoritative bodies addressing ESG risks (also referred to as **sustainability**) include the following:

- Issuance by COSO of *Enterprise Risk Management—Applying ERM to Environmental, Social, and Governance-Related Risks*
- Proposed reporting requirements by the SEC that would require domestic and/or foreign registrants to include **climate-related disclosures** in registration statements and periodic reporting (eg, Form 10-K)
- Papers issued by the FASB highlighting the connection between ESG-related matters and their effect on financial statements
- Issuance of *Considerations of ESG-Related Matters in an Audit of Financial Statements*, a practice aid released by the AICPA to support practitioners

The AICPA's practice aid defines the components of ESG as follows:

Environmental: Describes how an entity is exposed to and manages risks *and opportunities* related to the environment (eg, climate change, natural resource scarcity, pollution, waste)

Social: Applies to information about an entity's values and business relationships and addresses topics such as fair labor practices, the use of ethically sourced material in the production of products, product quality and safety, human capital such as employee health and safety, and diversity and inclusion policies and efforts

Governance: Relates to information about the system of rules, practices, and processes by which an entity is directed and controlled and addresses topics such as the structure and diversity of the board of directors, critical event responsiveness, and policies and practices related to lobbying, political contributions, bribery, and corruption

Environmental, Social, Governance (ESG)

Environmental	Social	Governance
• Climate issues	• Data privacy	• Board compensation
• Pollution	• Diversity	• Executive compensation
• Waste management	• Human rights	• Whistle-blower protection

A report by the Society for Corporate Governance found that these ESG issues often:

- Derive from a risk or impact **inherent in the core** operations or products;
- Have the potential to **meaningfully damage** a company's intangible value, reputation, or ability to operate; and
- Are accompanied by **persistent media interest**, organized stakeholders, and associated public policy debates that could magnify the impact of a company's existing position or practice and increase the reputational risk (or opportunity) created by a change in company policy or practice.

Given that management is responsible for the fair presentation of F/S, each entity must establish policies and procedures to identify and address ESG matters that affect its business and F/S. Each entity will have its own definition of ESG based on its business model; internal and external environment; product or services mix; and mission statement, vision, core values, and risk profile.

Many entities already have established ERM structures in place to identify, assess, manage, monitor, and communicate risks. Using the ERM processes, ESG concerns can be included and *prioritized* in the entity's risk profile, or a separate and distinct profile can be developed, with risk responses tailored to specific ESG concerns.

Mitigation strategies can then be developed and implemented. Along with risk comes *opportunities*, which should also be part of the overall ERM philosophy. These processes provide an avenue for boards and management to optimize outcomes, with the goal of enhancing capabilities to create, preserve, and ultimately realize value.

COSO's ESG Guide

COSO's *Enterprise Risk Management—Applying ERM to Environmental, Social, and Governance-Related Risks* was specifically designed to help entities apply ERM principles and practices to ESG-related risks. This guidance is intended to be used in conjunction with an established ERM framework.

The purpose of the COSO ESG guidance is to help an entity achieve the following:

- **Enhanced resilience:** An entity's medium- and long-term viability and resilience will depend on the ability to anticipate and respond to a complex and interconnected array of risks that threaten the strategy and objectives
- **Articulation of ESG-related risks:** ERM identifies and assesses risks for potential impact to the strategy and business objectives. Articulating ESG-related risks in a "common language" among all concerned parties brings ESG issues into mainstream processes and evaluations
- **Improved resource deployment:** Obtaining robust information on ESG-related risks enables management to assess overall resource needs and helps optimize resource allocation
- **Enhanced pursuit of ESG-related opportunities:** By considering both positive and negative aspects of ESG-related risks, management can identify ESG trends that lead to new opportunities
- **Realized efficiencies of scale:** Managing ESG-related risks centrally and alongside other entity-level risks helps to eliminate redundancies and better allocate resources to address the entity's top risks
- **Improved disclosure:** Improving management's understanding of ESG-related risks can provide the transparency and disclosure that investors expect and can achieve compliance with jurisdictional reporting requirements.

The COSO ESG guidance is formatted much like COSO'S ERM Framework, with the same five basic components:

- **Governance and culture for ESG-related risks:** Raise the *awareness levels* of the board of directors and executive management to ESG-related risks. Additionally, support a *culture of collaboration* among those who are responsible for ESG-risk management
- **Strategy and objective setting for ESG-related risks:** Examine the *value-creation process* to understand the impact of ESG risks in the short, medium, and long term
- **Performance for ESG-related risks:** Risks are identified, assessed, and prioritized, and responses are implemented
- **Review and revision for ESG-related risks:** Monitor and assess EGS-related risks. This step is critical to evaluating the effectiveness of implemented risk responses and modifying approaches as needed
- **Information, communication, and reporting for ESG-related risks:** Consult with *risk owners* to identify the most appropriate information to be communicated and reported internally and externally (ie, to support risk-informed decision-making)

Strategies to Mitigate Financial Risk

Representative Task (Application): Use strategies to mitigate financial risks (eg, market, interest rate, currency, liquidity)

Risk tolerance is a company's ability and willingness to incur losses while pursuing strategic goals. Leadership determines the company's risk tolerance by analyzing internal and external risk factors that could diminish the company's ability to achieve important goals or—at worst—threaten its solvency.

Appropriate and inappropriate factors that leadership should consider when determining risk tolerance include the following:

Appropriate Factors	Inappropriate Factors
• Flexibility to respond to adverse events	• Individual motivations
• Intensity of market competition	• Board of directors' agendas
• Regulatory and government environment	• Short-term operating pressures
• Ability to absorb losses and remain solvent	• Management compensation

Within a **risk management framework**, risk infrastructure encompasses the people and systems required to track risk exposures and perform basic quantitative analysis that allows for more in-depth risk assessment.

Enterprise Risk Management Framework	
Set Risk Governance Parameters	• Set strategic goals, risk tolerance, and risk budget (leadership) • Allocate capital to achieve goals (management)
Establish Risk Infrastructure	• Establish people and systems to support risk management • Collect risk data, test data, and create reports
Identify, Measure, and Monitor	• Analyze risk drivers and identify financial and nonfinancial risks • Track risk metrics and changes in risk exposures • Assess alignment or risk exposure and tolerance
Report and Strategize	• Communicate continually throughout organization • Determine which activities add value

Risk identification is the initial step in implementing **strategies to mitigate financial risks**. Financial risks originate directly in the financial markets and include the following.

Market Risk

Market risk premium is the *difference* between the **expected return** on a given investment and the **risk-free return** (ie, U.S. government-issued securities such as Treasury bills and bonds). The greater the difference, the larger the premium. The premium is essentially compensation to the investor for accepting greater risk.

Factors that affect the risk premium include length of maturity, relative liquidity, and relative seniority. In general, investments with a greater length of maturity have a greater risk premium than do short-term investments, due to increased uncertainty over their longer life span.

The expected return is calculated as follows:

$$\text{Expected return} = \left[\left(1 + \begin{matrix}\text{Real}\\\text{risk-free}\\\text{rate}\end{matrix}\right) \times \left(1 + \begin{matrix}\text{Expected}\\\text{inflation}\end{matrix}\right) \times \left(1 + \begin{matrix}\text{Expected}\\\text{risk premium}\end{matrix}\right)\right] - 1$$

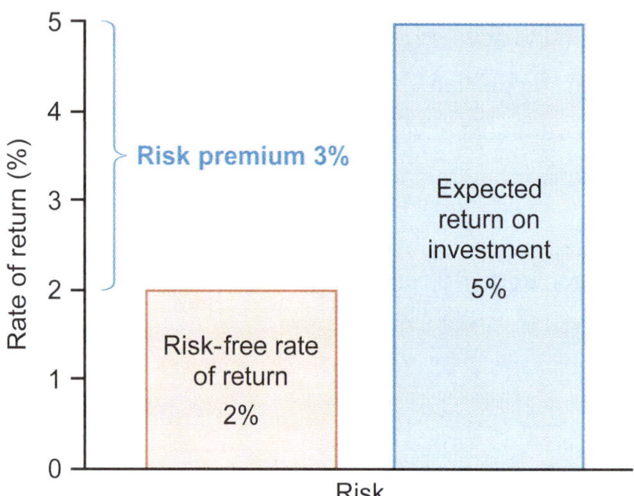

Companies manage market risk in the following ways:

- Shifting their financing sources from debt to equity, since equity can more easily accommodate temporary declines in the value of their assets
- Diversifying their income streams and the assets they hold; however, greater diversification may be accompanied by losses in managerial focus
- Using hedging strategies, such as purchasing instruments whose value will increase should the company, its competitors, or the economy as a whole experience difficulty
- "Shorting" the S&P 500 stock index (for short-term market risk)

Credit Risk

Credit risk is the risk that the parties that one has lent to, or that owe payments, may fail to pay. Standard techniques to deal with credit risk include the following:

- Diversifying one's customers
- Selling future streams of payments, that is, turning from being a lender who "originates to hold" and earns profits from interest payments to being a lender who "originates to distribute" and earns profits from origination fees

- Implementing internal control mechanisms to ensure that credit standards are appropriately tight
- Requiring greater guarantees from borrowers (eg, requiring larger down payments or other forms of collateral)
- Using derivatives, such as credit default swaps

Credit default swaps (CDS) are derivative instruments that **protect a lender against default** by its borrowers (they are essentially insurance). Under a CDS, a holder (ie, buyer) pays periodic premiums to an issuer (ie, seller). The CDS seller pays the buyer only in the case of default (similar to an insurance policy).

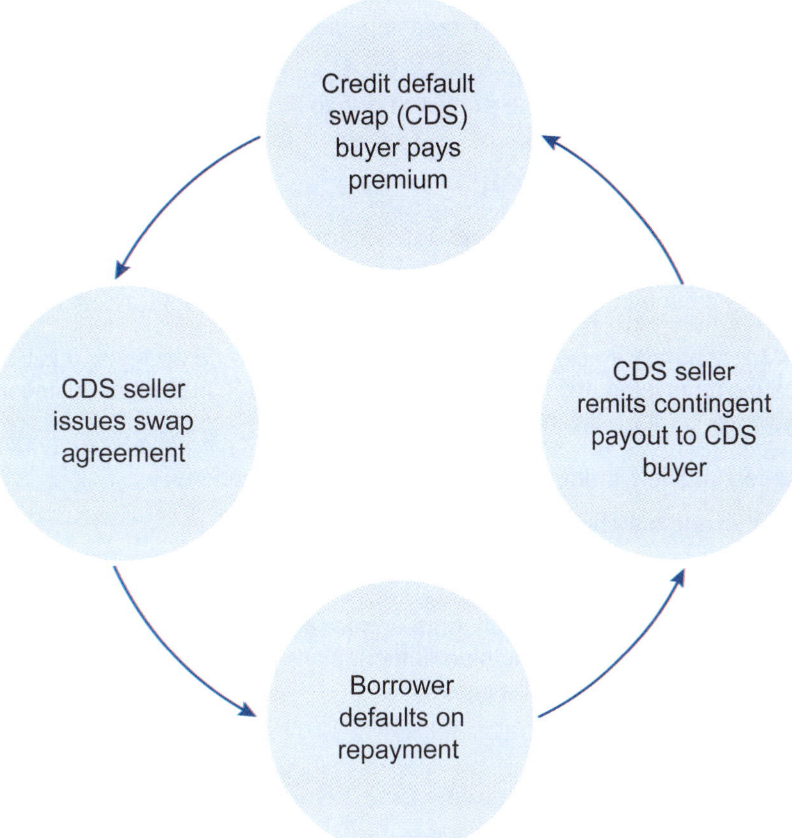

Liquidity Risk

Liquidity risk is the risk that while companies may be solvent on a long-term basis (ie, their long-term revenues outweigh their long-term costs), during a crisis situation, their short-term obligations might outweigh their access to liquid funds, forcing them to sell long-term assets at **"fire sale prices"** or at depressed prices, effectively making them insolvent in the short term and, hence, indefinitely.

Companies may manage their liquidity risk in the following ways:

- Matching the maturities of their assets and liabilities better, such that, as liabilities come due, some assets can be liquidated at full prices
- Maintaining a large cushion of liquid assets (cash and short-term securities)
- Maintaining a variety of long-term lines of credit with a variety of providers. Of course, the greater the number of lines, the more secure that they are, and the longer they extend into the future, the higher the fees they will involve

Interest Rate Risk

Interest rate risk is the risk that changes in **economy-wide interest rate levels** may adversely affect an entity's earnings. If the entity holds assets with longer maturities (eg, investment in bonds) and liabilities with shorter maturities (eg, accounts payable), interest rate increases may leave the entity with assets that reprice slowly and liabilities that reprice quickly. That is, assets continue to generate low interest rates established in previous years while the entity must now pay higher rates on most liabilities.

Interest rate risk can be **mitigated** in the following ways:

- Reducing assets with long maturities and increasing liabilities with long maturities
- Reducing fixed-rate long-term assets and increasing variable-rate long-term assets
- Using interest rate derivatives (including swaps); however, the fees for interest rate derivatives increase the further out one seeks to be protected due to increased risk

Systematic and Unsystematic Risk

Total business risk consists of systematic risk and nonsystematic risk. **Systematic risk** is inherent in the marketplace (ie, the economy) and affects all companies and industries. It cannot be reduced because entities do not control the source of the risk (eg, high interest rates, inflation, recessions).

Nonsystematic risk (or nonmarket risk) is *unique* to an industry or a company and includes poor earnings or labor strikes. Because nonsystematic risk occurs at the entity level, individual businesses can reduce or mitigate nonsystematic risk through diversification of the following:

- Income streams (eg, multiple products produced in multiple locations)
- Resource acquisition and distribution methods
- Asset/portfolio holdings

For example, if an entity relies solely on air transportation for distribution of sold goods, a pilot labor strike would severely impact its business. Diversification of the entity's transportation options (eg, rail and sea transportation) would mitigate the impact of a pilot strike.

Total Risk = Systematic Risk + Nonsystematic Risk	
Systematic Risk	**Nonsystematic Risk**
• Also known as "market risk" or "nondiversifiable risk" • Inherent in the market • Cannot be eliminated by diversification • Examples: interest rate shifts, stock market crashes	• Also known as "nonmarket risk" or "firm-specific risk" • Specific to a firm or industry • Can be eliminated by diversification • Examples: business litigation, cyberattacks

Working Capital

Representative Task (Analysis): Compare various strategies for managing the working capital of an entity.

Working capital is current assets less current liabilities. Managing working capital involves ensuring that the business has sufficient current assets to meet the firm's current liabilities (ie, obligations). Management can focus on any/all of the following items to manage working capital:

- Cash
- Short-term financing
- Marketable debt securities
- Receivables
- Inventory
- Current liabilities

Current assets are items expected to be converted to cash within one year or one operating cycle, whichever is longer (eg, cash and cash equivalents, accounts receivable, inventory). **Liquid assets** are current assets that can be converted easily into cash (eg, cash, marketable debt securities, accounts receivable). Certain current assets, such as inventory and prepaid expenses, are not considered quick assets because they cannot be quickly converted to cash.

Current liabilities are obligations due within one year or one operating cycle, whichever is longer (eg, short-term debt, accounts payable, accrued liabilities).

The components of working capital are included in several key liquidity ratios, including the following:

Liquidity Ratios	
Current Ratio	$\frac{\text{Current assets}}{\text{Current liabilities}}$
Quick Ratio*	$\frac{\text{Cash + Marketable securities + Accounts receivable}}{\text{Current liabilities}}$
Cash Ratio	$\frac{\text{Cash + Marketable securities}}{\text{Current liabilities}}$

**Also call the acid-test ratio*

The **cash ratio** is the most **conservative liquidity ratio** since it includes only the most liquid current assets in evaluating a company's ability to pay its current liabilities. Liquidity is how quickly an asset can be converted to cash at its current valuation. The higher the cash ratio, the better the company's ability to pay its current liabilities.

Working capital (WC) turnover measures how efficiently a company generates sales (revenue) from its current working capital. The turnover ratio is revenue divided by average WC. A high WC turnover suggests that the company is more efficient at using its short-term assets and liabilities to support sales.

$$\text{WC turnover} = \frac{\text{Revenue}}{\text{Average WC}}$$

Managing Cash

Businesses keep cash balances for several purposes:

- **Operations:** Funds to pay for ordinary expenses
- **Compensating balances:** Banks may require businesses to maintain minimum checking account balances as an alternative (noncash) form of compensation for bank services and loans
- **Trade (purchase) discounts:** Quick payment of bills may result in early payment discounts. For example, an entity may allow a 2% discount on a payable if payment is remitted within 10 working days; otherwise, the full amount is due within 30 days

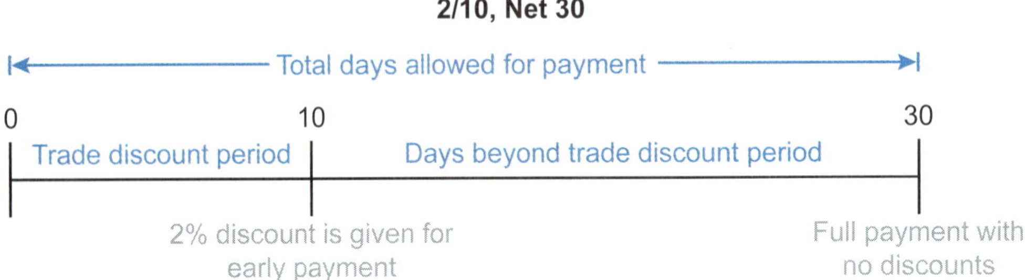

- **Speculative balances** to take advantage of unexpected business opportunities

The **cash conversion cycle (CCC)** measures the average number of days between a company's disbursement of cash to suppliers and receipt of cash from customers. Shortening the CCC improves profitability because longer CCCs require businesses to use more financing.

The CCC is made up of three distinct elements:

- **Inventory conversion period (ICP)** represents the average number of days it takes a company to convert inventory to sales
- **Receivable collection period (RCP)** is the average number of days required to collect accounts receivable
- **Payable deferral period (PDP)** represents the average number of days between buying inventory and paying for that inventory

Cash Conversion Cycle (CCC) Calculation

CCP = ICP + RCP - PDP

$$\text{Inventory conversion period (ICP)} = \frac{\text{Average inventory}}{\text{COGS}} \times 365$$

$$\text{Accounts receivable collection period (RCP)} = \frac{\text{Average receivables}}{\text{Credit sales}} \times 365$$

$$\text{Accounts payable deferral period (PDP)} = \frac{\text{Average payables}}{\text{Purchases or COGS}} \times 365$$

Managing Short-Term Financing

Companies typically have many options for short-term financing, including internal sources and financial intermediaries (eg, lines of credit). If an entity needs to improve its short-term liquidity, it should select the option with the *lowest financing cost*. Mismanaging capital can result in higher costs paid or a shortage of funds.

Internal Financing for Short-Term Liquidity Needs		
Operating Cash Flows	**Working Capital Efficiency**	**Converting Liquid Assets to Cash**
• Cash flow after dividends and interest payments	• Extending payable period • Reducing receivables period or delaying payments • Shortening asset conversion cycle	• Receivables • Inventories • Marketable securities • Bonds

Managing Marketable Debt Securities

To maximize earnings, businesses may choose to use various **short-term debt investments** of another entity, instead of cash (or zero-interest business checking accounts). Generally, if an entity acquires the debt securities of other entities, it is essentially becoming a creditor with a receivable from the other entity.

While holding the receivable, the entity will be receiving periodic interest payments and may be receiving periodic payments to reduce the principal. In other cases, the principal may be paid as a single lump sum at the end of the receivable's term. In choosing among these debt investments, the most important considerations are *liquidity and risk (safety)*. The classifications of marketable debt securities are the following:

Security	Classification	Balance Sheet Measurement	Holding Gains and Losses
Trading	Investor buys and sells within a short period of time to earn a profit	Fair value	Reported in net income
Available-for-sale	All other securities not classified as trading or held-to-maturity	Fair value	Reported in other comprehensive income
Held-to-maturity	Investor has intent and ability to hold until the due date for repayment	Amortized cost	n/a

Managing Receivables

Managing accounts receivable (receivables or A/R) includes setting up and updating credit approval mechanisms and monitoring the resulting receivables. Businesses' credit policies include four key elements:

- **Credit period:** The time buyers are given to make payments (typically 30 days for business buyers)
- **Discounts:** Price reductions for paying early (such as a 2% discount for paying within 10 days), with the full amount due in 30 days if the discount is not taken
- **Credit criteria:** Financial strength requirements for customers to be granted credit
- **Collection policies:** Methods employed to collect on receivables that are behind schedule

To generate immediate cash, a business may do the following with its receivables (A/R financing):

- **Pledging:** Involves borrowing cash and using part of the A/R (ie, 75%) as collateral to secure a loan. Age and creditworthiness of the receivables are taken into consideration by the lender. There is no change in control or transfer of ownership of the receivables. The entity, not the lender, still bears the risk of uncollectible accounts
- **Assignment of A/R:** A lending agreement whereby the borrower assigns an A/R for cash but must pay interest and usually a service charge on the advance. The company (borrower) agrees to use the collections from the receivables to repay the lender
- **Factoring with or without recourse:** The business may *sell receivables* to a financing company. Factoring may occur with or without recourse. When receivables are sold with recourse, the company (seller) **bears the risk** of uncollectible accounts. If sold without recourse, the **factor** will generally charge a higher fee to compensate for the additional risk it assumes for uncollectible accounts

Factored, Pledged, and Assigned Receivables

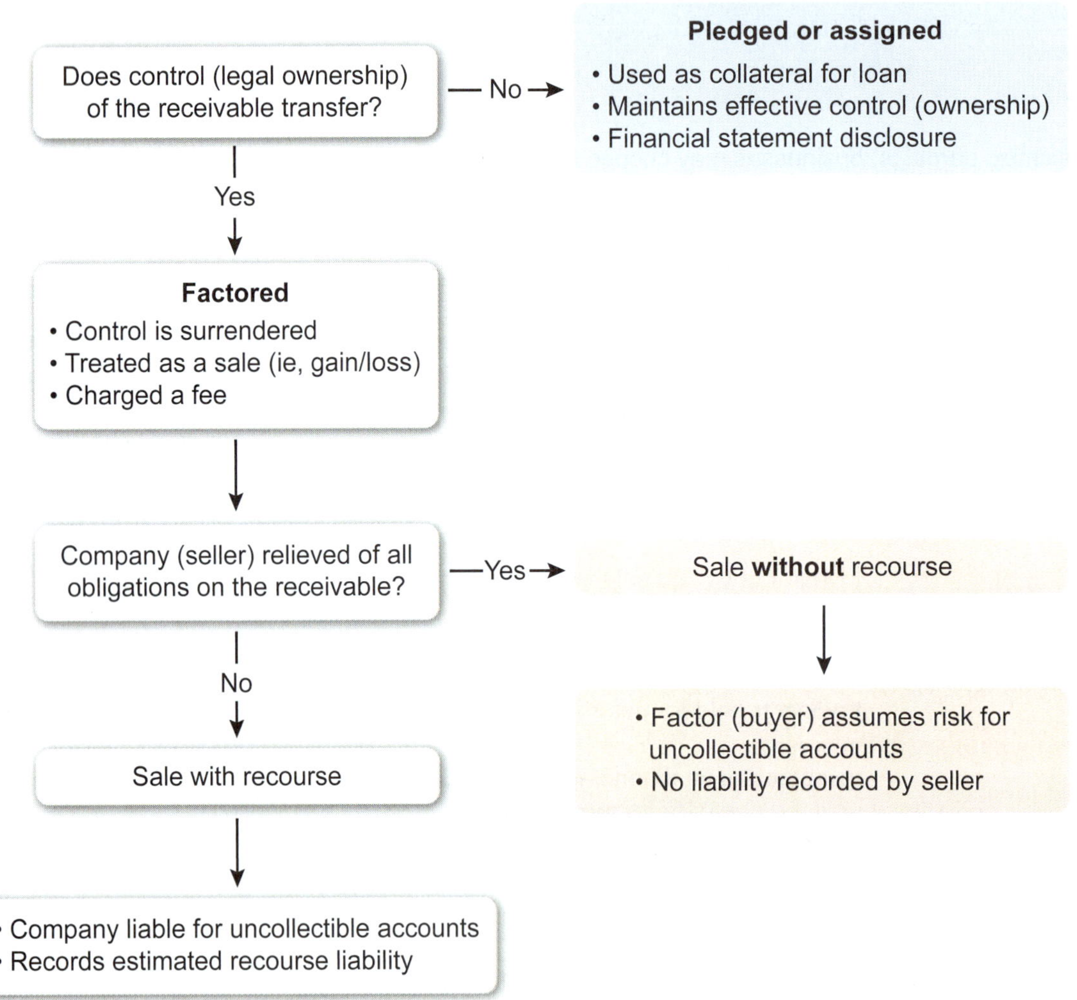

Managing Inventory

Budgeting for inventory involves determining when to place orders (or start production) to replace inventory and how much to purchase (or produce). Managing inventories requires weighing many potentially conflicting factors:

- Higher costs of carrying inventories would push businesses to reduce inventories to the extent possible
- Higher costs of placing small orders would probably push businesses to make fewer but larger orders, which would probably increase their inventories
- Longer lead times in the delivery of inventories would push businesses to carry larger inventories to avoid running out of products to sell
- Higher sales are also typically associated with higher inventory needs

Deciding when to order inventory involves calculating the **reorder point**. To do so, the business determines the quantity used per day and the lead time needed for orders to be filled. For example, if the company uses 25 units per day and an order normally takes 10 days to fill, then the order should be placed (at the latest) when the inventory balance consists of 250 (25 × 10) units.

Reorder Point
Average daily demand
× Average lead time
Reorder point without a safety stock
+ Safety stock
Reorder point with a safety stock

Of course, the time it takes to fill an order may vary somewhat, so businesses often use the maximum lead time rather than normal lead time to determine when to place orders. The difference between the two inventory levels is known as the **safety stock**. If, in the above case, the maximum lead time is 15 days, then an order might be placed when there are 25 × 15 = 375 units remaining, and the safety stock is 375 − 250 = 125 units.

Just-in-Time (JIT)

Some companies follow a **just-in-time (JIT)** philosophy to manage their inventories, which is based on a demand (ie, pull) approach, in contrast to traditional inventory management methods based on long-range sales forecasts (ie, push method).

To keep inventories low, businesses order as little as possible and order as close to the time when inventories are needed as possible. JIT may be used effectively in the following situations:

- The costs of storing (nonvalue-adding operations) inventory are high
- Lead times and costs per purchase order are both low
- Needs for safety stock are low because the business has good relationships with suppliers that are very reliable

Push	Pull

• Purchases based on anticipated need • Large lots/high inventory balances • Higher nonvalue-added costs (eg, waste, storage) • Poor supplier relationships • Lower quality, more defects • Poor communication	• Purchases based on actual need • Small lots/low inventory balances • Lower nonvalue-added costs (eg, waste, storage) • Strong supplier relationships • Higher quality, fewer defects • Strong communication

In a mature JIT system, units are in process for a relatively short period of time due to the efficiency of the system and the higher speed of manufacturing. As a result, traditional accounting approaches for keeping track of costs in work-in-process are not effective, and many companies adopt a *backflush costing* approach.

In a **backflush costing approach**, costs assigned to jobs will not be tracked in as much detail as in traditional costing systems. Under a backflush approach:

- All manufacturing costs are charged directly to cost of goods sold since little or no inventory is expected to remain at any point in time;
- At the end of an accounting period, the company determines if there are inventories; and
- When inventories exist on a reporting date, costs are allocated from cost of goods sold into the appropriate inventory accounts, such as finished goods using standard costs.

Economic Order Quantity (EOQ)

The **economic order quantity (EOQ)** formula is often used to estimate the **optimal number** of inventory units to be ordered at one time to minimize the sum of inventory costs. Inventory costs include carrying (ie, storage) and restocking placement (ie, ordering) costs.

The formula takes into account the annual usage of inventory (A), costs involved in placing orders (P), and storage costs for carrying inventory (S).

Economic Order Quantity Graph

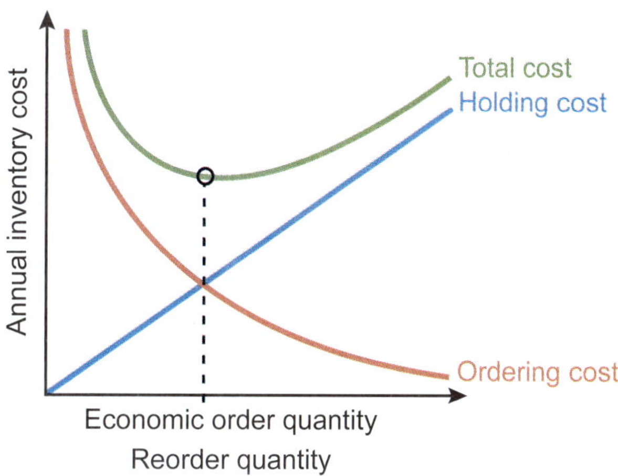

Impact of Proposed Transactions

Representative Task (Analysis): Derive the impact of a proposed transaction on key performance measures of an entity.

Key performance measures, more commonly known as **key performance indicators (KPI)**, provide feedback to management that evaluates how well a person, division, or entity is accomplishing its goals. At the entity level, KPIs assess progress toward **achieving strategic goals**.

KPIs should be assigned to an individual who has the ability to measure achievement and allocate resources required for improving the measure. As with all performance measures, KPIs should be continually monitored and revised as necessary.

Annie's Artworks, Inc., mass produces paintings by the great masters. Management is considering a change in how the company addresses production quality issues. Currently, Annie's spends 50% more on corrective actions (such as free replacements for flawed paintings) than on preventive actions.

Management believes that a one-time cash outlay of $250,000 for a high-quality digital printer will result in a decrease in warranty costs of $400,000. Determine the potential impact on the following KPI related to the specific department listed:

Department	KPI Example	Impact on KPI (Solutions)
Finance	Working capital ratio	Decrease due to use of cash but potential increase from more sales
Marketing	Return on Ad Spend	No effect (could potentially reduce marketing if product's reputation improved)
Sales	Sales per employee	Potential increase due to improved quality of product
IT	Server downtime	No effect
Customer Service	Average number of tickets	Potential improvement due to fewer complaints

SWOT Analysis

Representative Task (Analysis): Interpret an entity's strengths, weaknesses, opportunities, and threats (SWOT) analysis to assess the entity's options to achieve its overall business strategy.

One method of comparing business strategies is to engage in a formal analysis of an entity's strengths, weaknesses, opportunities, and threats (ie, SWOT analysis) from both an internal and external perspective.

- **Strengths:** Includes internal areas that the company excels at and with which it is able to differentiate itself from its competitors (eg, strong brand loyalty, low debt balance sheet, unique product or service)
- **Weaknesses:** Includes internal areas requiring improvement in order to reach an entity's optimal performance level (eg, high employee turnover, high levels of debt, aging equipment)
- **Opportunities:** Focuses on external factors that provide an advantage over competitors (eg, ability to increase market share of electric car sales due to patented cutting-edge technology)
- **Threats:** Focuses on external factors that represent potential harm to the entity (eg, supply chain issues in obtaining raw materials in a timely manner to meet production demands)

Consider the following SWOT analysis for Versatile Vaccine, a global manufacturer specializing in pandemic-related virus vaccines. Versatile Vaccine's business strategy is to *globally* provide effective vaccines while continuing to expand operations and increase profitability.

The visual overview of Versatile Vaccine's SWOT analysis quickly shows the company's position. Each section represents key insights and interconnectivity of opportunities and threats, advantages and disadvantages.

Once identified, the analysis leads to alignment of a strategic vision by all groups within an organization. Key areas can be analyzed further with data provided from company results, economic conditions, and competitor information.

Versatile Vaccine SWOT Analysis

Strengths

- World market share of 68%
- Innovative and cutting-edge technology

Weaknesses

- Quality control issues at some production sites
- Global backlog on raw materials

Opportunities

- Increasing demand for new variations due to virus mutation
- Relatively few major competitors

Threats

- Increasing competition from rival vaccine manufacturers
- Increasing cost of raw materials

Strengths

With an estimated 68% of the world market, Versatile Vaccine has a strong and influential position. Combined with its innovative and cutting-edge technology, it is well situated for rapidly and effectively addressing evolving strains of viruses and maintaining its position as a global power player in the industry.

Weaknesses

Quality control issues have resulted from the significant amount of overtime required to meet global demand. This has led to some vaccine batches being recalled from distribution. Patient trust in the brand is beginning to erode, which may allow competitors to obtain larger market share. Although global backlog on the availability of raw materials is a significant issue, the backlog affects all the companies in this industry, so it is not unique to Versatile.

Opportunities

Due to mutation of the virus, demand for new vaccine variations will increase over time. The global market is expanding as more individuals are eligible to receive new variations of the vaccine (eg, vaccines are now available for very young children). With relatively few major competitors, Versatile Vaccine can rapidly roll out new products, provided that quality control issues can be addressed.

Threats

Current dominance in the global markets is not guaranteed. Rivals, who have a stronger reputation for quality, are beginning to ramp up production, which is a concern for Versatile Vaccine. In response to competitor threats, Versatile Vaccine has begun to lower some of its prices, which will reduce profit margins. This reduction in profit is further compounded by the increased cost of raw materials, as Versatile Vaccine must now compete with competitors for a limited supply of vaccine components.

Conclusion

Versatile Vaccine is in a relatively strong position to achieve its objectives for continued growth and profitability. It does need to focus on improving the quality control issues before other competitors gain market share. Additionally, profit margins should be carefully monitored and improved where feasible.

2.05 Economic and Market Influences on Business

Supply and Demand

Representative Task (Application): Determine the effect of supply and demand and elasticity measures on a product.

Economics is the study of how we allocate scarce resources to satisfy unlimited wants. **Microeconomics** is the study of the decisions of, and interactions among, various individual economic agents (households and firms) in a market setting. Macroeconomics is the study of interactions of these agents at the aggregate level and involves broader issues of economic growth, business cycles, inflation, and unemployment.

- Both households and firms act as buyers in the economy, providing demand for products (eg, goods, services) and factor resources (eg, labor, capital, land) in their respective markets
- Both households and firms act as sellers in the economy, providing the supply of factor resources and products, respectively
- The interaction of demand and supply determines the price, the quantity produced and consumed, and the allocation of products and factor resources

Supply

A **supply curve** shows the *direct relationship* between the price of a product or service and the quantity that a group of producers and/or sellers is willing to supply at a particular time (ie, the quantity supplied). On a graph, a change in the price of the product is indicated by a movement along the supply curve. For instance, as the price of a product increases (eg, from 10 to 20), the quantity supplied by sellers increases (eg, from 30 to 50).

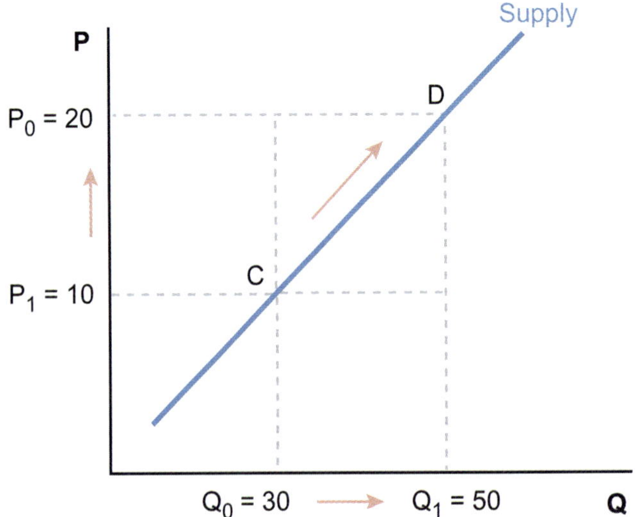

On the other hand, the **supply curve shifts** if there are changes in relevant factors other than a change in price. Economists use a variety of terms to describe supply curve shifts:

- **Changes in the supply curve where *quantity supplied increases* for each price** are described as "the supply curve shifts outward" (not upward), "the supply curve shifts to the right," or "supply increases"
- **Changes in the supply curve where *quantity supplied decreases* for each price** are described as "the supply curve shifts inward" (not downward), "the supply curve shifts to the left," or "supply decreases"

Below we show a supply curve shift to the right from S_0 to S_1. Note that at a price of 20, sellers supply 70 instead of 50 units. Alternatively, for a quantity of 50, sellers charge a (lower) price of 10 instead of 20.

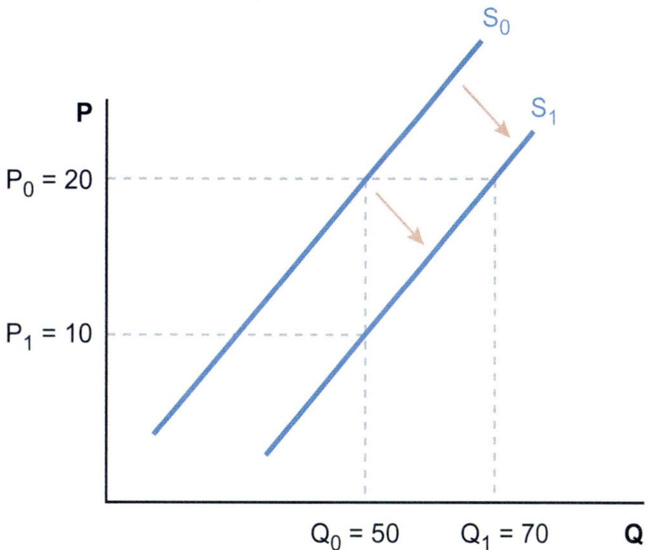

There are various reasons why supply curves may shift. Some factors exhibit a **direct relationship** with the supply curve, meaning that increases in that factor cause the supply curve to shift outward (or supply to increase). Here are some examples:

- **Number of producers:** More producers normally increase the quantity supplied of a product at a given price. Entry by foreign suppliers into the U.S. auto market increases the supply of cars in the U.S.
- **Government subsidies:** Additional funding permits producers to purchase more inputs and, thus, increase quantity supplied at any given price
- **Price expectations:** When higher prices are expected, producers will increase their quantity supplied at any given price
- **Technological advances:** Technological advances generally reduce production costs; hence, producers generally will increase their quantity supplied at any given price with an increase in technological advances

Other factors exhibit an **inverse relationship** with the supply curve, meaning that increases in that factor cause the supply curve to *shift inward* (or supply to decrease). Some examples include the following:

- **Increases in production costs** (eg, production taxes): When higher costs are expected, producers will decrease their quantity supplied at a given price
- **Prices of other products:** An entity producing both products A and B may decrease supply of one item if the other item becomes more profitable

Price Elasticity of Supply

Price elasticity is a measure of how sensitive quantity supplied is to a change in price. It tells us how a change in price will affect the quantity supplied by firms; that is, it measures the responsiveness of firms to a price change.

$$\textbf{Price Elasticity of Supply }(\mathbf{E_s}) \text{ (Elasticity of Supply)} = \frac{\text{Percentage change in quantity supplied}}{\text{Percentage change in price}}$$

Owners of factors of production (labor, natural resources, capital, and entrepreneurship) aim to shift those factors to their most productive uses. These efforts are reflected in **economic rents** or **surpluses**, which are the excess of the payments for these factors when used most productively over their best alternative use (ie, opportunity cost).

Demand

A **demand curve** shows the *inverse relationship* between the price and the quantity of a product or service that a group of consumers is willing and able to buy at a particular time (ie, the quantity demanded). On a graph, a change in the price of the product is indicated by a movement along the demand curve. For instance, as the price of a product increases (eg, from 10 to 20), the quantity demanded by buyers decreases (eg, from 50 to 30).

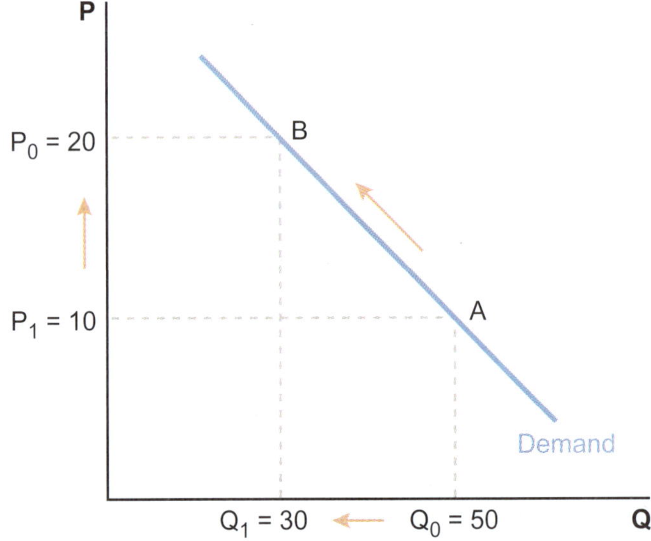

Remember that the **Demand** curve, starting with a *D*, slopes **Down**, also starting with a *D*.

Similar to the supply curve, a demand curve shifts if there are changes in relevant factors *other than a change in price*. Economists use a variety of terms to describe demand curve shifts:

- **Changes in the demand curve where quantity demanded becomes larger for each and every price** are described as "the demand curve shifts upward," "the demand curve shifts outward," "the demand curve shifts to the right," or "demand increases"
- **Changes in the demand curve where quantity demanded becomes smaller for each and every price** are described as "the demand curve shifts downward," "the demand curve shifts inward," "the demand curve shifts to the left," or "demand decreases"

Below we show an upward demand curve shift from D_0 to D_1. Note that at a price of 20, consumers are willing and able to purchase 50 instead of 30 units. Alternatively, for a quantity of 30, consumers are willing and able to pay a price of 27 instead of 20.

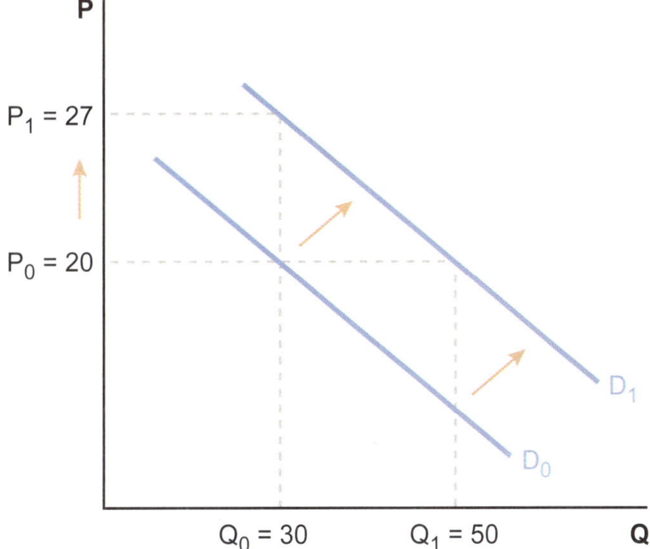

There are various reasons why demand curves may shift. Some factors exhibit a **direct relationship** with the demand curve, meaning that increases in that factor cause the demand curve to *shift upward* (or demand to increase). Some examples include the following:

- **The price of a substitute good:** When product A may be an acceptable alternative to product B, an increase in the price of product A will make product B more attractive (eg, some consumers will shift from buying product A to product B). For example, an increase in the price of hamburgers will increase the demand for hot dogs
- **Expectations of price changes:** Consumers are more likely to buy now if they think prices will increase in the future. For example, if cigarette taxes are expected to double next year, some buyers will bring forward some of their purchases, increasing demand this year until the tax increase goes into effect
- **Income (for normal goods):** For many goods (eg, cars or smartphones), when incomes increase (wealth increase), demand increases
- **Extent of the market:** New consumers may increase demand, therefore increasing the size of the market. For example, the removal of trade barriers by foreign governments will increase the demand for American products that can be exported. A baby boom will increase demand for baby food. A large inflow of immigrants from a country to the U.S. will increase demand for that country's ethnic food in the U.S.

Other factors exhibit an **inverse relationship** with the demand curve, meaning that increases in that factor cause the demand curve to *shift downward* (or demand to decrease). Some examples include the following:

- **The price of a complement good:** When products are normally used together, an increase in the price of one of the goods decreases demand for the other. For example, an increase in the price of chips will cause a downward shift in the demand for salsa
- **Income (for inferior goods):** For some goods (eg, used cars), when incomes increase (wealth), demand decreases as consumers shift their spending to other goods (eg, new cars)
- **Consumer boycotts:** An organized boycott will, if effective, temporarily decrease the demand for a product. For example, members of unions commonly refuse to buy from businesses that are involved in labor disputes

Price Elasticity of Demand

Barring shifts in the demand curve, a firm expects the quantity demanded for its product to decrease as the price increases. A smaller level of sales (ie, quantity demanded) could reduce the firm's total revenue (price × quantity). Alternatively, a higher price could increase the firm's total revenue.

$$\textbf{Price Elasticity of Demand } (\mathbf{E_d}) \text{ (Elasticity of Demand)} = \frac{\text{Percentage change in quantity demanded}}{\text{Percentage change in price}}$$

$$E_D = \frac{\dfrac{\text{Change in quantity demanded}}{\text{Average quantity demanded}}}{\dfrac{\text{Change in price}}{\text{Average price}}}$$

Whether total revenue will increase or decrease when prices change turns out to depend on the price elasticity of demand (ie, "elasticity of demand"). This concept measures how responsive the quantity demanded (of a good or service) is to a change in price.

Elasticities are commonly computed using the **arc method** or relative to the midpoint (or average) between conditions before and after a change, instead of relative to conditions "before" the change.

Using the formula shown above, price elasticities of demand technically yield negative answers (either the change in quantity demanded or the change in price will be negative while the other is positive). When interpreting price elasticities of demand, it is customary to ignore the negative sign (or to report its absolute value).

- **Elastic:** E_d is greater than 1, and total revenue will decline if the price is increased
- **Inelastic:** E_d is less than 1, and total revenue will increase if the price is increased
- **Unit elastic:** E_d is equal to 1, and total revenue is *not sensitive* to price changes

Assume a firm can sell 110 units for a product that is priced at $9 per unit. Thus, its total revenue currently would be 110 × $9 = $990. The firm is considering a price increase of $2 per unit, or 20% (under the arc method).

If the 20% price increase caused quantity demanded to decrease from 110 to 80 or by 30 units (30/95 avg Q decrease = 31.6%), *price elasticity of demand would be 1.58* (31.6% / 20%), and *demand would be elastic*. Total revenue would decline to 80 × $11 = $880.

If the price increase caused quantity demanded to decrease only from 110 to 100, or by 10 units (9.5%), *price elasticity of demand would be 0.48* (9.5% / 20%), and *demand would be inelastic*. Total revenue would increase to 100 × $11 = $1,100.

Goods that represent a larger fraction of consumers' budgets tend to be elastic (automobiles), and those that represent a smaller fraction of consumers' budgets tend to be inelastic (table salt).

	More Inelastic	**More Elastic**
Variable Substitutes	Few or none	Many
Nature of Good	Nondiscretionary	Discretionary
Portion of Budget	Small	Large

Elasticities are often larger if **more time elapsed** while the compared changes took place. For instance, in the short run, consumers may not be able to reduce their consumption of gasoline significantly when there is an increase in gasoline prices (ie, consumers' gasoline purchases are less responsive to price changes in the short term).

However, over longer periods, consumers can switch to more efficient cars, change their work arrangements to reduce driving needs, and reduce their consumption of gasoline. The longer they have to adjust, the more they can reduce their gasoline consumption in response to price increases (ie, consumers' gasoline purchases are more responsive to price changes in the long term; consumers' demand for gasoline is more elastic over the long term).

Income Elasticity of Demand

$$\text{Income Elasticity of Demand} = \frac{\text{Percentage change in quantity demanded}}{\text{Percentage change in income}}$$

Income elasticity of demand measures the effect of changes in (consumer) income on changes in the quantity demanded of a product. All elasticities (not just price elasticity of demand) may be computed using the arc method.

A positive income elasticity indicates a **normal good**, which means that as consumer income increases, the quantity demanded of the normal good also increases. A negative number indicates an **inferior good**, so as income increases, the quantity demanded of the inferior good will decrease.

For example, if incomes increase and the quantity demanded of new cars also increases, new cars are a normal good. However, if incomes increase and the quantity demanded of used cars decreases, used cars are an inferior good.

Cross-Price Elasticity of Demand

Cross-price elasticity measures the sensitivity of demand for one good relative to the price change of another good and is used to determine if two different goods are substitutes or complements.

$$\text{Cross-Elasticity of Demand} = \frac{\text{Percentage change in } \textbf{quantity demanded} \text{ for product X}}{\text{Percentage change in the } \textbf{price} \text{ of product Y}}$$

Complements are products or services that tend to be **consumed together** (eg, vehicles and tires). An increase in the consumption of any good tends to coincide with an increase in the consumption of its complements, and vice versa. **Substitutes** are different goods that satisfy the same want (eg, Coke and Pepsi). An increase in the price of a good will cause some consumers to buy less of the more expensive good and more of other goods that satisfy the same want.

	Cross-Price Elasticity	Example
Complements	Negative	Vehicles and tires
Substitutes	Positive	Coke and Pepsi

Since complements are consumed together, cross-price elasticity for complements is negative. Substitutes exhibit positive cross-price elasticity. If cross-price elasticity is zero, the products are **unrelated**.

For example, if the price of butter increases by 10% and the quantity demanded of margarine increases by 12%, .12 / .10 = 1.2, then their cross-elasticity of demand is positive, and they are *substitutes*. However, if the price of chips increases by 10% and the quantity demanded of salsa decreases by 12%, −.12 / .1= −1.2, then their cross-elasticity of demand is negative, and they are *complements*.

Market Equilibrium

Generally, as long as governments do not interfere, prices, quantities supplied, and quantities demanded adjust to an equilibrium level, where there is adequate supply to satisfy buyers and adequate demand. Equilibrium is that point where demand and supply curves cross in the graph below.

At the equilibrium price, **quantity demanded = quantity supplied**, so all the goods offered for sale will be sold.

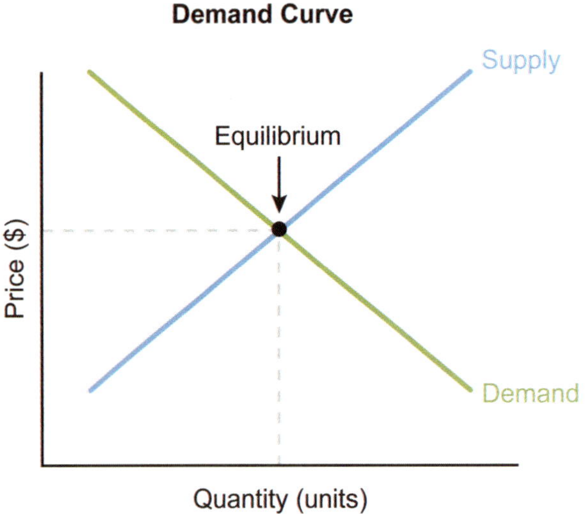

Market Adjustments to Equilibrium

In the absence of government intervention, most shifts in demand and supply lead to somewhat predictable changes from an initial combination of equilibrium price and equilibrium quantity to a new combination, as shown in the graphs below:

Comparing an Initial and New Equilibrium Resulting from an Increase in Demand

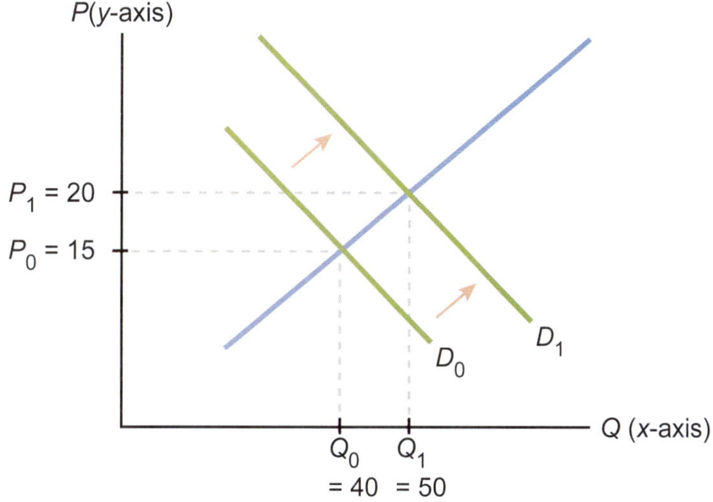

Comparing an Initial and New Equilibrium Resulting from an Increase in Supply

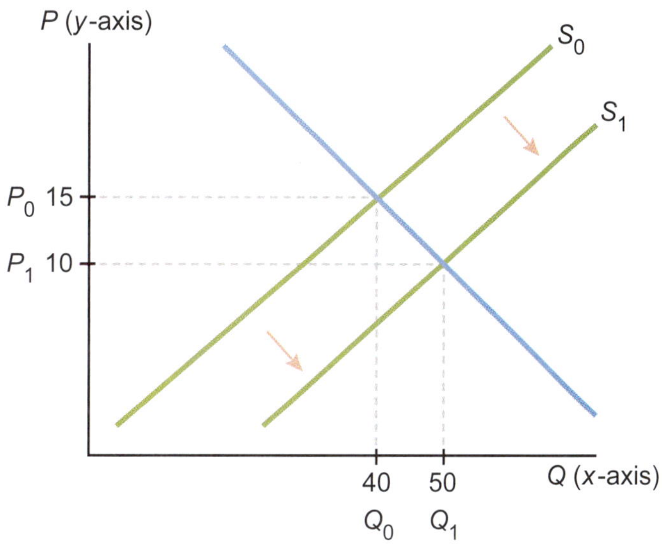

However, some shifts are not as easy to predict, as in a situation in which both the supply curve and the demand curve shift. Assume that product demand increases while product supply decreases *simultaneously*. The combination of shifts results in a **price increase**; however, the **effect on quantity is uncertain** unless exact amounts are provided. This combination of shifts affects quantity in opposite directions; the increase in demand leads to an increase in quantity, while the decrease in supply results in a decrease in quantity.

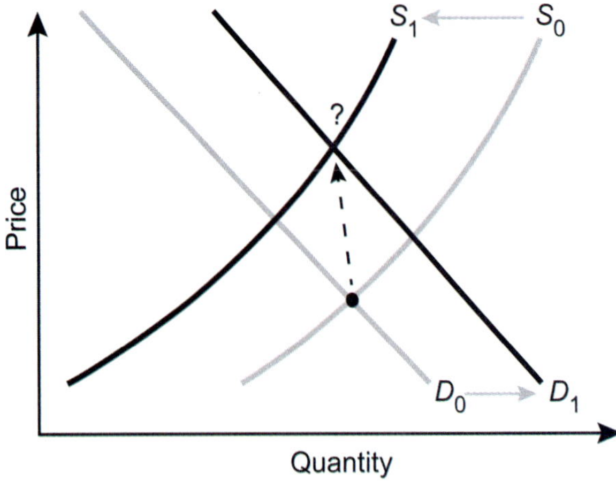

Below we summarize the changes in equilibrium price and quantity resulting from various shifts in supply and demand curves:

Demand	Supply	Equilibrium Price	Quantity Purchased
Increase	No change	Increase	Increase
Decrease	No change	Decrease	Decrease
No change	Increase	Decrease	Increase
No change	Decrease	Increase	Decrease
Increase	Increase	Uncertain	Increase
Decrease	Decrease	Uncertain	Decrease
Increase	Decrease	Increase	Uncertain
Decrease	Increase	Decrease	Uncertain

Government Actions That Affect Equilibrium

If governments impose a **price ceiling** (eg, setting the maximum legal price at which a product or service may be sold at $7) **below equilibrium** (ie, $15), the quantity demanded (ie, 56) will exceed quantity supplied (ie, 24), resulting in **shortages** of goods. For example, the graph below shows that there are 32 (ie, 56 units demanded − 24 units supplied) additional units that consumers would like to purchase at the $7 price.

If governments impose a **price floor** (eg, setting the minimum legal price at which a product or service may be sold at $17) above equilibrium, the quantity supplied (ie, 52) will exceed quantity demanded (ie, 28), resulting in unpurchased **surpluses** of goods.

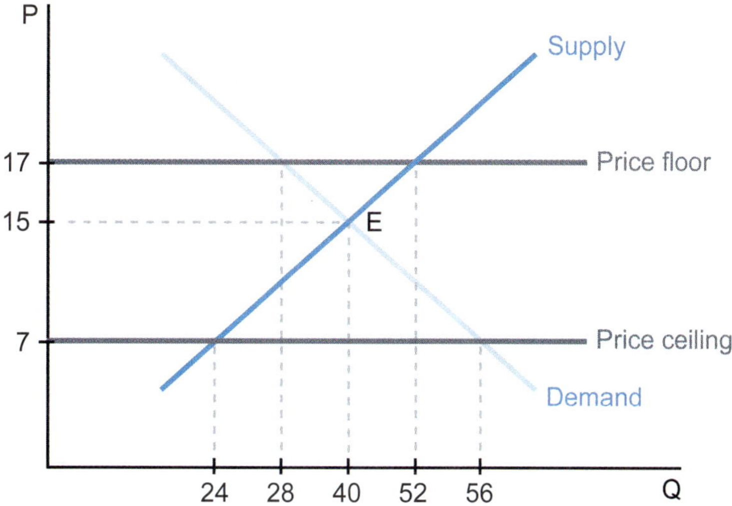

Notice that there are 24 additional units (ie, 52 supplied − 28 demanded) that suppliers would like to sell at the $17 price, but there is not enough demand. For example, a minimum wage for unskilled workers results in higher unemployment rates for unskilled workers.

Inflation

Representative Task (Application): Calculate the effect of inflation on a product's real price or an entity's investments, debt, and future expenses.

Price Indexes

Price indexes are used to measure overall price levels in the economy. The percentage change in a price index is the inflation rate.

Inflation Measure	Includes	Also Known As
Consumer price index (CPI)	Consumption goods	Headline inflation
Personal consumption expenditures (PCE)	Consumption goods	Alternate to CPI
Core inflation	CPI basket except food and energy	–
Producer price index (PPI)	Business inputs	Wholesale price index
GDP deflator	All economic output	–

The **consumer price index (CPI)** is widely followed as the "headline" measure of an economy's consumer goods inflation.

A worker earned and spent $40,000 in 2002, when the CPI was 180. The same worker earned and spent $50,000 in 2012, when the CPI was 230. Converting the $40,000 from 2002 into 2012 dollars, one finds that the income in 2002 purchased the equivalent of $51,111 in 2012 (= $40,000 × 230 / 180). Thus, the worker's real income is 97.8% ($50,000 / $51,111) of what it used to be (ie, it fell by 2.2%).

The **personal consumption expenditures (PCE)** index is similar to the CPI, but it adjusts for known biases in the CPI. The PCE index includes goods and services bought by consumers (ie, not businesses or governmental entities) and also does not include exports. The PCE index does reflect inflation/deflation and incorporates consumer behavior. For example, if the price of seafood increases, consumers may switch to chicken.

The **core inflation index** is similarly constructed, but it excludes food and energy. The image below depicts the year-over-year change in US CPI (green line) and core CPI (blue line) over a 10-year period. The long-term trend in core CPI is fairly steady, while headline CPI is more volatile. Therefore, core inflation is generally considered a better indicator of long-run inflation trends because volatile items like food and energy are removed from the index.

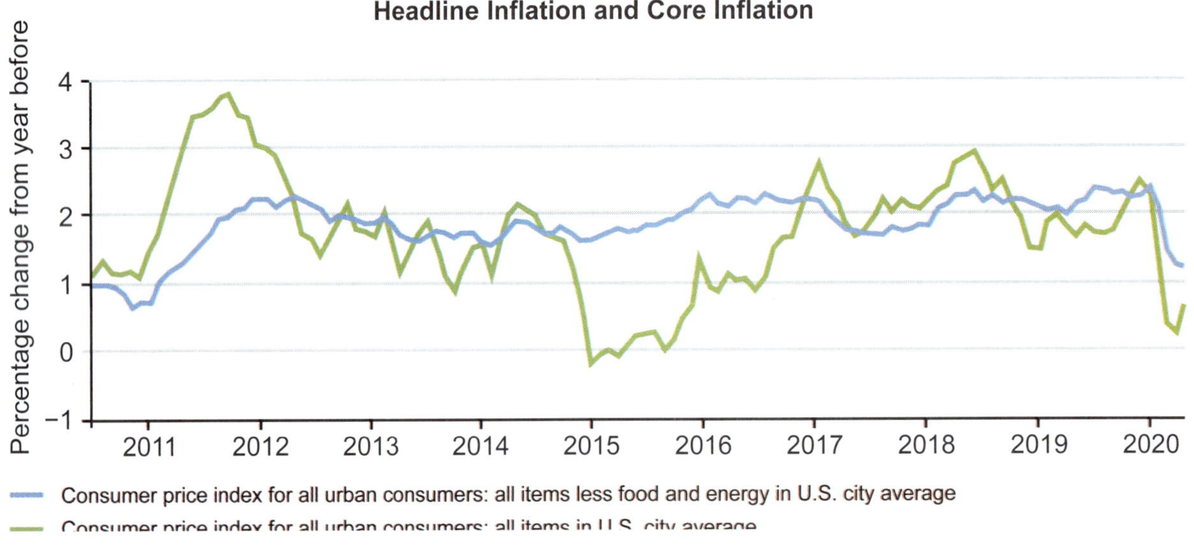

The **producer price index (PPI)** compares the price of a fixed basket of goods received by producers at the wholesale level, instead of focusing on the prices paid at the retail level by consumers.

The **GDP deflator** is the most comprehensive measure of price levels, including prices paid by all parties included in GDP instead of only consumers. The GDP deflator is the index used to convert nominal GDP into real GDP.

Nominal GDP measures a country's *current* economic output at current prices; it can overstate the growth of real economic activity if there has been inflation. *Real GDP* measures current economic output at *base period* prices. Comparing the two measures reveals the effect of price changes, separate from the actual growth in output.

The **GDP deflator** is simply the ratio of nominal GDP to real GDP. The GDP deflator measures the effect of the change in price level (eg, inflation) on an economy's GDP from a given base year. It "deflates" the effects of inflation to arrive at a "real" level of output, unaffected by price changes.

$$\textbf{GDP deflator} = \frac{\text{Value of current-year output at current-year prices}}{\text{Value of current-year output at base-year prices}} \times 100$$

Diamond Co. uses a material that cost $195 per ton at the beginning of the year and $200 per ton at the end of the year. The industry experienced 4% inflation during the year. Determine the change in the real cost of Diamond's material.

The nominal value of materials increased by $5 ($200 − $195). In percentage terms, this increase in nominal value is 2.56% [((200 − 195) / 195) × 100].

In percentage terms, the change in real value equals the difference between the change in the nominal value and the inflation rate: 2.56% − 4.00% = (1.44%).

The material's cost in real terms (ie, cost after taking the effect of inflation into account) actually **decreased by 1.44%**, which is a **$2.80** ($195 × .0144) **per ton decrease**.

Types of Inflation

Expected versus Unexpected

Expected inflation is the level of inflation that is anticipated, whereas **unexpected inflation** is the level of inflation above or below expectations. There are certain costs associated with expected and unexpected inflation.

Counterparties to commercial and financial contracts are concerned with the real value—the inflation-adjusted purchasing power—of their payables or receivables, so *contract terms reflect expected inflation*. When inflation is close to expectations, nominal payments and receipts reflect the real values implied by the original contract. If inflation differs from expectations, the real value of payments changes, causing unanticipated gains and losses.

However, when inflation *exceeds expectations*, money loses its purchasing power faster than expected. Those who owe fixed payments (ie, nominal amounts) benefit from paying in depreciated currency. Higher-than-expected inflation results in a transfer of real wealth from creditors to debtors.

Impact of Inflation Differing from Expectations

	Group Benefiting	Rationale
Inflation > Expectations	• Borrowers • Purchasers under fixed-price contracts	Payments made have less purchasing power than expected
Inflation < Expectations	• Lenders • Retirees with fixed pension benefits	Income received has more purchasing power than expected

Demand-Pull versus Cost-Push

Economists identify two different types of inflation:

Demand-pull inflation stems *from increased demand*. Here, the increased demand cannot easily be met by expanding output, allowing producers to raise prices (ie, prices are being "pulled up" by the increase in demand). In some instances, increasing demand results from excess money creation; consumers competing to buy goods **bid up overall prices**. In other cases, a growing economy is constrained by production capacity (ie, high capacity utilization).

Cost-push inflation results from decreased supply. Here, costs of widely used factor inputs increase; rising input costs for labor or commodities reduce business profit margins. Businesses often raise selling prices in response, leading to higher inflation rates.

	Definition	**Causal Factors**
Cost-Push	Rising input costs lead to higher prices	• Increasing wages • Rising commodity prices
Demand-Pull	Increasing demand causes higher prices	• Money supply increases • High capacity utilization

Disinflation and Deflation

Disinflation is an economic environment with positive but *falling inflation rates* (ie, a slowdown in inflation). Price levels are still rising but at a slower rate than previously (eg, inflation rate declines from 6% to 4%). Aggregate price levels are increasing but at a decreasing rate. Disinflation can result from tight monetary policy intended to prevent an economy from overheating.

Deflation describes *negative* inflation. Deflation is more ominous and occurs during economic contraction. It is often paired with reduced spending and high unemployment. Deflation increases the value of money, incentivizing citizens to hold more savings while waiting for prices to fall even further. Deflation transfers real wealth from debtors to creditors.

Hyperinflation

Hyperinflation describes an environment in which inflation is *increasing rapidly* and is effectively *out of control*. Hyperinflation can occur during severe shortages or an economic crisis, but the most common cause of hyperinflation is *too much money* in circulation without the backing of real economic activity.

Hyperinflation quickly erodes the value of the currency, and citizens respond by converting as much money as possible into real goods. Hyperinflation devastates private savings through rapid devaluation, often resulting in bank runs.

Stagflation

Stagflation describes a combination of high inflation, a high level of unemployment, and below-potential GDP growth (eg, inflation > 12% and unemployment > 10%). A distinguishing feature of stagflation versus other types of inflation is that central banks typically lack the tools to combat it and instead rely on the economy to self-correct.

For example, central banks often employ short-term restrictive monetary policies such as raising interest rates to combat "normal" inflation. However, if an economy is experiencing stagflation, these same policies could further depress GDP growth and increase the already high unemployment level.

Economic Conditions and Inflation

	Price Levels	Inflation Rate
Inflation	Increasing	Positive
Disinflation	Increasing at a slower rate	Positive and decreasing
Deflation	Decreasing	Negative
Hyperinflation	Increasing very rapidly	Very high
Stagflation	Increasing	High

Effect of Inflation

Inflation will probably impact a company's costs and revenues. A company with a stronger relative market position than its peers is better able to raise its prices without a significant reduction in sales volumes and thus more likely to maintain profitability.

Factors to Consider: Effect of Inflation (Deflation) on Operations	
Sales	**Costs**
• Elasticity of demand	• Elasticity of demand
• Competitors' pricing strategies	• Competitors' pricing strategies
• Company's relative market position	• Company's relative market position
• Industry structure	• Industry structure

Management should consider the effects of inflation on the company's revenues and costs. Costs are directly related to inflation (deflation), which can increase (decrease) input costs, especially if alternative resources are not available. A company's pricing strategy in response to a change in costs may indirectly impact revenues.

During periods of rising costs, a company can either:

- Pass the cost increases on to its customers through increased prices, or
- Maintain prices and risk contracting margins.

A company with a stronger relative market position than its peers (eg, strong brand name, unique products) is better positioned to raise its prices without a significant reduction in sales volumes and thus more likely to maintain profitability.

Entity Risks

Representative Task (Application): Calculate and use ratios and measures to quantify risks associated with risks of an entity (eg, interest rates, currency exchange, prices).

Overview

Some sources of information, like financial statements, require analysis to find indications of risks. Other sources explain and discuss risks, either voluntarily or as required by accounting standards and/or securities regulation.

A company's *financial statements* are the primary source of information for identifying the following:

- Financial risks, which can be measured with leverage (ie, solvency) ratios, liquidity ratios, or bankruptcy prediction models such as the Altman model
- Operating risks, indicated by problems such as decreasing profit margins and volatile cash flows
- Other risks, especially from disclosures contained in the accompanying notes

GAAP requires companies to disclose a quantitative and qualitative analysis of their exposure to financial market risks due to interest rates, foreign exchange rates, and commodity prices. Generally, a company will describe the exposed instruments (eg, floating-rate debts, exports priced in a foreign currency) and quantify the company's loss given a certain change (eg, 1%) in the market rate to which it is exposed.

Interest Rate Risk

Entities that typically hold assets with longer maturities (eg, long-term mortgage loans) and liabilities with shorter maturities (eg, certificates of deposit with maturities under one year) face **interest rate risk**. This is the risk that negative changes in economy-wide interest rates may adversely affect earnings, asset value, liability value, and equity value.

A **negative interest rate gap occurs when entities have** assets that reprice slowly (eg, banks will continue to pay the low interest rates they started charging in previous years) and fewer liabilities that reprice quickly (eg, banks will pay higher rates on most liabilities quickly).

Risk management strategies include the following:

- Reducing the amount of assets with long maturities and increasing the amount of liabilities with long maturities (ie, improve matching of maturities)
- Reducing the amount of fixed-rate long-term assets and increasing the amount of variable-rate long-term assets
- Using interest rate derivatives, although fees can be significant

Price Risk

Price risk addresses the probability that the cost of goods and services will change and have a negative impact on earnings. There is a broad range of items that can fall into this category, from the cost of labor or raw material to the cost of a multiyear project that an entity is bidding on. Price risk is also frequently used in portfolio management.

Businesses need to reflect price risk in their **pricing strategies**. For longer-term projects, price fluctuations need to be tracked over the life of the project, with adjustments made to cost and profit projections as needed.

Exchange Rate Risk

Fluctuations in currencies' exchange rates are ultimately based on relative changes in the supplies and demands of those currencies. Companies considering decisions regarding short-term international trade and long-term international investments face these types of (nominal and real) **exchange rate risks**.

Currency (or Foreign Exchange) Risk	
Transaction Risk	• The risk an entity faces when it buys product(s) from a foreign company (ie, product denominated in the selling company's currency) or has receivables in a foreign currency • Entities can manage this risk by matching as many revenues and costs in the same currency as possible for each market an entity operates in
Translation Risk	• Losses faced by a parent company owning a foreign subsidiary when the subsidiary's financial statements, which are denominated in that country's currency, are translated into the parent company's currency • Translation gains/losses are reflected on the balance sheet as other comprehensive income (OCI) • Companies manage translation risk by negotiating related asset and liability transactions in the same currency
Economic Risk	• The volatility of a company's market value when it is continuously subjected to currency fluctuations (also called forecast risk)

The aggregate risk consists of transaction risk, translation risk, and economic risk. The most effective mitigation strategy is to negotiate that prices and payments must be denominated in U.S. dollars. Additional risk management techniques include the following:

Risk Management Strategies	
Options (Put, Call)	Option to purchase or sell at a stated price and time frame
Forwards or Futures	Obligation to purchase or sell at a preset price on a future date
Money Market Hedges	A pays B in one currency, and B pays A in another currency
Currency Swaps	Borrowing money in one currency and repaying using an existing receivable agreement in another currency
Currency Selection	Using same currency for related assets and liabilities or related revenues and expenses.

An exporter enters into a contract to supply goods to a foreign buyer. The contract requires the payment in foreign currency 120 days after delivery. Recently the foreign currency has experienced many fluctuations. The exporter may incur a loss on this contract at the time payment is received due to such fluctuations. What action can the exporter take to avoid such loss?

Fluctuating currency creates *transaction risk*, which is the risk due to a time delay between entering into a contract and settling it. This ultimately affects the expected return on the transaction and includes foreign exchange risk, commodity risk, interest rate risk, and time risk.

Companies can manage transaction risk by using derivatives or a hedging contract such as a **forward contract**. Forwards are specifically negotiated contracts in which two parties agree to exchange some quantity of a commodity (eg, currency) at a preset price on a future date. Generally, one of the parties is a financial institution.

Under a forward contract, if the exchange rate is higher in 120 days than the forward's contract rate, the exporter owes the financial institution the incremental difference, and vice versa. Although forwards do not entirely eliminate the risk, they significantly mitigate it.

Exchange Rate

An exchange rate is the price of a country's currency in relation to another country's currency. Under a freely fluctuating (floating) exchange rate system, the exchange rate is primarily affected by **supply and demand** for the country's currency. Supply and demand for the currency is driven by imports and exports. Additional commonly cited factors that affect foreign exchange rates include the following:

- Inflation
- Interest rates
- Government intervention
- Long-term economic stability

Freely fluctuating exchange rates automatically adjust the value of currencies to correct imbalances in trade and investment between countries (ie, balance of payments).

Types of Exchange Rate Systems	
Freely Fluctuating (Floating)	Exchange rates that move freely, set by the supply and demand for the currency
Fixed	The country's central bank buys and sells foreign currencies as needed to maintain its exchange rate, "fixed" related to the currency of a key trading partner
Managed	A mixture of floating and fixed exchange rate systems

Exchange rates may be expressed by dividing by either currency, for example, if €1 (ie, 1 euro) buys $1.25, the exchange rate may be expressed as €1 = $1.25, or $1 = €0.80. In a table listing multiple exchange rates for one currency, it is customary to express all exchange rates on the same basis, for example, how many units of the various foreign currencies it takes to buy $1. It is also customary to choose the "direction" of the exchange rates that ensures that most exchange rates are greater than 1 (ie, $1 = 80 yen, instead of $0.0125 = 1 yen).

Commonly cited exchange rates between currencies include the following:

- The **spot rate** is the exchange rate at which a financial party (eg, a financial institution, a currency dealer) will exchange two currencies at this time (ie, "on the spot").
- The **forward rate** is the exchange rate at which a financial party will exchange two currencies at a specific future date (called the settlement date), for example, three months later.

In forward markets, one currency is at a premium (or discount) if its forward rate is higher (lower) than the spot rate (both rates expressed per the foreign currency), that is, if it is expected to appreciate (depreciate). For instance, according to the spot rate, 1 Kuwaiti dinar may equal \$3.57, and according to the three-month forward rate, 1 Kuwaiti dinar may equal \$3.53. In this case, there is a discount since the Kuwaiti dinar will be worth less in the future (ie, it will buy fewer dollars). The size of the forward premium (or discount) is expressed in annual terms as follows:

$$\frac{\text{Forward rate} - \text{Spot rate}}{\text{Spot rate}} \times \frac{\text{Months in a year}}{\text{Months in the forward period}}$$

$$\frac{3.53 - 3.57}{3.57} \times \frac{12}{3} = 4.5\%$$

Cross Exchange Rate

A **cross rate** is an **implied exchange rate** between two currencies that is derived from quoted exchange rates. The cross rate for any pair of currencies is obtained by multiplying two quoted exchange rates, each containing one of the currencies from the pair and a **common currency** (eg, U.S. dollar). Speculators also use cross exchange rates to make interest rate plays and a quick profit in trading back and forth between the three currencies.

One euro (€) will buy U.S. \$1.48, and a British pound sterling (BPS) will buy U.S. \$2.06. Determine the cross rate of euros per pound. The cross rate of one euro per BPS is 1.39. Here, the currency pair is the euro and the British pound sterling (BPS), and the home currency is the U.S. dollar (USD). The exchange rate can be determined through a currency pair's relationship to a widely traded third currency (the USD here).

$$\frac{\text{Currency 1}}{\text{Currency 2}} = \frac{\text{Currency 1}}{\text{Currency 3}} \times \frac{\text{Currency 3}}{\text{Currency 2}}$$

$$\frac{\text{Euro}}{\text{BPS*}} = \frac{\text{Euro}}{\text{USD}} \times \frac{\text{USD}}{\text{BPS}}$$

**British pound sterling*

Restate each exchange rate as a function of USD (or desired currency), as follows:

- If €1 = \$1.48, then \$1 = €0.676 (€1 / \$1.48)
- If £1 = \$2.06, then \$1 = £0.485 (£1 = \$2.06)

Substitute the restated rate for the euro and the pound and solve as follows:

$$\frac{\text{Euro}}{\text{BPS}} = \frac{\text{Euro}}{\text{USD}} \times \frac{\text{USD}}{\text{BPS}} = \frac{.676}{1.00} \times \frac{1.00}{.485} = \mathbf{1.39}$$

Currency Depreciation Risk

A significant **decline** in the exchange rate of the U.S. dollar (USD) means that the USD has **depreciated** and foreign currencies have appreciated. In other words, foreign entities will be able to *purchase more units* of the USD for *less cost*. This makes exports from the U.S. highly desirable because the relative cost of those exports has fallen. However, since the USD now purchases less, the cost of imports from foreign countries has risen. Since consumers will have to pay more for those imports, import sales will decline.

Economic Effects of a Currency Depreciation

When the U.S. dollar depreciates against a foreign currency

U.S. import prices* RISE — U.S. export prices* FALL

↓

Changes in import and export prices will affect demand

Import sales will SHRINK — Export sales will GROW

↓

This affects several key economic indicators

Domestic production ↑ — Trade deficit ↓ — Domestic jobs ↑

**The value of the currency increases/decreases, making items more/less expensive.*

A U.S. company is purchasing inventory components from a company in a foreign country. The price of the company's routine inventory order is 100,000 foreign currency units (FCUs), and the exchange rate at the time of the last order was $1.45 per one FCU. The exchange rate changes to $1.60 per one FCU, and the U.S. company orders *half* of its normal quantity. Determine the invoice difference from the last order.

The net invoice amount decreased by **$65,000**. When a foreign country's currency strengthens (as in a change from $1.45 to $1.60 per FCU), products from that country become *more expensive* for purchasers in the U.S.

Even though the exchange rate increased, causing imports to be more expensive, the size of the order decreased, resulting in a **$65,000 net decrease** in the invoice amount. The invoice difference between orders is calculated as follows:

FCU	Exchange Rate	Invoice Amount
100,000	$1.45	$145,000
50,000	$1.60	80,000
		$ 65,000

Investment Risk

Risky assets have both systematic and nonsystematic risk. Total risk of an asset comprises both types of risk. **Systematic risk** (market risk) is the intrinsic risk of the financial system and cannot be reduced or eliminated. It is associated with macroeconomic risks that impact all assets (eg, wars, recessions, interest rates). **Nonsystematic risk** usually refers to the risk of an individual company or an industry (eg, a pharmaceutical company facing a class-action lawsuit due to a poorly performing vaccine).

Systematic vs. Nonsystematic Risk	
Systematic Risk	**Nonsystematic Risk**
• Also known as market risk or nondiversifiable risk • Inherent in the market • Cannot be eliminated by diversification • Examples: interest rate shifts, stock market crashes	• Also known as nonmarket risk or firm-specific risk • Specific to firm or industry • Can be eliminated by diversification • Examples: business litigation, cyberattacks

Country Risk

Country risk relates to the uncertainties of conducting business in a foreign location. Political and economic factors are two of the more important risks. *Political risks* arise from actions taken and decisions made by the country's politicians (eg, increased regulations). *Economic (ie, financial) risks* are typically associated with the nation's ability to repay its external debts.

Country Risk Components

Opportunity Cost

Representative Task (Application): Calculate the opportunity cost of a business decision.

Opportunity cost refers to the *benefit given up* from not using a resource for another purpose (the forgone dollar benefit of the alternative *not* selected).

Opportunity Cost

Alternative rejected

Alternative selected

Opportunity cost = forgone value of rejected alternative

For example, if a worker accepts a job paying $60,000 instead of another offering $50,000, the worker incurred an opportunity cost of $50,000 by doing so. Remember, it does not matter which number is larger. Opportunity cost is simply the *amount forfeited* by the choice made.

Countries often engage in international trade to obtain goods or services more economically. Trading according to comparative advantage allows each country to focus on goods that it can **produce more efficiently** while importing other goods that are less efficient to produce domestically. A country's **comparative advantage** is determined by opportunity costs, which measure the cost of producing a good in terms of the forgone production of another good.

The country that has the *lowest* opportunity cost of producing a good has the comparative advantage.

Assume the following monthly output per worker for pants and zippers in three countries:

	Pants	Zippers
Country A	30	165
Country B	45	180
Country C	50	250

These three countries trade only with each other. Determine which country *most likely* has the greatest comparative advantage in producing zippers.

	Opportunity Cost for Producing One Zipper
Country A	30 / 165 = 0.18
Country B	45 / 180 = 0.25
Country C	50 / 250 = 0.20

Country A *sacrifices the smallest quantity* of pants by producing zippers instead (ie, Country A gives up less). Therefore, it has the *lowest opportunity cost* and, consequently, a comparative advantage in producing zippers.

Industry Analysis

Representative Task (Analysis): Interpret the impact of market influences on an entity's business strategy, operations, and risk (eg, sourcing production inputs, innovating to develop or diversify product offerings, seeking new markets, undertaking productivity or cost-cutting initiatives).

Overview

Market influences are items that affect the economy, an industry, and/or an individual business. These items can affect both profitability and operating strategies. Businesses need to understand and interpret the impact of market influences as part of their strategic planning and ongoing revisions to the overall business plan.

We will first start by examining industry-level concerns and then take a deeper dive into the individual entity's assessment of market influences.

Industry Life Cycle

Industries evolve over time and experience different levels of growth and profitability in each stage of their life cycle. Each stage exhibits *different characteristics* that affect the competitive dynamics of an industry, such as level of product demand, intensity of competition, and excess capacity. Understanding what phase a business is in is key to developing appropriate business strategies.

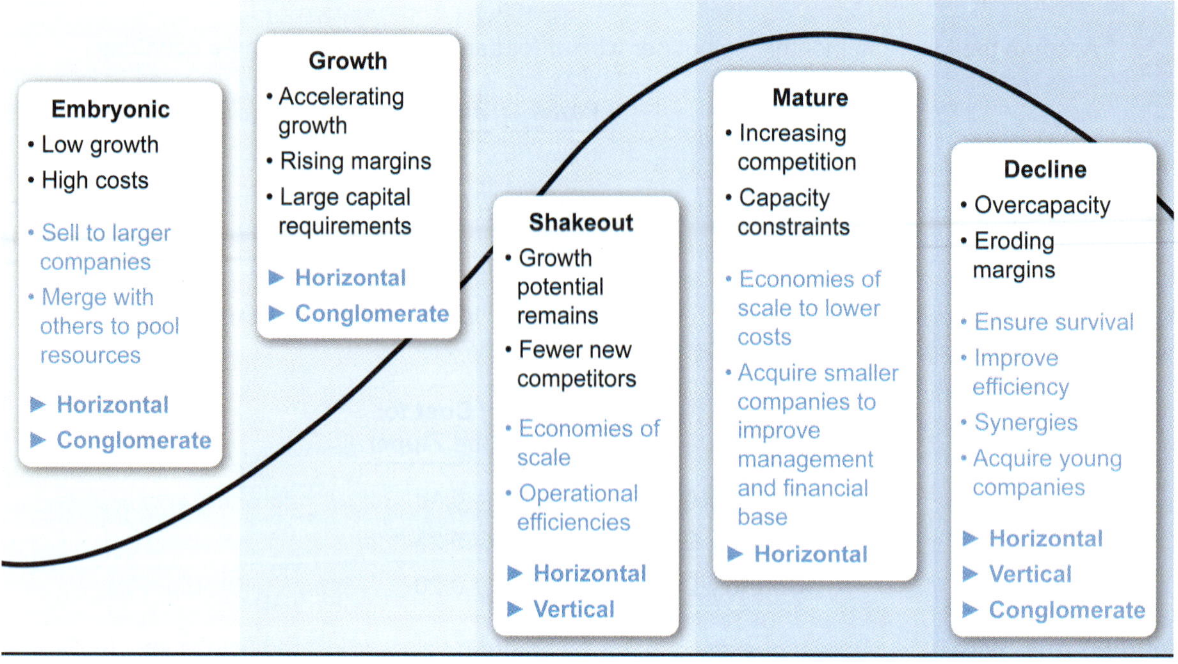

For example, a large breakfast cereal manufacturer is in the **mature phase**. To compete on a national level, there are high barriers to entry in this industry. New growth tends to come from variations to existing products, like adding gluten-free options for existing brands.

Industry Capacity

When an industry is at or near capacity, an increase in demand may create pricing power and enhance profitability for firms within that industry. The duration of the pricing power depends on the ability of firms to increase capacity: the more rapidly capacity is added, the sooner price competition will return, with a resulting loss of pricing power.

The lead time to add capacity depends on the industry's critical input. The critical input needed for providers of professional or financial services to expand capacity is productive employees. In contrast, goods producers and manufacturing or transportation service providers need to acquire fixed capital.

Industry Capacity Expansion Considerations

	Sector	Examples	Critical Input	Lead Time
Services	• Professional • Financial	• Legal, advertising • Asset management, insurance	Productive employees	Short
	• Transportation • Production	• Airlines, dry-bulk shipping • Oil services, contract manufacturing	Fixed capital	Long
Goods	• Manufacturing	• Automobile, pharmaceuticals	Fixed capital	Long

Industry Concentration

Industry concentration is a key component of strategic industry analysis and refers to the concentration of market share among firms in an industry. **Concentrated industries** consist of a few big players with relatively large shares of the market, whereas fragmented industries consist of many small players with relatively small shares of the market.

Fragmented industries often exhibit high price competition for the following reasons:

- Large firms may have more difficulty coordinating on strategy effectively
- Small firms aim for market share gains by undercutting competitors' prices
- Firms in general tend to view themselves as individual companies rather than as members of a larger group

Industry Market Share

Market *stability* is characterized by high barriers to entry, high switching costs, and a slow rate of product innovation. Market *instability* has the opposite characteristics.

	Market Share Stability	**Market Share Instability**
Entry Barriers	High	Low
Switching Costs	High	Low
Rate of Product Innovation	Slow	Rapid

Porter's Five Forces

Porter's Five Forces is a framework for strategic analysis that examines an **industry's competitive environment** to assess whether the conditions favor economic profits. Favorable competitive environments may allow existing companies to protect and grow economic profits.

Force	Description	Factors
Threat of new entrants	Increased competition can lower profits, but barriers to entry can protect them	• Economies of scale • Brand loyalty • Switching costs • Fixed costs • Regulation
Bargaining power of suppliers	Increased input costs lower profit margins	• Ease of product substitution • Concentration of suppliers • Switching costs

Force	Description	Factors
Bargaining power of buyers (customers)	Limited prices lower profit margins	• Customer concentration • Switching costs • Vertical integration
Threat of substitutes	Increased competition can lower sales quantities and/or prices	• Similarities in function • Utility of substitutable products
Rivalry among existing competitors	Increased competition lowers prices and profit margins	• Industry fragmentation • Degree of product differentiation • Barriers to exit

The purpose of the analysis is not only to understand the competitive dynamics but also to recognize the fundamental investment merits of the industry. Structural industry attributes can vary dramatically, generating vastly different economic return profiles. Some industries generate consistent profits through an economic cycle, whereas other industries struggle to generate economic profits, even during a sustained economic expansion.

Demand and Supply Analysis

Demand analysis is conducted to estimate a **firm's** current and future revenue. Factors considered include the following:

- **Size of the market:** Potential unit sales and prices and forecasted rates of change
- **Industry product:** Either differentiated (eg, make/model of automobiles) or homogeneous (eg, mobile phone service)
- **External influences:** Sensitivity of industry revenues to changes in the economy (eg, GDP growth), demographics (eg, age distribution of population), and social attitudes (eg, tobacco use, income inequality)
- **Business opportunities:** Revenue potential from introducing new products or entering new markets

Supply analysis at the **firm level** aids in gaining an understanding of the company's ability to supply product to customers. The analysis revolves around the competition for resources and production capacity. Factors in supply analysis include the following:

- **Input sources:** Competition or concentration in industries that supply inputs and availability of substitute resources
- **Industry capacity:** Current capacity and anticipated expansions and the ease or difficulty of adding capacity
- **Firm capacity:** Output potential and cost structure
- **International factors:** Potential impact of import competition on supply and prices in the product market; impact on input prices from exports to foreign competitors
- **Proprietary products and trademarks:** Possibility of restraining output below capacity to maintain the value of products and trademarks

Analysis of Company Products and Services	
Demand	**Supply**
• Market size • Product differentiation • Economic and demographic factors • Opportunities	• Input sources • Capacity • Import/export considerations • Proprietary products

Product Differentiation

Product differentiation involves developing a range of slightly different products that are more attractive to one's target markets or simply to ensure that they differ substantially from competitors' offerings. This strategy will (1) make the firm's sales less responsive to changes in the prices charged by other competitors, (2) allow the firm to charge different prices (ie, some higher) for different products, and (3) ultimately allow the firm to charge higher prices than otherwise (and potentially higher than those of one's competitors).

Products may differ in many ways:

- **Physical differences:** Individual features, quality, appearance
- **Perceived differences:** Image, brand name, advertising
- **Customer support differences:** Return policies, technical support

Cost Leadership

Businesses concentrate on *cutting the costs* of producing, selling, and distributing a firm's range of products. These strategies include the following:

- **Process reengineering:** In-depth redesigns of a firm's existing processes to improve performance
- **Lean manufacturing:** Identifying and removing the misuse of resources in a firm's existing production processes
- **Supply chain management:** Sharing relevant information in the chain of supply that ranges from the final consumer to the various levels of suppliers, independently of whether each step took place within one's firm or not. For example, all steps of the chain, from retailers to wholesalers to suppliers and suppliers' suppliers, might be able to operate with leaner inventories overall if each party shared more readily its plans and forecasts

SWOT Analysis

SWOT analysis consists of an assessment of an entity's strengths, weaknesses, opportunities, and threats (ie, SWOT), from both an internal and external perspective. SWOT analysis is covered in detail under the BAR *Risk Management* section.

Entities perform strategic analyses (eg, Porter's Five Forces) to understand their industry's competitive environment. Entities then tailor their business strategy and operations to gain competitive advantage within their industry.

Assume that Sophie Co. manufactures and sells sponges and mops. An analysis of the industry's competitive environment shows the following:

- There are many suppliers of inputs in the industry. Firms can switch suppliers of inputs easily. Firms generally do not have strong alliances with suppliers of inputs
- Many firms operate in the industry. Products typically have equal performance across firms
- Customers do not have significant preferences or brand loyalty. Customers' switching costs are low
- Up-front costs associated with entering the industry are low. The industry has not seen significant growth in recent years

Task 1: Complete the analysis below using Porter's Five Forces. Enter one of the following options: High, Low, Need more information.

	Forces	Options
1	Threat of new entrants	**High** / Low / Need more information
	There are no significant up-front costs to entering the industry, and customers do not have preexisting preferences or significant brand loyalty.	
2	Bargaining power of suppliers	High / **Low** / Need more information
	There are many suppliers of inputs, and firms can switch suppliers easily. Firms generally do not have strong alliances with suppliers.	
3	Bargaining power of buyers	**High** / Low / Need more information
	Many firms operate in the industry, so there are many options for customers to choose from. Additionally, customers' switching costs are low.	
4	Threat of substitutes	**High** / Low / Need more information
	Products typically have equal performance across firms. Many substitutes are readily available to customers because many firms operate in the industry.	
5	Rivalry among existing competitors	**High** / Low / Need more information
	Many firms operate in the industry. Customers do not have strong brand preferences or loyalty. The market is not growing significantly, so firms are competing for a larger piece of a consistent pie.	

Task 2: Enter one of the following options: Product differentiation or Cost leadership.

Task	Options
Determine which competitive strategy would be most effective for Sophie Co.	Product differentiation / **Cost leadership**

In this industry, customers have high bargaining power and low switching costs. Additionally, many firms exist in the industry, and products across firms have equal performance. This means that customers are more price sensitive because they can easily switch between the many options available, and quality is consistent among available options. Customers are probably looking for the lowest price option.

There are many suppliers of inputs, and suppliers currently do not have alliances with firms. This means that Sophie Co. can evaluate its suppliers regularly and choose its supplier on the basis of the cheapest option. Sophie Co. may also be able to seek out a specific firm and attempt to create a mutually beneficial alliance with it. This would lead to cheaper inputs in Sophie Co.'s production.

Sophie Co. should execute a cost leadership strategy. If Sophie Co. can sell at a lower price than its competitors, it can gain a larger portion of market share. If Sophie Co. cannot sell at a lower price than its competitors, it may be able to earn a higher profit through lower total costs.

Task 3: Determine which tactics Sophie Co. can use to execute its chosen strategy. Enter either Yes or No in the Options column.

	Tactics	Options
1	Sourcing higher-quality production inputs	Yes / **No**
	Under cost leadership, firms aim to produce a product more efficiently and at a cheaper cost. Higher-quality inputs typically cost more. This would not be conducive to Sophie Co.'s strategy.	
2	Seeking new markets	**Yes** / No
	Sophie Co. may be able to use its existing manufacturing process to efficiently create a new, related product in a different market.	
3	Innovating to diversify product offerings	Yes / **No**
	Innovating to diversify product offerings is costly. Sophie Co. would probably have to charge customers more to cover the increased costs. Customers in this industry are price sensitive, so this would not be beneficial for Sophie Co.	
4	Undertaking productivity initiatives	**Yes** / No
	Productivity initiatives (eg, lean manufacturing, supply chain management) can reduce costs and reduce time of delivery of goods. This can lead to an increase in Sophie Co.'s market share or a higher profit for Sophie Co.	

Acquisition and Divestiture Opportunities

Representative Task (Analysis): Compare acquisition and divestiture opportunities on the basis of given market analysis and investment criteria.

Acquisitions and Mergers

Mergers are a type of acquisition that specifically refer to a company's purchase and *full takeover* of another, typically smaller, company. The new entity will generally have a larger market share and can thereby reduce competition.

- **Horizontal mergers** occur where the target is in the *same line of business* as the acquirer's core business and is often a competitor or unit of a competitor. Horizontal mergers can grant companies economies of scale by reducing duplicate resources and departments and greater pricing power while reducing the number of competitors in the market
- **Vertical mergers** occur when the target is in the *acquirer's supply chain* (eg, supplier, distributor). Vertical mergers can help companies secure the supply of a resource or increase the potential customer base through new or improved distribution channels
    - **Forward integration** exists when the target is *downstream* from the acquirer in the supply chain, such as a *distributor*. The target can increase the acquirer's potential customer base through new or improved distribution channels
    - **Backward integration** exists when the target is *upstream* from the acquirer in the supply chain, such as a *supplier*. In such a case, the vertical merger can help the acquirer secure the supply of a resource, ensure better quality, or lower its costs
- **Conglomerate mergers** occur when the target is *unrelated* to the acquirer's core business, providing diversification. However, conglomerates are typically viewed as inefficient managers of capital, and investors can usually achieve diversification more efficiently through their own portfolios

Mergers that **create value for shareholders** tend to share several characteristics:

- The premium is relatively low
- The number of bidders is low (a larger number of bidders tends to drive up the price)
- Investors' initial reaction to the news is positive

Another reason companies undertake mergers and acquisitions is to enter a **new and unfamiliar market** more quickly and with less risk than could be done through internal development, thereby **increasing market power**.

Motivations for Mergers and Acquisitions	
Financially Driven	• Synergies • Growth • Tax considerations

Motivations for Mergers and Acquisitions	
Strategically Driven	• Increasing market power • Acquiring unique capabilities and resources • Unlocking hidden value • Cross-border motivations • Diversification
Management Driven	• Management's personal incentives (eg, compensation, prestige) • Bootstrapping earnings

Companies pursuing an **acquisition** have the following options:

- **Acquire the target company's stock:** The acquirer will use cash or its own stock (or both) to purchase the stock of the other company. By doing so, it acquires control over the entire company, including the company's assets and liabilities
- **Acquire assets of the target company (eg, a division):** Usually the acquisition is in exchange for cash. The acquirer will typically try to structure the transaction to acquire just the assets and avoid assuming any associated liabilities

Stock Acquisition	Asset Acquisition
• Must be approved by 50% (or more) of target's shareholders	• Usually does not require shareholder approval unless assets are significant
• Acquirer assumes target's liabilities	• Acquirer usually only assumes assets
• Simpler: less likely to require renegotiations and amendments to contracts	• More complex: more likely to require renegotiations and amendments to contracts
• More likely to require regulatory approval	• Less likely to require regulatory approval

The process of acquiring a company's assets is often quicker than a stock purchase. Stock purchases will transfer the target's liabilities since the acquirer is purchasing ownership (ie, equity) of the target, which includes its assets and liabilities. Most asset purchases do not transfer the associated liabilities since the acquirer is purchasing only the assets.

Stock purchases are also more likely to require regulatory and shareholder approval. Many asset purchases, unless they are for a significant portion of the target company's assets, will not require any regulatory approval. However, the required renegotiations and/or amendments of existing contracts and asset-related legal documents make the process more complex overall. The acquisition of stock is less likely to require such renegotiations and amendments.

An acquisition attempt can be either friendly or hostile. **Friendly takeovers** are those in which the target company's management is receptive to the deal and the two sides enter into merger discussions after the initial pitch. If the discussions result in a mutual agreement, a definitive merger agreement will be made and presented to shareholders for approval.

Hostile takeovers are those in which the target company's management rejects the deal. The acquirer has one of several options to try to complete the transaction despite management's resistance:

- **Bear hugs:** The acquirer takes the merger proposal directly to the target's board of directors, effectively bypassing the management team

Hostile "Bear Hug" Takeover

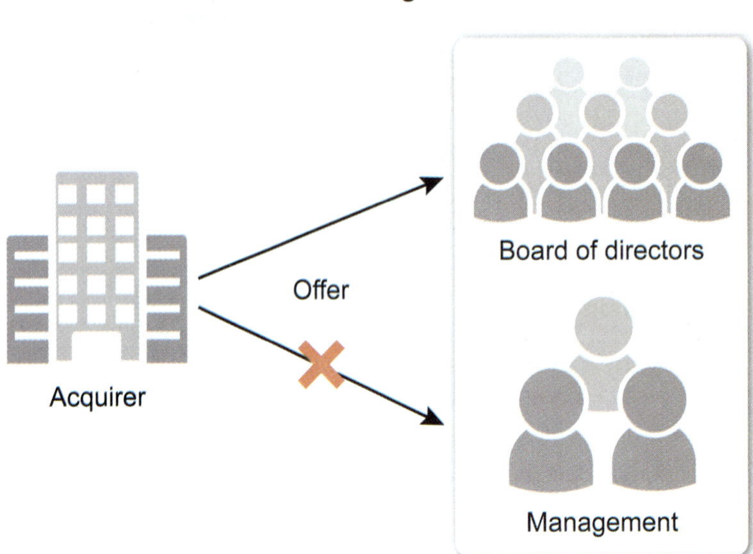

- **Tender offer:** The acquirer tries to buy the target company directly from its shareholders by offering them an opportunity to submit (ie, tender) their shares for compensation
- **Proxy fight:** The acquirer aims to elect new, selected members to the target's board of directors through a shareholder vote. The proposed slate of electors is approved by regulators and then sent to the target company's shareholders. If elected, the new acquisition-friendly board members then approve the transaction

Defenses

Companies that want to remain independent and protected against potential takeover attempts may construct **pre-offer takeover defense mechanisms**. Pre-offer mechanisms typically fare better than post-offer mechanisms in court when hostile takeover attempts are litigated. If a post-offer mechanism is used, the target faces a higher burden of proof that the mechanism is meant to protect its shareholders, not just management.

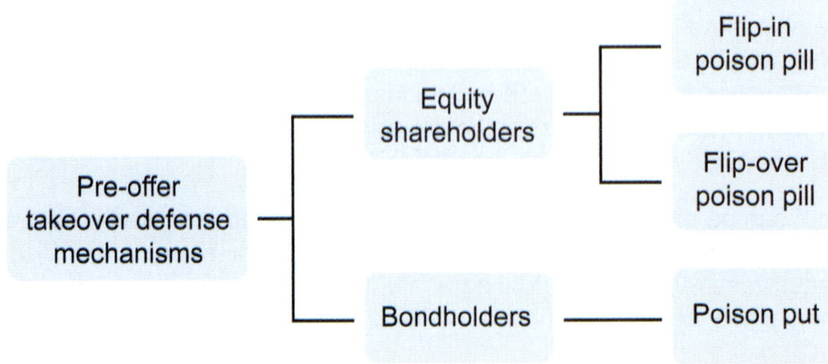

- **Poison puts** are a pre-offer takeover defense mechanism that allows bondholders to sell (ie, put) their bonds back to the target company in the event of a takeover. The put price is typically at or above par. Potential acquirers are forced to immediately pay the bondholders or refinance the target's debt, which requires additional cash and makes the acquisition both more expensive and more difficult.
- **Poison pills** allow the target's shareholders to purchase new shares at a discount to the current stock price once a certain ownership threshold (eg, 25%) has been reached. This makes it more expensive for acquirers to purchase the company. Flip-in poison pills allow shareholders to purchase shares of the target company; flip-over poison pills allow them to purchase shares of the acquiring company.
- If pre-offer takeover defense mechanisms do not deter a hostile bidder's takeover attempt, the target company can pursue a post-offer mechanism. The **crown jewel defense** is a post-offer takeover defense mechanism in which the company sells a key asset, division, or subsidiary (ie, the crown jewel) to a third party

Crown Jewel Defense

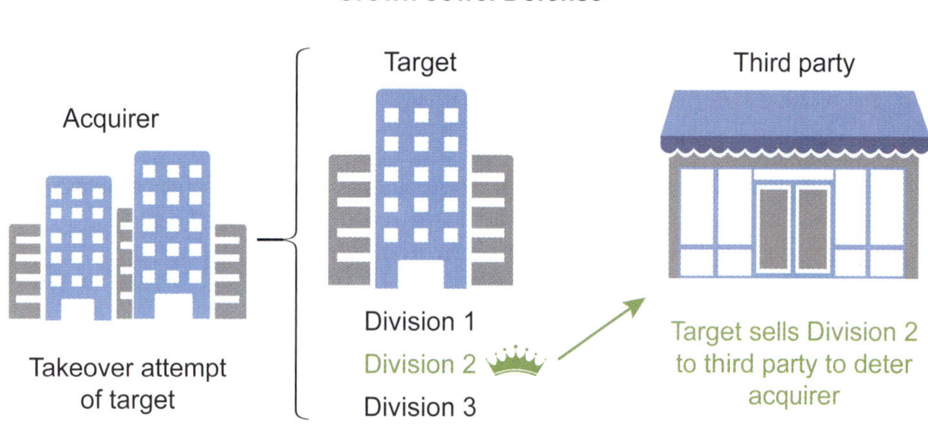

The goal of the sale is to deter a hostile bidder by divesting an asset that the bidder is seeking to purchase. This can make an acquisition of the rest of the company less compelling or even irrelevant, such that the bidder will end the takeover attempt. However, given the timing of the sale, courts are likely to scrutinize this strategy and may find it illegal and not in the shareholders' best interests.

Other post-offer takeover defense mechanisms include the following:

Mechanism	What Target Does	How It Deters Buyers
"Just say no"	Lobbies its board and shareholders to reject offer	Buyer may be forced to adjust bid or reveal more of its strategy to get approval
Litigation	Files lawsuit against acquirer for breach of securities law or competition law	Can take significant time and resources, with unknown outcome
Greenmail	Agrees to repurchase its shares from acquirer, potentially at a premium; effectively a payoff or "ransom" to acquirer	Acquirer usually agrees not to attempt another takeover
Share repurchase	Repurchases shares from any willing shareholder	Increases costs of shares in the market; can increase target's leverage if debt is used

Mechanism	What Target Does	How It Deters Buyers
Leveraged recapitalization	Issues a large amount of debt to fund share repurchases	Dramatically changes target's capital structure
Pac-Man	Makes counteroffer to acquire acquirer	
White knight	Seeks a third party to acquire the company instead, often at a higher price	Can cause a bidding war that may make the winner overpay for the target (ie, "winner's curse")
White squire	Seeks a third party to purchase a significant minority stake	Minority stake may be large enough to block takeover attempt

Restructuring (Divestitures)

Restructuring (ie, divestitures) typically refers to ways that companies seek to become more efficient: smaller but more profitable. This is a type of **exit strategy** whereby an entity only retains ownership of the profitable components of the business. The entity may be **severely in need of cash** or, on occasion, may divest of a component due to legal, political, social, or environmental reasons.

Common Forms of Divestiture	
Direct Sale	• Sale to third party
Equity Carve-Out	• Creation of new legal entity • Sale of portion of equity to outsiders
Spin-Off	• Creation of new legal (ie, independent) entity • Parent company's shareholders receive shares in entity proportional to ownership of parent • Also called a "spin-out" or "starburst"
Split-Off	• Creation of new legal entity (ie, subsidiary) • Parent company's shareholders are offered ownership in the new subsidiary in exchange for shares of parent
Liquidation	• Breakup of a company, division, or subsidiary with piecemeal selling of assets (eg, bankruptcy)

Sapphire, Inc., is part of the biotech industry, which has recently transitioned from the growth phase to the shakeout phase of the industry life cycle. During both the embryonic and growth phases of the life cycle, Sapphire was a frequent acquirer of other entities and plans to continue acquiring companies in the shakeout phase.

Management plans to restructure the company's current business to streamline its operations before making any further acquisitions. Sapphire intends to accomplish the restructuring by creating a new entity and completing a spin-off of all its divested business into the new entity.

Exhibits

Exhibit 1: Factors Impacting Restructuring Option

Based on my market research, the following factors support Sapphire management's decision to restructure the company's business to streamline operations:

Factor 1: Sapphire has the opportunity to shift its production to a developed country that has invested heavily in the capability of manufacturing Sapphire's products at lower cost.

Factor 2: Sapphire faces potential supply shortages for a certain component for one of its products after a supplier went bankrupt.

Factor 3: The profitability of one of Sapphire's previous acquisitions has not improved after years of continued investment.

Lee Langston

Internal Research Analyst

Exhibit 2: Spin-Off Choices

Sapphire has several choices related to the creation of a separate entity and spin-off of all diversified business, as follows:

Choice 1: Sell a portion of the equity in the separate, independent entity to outsiders.

Choice 2: Provide its shareholders equity in the separate, independent entity proportional to their Sapphire ownership.

Choice 3: Provide its shareholders equity in the separate, independent entity in exchange for Sapphire shares.

Lee Langston

Internal Research Analyst

Indicate the proper option for each of the independent situations listed in the table below relating to Sapphire's plans.

Situation 1	Options
Given where the biotech industry is in the industry life cycle and Sapphire's objectives to streamline, determine which type of merger Sapphire is least likely to undertake.	A. Vertical B. Horizontal **C. Conglomerate**

Companies can acquire a portion of—or merge with—another company for several reasons, often related to the current phase of the industry life cycle. In the **shakeout phase**, growth potential remains, but growth has slowed compared with the previous phase.

As growth slows, fewer new competitors enter the industry. In this situation, a common rationale for acquisitions and mergers is to **achieve economies of scale** and **operational efficiencies** that maintain margins. To do this, companies are most likely to undertake horizontal and/or vertical mergers.

Vertical mergers allow companies to more closely control their production or distribution process, which often helps them achieve cost savings. Horizontal mergers allow companies to consolidate operations and eliminate duplicate resources and departments. For a **conglomerate merger**, the target is unrelated to the acquirer's core business, thus achieving economies of scale. Note that operational efficiencies are unlikely to occur.

Situation 2	Options
Determine which of the factors best justifies Sapphire's intention to restructure.	A. Factor 1 B. Factor 2 **C. Factor 3**

Periods of increased restructuring often follow an active period of mergers and acquisitions as the acquiring entity decides to divest assets, a division or a subsidiary related to a previous merger that did not work out as expected.

A common acquisition rationale is that a company believes it can unlock a target company's hidden value by managing it better than the target company did on its own. If this plan fails, the acquirer may seek to cut its losses and divest the business rather than continuing to invest more money into it (**Exhibit 1**).

Moving production to a country with lower production costs and locking in supply to avoid a shortage are common rationales for mergers and acquisitions but are less likely to be accomplished directly by restructuring.

Situation 3	Options
To perform the spin-off after creating a separate entity, determine which method Sapphire is most likely to use.	A. Choice 1 **B. Choice 2** C. Choice 3

Restructuring typically refers to ways that companies seek to become more efficient (ie, smaller but more profitable). Companies typically restructure in one of three ways:

- Sell assets directly to another company. This can be done as a direct sale or equity carve-out
- Liquidate by breaking up the company and selling its assets individually
- Create a new legal entity in which existing shareholders receive ownership. This can be done through one of two ways:
  - Spin-off: Creating a new legal entity and issuing shares of that entity to shareholders of the parent company, which gives them the **same proportional ownership** in both companies
  - Split-off: Creating a new legal entity and offering shareholders of the parent company shares of the separate entity in exchange for their parent company shares
- To accomplish the spin-off, Sapphire will issue shares to existing shareholders in the same proportions as their ownership in Sapphire (eg, each shareholder will have the same proportional ownership in both companies)

BAR

Area II: Technical Accounting and Reporting

BAR 3

Indefinite-Lived Intangible Assets, Including Goodwill

BAR 3: Indefinite-Lived Intangible Assets, Including Goodwill

3.01 Indefinite-Lived Intangible Assets, Including Goodwill

Overview

Intangible assets refer to a company's assets that lack physical substance and provide economic benefits through the rights and privileges associated with their possession. They may have finite or indefinite lives. The Financial Accounting and Reporting (FAR) exam covers finite lived intangible assets, while the BAR exam covers indefinite lived intangible assets, notably goodwill.

Indefinite lived assets (eg, trademarks) do not have an expiration date, which means that it is difficult to determine total life. In other words, the asset lacks a regulatory, competitive, contractual, or economic time frame.

Internally generated intangible assets are *not recorded* on the balance sheet as their value cannot be independently determined. Examples of such assets include the following:

- Knowledge
- Customer loyalty
- Desirable physical location of the business
- Internally generated goodwill

Goodwill is an unidentifiable intangible asset because its value cannot be directly determined. It is the excess of what a buyer is willing to pay for a business over the value of the **net identifiable assets** on the books of the acquired company.

Initial Value of Goodwill

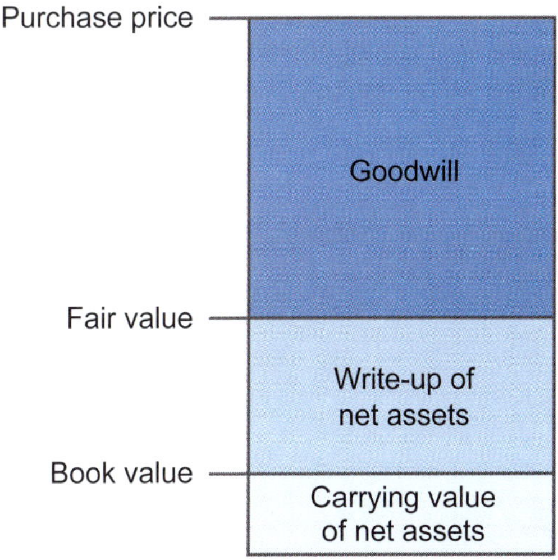

Since it is impossible to verify the value of goodwill in the absence of an actual transaction, it is *only recorded* on the balance sheet when it results from the purchase of another business.

Impairment Indicators

Representative Task (Remembering & Understanding): Recall impairment indicators for goodwill and other indefinite lived intangible assets.

Intangible assets with indefinite useful lives are tested at least annually for **impairment** (ie, a decline in the recorded value of the asset). Testing for impairment may also be required during the year if conditions indicate that impairment may have occurred.

For indefinite lived intangibles, impairment is tested by comparing the fair value of the asset to its carrying value. Various **qualitative factors** can be evaluated to determine whether the carrying value of an intangible asset has been impaired.

Conditions that may cause impairment include the development of new technology (which minimizes or eliminates the value of existing technology) and economic changes. Note that qualitative assessment is *optional*, not mandatory.

Qualitative factors include the following:

- Macroeconomic conditions, such as general limitations on the availability of capital
- Industry and market considerations, such as an increase in the competitive environment
- Cost factors, such as increases in the costs of raw material or labor
- Overall financial performance, such as declining profits or cash flows
- Events specific to the entity, such as changes in management
- Events affecting the reporting unit, such as a change in the composition of its assets
- In some cases, a sustained decrease in stock price
- Other relevant events or circumstances that affect a reporting unit's carrying value or fair value of net assets

If the qualitative assessment indicates that impairment is unlikely (ie, less than 50% chance), further testing is not required. Additional **quantitative assessment** is required if impairment is more than likely.

Intangible Assets with Indefinite Lives: Impairment Testing

TM Trademarks
Goodwill
Tested annually for impairment

↓

Qualitative assessment:
Industry-specific factors indicate more likely than not that asset is impaired?

Yes ↓

Quantitative assessment:
Is carrying value (CV) > fair value (FV)?

No → **No impairment**

Yes ↓

Asset impaired: FV is new CV
Impairment loss recognized
Subsequent reversals prohibited

Carrying Values

Representative Task (Application): Calculate the carrying amount of goodwill and other indefinite lived intangible assets reported in the financial statements (initial measurement and impairment) and prepare journal entries.

Initial Carrying Amount

If one entity acquires 100% of another entity, it is assumed that the fair value of the consideration given is the fair value of the entity reported (ie, that the purchaser is paying a fair price).

That amount will be compared to the net of:

- The fair value of all identifiable tangible and intangible assets acquired, which may include assets that are not on the financial statements of the acquired entity, minus
- The fair value of all liabilities assumed.

Equity Method: Excess Purchase Price Over Net Assets

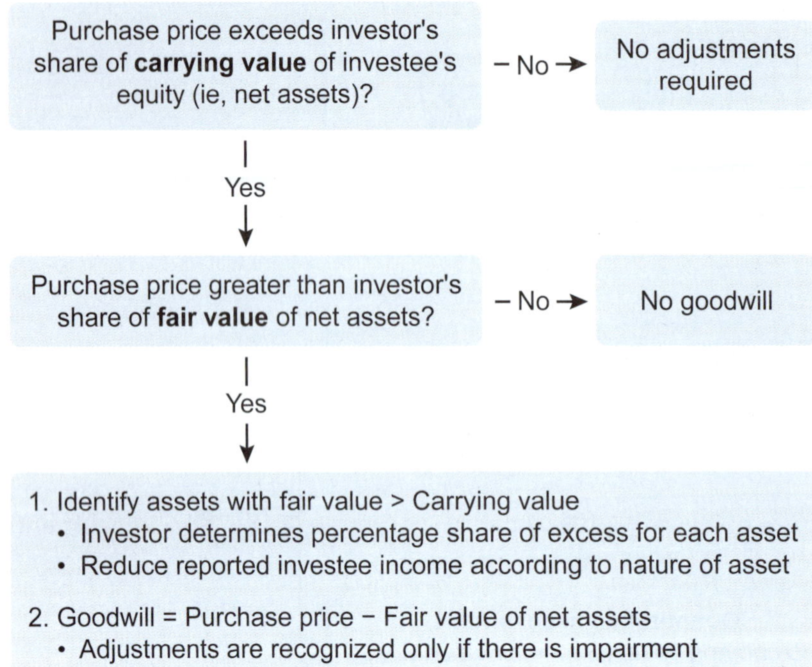

If the fair value of the underlying net assets is less than the fair value of consideration given, the difference is recognized as **goodwill** by the acquiring entity.

If the fair value of the underlying net assets exceeds the fair value of consideration given, the difference is recognized as a **gain on bargain purchase** by the acquiring entity.

Assume one entity acquires all of the stock of another entity for $1,000,000. The acquired entity has the following assets and liabilities:

	Book value	Fair value
Current assets	$350,000	$ 350,000
Plant and equipment, net	600,000	850,000
Intangibles, excluding goodwill	0	100,000
Total identifiable assets	$950,000	$1,300,000
Liabilities assumed	(500,000)	(500,000)
Value of underlying net assets	$450,000	$ 800,000
Total consideration		1,000,000
Goodwill		**$ 200,000**

Now assume that the total consideration was $700,000 rather than $1,000,000. That means the entity was acquired for less than the fair value of the net assets of $800,000, and a gain on bargain purchase of $100,000 results.

Goodwill is assigned to the **reporting unit** (ie, operating segment or one level below) that receives the benefit of the acquired business.

Assignment of Goodwill

Company

Reporting Unit A (microchip production)	Reporting Unit B (code development services)	Reporting Unit C (consulting services)

Acquired business
(microchip development lab)

Assume that Tally Corp., a public entity, has goodwill that consists of five reporting units from three acquisitions.

In the first acquisition, the assets and liabilities of the subsidiary were integrated into Tally's books.

The second acquisition involves an additional payment to the seller if certain results are achieved. As a result, separate books are maintained for the subsidiary.

The third acquisition involves two separate managers, each running a different department. As a result, two separate sets of books and records are being maintained for this acquisition, one for each department, with goodwill separately allocated to each one.

Tally Corp. is preparing financial statements and performing an impairment evaluation on its reported goodwill. Determine how many separate impairment evaluations Tally is required to perform.

Tally has goodwill from three acquisitions:

- The first acquisition assigned goodwill to Tally
- The second acquisition assigned goodwill to the acquired subsidiary
- The third acquisition assigned goodwill to two departments, each with its own set of books and records

If a separate set of books and records is maintained, it counts as a reporting unit. Since Tally assigned goodwill to four different reporting units, it must perform **four separate impairment** evaluations in each reporting period.

Other **indefinite lived intangible assets** (eg, trademarks) are recognized when purchased, at **cost**.

Testing for Impairment

If the optional qualitative testing indicated that an asset may have been impaired, additional **quantitative assessment** is required. For indefinite lived intangibles, impairment is determined by comparing the fair value (FV) of the asset to its carrying value (CV). If the FV is less than the CV, the asset is permanently written down. If the FV exceeds the CV, no adjustment is permitted.

Goodwill is tested for impairment at least annually by comparing the CV of the reporting unit (including goodwill) to its FV. The CV of the reporting unit will be known to the entity because it is the amount reflected in the books and records being maintained for the reporting unit. The FV will represent the amount that the entity would be able to sell the reporting unit for in an orderly transaction between market participants.

Push Corporation acquired all of the outstanding stock of Shove, Inc. for $7,500,000 at a time when Shove's identifiable net assets had a fair value of $6,900,000. As a result, goodwill of $600,000 was recognized. Push maintains separate accounting records for Shove, which is considered a separate reporting unit.

During the current period, due to some very aggressive marketing tactics, Shove's reputation was damaged, and Push has determined that it is more likely than not that the goodwill has been impaired. As a result, Push will perform a quantitative impairment test in relation to Shove's goodwill.

The carrying value is determined as follows:

Cash	$ 350,000
Accounts receivable	1,250,000
Inventories	3,000,000
Other current assets	200,000
Plant and equipment	5,750,000
Intangibles	2,000,000
Goodwill	600,000
Total	$13,150,000
Current liabilities	(950,000)
Long-term debt	(4,100,000)
Carrying value of reporting unit	**$ 8,100,000**

The fair value is determined by outside experts, using an appropriate valuation technique. The fair value was determined to be $7,900,000

Impairment loss is $200,000 ($8,100,000 CV – $7,900,000 FV)

Impairment loss (I/S – continuing ops)	200,000	
Goodwill		200,000

Going forward, goodwill is now $400,000 ($600,000 – $200,000). The impairment loss of $200,000 is recognized on the income statement.

If the value of goodwill is written down due to impairment, the adjusted amount becomes the goodwill's new carrying value. This amount is used for comparison in future assessments. Due to **conservatism**, subsequent recoveries of a previously recognized impairment loss are not recognized even if the FV of goodwill is higher than its CV.

Accounting Alternatives for Certain Nonpublic Entities (Goodwill)

To reduce the cost and complexity associated with frequent impairment testing, there are two approaches available to **private companies and not-for-profit organizations**. Eligible entities can elect to follow one or both alternatives.

Goodwill Accounting Alternatives for Nonpublic Entities

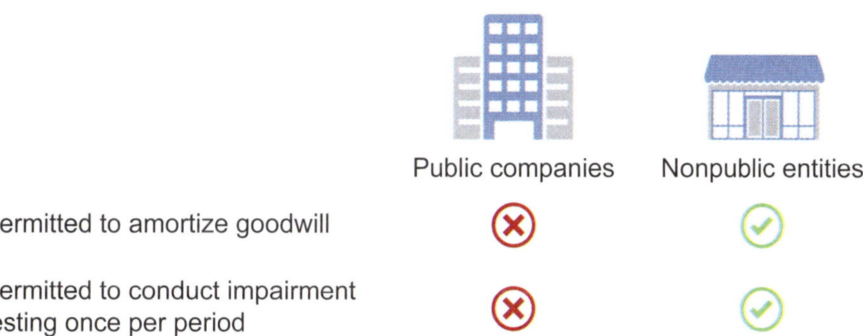

First Alternative

This option allows eligible entities to **amortize goodwill**.

- Goodwill will be amortized on a straight-line basis over its useful life, not to exceed **10 years**. The carrying value decreases each period, making it less likely that goodwill will be impaired
- Like a public entity, goodwill is still tested for impairment if a triggering event occurs indicating that the fair value of the entity (or reporting unit) has fallen below its carrying value
- Eligible entities may perform a *qualitative assessment* to determine if it is more likely than not (ie, greater than 50% probability) that goodwill has been impaired. If this assessment indicates that impairment is unlikely, no further testing is required. If it reveals that goodwill is more likely than not to be impaired, goodwill is tested for impairment (ie, *quantitative assessment*)
- Entities that elect this alternative have the option of performing **impairment tests** at the **entity** level or the **reporting unit level**. If the entity level is elected, the entity will combine all components of goodwill and perform a one-step impairment test for the entity as a whole
  - Since goodwill cannot be reduced below zero, if the amount of the impairment loss exceeds the carrying value of goodwill, the entity must evaluate its other assets to determine whether additional impairment losses should be recognized

Second Alternative

This option **reduces frequency** of goodwill impairment testing. **Triggering events** should be monitored and evaluated *throughout* the reporting period. Under this alternative, eligible entities are allowed to effectively test for triggering events and impairment only once, as of the end of each reporting period (ie, annual or interim).

Disclosure Requirements

The selection to use either (or both) of these accounting alternatives, as well as the selection to test impairment at the entity level, is disclosed in the *Summary of Significant Accounting Policies*. Required disclosures for goodwill impairment losses and specific goodwill transactions are generally recognized in a separate goodwill note.

BAR 4
Internally Developed Software

BAR 4: Internally Developed Software

4.01 Internally Developed Software

Overview

Computer software costs (developed for internal use or sale) have a unique treatment in that research costs are expensed while development costs are capitalized. These costs include any expenditures after technological feasibility is established, through the creation of product masters.

Capitalized software costs are amortized over their useful lives, using the straight-line or relative sales value approach (whichever results in greater amortization).

Representative Task (Remembering & Understanding): Recall the criteria necessary to capitalize software developed for internal use or software developed for sale in the financial statements.

Software Developed for Internal Use Only

If computer software is developed for internal use, costs incurred in the preliminary project stage and in training, data conversion, reengineering, and maintenance should be expensed. Costs incurred during the application development stage and for upgrades and enhancements are capitalized and amortized on a straight-line basis.

Capitalization of costs should cease when the software project is substantially complete and ready for its intended use (ie, postimplementation stage costs should be expensed). If the entity later decides to market the software to outsiders, net proceeds received are first applied to the carrying amount of the software until it reaches zero and then recognized as revenue.

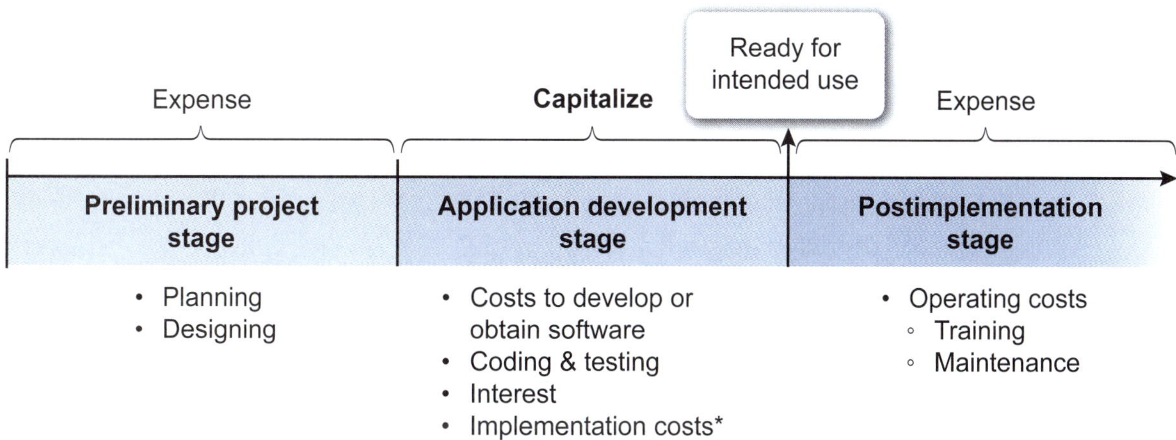

**Capitalized implementation costs do not include costs for training, data conversion, reengineering, and maintenance; these costs must be expensed.*

Software Developed for Sale

In the case of computer software developed to sell, lease, or market as a product, the costs associated with converting a technologically feasible program into final commercial form are **capitalized** (ASC 985). **Technological feasibility** is established when it has been proven that it is possible to create the desired software. Typically, this is shown through creation of a beta version (working model) of the software.

- Costs **prior** to **technological feasibility** are **expensed** as research and development (R&D)
- Costs incurred **after** software **sales** begin are inventoried and included in **cost of sales**

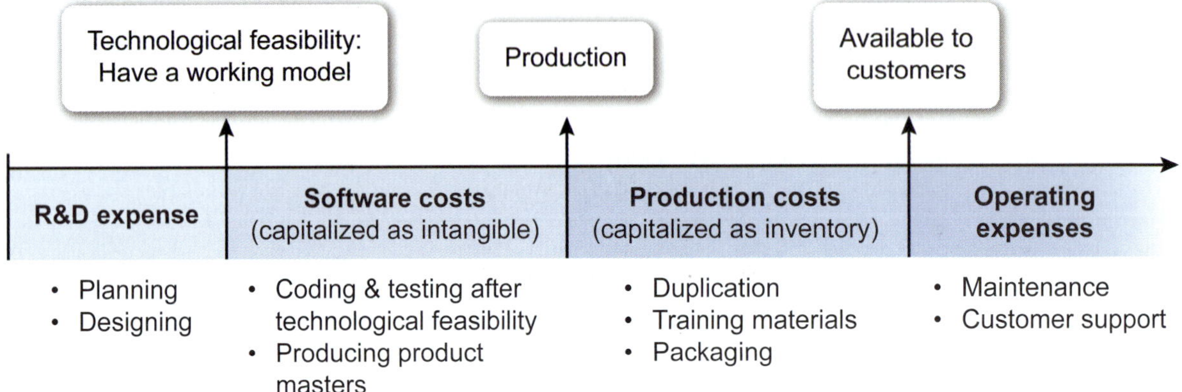

Capitalized Software Costs and Related Amortization

Representative Task (Application): Calculate capitalized software developed for internal use or software developed for sale to be reported in the financial statements and the related amortization expense.

Costs to be capitalized are recorded as a computer software asset.

A company began developing computer software to be sold as a separate product. The following costs were incurred:

Planning coding & testing before technological feasibility	$30,000
Coding & testing after technological feasibility	20,000
Creation of product masters	5,000
Production of physical units	2,000

Determine how the costs should be classified:

- $30,000 of costs before technological feasibility are expensed as research
- $25,000 ($20,000 + $5,000) of costs after technological feasibility (including creating product masters) are capitalized as computer software development cost (asset)
- $2,000 of production costs are capitalized as inventory

Amortization of capitalized software costs, which **increases cost of sales**, is calculated using a two-step process:

1. Amortization is calculated using the more conservative of **straight-line** and the **relative sales value approach**; that is, the *larger* of the two amounts will be recognized as amortization expense:
   - The straight-line amount is calculated by dividing the remaining carrying value by the remaining useful life, as of the beginning of the period
   - The amount under the relative sales value approach is calculated by establishing a ratio with the current period's sales in the numerator and the total estimated sales for the remaining life of the software, including the current period's sales, in the denominator. Amortization is equal to the ratio multiplied by the carrying value of the software as of the beginning of the period
2. The new carrying value of the software, after amortization from Step 1, is compared to the net realizable value (NRV) of the software

Net realizable value of internally developed commercial software =

Expected future software sales − Costs of completion, disposal & maintenance

If the carrying value is greater than NRV, the **excess** is also **written off** as amortization expense. For purposes of this calculation, the NRV of the software is the amount expected to be generated from future sales less the costs associated with completion, disposal, maintenance, and customer support.

Amortization of Internally Developed Commercial Software Costs

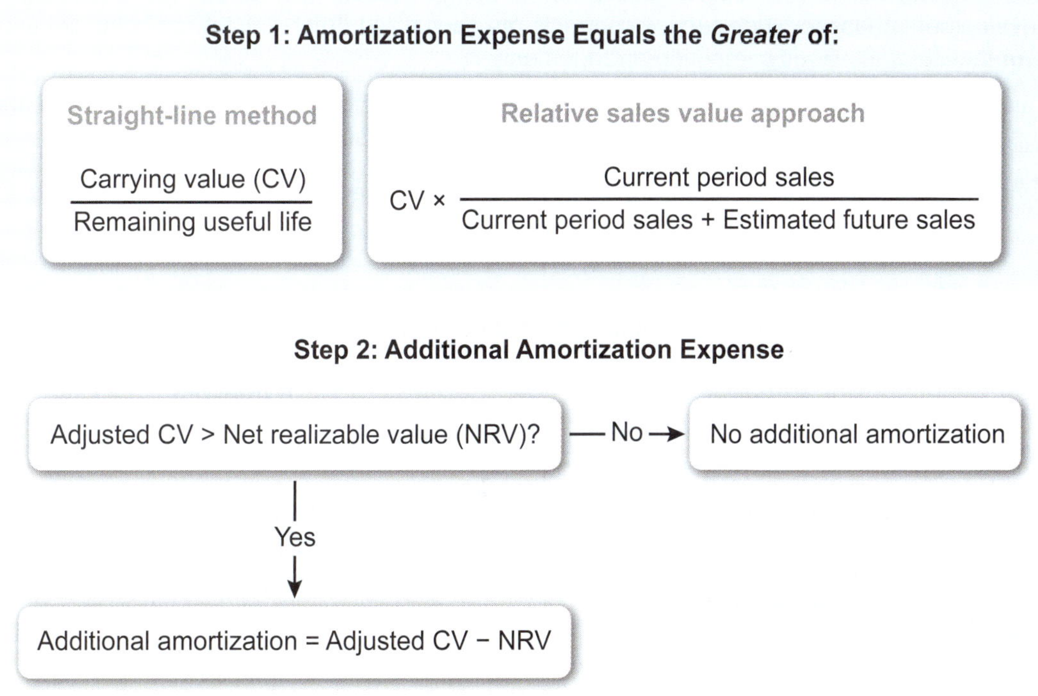

Assume a company has capitalized software costs with a five-year useful life. Revenues for the first year are expected to be $100,000, out of lifetime expected revenues of $400,000.

- Annual straight-line amortization would be 1/5, or 20%
- Relative sales value is 25% ($100,000 revenue / $400,000 expected lifetime revenue) annually

Amortization will be 25% of carrying value (larger amount). If the company's carrying value (after amortization) is $2,850, with a NRV of $2,400, the excess $450 ($2,850 – $2,400) is written off as amortization expense.

Cloud Computing Arrangements

When an entity enters a **cloud computing arrangement** (eg, hosting arrangement), an analysis is performed to determine whether some or all of the arrangement includes a software license.

- If the arrangement is considered a **software license**, the entire cost, including the present value of future payments, is treated as an intangible and accounted for like other licenses. The cost will be capitalized, and a determination will be made as to whether it has a finite useful life
- If the arrangement does not include a software license, the entire amount is treated as a **service contract**, with the expense recognized in the period in which the benefit is derived
  - Note that implementation costs (eg, setup, other up-front costs) incurred during the application development phase for such service contracts are capitalized. Such capitalized costs are amortized over the life of the cloud computing arrangement
  - This does not include costs for *training, data conversion, reengineering, and maintenance*; these costs must be *expensed* (ie, same treatment as internal use software)

If the arrangement represents a **combination** of a service contract (eg, hosting arrangement) and a software license, the total cost will be *allocated* between the two services

Costs Capitalized for Cloud-Based Software	
Capitalized	**Expensed**
• Purchase of software and software licenses	• Training
• Third-party software development fees	• Manual data conversion
• Coding and testing	• Reengineering
• Purchase of external materials	• Maintenance and technical support

BAR 5
Revenue Recognition

BAR 5: Revenue Recognition

5.01 Revenue Recognition

Overview of Business Analysis and Reporting (BAR) Coverage

As covered in Financial Accounting and Reporting (FAR), all entities that enter into **contracts with customers** are subject to the revenue recognition standard (ASC 606). The standard requires that customer contracts meet the following **criteria**:

- The parties have approved the provisions and have *committed to perform*.
- The *rights* in the contract and the *payment terms* can be identified.
- The contract has commercial *substance*.
- *Collection is probable* (ie, customer has the ability and intent to pay).

Revenue recognition occurs when an entity satisfies a performance obligation by transferring a good or service to a customer. The core revenue recognition principle consists of two components:

- Revenue is to be recognized upon the transfer of promised goods and services to customers; and
- The amount of revenue recognized represents the consideration the entity expects to receive in exchange for those goods and services.

Revenues are recognized by applying a *five-step* process:

5-Step Revenue Recognition Process

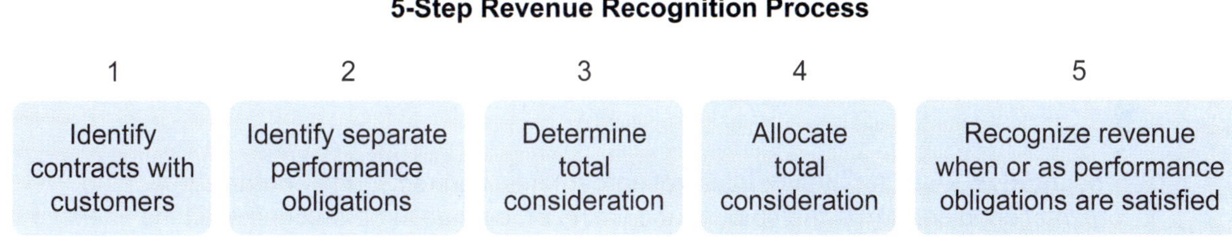

Revenue Arrangements That Are Not Contracts with Customers

An entity may enter into an arrangement that has some of the characteristics of a revenue-related contract in that it involves providing goods/services in exchange for compensation. It may not, however, meet all of the criteria to be a contract. As long as the arrangement does not meet the criteria (eg, either or both parties can terminate the agreement without penalty), all amounts received will be recognized as a *liability*.

Entry To Recognize Liability		
Cash	XX	
Deferred revenue		XX

The arrangement will be reevaluated every reporting period to determine whether it has met the criteria, at which time the method of accounting will be changed to the 5-step process.

Entry To Record Revenue		
Deferred revenue	XX	
Revenue		XX

If the criteria are never met, the liability is *derecognized* and treated as *revenue* when *consideration* received from the customer is *nonrefundable* and *one* of the following scenarios applies:

Liability Is Derecognized And Revenue Is Recorded		
Scenario 1	**Scenario 2**	**Scenario 3**
The entity has no remaining obligations, and All, or substantially all, of the consideration has been received.	The arrangement has been terminated.	Consideration received relates to goods/ services, the control of which, has been transferred; and The entity has stopped transferring goods/ services, and neither has an obligation to, nor intends to, provide any additional goods/services.

The material covered in this chapter is specifically tailored to meet the representative tasks related to BAR. For more in-depth coverage, refer to the Revenue Recognition material presented in FAR.

Amount and Timing of Revenue Recognition

Representative Task (Analysis): Interpret agreements, contracts, and/or other supporting documentation to determine the amount and timing of revenue to be recognized in the financial statements using the five-step model.

Testing scope

The representative task shown above is classified as an Analysis skill level in the July 2024 AICPA Blueprint. **Analysis skills** are tested through the task-based **simulation** format. As such, we will use different scenarios and contracts to determine the amount and timing of revenue an entity recognizes using the five-step model.

Keep in mind that every business records revenue. Retail businesses record revenue at the point of sale. Contractors record revenue over the construction contract. It's important to understand what the business provides, when they provide it, and how they provide it in order to properly recognize revenue.

Single performance obligation

Let's look at an entity that provides financial consulting services. In this scenario, Financial Consultants, Inc. (FCI) has been engaged to provide accounting services to Designer Concepts using the following consultant agreement.

Financial Consultants, Inc.

Consultant Agreement

This consultant agreement ("Agreement") is entered into by and between Concepts ("Firm") and Financial Consultants, Inc., a Delaware corporation ("FCI"), and is effective as of May 1, Year 1 (the "Effective Date").

OBJECTIVES AND SCOPE

Maintenance of Firm's Books and Records: FCI will maintain the books and records of the Firm, handling all accounting related functions, including invoicing, payables, receivables, vendor management, treasury, and monthly close process.

Payroll Processing: FCI will process the payroll for the Firm under its current cycle and frequency, utilizing the current payroll processing service. FCI will maintain all employee records and process all necessary tax filings.

Financial Reporting (Firm): On a monthly basis, FCI will provide:

- Financial statements for the Firm to all of its relevant stakeholders, including executive management, shareholders, and financial institutions, where applicable.
- Year-end reporting and presentations for the Firm's annual update to investors.
- Required certifications to meet any banking covenants.

Financial results can be presented on a comparative basis, both to budgets and forecasts, and to prior periods.

Performance obligation(s) in section 1

2. CONSULTANT COMPENSATION

In consideration of FCI's agreement to provide the services outlined above, the Firm will compensate FCI as follows:

Retainer: Firm agrees to pay FCI a monthly retainer in the amount of $4,500.00 (the "Retainer"). The Retainer will be invoiced monthly in arrears.

Billing: FCI will bill the Firm on a monthly basis for the Retainer in arrears. The Firm will pay all invoices within seven (7) days of receipt, and any invoice not paid within 30 days of receipt will incur interest on the unpaid balance at a rate of 1.5% per month. The Firm shall further pay to FCI all reasonable expenses incidental to the collection of overdue amounts under this agreement, including but not limited to attorney's fees actually incurred.

3. TERM OF AGREEMENT

This Agreement will be on a month-to-month basis. Either party may terminate this Agreement, with or without cause, upon thirty (30) days' advance written notice to the other, unless otherwise mutually agreed upon.

Total consideration in section 2

IN WITNESS WHEREOF, the parties have duly executed this Agreement as of the Effective Date.

Designer Concepts	**Financial Consultants**
By: *Lucy Brown*	By: *Bill Smith*
Owner	President

www.financialconsultants.com

FCI should recognize revenue using the 5-step process.

Step 1: Identify contracts with customers	FCI has a **signed consultant agreemen**t (ie, contract) with Designer Concepts indicating that all parties have approved of this contract and committed to perform on their obligations. The payment terms can be identified, and the contract has commercial substance (ie, risk, timing, or cash flows will change for the parties as a result of the contract).
Step 2: Identify separate performance obligations	In *Section 1 (Objectives and Scope)* of the contract, FCI has agreed to maintain Designer Concepts' books and records, perform payroll processing, and provide financial reporting. While these are three distinct tasks, they are all part of *one monthly retainer for services*. The services aren't sold separately. Therefore, this is **one performance obligation** to provide accounting services.
Step 3: Determine total consideration	In *Section 2 (Consultant Compensation)* of the contract, Designer Concepts has agreed to pay FCI **$4,500 per month** for services. This amount is billed in arrears (ie, after services have been provided each month).
Step 4: Allocate total consideration	Because FCI has only one performance obligation, accounting services, it allocates the entire $4,500 revenue to the services provided.
Step 5: Recognize revenue when or as performance obligations are satisfied	FCI satisfies its performance obligation to provide accounting services each month. The agreement is a month-to-month contract as detailed in the Section 3 Term of Agreement Section. FCI **recognizes $4,500 in revenue monthly** as it satisfies its performance obligation.

Multiple performance obligations

Let's look at an entity that provides software and technical support services. In this scenario, Smart Tech, Inc. (ST), has a contract to sell Jefferson Company a software license for TechERM, provide installation services, and provide technical support services for three years. ST normally sells each service separately to its customers but has bundled these services together for Jefferson Company. ST typically completes installation services in 5 to 10 business days after work begins.

SMART TECH, INC.

Sales Agreement

This sales agreement ("Agreement") is entered into by and between Jefferson Company ("Customer") and Smart Tech, Inc., a Delaware corporation ("ST"), and is effective as October 1, Year 1 (the "Effective Date").

OBJECTIVES AND SCOPE

Software License: ST grants customer a royalty-free, revocable, limited, non-exclusive license during the term of this agreement to possess and use a copy of TechERM software. ST maintains all rights, titles, and interest in the copyrights and other intellectual property in TechERM. The trademarks, logos, designs, and service marks appearing in TechERM are registered to ST.

Installation Services: ST will install TechERM on all customer's desktop computers and servers. ST will ensure that software is working on all machines.

Technical Support: ST will provide technical support, including all software updates to customer for a period of 3 years after successful installation of TechERM software.

Performance obligation(s) in section 1

2. COMPENSATION

In consideration of ST's agreement to provide the software license and services outlined above, the customer will compensate ST as follows:

Software License: Customer agrees to pay ST a one-time, nonrefundable license fee of $15,000 for the use of TechERM software. The customer has unlimited access to the software as of the Effective Date of this contract.

Installation Services: Customer agrees to pay ST a one-time installation fee of $5,000 for the installation of TechERM software on all customer's computers.

Technical Support: Customer agrees to pay ST $6,000 per year over a period of three years for technical support and updates related to the TechERM software. The technical support period will begin after successful installation of the Tech ERM software.

Billing: ST will bill the customer $20,000 as of the effective date of this contract for the Tech ERM license and installation services. Upon successful installation of TechERM, customer will be billed $6,000 for annual technical support, and then $6,000 annually thereafter for the next two years.

The customer will pay all invoices within seven (7) days of receipt, and any invoice not paid within 30 days of receipt will incur interest on the unpaid balance at a rate of 1.5% per month. The customer shall further pay to ST all reasonable expenses incidental to the collection of overdue amounts under this agreement, including but not limited to attorney's fees actually incurred.

Total consideration in section 2

IN WITNESS WHEREOF, the parties have duly executed this Agreement as of the effective date.

Designer Concepts	**Financial Consultants**
By: *Daphne Blake*	By: *Norville Rogers*
Owner	President

ST should recognize revenue using the 5-step process.

Step 1: Identify contracts with customers	ST has a **signed sales agreement** (ie, contract) with Jefferson Company indicating that all parties have approved of this contract and committed to perform on their obligations. The payment terms can be identified, and the contract has commercial substance.
Step 2: Identify separate performance obligations	In *Section 1 (Objectives and Scope)* of the contract, ST has agreed to sell a software license for TechERM to Jefferson, install the software on all Jefferson's computers, and provide technical support for three years. ST normally sells each service separately, and each is listed separately in the contract. Therefore, there are **three separate performance obligations:** software license, installation services, and technical support.
Step 3: Determine total consideration	In *Section 2 (Consultant Compensation)* of the contract, Jefferson has agreed to pay ST $20,000 **($15,000 software license + $5,000 installation)** as of contract's effective date. Jefferson has also agreed to pay **$6,000 per year** for technical support for **3 years** upon successful installation of the TechERM software for a total of $18,000 ($6,000 × 3 years).
Step 4: Allocate total consideration	The contract specifies the amount to be allocated to each performance obligation: Software license = $15,000 Installation = $5,000 Technical support = $6,000 per year for 3 years
Step 5: Recognize revenue when or as performance obligations are satisfied	**Software license:** This is a nonrefundable one-time license fee granting Jefferson unlimited use of the TechERM software as of the contract's effective date. ST recognizes $15,000 in revenue *when the license is granted* (ie, at a point in time) on October 1, Year 1.

Installation services: ST bills Jefferson for the installation services as of the contract's effective date. However, ST has not satisfied the performance obligation until the *installation is complete*. Because ST typically completes installation services within 5 to 10 business days after work begins, there is not a material difference between contract inception and service completion. Therefore, ST can recognize $5,000 in revenue in October, Year 1. However, if installation services require a more material amount of time to complete, the revenue should be deferred until the performance obligation has been satisfied (ie, at a point in time).

Technical support: The $6,000 technical support fee is billed annually in advance. ST has an obligation to provide services for a full year. The *revenue is recognized as the support obligation is satisfied* (ie, over time) at a rate of $500 per month ($6,000 annual fee / 12 months).

Reconciliation of Sales Subledger and General Ledger

Representative Task (Analysis): Interpret source data and outputs from data analytic techniques (eg, reports, visualizations) to detect, investigate and resolve potential discrepancies (eg, errors, outliers, unexpected contract elements) in the recognition of revenue in the financial statements using the five-step model.

Potential discrepancies are often identified by comparing the general ledger to the subledger. The **general ledger** is the central **record-keeping** system for an entity's **accounting transactions**. Account balances in the general ledger are supported by **detailed account records** kept in separate subsidiary ledgers (ie, **subledgers**). General ledger balances are reported in the entity's financial statements (F/S).

The subledgers provide more **granular details** for specific types of transactions like customer accounts, vendor accounts, fixed assets, etc. The total of the subledger each period should match the total reported in the general ledger. Subledgers help to organize and control transaction level data that flows into F/S.

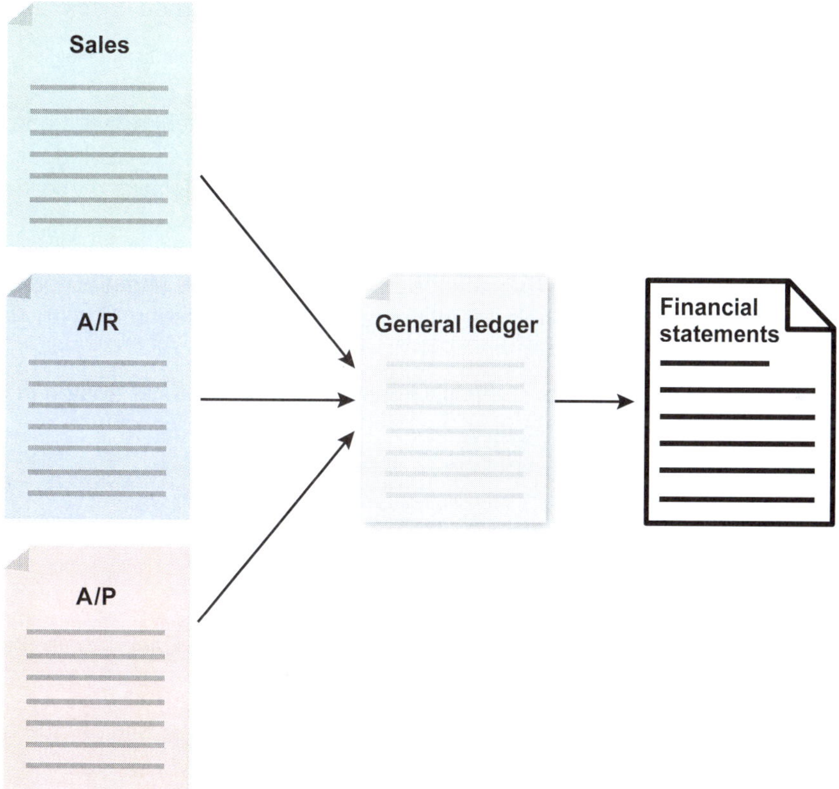

There are times when amounts are included in the subledger but not in the general ledger. In a computerized accounting system, this can happen when a transaction is entered in the sales subledger but not posted due to a failed posting process or the data entry clerk not having system permissions to post the transaction.

For example, a sales clerk has system permission to enter sales and record returns. Once the transaction is entered in the sales journal, it is routed to the manager for approval and posting to the general ledger.

The manager had a personal emergency and left work without approving sales transactions for the day and never went back to approve that day's activity. The sales journal is correct, but the general journal is not because the sales transactions were not approved and posted.

Likewise, an accounting clerk may post a general journal transaction that impacts the sales account but does not record it in the sales subledger.

For example, a customer's check was returned from the bank due to insufficient funds. The accountant recorded the transaction as a credit to cash for the returned check and a debit to the sales account in the general ledger, but there was no corresponding entry in the sales ledger.

In this case, the sales subledger will not match the sales general ledger account. The accountant should have credited the accounts receivable subledger for the customer's returned check, not sales.

It is important to make sure that the total of the items in the subledger matches to the corresponding account in the general ledger by performing a reconciliation that compares the subledger to the general ledger to identify any discrepancies. Generally, the reconciliation process follows these steps:

- Compare the ending balances of the general ledger to the subledger.
- Identify any differences by confirming beginning balances (for balance sheet accounts), ensuring daily postings from the subledger to the general ledger match, and researching any nonrecurring or unusual transactions.
- Investigate reasons for the differences. Typically, these are errors or items posted in the general ledger and not the subledger or vice versa.
- Adjust the appropriate ledger.
- Compare adjusted balances.

Example

Let's look at an example. Blue Company manufactures and sells engines. Each month the sales subsidiary ledger is reconciled to the general ledger. Additional information:

- All sales are on account and must be approved by a manager before posting to the accounting system general ledger.
- Blue uses a perpetual inventory system.
- Sales returns are recorded in the Sales Returns and Allowances contra account.

The first step in the monthly reconciliation between the sales journal and the general ledger is to compare the ending balances. For January, Year 1, Blue discovers that there is a $37,100 discrepancy.

Sales journal balance	$ 334,620
General ledger balance	(297,520)
Difference	$ 37,100

Next, Blue identifies the differences. There are no beginning balances for sales.

- In confirming the daily sales journal postings, the $16,300 sale to Dixon Company (invoice #108) is missing from the general ledger.
- There are three general journal entries totaling $20,800 ($12,400 + $3,800 + $4,600) that are in the general ledger but not in the sales journal.
- These two discrepancies equal the $37,100 difference ($16,300 + $20,800).

Blue Company Sales Journal
January, Year 1

Date	Customer	Invoice	Amount
4-Jan	Dixon Company	104	$ 67,200
8-Jan	Mick, Inc.	105	23,900
14-Jan	Feely Enterprises	106	54,000
20-Jan	Board Industries	107	81,400
23-Jan	Dixon Company	108	16,300
26-Jan	Board Industries	109	49,100
30-Jan	Daisy Chains	110	30,000
31-Jan	Mick, Inc.	111	12,720
			$ 334,620

Difference between sales journal and general ledger = $37,100 ($334,620 − $297,520)

Blue Company General Ledger

Account: Sales					**Account Number: 400**	
					Balance	
Date	**Description**	**Reference**	**Debit**	**Credit**	**Debit**	**Credit**
Year 1						
4-Jan	Post from sales journal	SJ		67,200		67,200
8-Jan	Post from sales journal	SJ		23,900		91,100
14-Jan	Post from sales journal	SJ		54,000		145,100
18-Jan	NSF check	GJ	12,400			132,700
19-Jan	Customer return	GJ	3,800			128,900
20-Jan	Post from sales journal	SJ		81,400		210,300
25-Jan	Post from sales journal	GJ	4,600			205,700
26-Jan	Customer return	SJ		49,100		254,800
30-Jan	Post from sales journal	SJ		30,000		284,800
31-Jan	Post from sales journal	SJ		12,720		297,520

Account: Sales returns and allowances					**Account Number: 401**	
					Balance	
Date	**Description**	**Reference**	**Debit**	**Credit**	**Debit**	**Credit**
Year 1						
19-Jan	Dixon Company	GJ	4,500			4,500
25-Jan	Dixon Company	GJ	5,870			10,370

SJ = Sales Journal GJ = General Journal

To investigate the differences, Blue reviews the postings to the January, Year 1, sales journal and general journal.

$16,300 Sale to Dixon Company: Invoice #108 to Dixon Company (23-Jan) was posted to the sales journal but not to the general ledger. While researching the missing posting, Blue discovered that the sales manager did not review and approve the sales from that day when he left early because of a personal emergency. The manager forgot to approve the day's activity to the accounting system. To correct this, the posting was processed, and the sale was added to the general ledger. This posting *increases* the general ledger balance.

Blue Company General Journal *(January, Year 1)*

Date	Account	Debit	Credit
18-Jan	Sales	12,400	
	Cash		12,400
	Nonsufficient funds check return		
19-Jan	Sales	3,800	
	Sales returns and allowances	4,500	
	Accounts receivable – Dixon Company		4,500
	Cost of goods sold		3,800
	Customer return		
25-Jan	Sales	4,600	
	Sales returns and allowances	5,870	
	Accounts receivable – Dixon Company		5,870
	Cost of goods sold		4,600
	Customer return		

General journal entry (18-Jan): A customer check for $12,400 was returned due to nonsufficient funds at the bank. The customer's *account receivable should be debited*, not sales. The customer didn't have the funds available to pay for the purchase. By debiting accounts receivable, the customer's obligation is reinstated on Blue's books.

The original entry to the general ledger account reduced the sales account balance. When the general journal entry is corrected to debit accounts receivable, the $12,400 reduction is removed from the sales general ledger account, and the *sales account balance increases*. Blue makes the following journal entry on January 31 to correct the error:

Account	Debit	Credit
Accounts receivable	12,400	
Sales		12,400
Correct nonsufficient funds entry from 18-Jan		

General journal entries (19-Jan and 25-Jan): For both entries, Dixon Company returned goods to Blue. Because Blue uses a perpetual inventory system, the cost of the goods returned is debited to *Inventory (not Sales)* and credited to Cost of goods sold. The sales price of the goods sold is debited to Sales returns and allowances and credited to accounts receivable.

The original entry to the general ledger account reduced the sales account balance. When the general journal entries are corrected by debiting Inventory, the $3,800 and $4,600 reductions to the sales account in the general ledger are removed, and the *sales account balance increases*. Blue makes the following journal entries on January 31 to correct the error:

Inventory	3,800	
Sales		3,800
Correct customer return entry from 19-Jan		

Inventory	4,600	
Sales		4,600
Correct customer return entry from 25-Jan		

Once all adjustments and correcting journal entries are recorded, Blue compares the adjusted balances of the sales journal and the general ledger to ensure that the balances are reconciled.

Sales journal original balance	$334,620	General ledger original balance	$297,520
(No adjustments required)		Add missing Dixon sale (invoice #108)	16,300
		Remove reduction for NSF check (18-Jan)	(12,400)
		Remove customer return (19-Jan)	(3,800)
		Remove customer return (25-Jan)	(4,600)
Sales journal balance	$334,620	General ledger adjusted balance	$334,620

The adjusted balance for sales in the general ledger is $334,620. This matches the sales journal balance, and the reconciliation is complete. The corrected sales general ledger account is below

Blue Company General Ledger

Account: Sales					**Account Number: 400**	
					Balance	
Date	**Description**	**Reference**	**Debit**	**Credit**	**Debit**	**Credit**
Year 1						
4-Jan	Post from sales journal	SJ		67,200		67,200
8-Jan	Post from sales journal	SJ		23,900		91,100
14-Jan	Post from sales journal	SJ		54,000		145,100
18-Jan	NSF check	GJ	12,400			132,700
19-Jan	Customer return	GJ	3,800			128,900
20-Jan	Post from sales journal	SJ		81,400		210,300
23-Jan	Post from sales journal	SJ		16,300		226,600
25-Jan	Customer return	GJ	4,600			222,000
26-Jan	Post from sales journal	SJ		49,100		271,100
30-Jan	Post from sales journal	SJ		30,000		301,100
31-Jan	Post from sales journal	SJ		12,720		313,820
31-Jan	Correct NSF entry 18-Jan	GJ		12,400		326,220
31-Jan	Correct return 19-Jan	GJ		3,800		330,020
31-Jan	Correct return 25-Jan	GJ		4,600		334,620

Total of corrections = $37,100
($16,300 + $12,400 + $3,800 + $4,600)

Using Data Analytics to Detect, Investigate, and Resolve Discrepancies

Data analytics can be used to efficiently identify potential discrepancies in the recognition of revenue. Many entities use data analytic techniques to **generate outputs** (eg, reports and visualizations) using **source data**, such as sales orders, sales invoices, detailed account records, etc. Entities then **analyze** outputs for patterns, trends, and correlations to detect potential discrepancies and resolve any confirmed errors. Flagged irregularities may require additional investigation prior to taking any corrective action.

Example

Assume Dennis Company manufactures and sells office supplies and office furniture. Dennis uses data analytics to analyze its revenue each quarter. Dennis prepares a visualization of revenue per quarter as follows:

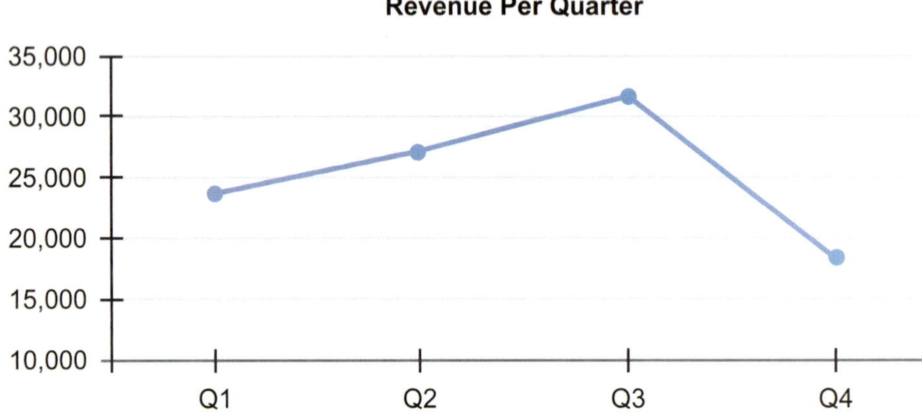

Data analytics is beneficial for organizing and evaluating large amounts of data. Visualizations are helpful in identifying discrepancies when manual review would be inefficient. However, because visualizations are often created using high-level data, alternative techniques must be used to understand the cause of the discrepancies.

Here, Dennis Company's revenue steadily increased quarter-over-quarter for Q1 through Q3. However, the company saw a significant decrease in revenue in Q4 as compared to prior quarters. Dennis takes a closer look to understand the cause of this outlier quarter.

Dennis uses the sales journal to prepare a visualization of Q3 revenue compared to Q4 revenue, segmented by customer:

Dennis Company - Sales Journal - 4th Quarter

Date	Customer	Invoice/ Credit Memo	Amount
10-Oct	Irvin IT Support	205	$ 4,300
27-Oct	Bell Banking	202CM	(5,500)
8-Nov	Moore Marketing	206	9,000
23-Nov	Cole Cybersecurity	207	800
30-Nov	Bell Banking	208	4,400
6-Dec	Moore Marketing	209	2,400
19-Dec	Irvin IT Support	210	3,200
			$18,600

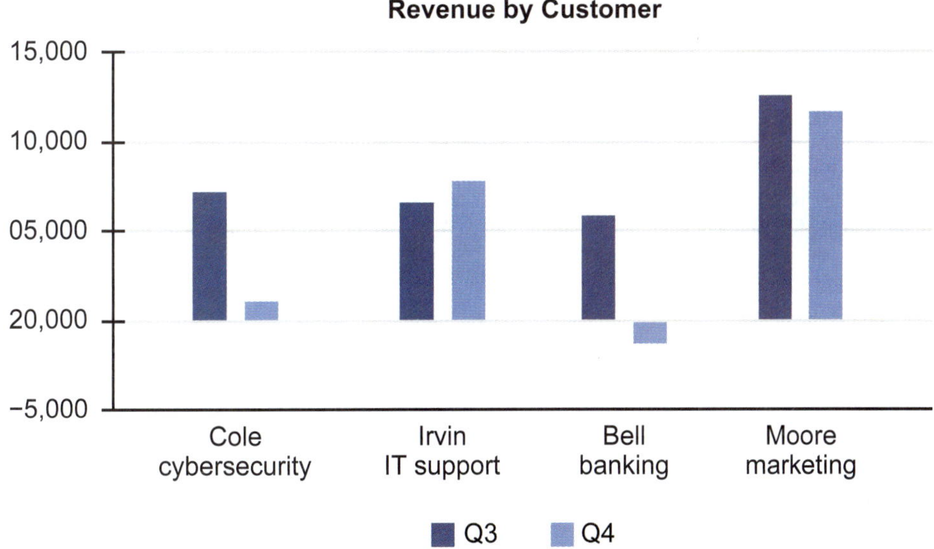

Dennis Company identifies Cole Cybersecurity and Bell Banking as outliers in Q4. Dennis compares the above visualization to the source data from customer invoices and the sales journal to investigate both customer accounts. For each customer account, the relevant invoices are presented first, and then the explanations follow.

Cole Cybersecurity:

INVOICE

Dennis Company
123 Surface Lane
Detroit, MI 48226

INVOICE NO: 207
INVOICE DATE: 23-Nov

Bill to:
Cole Cybersecurity
456 Sediment Circle
Ann Arbor, MI 48104

Item:	QTY	PRICE PER UNIT	AMOUNT
Large Oak Writing Desk	14	$400.00	$5,600.00
Premium Gray Computer Chair	8	$300.00	$2,400.00
		Subtotal	$8,000.00
		Fees/Discounts	$0.00
		Total	$8,000.00

Based on the above visualization, in Q3, Cole Cybersecurity accounted for about $7,000 of Dennis's revenue. Then, in Q4, Cole accounted for less than $1,000 of Dennis's revenue. After reviewing Cole's Q4 invoice, a transcription error was detected. Invoice #207 was recorded in the sales journal for $800, when it should have been recorded for $8,000. As a result of this error, Dennis's Q4 revenue is understated by $7,200. Dennis should make the following journal entry to correct the error:

	Debit	Credit
Accounts receivable	7,200	
Sales		7,200

Bell Banking:

INVOICE

Dennis Company
123 Surface Lane
Detroit, MI 48226

INVOICE NO: 202
INVOICE DATE: 24-Aug

Bill to:
Bell Banking
789 Crown Blvd
Toledo, OH 43604

RETURNED

Item:	QTY	PRICE PER UNIT	AMOUNT
X-Large Cherry Drawing Desk	8	$687.50	$5,500.00
		Subtotal	$5,500.00
		Fees/Discounts	$0.00
		Total	$5,500.00

Items were returned on October 27

INVOICE

Dennis Company
123 Surface Lane
Detroit, MI 48226

INVOICE NO: **208**
INVOICE DATE: **30-Nov**

Bill to:
Bell Banking
789 Crown Blvd
Toledo, OH 43604

Item:	QTY	PRICE PER UNIT	AMOUNT
Large Cherry Drawing Desk	8	$540.00	$4,320.00
Black Writing Pad	4	$20.00	$80.00
		Subtotal	$4,400.00
		Fees/Discounts	$0.00
		Total	$4,400.00

Based on the above visualization, in Q3, Bell Banking accounted for over $5,000 of Dennis's revenue. Then, in Q4, Bell's contribution to Dennis's revenue was a net negative. However, this significant change is not the result of an error. Bell purchased 8 X-Large desks in Q3 (invoice #202). Then, in Q4, Bell returned the X-Large desks and replaced them with Large desks (invoice #208). The return was approved by management and recorded correctly. No additional work is required.

In a simulation with many exhibits, such as this, it is easy to overlook key items. When reviewing source data, pay close attention to:

- Important dates (eg, dates in the invoices and sales journal)
- Identifying numbers (eg, invoice numbers)
- Item names
- Amounts charged for each item

BAR 6
Stock Compensation

BAR 6: Stock Compensation

6.01 Stock Compensation

Share-Based Arrangements

Representative Task (Remembering & Understanding): Recall concepts associated with share-based arrangements (eg, grant date, vesting conditions, inputs to valuation techniques, valuation models).

Share-based arrangements are a type of **deferred** compensation with a focus on long-term performance, usually with **no cash payments**. Compensation is typically based on a fair value calculation and expensed during the service period. Share-based compensation can be equity-settled or cash-settled.

Forms of Share-Based Compensation

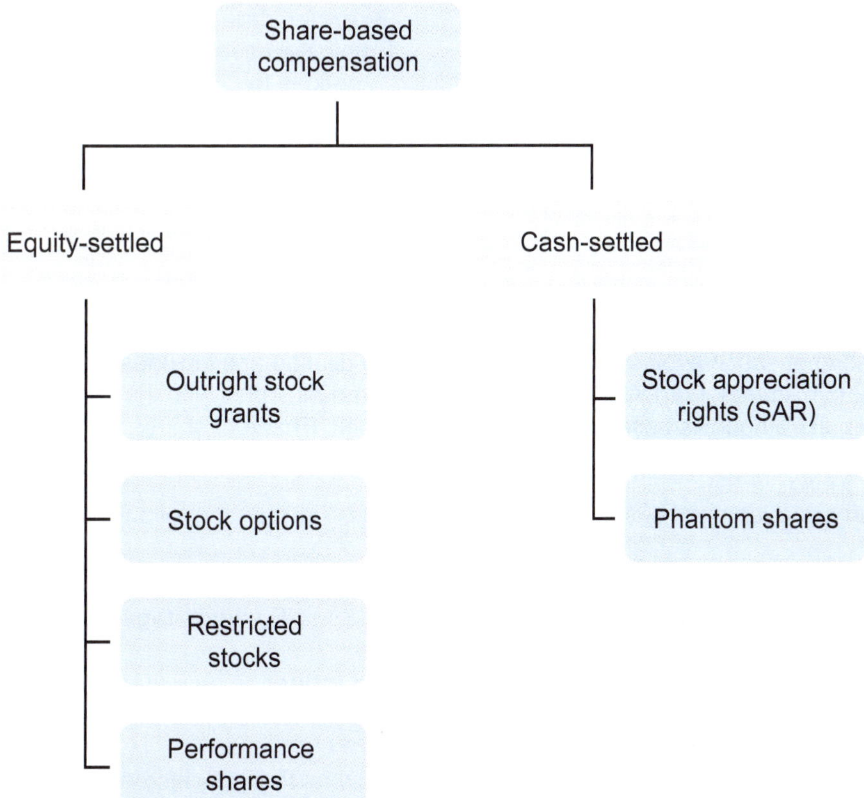

Common **equity-settled** share-based compensation includes the following:

- **Outright stock grants**
- **Stock options**

- **Restricted stocks**, which must be returned to the company if the employee does not meet the conditions (eg, if employee resigns or does not achieve certain performance goals)
- **Performance shares**, whose amount depends on the company meeting performance goals, like a determined level of net income or ROE

Both stock grants and stock options are designed to motivate and retain employees. By tying part of their compensation package to grants or options, the employee benefits when the company benefits. As the company's stock appreciates in value, so too does the employee's compensation.

For both stock grants and stock options, the company **records** the expense according to the **Fair Value (FV)** of the security granted. Stock grants are expensed according to their market value at the grant date, but stock options require the use of a **valuation model**, such as the binomial or Black-Scholes model (discussed later).

Employee stock options are regular call options wherein the employee can purchase a set amount of the company's stock at a predetermined price for a specific period of time. Stock options can be exercised at any point during the specified time frame (ie, there is no vesting period). The employee is not required to exercise the option and can simply let it lapse.

Stock grants vest over a period of time; they cannot be sold until the vesting date is reached. For example, an employee may receive a stock grant that vests ratably over a three-year period of time. This encourages the employee to remain with the company for at least that period of time in order to realize the full benefit of the grant.

Stock grants have several key dates to remember:

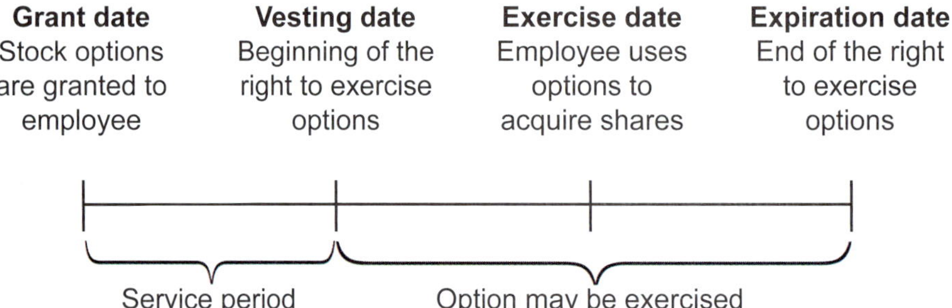

Cash-settled compensation avoids shareholder ownership dilution and includes stock appreciation rights (SAR) and phantom shares. For SAR, the compensation amount varies with the company's stock price. For phantom shares, the amount is based on a hypothetical stock. Phantom shares can be used by private or illiquid companies or by business units within a company.

Advantages and disadvantages of share-based compensation include the following:

Advantages	Disadvantages
• Employee **motivation** with the possibility of higher earnings	• **Limited influence** over firm value or stock price may weaken motivation
• Incentive to **align interests** of shareholders and employees	• Stock ownership may increase **risk aversion**, leading to less profitable projects • Asymmetrical payout of options may increase **risk appetite**, leading to riskier projects
• Potentially **no cash** disbursements required	• Equity-settled compensation can cause **dilution** of shares

Vesting

Compensation expense is recognized over the service period. If there is no vesting, then recognition occurs on the grant date. If the award is conditional (eg, percentage of market share), then recognition occurs over the estimated service period.

Vesting conditions are determined on the basis of the terms of the option.

If the option is *immediately exercisable*, it indicates that the compensation is for services already rendered.

- Therefore, on the date of grant, the total amount of compensation will be recognized as compensation expense

If the options are *not immediately exercisable*, the compensation will be recognized over the period from the grant date through the date on which the options become exercisable.

- When options become exercisable, they are said to be vested on such date
- The period of time is referred to as the service (ie, vesting) period

Common vesting schedules include the following:

- **Cliff vesting:** Benefits received at a specific point in time rather than gradually securing portions of the benefits over time. An example is options vesting all at once or 100% after two years of service
- **Graded vesting:** Benefits received gradually by a certain amount each year until fully vested. An example is options vesting 20% per year over five years until 100% vested

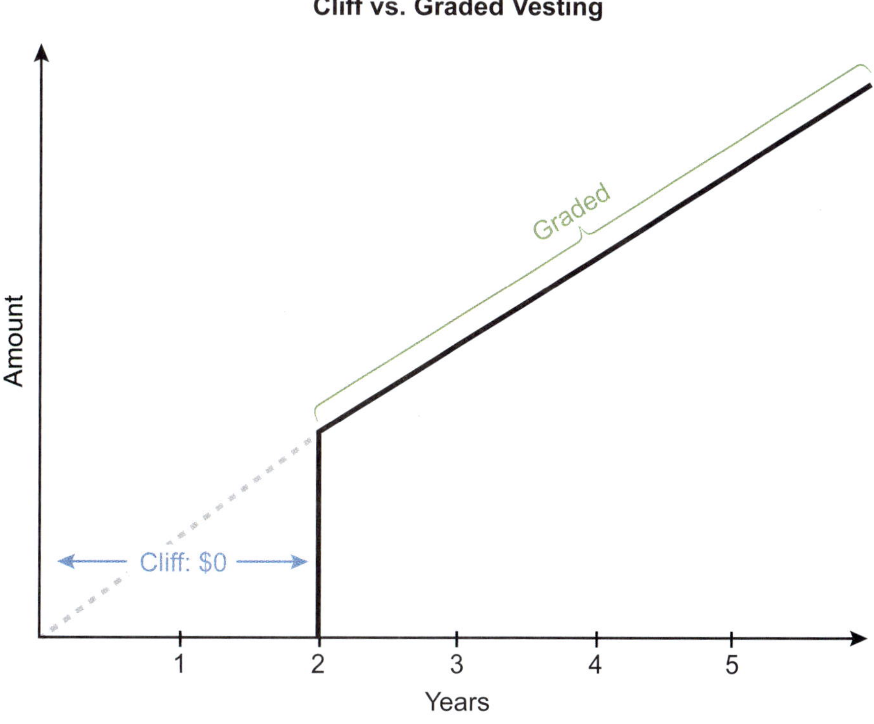

Assume that on January 1, Year 5, Siobhan Inc. granted its employees 300 shares of stock that vest at the end of two years. On the grant date (ie, 1/1/Year 5) the FV of each share was $12.

Determine the amount of compensation expense that Siobhan will recognize at the end of Year 5.

As a result of the grant, Siobhan will recognize a total of $3,600 (300 shares × $12) in compensation expense over the two-year vesting period. The company should recognize $1,800 ($3,600 / 2 years) at the end of Year 5 and Year 6.

Recognition of Compensation Expense for Restricted Stock Awards

Step 1: Determine fair value (FV) of stock awards on grant date
Step 2: Record compensation expense pro rata over vesting period

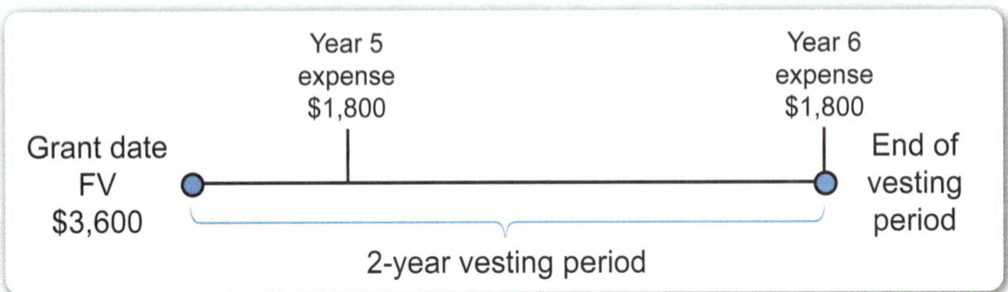

External Compensation Arrangements

Shares of stock can also be issued *externally* to vendors, lawyers, or others who provide goods or services to the entity. The expense is recognized in the period that goods/services are provided (to match the benefits from having use of those services).

The value of the goods/services (ie, the expense) is recorded using the stock's FV on the measurement date. For employment contracts, this is the contract's execution date. Because contract completion time can vary, the execution date provides a definite date on which the expense for services can be measured. The stock is recorded at par value, and APIC is recorded for any excess of FV over par.

Assume that Morgan was engaged to perform consulting services for Derrick. Morgan's compensation for these services consisted of 1,000 shares of $10 par value common stock. On the execution date of the employment contract, the stock had a FV of $45 per share. When Morgan's services were completed, the FV had increased to $50 per share. Derrick estimated that Morgan's services were worth $100,000 in cost savings to the company.

Determine the amount that APIC should increase by this transaction.

The expense is recorded on the execution date, when the FV of the shares was $45 per share, with the following journal entry:

Compensation Expense ($45 x 1,000 shares)	45,000	
Common stock (1,000 shares × $10 par)		10,000
APIC ($35 × 1,000 shares)		35,000

Noncompensatory Stock Plans

Stock awards that *do not involve recognition* of compensation expense are considered **noncompensatory plans**. As an example, companies may allow employees the opportunity to purchase shares of company stock at a discounted price through voluntary payroll withholdings (eg, **employee stock purchase plan**, or ESPP).

To be considered noncompensatory, certain criteria must be met.

- The plan satisfies either of the following conditions:
  - The terms are comparable, and no more favorable than terms offered to any shareholder holding the same class of stock that is the subject to the plan; **or**
  - Any purchase discount below fair value at issuance is no greater than the costs that would have been incurred in a public offering of the securities, which is assumed to be the case if the discount is 5% or less without further justification. Generally, a purchase discount greater than 5% that cannot be justified results in compensation expense for the entire amount of the discount.
- The plan is available to substantially all employees meeting limited employment requirements
- The plan provides no special option features other than the following:
  - Permitting employees a period not to exceed 31 days to enroll in the plan once the purchase price has been determined
  - The purchase price is determined based on the market price on the date of purchase
    - Employees may be permitted to cancel participation before the purchase date
    - Upon cancellation, employees would be refunded amounts previously paid

No entry is reported for the granting of noncompensatory options or upon their expiration, and the exercise of such options is recorded as a simple issuance of shares at the exercise price paid by the employee.

Assume that a company issues noncompensatory stock allowing all employees to purchase 1,000 shares in the company's $10 par value stock at a 5% discount. The stock has a fair value of $40 per share, but employees would only pay $38 ($40 × 95%) a share.

The journal entry to record the issuance of the stock is as follows:

Cash ($38 × 1,000 shares)	38,000	
Common stock (1,000 shares × $10 par)		10,000
APIC ($28 × 1,000 shares)		28,000

Compensatory Stock Plans

Any share-based compensation plan that does not meet all of the above criteria is **compensatory** (ie, the plan will result in the recognition of compensation expense). A share-based transaction with employees/nonemployees will always be *measured at the fair value* of the equity instruments issued.

The cost of goods obtained or services received from employees/nonemployees in a share-based transaction will generally be equal to either:

- The fair value of equity instruments issued as of the grant date; or
- The fair value of liabilities incurred.

If, however, the grantee pays (or is obligated to pay) an amount in exchange for the instruments granted, then that amount must be subtracted from the cost of goods obtained or services received.

Assume that Grantee pays $10 at the grant date for an option with a fair value of $100 received in exchange for services provided by Grantee. The cost of the services is $90.

Valuation Inputs and Models

If stock options are traded in active markets, the FV is readily determinable. In other cases, particularly when dealing with nonpublic entities, the FV of the stock options is not readily determinable. When the FV of stock options is not readily determinable, an **option pricing model** will be used.

A reliable model will take into account such factors as the exercise price, the expected life of the option, the current value of the underlying stock, and the volatility of the underlying stock's price, dividends, and the risk-free interest rate.

The FV of stock options is *affected by assumptions* used in the valuation model, including the risk-free rate. Therefore, changes to the assumptions can change the expense recorded for the options. A higher risk-free rate increases the required rate of return, which, all else equal, results in a greater FV for the options. A greater FV means a larger stock option expense and a smaller net income.

Stock option compensation plans: effects from changes in assumptions	
Increase in:	**Effect on fair value of stock options**
Volatility of stocks	Increase
Estimated life of options	Increase
Risk-free interest rate	Increase
Dividend yield of stocks	Decrease

Two common option pricing models include the binomial distribution model and the Black-Scholes model. The **Binomial** model does the following:

- Evaluates the fair value that the option can take in one period of time
- Allows the assumption that the option may be exercised at any time
- Includes only two possibilities for fair value: either positive (in the money) or zero (out of the money)

The **Black-Scholes-Merton** model assumes the following:

1. No dividends are paid out during the life of the option
2. Market movements are random and not predictable
3. There are no transaction costs in buying the option
4. The risk-free rate and volatility are known and are constant
5. Returns of the underlying (stock) are normally distributed
6. The option can only be exercised at expiration (European)

Determining Compensation Cost

Representative Task (Application): Use a given fair value measurement of a share-based payment arrangement classified as equity and prepare journal entries to recognize compensation cost.

When fair value (FV) can be determined with some degree of reliability, the entity will value stock options using the **binomial distribution method**. IF FV *cannot be determined* with any degree of reliability, then the entity will value stock options using the **intrinsic method**. Examples of both methods are provided next.

Binomial Distribution Model

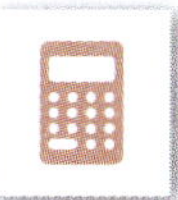

Assume that a company's stock is selling at $30 per share when it issues stock options to key employees. The option gives employees the right to purchase company stock at $30, exercisable for a period starting in two years and ending in five years.

The risk-free interest rate is 5%, the present value of $1 for two periods at 5% is 0.91, and the present value of $1 for five periods at 5% is 0.78.

The company estimates that 30% of the options will expire without being exercised, that 50% will be exercised in two years, at their earliest possible date, with the stock selling at an average $40 price, and that 20% of the options will be held as long as possible and exercised in five years, just before expiration, at an average $50 price.

The *gain to the employees* who exercise the options will be the amount by which the value of the stock received exceeds the exercise price on the date of exercise. The fair value of the option under the binomial distribution method is $7.67, calculated as follows:

Result	Stock price	Exercise price	Gain	PV factor	PV	%	Weighted value
Expire	–	–	–	–	–	30%	–
Exercise in two years	$40	$30	$10	0.91	$ 9.10	50%	$4.55
Exercise in five years	$50	$30	$20	0.78	$15.60	20%	$3.12
Fair value							**$7.67**

Under the **binomial distribution model**, if a company issued 100,000 options to employees that vest over three years with an expected turnover rate of 2% per year, the number of options expected to be exercisable will be calculated as follows:

- Year 1: 2% will terminate employment, resulting in forfeitures of 2% × 100,000 or 2,000, leaving 98,000 options.
- Year 2: An additional 2% will terminate employment, resulting in forfeitures of 2% of 98,000 or 1,960, leaving 96,040 options.
- Year 3: An additional 2% will terminate employment, resulting in forfeitures of 2% of 96,040 or 1,921, leaving **94,119** options that are estimated to become exercisable.

Total compensation expense will be 94,119 multiplied by the fair value per option and will be recognized over the three-year vesting period.

Assume that the 100,000 options, issued on January 1, Year 1, each give the employee the right to buy one share of the company's $10 par value common stock for $34, its current selling price. The option can be exercised after January 1, Year 4, if the employee remains in service with the company, and the option expires on December 31, Year 6.

The company is using the fair value method, and the value at January 1, Year 1, using the binomial distribution model is estimated at **$6** per option. Since the employee must remain for three years before the option can be exercised, the compensation expense is allocated over that time. At December 31, Year 1, 2, and 3, the following entry is recorded:

Compensation expense	188,238	
Deferred compensation		188,238

Assuming that the entity's actual turnover is the same as estimated turnover, the same entry will be made every year. If actual turnover differs, the amounts will be adjusted prospectively.

At the time the options are exercised the journal entry would be as follows:

Cash (94,119 × $34)	3,200,046	
APIC-Stock options outstanding (94,119 × $6)	564,714	
Common stock (94,119 × $10)		941,190
APIC Common stock (94,119 × $30)		2,823,570

Intrinsic Method

Under the intrinsic method, the options are measured on the basis of the difference between the exercise price and the fair value of the share on the measurement date.

- If the fair value of the stock is greater than the exercise price, compensation will be equal to the difference multiplied by the number of options
- If the fair value of the stock is equal to or lower than the exercise price, there will be no compensation

No entry is required at the time stock options are granted, although many entities will recognize deferred compensation for the total amount, the number of options multiplied by the fair value of an option, with a credit to APIC from stock options outstanding.

The entity must make an accounting policy election as to how to measure the total amount of compensation, which is based on the number of options that are expected to vest and become exercisable. The **two methods** that the entity will choose between will be:

- To estimate the number of options expected to be forfeited before becoming exercisable; or
- To account for forfeitures when they occur.

Nonpublic entities may make a one-time election to use the intrinsic method, which is an irrevocable election.

For the **intrinsic method**, assume the same facts and circumstances as used above in the binomial example. In addition, assume that actual forfeitures were 2,100 in Year 1, 2,250 in Year 2, and 1,950 in Year 3.

On the date of grant (January 1, Year 1), the entry is based on the total 100,000 options at $6:

Deferred compensation	600,000	
APIC-Stock options outstanding		600,000

To recognize compensation expense on December 31, Year 1, 1/3 of the total compensation, $600,000/3 or $200,000, is recognized:

Compensation expense	200,000	
Deferred compensation		200,000

Year 1 forfeitures are then recognized. With 2,100 options forfeited, at $6 each, total forfeitures will be $12,600, 1/3 of which relates to Year 1 ($4,200) with the remaining 2/3 ($8,400) relating to Years 2 and 3:

APIC-Stock options outstanding	12,600	
Compensation expense		4,200
Deferred compensation		8,400

This reduces deferred compensation to $600,000 − $200,000 − $8,400, or $391,600.

To recognize compensation expense at December 31, Year 2, 1/2 of the remaining deferred compensation, $391,600 / 2 or $195,800, is recognized:

Compensation expense	195,800	
Deferred compensation		195,800

The forfeitures for Year 2 are then recognized. With 2,250 options forfeited, at $6 each, total forfeitures will be $13,500, 2/3 of which relates to Years 1 and 2, with the remaining 1/3 relating to Year 3:

APIC-Stock options outstanding	13,500	
Compensation expense		9,000
Deferred compensation		4,500

This reduces deferred compensation to $391,600 − $195,800 − $4,500 or $191,300.

To recognize compensation expense at December 31, Year 3, the remaining deferred compensation, $191,300, is recognized:

Compensation expense	191,300	
Deferred compensation		191,300

The forfeitures for Year 3 are then recognized. With 1,950 options forfeited, at $6 each, total forfeitures will be $11,700, all of which will be recognized:

APIC-Stock options outstanding	11,700	
Compensation expense		11,700

Share-Based Payments Classified as Liabilities

Representative Task (Application): Use given fair value measurements of a share-based payment arrangement classified as a liability to prepare journal entries to recognize compensation cost.

Although stock options often provide a nice benefit to employees (or nonemployees), there are limiting factors that may make it difficult for grantees to exercise them.

- They must have the cash to pay the exercise price.
- They will be taxed in the period of exercise on the basis of the difference between the stock's market value and the option price.

To make certain that grantees have the opportunity to take advantage of a share-based compensation plan, entities will often use an alternative compensation method, such as **stock appreciation rights (SAR)**. A SAR works similarly to a stock option:

- It is granted to employees (or nonemployees), specifying an option price
- It is generally not immediately exercisable and vests over a period from the grant date to the exercise date at a future time
- It is generally exercisable for a certain length of time

A SAR may be exercised at any time from the vesting date to the expiration date. When it is exercised, rather than purchase a share of stock for the exercise price, the employee will be compensated for the difference between the market value of the share on the exercise date and the exercise price **(measurement date = settlement/exercise date)**.

For publicly held companies, compensation related to share-based plans classified as liabilities is the same as for those classified as equity in that both are recognized on the basis of FV. The measurement date, however, is the *date of settlement*.

Nonpublic entities may recognize share-based payment arrangements as liabilities either at FV or at intrinsic value and will make a policy decision as to which.

Since the share-based payment will be made in **cash**, rather than through the issuance of shares, the transaction results in the **recognition of a liability** instead of equity. Unlike stock option rights, where the total amount of compensation for the plan is determined on the grant date, compensation in a SAR plan is *measured in each reporting period*.

Assume that an entity has given its president 100 stock appreciation rights (SARS) on January 1, Year 1, exercisable on December 31, Year 3 and expiring on December 31, Year 5. The stock price on various dates was as follows:

January 1, Year 1	$20
December 31, Year 1	23
December 31, Year 2	26
December 31, Year 3	25
December 31, Year 4	27
December 31, Year 5	30

In Year 1, the stock increased to $23 (a $3 increase), indicating total compensation of $300 ($3 × 100 rights). Since only 1/3 of the vesting period has elapsed, only 1/3 of the compensation expense will be recognized:

Compensation expense	100	
Liability for appreciation rights		100

In Year 2, the stock increased to $26 (a total increase of $6). Total compensation was therefore $600 ($6 × 100 rights). Since 2/3 of the vesting period has elapsed, 2/3 of the compensation expense, $400, has been incurred. Compensation expense of $100 was previously recognized, requiring recognition of an additional $300 in the current period:

Compensation expense	300	
Liability for appreciation rights		300

At the end of Year 3, the stock price has declined to $25 per share, indicating total compensation expense of $500 ($5 × 100). Since $400 has been incurred in the preceding two periods, an additional $100 in compensation expense will be recognized in the current period.

Compensation expense	100	
Liability for appreciation rights		100

As of December 31, Year 4, the SARs have not been exercised. As a result, the liability is remeasured with any adjustment recognized in the current period as an increase or decrease to compensation expense. Since the price is now $27, total compensation is $700. This is compared to the $500 recognized to date requiring additional compensation expense of $200.

Compensation expense	200	
Liability for appreciation rights		200

Finally, on December 31, Year 5, when the SARs are nearing expiration, the president exercises them. At that point, the value of the stock is $30 per share, indicating total compensation of $10 per share or $1,000. The liability has a balance of $700, requiring the following entry:

Compensation expense	300	
Liability for appreciation rights	700	
Cash		1,000

Disclosures for Share-Based Payment Arrangements

The following disclosures are required for share-based payment arrangements:

- A description of the general terms under the arrangement that include requisite service period(s), vesting requirements, maximum term of options granted, number of shares authorized for grants of options, and the entity's policies for issuing shares upon option exercise (ie, new shares or treasury shares), estimating forfeitures
- The number and weighted-average exercise of prices of each group of options, including options that have service and performance-based conditions for exercise
- Weighted average grant-date fair value of options granted
- Description of methods used in measuring compensation cost
- A description and disclosure of the significant assumptions used to estimate fair value, including the following:
  - Discussion of the method or model used
  - Expected volatility and the methodology used for its estimate
  - Methodology used for expected dividends during contractual term
  - Risk-free rate(s) used in the methodology
  - Methodology used for estimating discounts for post-vesting restrictions
- Total compensation cost recognized for the year, including the cost for nonvested awards
- The number and weighted-average exercise prices for each group of share options:
  - Outstanding at the beginning and ending of the year
  - Exercisable at the end of the year
  - Granted, exercised, forfeited, and expired during the year
- The number and weighted-average grant-date fair value for share options:
  - Nonvested at the beginning and ending of the year
  - Granted, vested, and forfeited
- Overall disclosures generally required for each year that an income statement is presented

BAR 7
Research & Development Costs

BAR 7: Research & Development Costs

7.01 Research & Development Costs

Accounting for Research and Development Costs

Representative Task (Remembering & Understanding): Identify research and development costs and classify the costs as an expense in the financial statements (F/S).

Representative Task (Application): Calculate the research and development costs to be reported as an expense in the F/S.

Businesses acquire knowledge through research and development (R&D):

- Research is aimed at the discovery of new knowledge, with the hope that it will result in a new product or process or a significant improvement to an existing product or process
- Development is the conversion of that new knowledge into a plan or design for a new product or process

Matching R&D costs to benefits is difficult because much of the work may result in failure, or the benefits are of indefinite value and duration. As a result of this uncertainty, most R&D costs are expensed as incurred, in accordance with the conservative ideal of not understating expense.

Accounting for Research and Development (R&D) Costs

Expense immediately:
- Materials used
- Labor for design and development

Capitalize and expense over time:
- Equipment and facilities (long-lived assets)
- Purchased or developed intangibles

There are two exceptions to the "expense" rule:

- Equipment and/or buildings that have an **alternative future use**. These assets are capitalized and depreciated over the asset's useful life (not the R&D life)
- R&D activities performed for others under a **contract**. Here, the party that is paying for the R&D (the acquirer) will expense the cost as R&D

ASC 730 requires total R&D costs charged as an expense to be presented on the income statement in each period. The amount of R&D is required to be disclosed in the financial statements.

R&D Production Costs

Costs directly related to current revenue should not be treated as R&D costs. The following costs are considered part of cost of sales and are capitalized and recognized as appropriate:

- Research performed for others for a fee
- Periodic design changes to existing products
- Costs for setting up production of a commercially viable product

Research and development costs: *Expense as incurred* vs. **Production costs:** *Include in cost of inventory*

Research

- Discovering new knowledge
- Developing new products
- Improving existing products

Development

- Converting knowledge into plans
- Designing new products
- Testing new products

Production

- Making periodic design changes
- Incurring set-up costs for viable products
- Conducting market research for existing products

Assume that the following costs were incurred during the current year:

Design of tools, jigs, molds, and dies involving new technology	$125,000
Testing and construction of a prototype	160,000
Troubleshooting in connection with breakdowns during commercial production	100,000
Legal work in connection with a patent application	110,000

Determine the amount that should be reported as R&D expense in the income statement.

Costs related to existing commercial activities (eg, troubleshooting, legal work) are current-period expenses and therefore excluded from R&D. R&D expense is $285,000:

Design of tools, jigs, molds, and dies involving new technology	$125,000
Testing and construction of a prototype	160,000
Total R&D expense	**$285,000**

BAR 8
Business Combinations

BAR 8: Business Combinations

8.01 Business Combinations

Business vs. Asset Acquisition

Representative Task (Remembering & Understanding): Recall concepts associated with the accounting for business combinations (eg, business vs. asset acquisition, contingent consideration, measurement period adjustments).

To determine the proper recording requirements for an **acquisition**, the entity must first determine if it acquired a *business* or a *group of assets*. Making the proper determination is critical because of the impact this decision will have on future earnings. Examples include the following:

	Business acquisition	Asset acquisition
Purchase price allocation	Allocate to identifiable assets and liabilities assumed measured at FV	Allocate to noncurrent, nonfinancial assets at relative FV
Acquisition-related costs	Expensed as incurred	Capitalized as part of acquired assets and depreciated
In-process R&D costs	Capitalized as an indefinite-lived intangible asset	Expensed provided IPR&D has no alternative future use
Goodwill	Capitalized as an indefinite-lived intangible asset	No recognition
Bargain purchase (BP)	Recognized immediately in earnings	Allocate a BP amount only to certain nonfinancial assets using FV
Contingent consideration	Recorded at FV and adjusted to market value each period	Generally recorded only when probable and reasonably estimable
Assembled workforce	Recognized as part of goodwill	Recognized as a distinct intangible asset

ASC 805 defines a **business** as an integrated set of activities (set) capable of providing a return. A set must have an input and a substantive process that significantly contribute to the ability to create an output(s).

ASC 805 provides the following definitions for these key terms:

- **Input:** An economic resource that creates an output when at least one process is applied
- **Process:** A system, protocol, or rule that creates an output when applied to an input
- **Output:** The result of applying a process to an input that generates one of the following:
  - Goods/services to customers
  - Investment income
  - Other revenues

Screen Test

ASC 805 provides a framework or screen test to determine if an input and substantive process exist, as well as the criteria for sets without outputs. When determining if a set is capable of functioning as a business, the assessment should be based on a market participant view rather than the entity-level perspective.

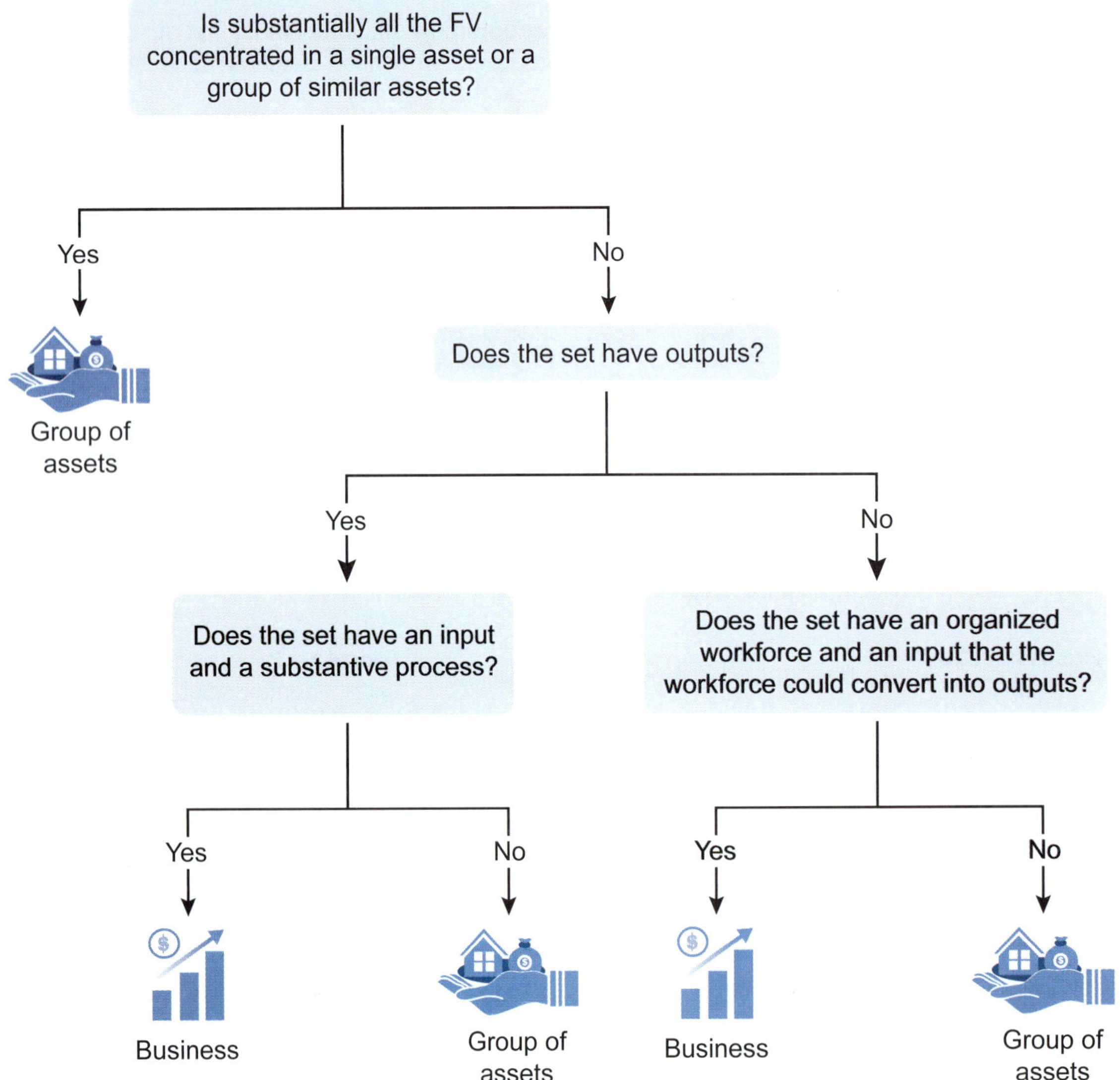

The screen test uses the term "similar assets." ASC 805 lists the following assets as examples of items that should not be considered similar (ie, cannot be grouped together as one):

- An intangible asset and a tangible asset
- A financial asset and a nonfinancial asset
- Items from different classes of financial assets (eg, receivables and held-to-maturity investments)
- Items from different classes of tangible assets (inventory versus property)
- Items from different class of intangible assets (goodwill versus patents)
- Assets that are in the same major asset class but have significantly different risk characteristics (eg, AAA bonds versus CCC bonds)

If the acquisition *includes outputs*, then the set must meet at least one of the following conditions to qualify as a *business*:

- Employees (ie, workforce) can perform an acquired process critical to converting acquired inputs into outputs
- Acquired contract provides access to the workforce
- Acquired process significantly contributes to the ability to produce outputs, and the process cannot be replaced without significant cost, effort, or delay
- Acquired process significantly contributes to the ability to produce outputs, and the process is unique or scarce

If the acquisition *does not include* outputs, the acquired set must include *both* of the following criteria to qualify as a business:

- Includes the organized workforce listed in the first condition above
- Includes an input that the workforce can convert into outputs

If an acquisition *fails to qualify* as a business acquisition, then the transaction is treated as an **asset acquisition**. Asset acquisitions are accounted for using a cost accumulation model, according to ASC 805-50. As with general asset acquisitions, transaction costs are allocated to the acquired assets on a relative fair value basis. There is no goodwill or bargain purchase option recognition.

Contingent Consideration

Contingent consideration (also known as an earn-out) is an obligation on the part of the acquirer to potentially transfer additional equity or assets **in the future** to the acquiree, assuming that certain criteria are met. The terms would be included in the acquisition agreement.

Because contingent consideration is an unknown future amount, it is recognized at FV as of the *acquisition date* estimated amount and is included in the acquisition consideration. The actual contingent payments will occur if the performance targets are met; therefore, total consideration represents the FV of acquirer shares plus the FV of contingent consideration.

Venus Co. issues 60,000 shares of $10 par value common stock to acquire 100% of Zeus, Inc. The market value of Venus's common stock is $20, for a total fair value of $1,200,000. On the acquisition date, the fair value and book value of Zeus's net assets was $1,500,000.

Venus also agreed to pay an additional $400,000 at year end if Zeus's customer base increased by 20%. On the date of acquisition, Venus estimated that there was a 75% probability that Zeus would achieve the growth target.

Determine the amount of contingent liability and prepare the journal entry that should be recorded by Venus.

The contingent liability is the total amount of the required increase times the probability of achieving that increase, or $300,000 ($400,000 × 75%).

Investment in Zeus, Inc.	1,500,000	
Estimated liability for contingent consideration		300,000
Common stock (60,000 × $10)		600,000
APIC ($1,200,000 − $600,000 common stock)		600,000

Measurement Period Adjustments

The acquirer may believe that the fair values of some of the individual identifiable assets acquired and liabilities assumed could not be reliably determined on a timely basis. If the acquirer is required to prepare consolidated F/S *prior* to being able to obtain a more accurate measurement, the following procedures will be applied:

- The asset or liability for which a reliable fair value has not been determined will be recorded at management's best estimate based on information that is available, with that amount referred to as a **provisional value**
- As a result of using the provisional values, the amount reported as goodwill may be over- or understated, depending on the overstatement or understatement of the assets and liabilities recorded at their provisional amounts
- Depreciation, amortization, interest income or expense, and other revenue and expense items that are affected by those values are recognized as if the provisional amounts are the actual fair values, and the consolidated F/S are prepared accordingly

The entity then has *one year* from the date of acquisition, referred to as the **measurement period**, to obtain a more reliable measurement. If management is unable to do so, the provisional amounts are accepted as the actual amounts, and the items are accounted for as comparable items would be. Neither the items nor their I/S effects will be adjusted.

If, on the other hand, management can obtain a more reliable measurement, the following procedures will be followed:

- The assets or liabilities will be adjusted to the amounts that would have been their carrying values as of the balance sheet date if they had originally been recorded at their more reliable amounts
- Measurement period adjustments are offset against goodwill or bargain gain

- The I/S effects, including such items as depreciation and amortization expense, interest net of amortization of discount or premium, and other items that would have been affected by the change in carrying value will be recalculated as if the appropriate amount had been used on the date of acquisition
- Current period amounts are adjusted to reflect the correct amounts that would have been reported if the assets and liabilities had been originally recorded at the appropriate amount
- New assets and liabilities that existed (but had not been identified) may be recognized

Jill Corp. acquired 100% of Jack, Inc. on June 1, Year 4, for $6,000. Provisional fair values were assessed on Jack's assets and liabilities at that time. Final acquisition values were identified at year end, November 30, Year 4.

	Book value	Provisional fair value	Final fair value
Current assets	2,000	2,000	2,000
Long-term assets	5,000	4,000	3,500
Current liabilities	1,500	1,500	1,400
Long-term liabilities	500	500	500
Common stock	1,000		
Additional paid-in capital	3,000		
Retained earnings	1,000		
Totals		**4,000**	**3,600**

Determine the following:

Goodwill on June 1, Year 4, based on the provisional fair values

Goodwill = $2,000 ($6,000 purchase price − $4,000 provisional fair value)

Goodwill adjustment required on November 30, Year 4, for final fair values

Goodwill = $2,400 ($6,000 purchase price − $3,600 provisional fair value)

Goodwill increased by $400

Journalize the consolidating work paper eliminating journal entry for provisional values and to record the final fair values

Common stock	1,000	
Additional paid-in capital	3,000	
Retained earnings	1,000	
Goodwill	2,000	
Investment in subsidiary		6,000
Long-term asset adjustment		1,000

Goodwill (net/plug amount)	400	
Current liabilities	100	
Long-term assets		500

Consideration Transferred

Representative Task (Application): Calculate the consideration transferred in a business combination.

Representative Task (Application): Prepare journal entries to record the identifiable net assets acquired in a business combination that results in the recognition of goodwill or a bargain purchase gain.

The acquirer will recognize **consideration given**, if any, at its **fair value**.

- Any assets transferred are included at fair value, with any difference between fair value and book value treated as a gain or loss on disposal
- Stock issued is recognized at fair value with a credit to common stock for any par or stated value and another credit to additional paid-in capital for the difference

West, Inc. acquired 60% of East Co.'s outstanding common stock. West paid $800,000 to acquire the stock. West plans to relocate East's company headquarters, which is expected to cost between $100,000 and $300,000. The present value of the probability adjusted relocation cost is $240,000.

Determine the amount of West's acquisition consideration to acquire East.

West's **acquisition consideration** is the *fair value* of the consideration given in exchange for a controlling financial interest in East, or **$800,000**. The cost of relocating East initiated by the acquirer may be partially or fully capitalized when incurred by the acquirer but is not included as part of the acquisition consideration.

Most **costs incurred** in relation to the transaction will be **recognized as expense** when incurred. This includes the following:

- Any general expenses incurred
- Costs directly related to the acquisition, such as attorney or appraiser fees
- Indirect costs, such as the costs of printing new stationery or developing new training manuals, finder fees

One **exception** to the rules regarding expensing items is the treatment for the cost of issuing and registering debt and/or equity securities issued in conjunction with the business combination.

Acquisition-related costs of the acquirer	
Type of cost	**Treatment**
Cost of registering and issuing stock	Reduce additional paid-in capital
Cost of issuing debt securities (bonds)	Record as a contra-liability and amortize issue costs
All other acquisition fees (eg, appraisals, legal fees)	Expense in current period

Dayton Co. issues 300,000 shares of $5 par value common stock to acquire Columbus Co. in a business combination accounted for under the acquisition method. The market value of Dayton's common stock is $10. Legal and consulting fees incurred in relationship to the purchase are $110,000. Registration and issuance costs for the common stock are $40,000.

Determine the amount that should be recorded in Dayton's **additional paid-in capital** account for this business combination.

Dayton records its investment in Columbus at the market value of the stock, $3,000,000 ($10 × 300,000 shares). Because the total par value of the shares is $1,500,000 ($5 × 300,000), APIC is also initially $1,500,000 [($10 − $5) × 300,000]. The $40,000 stock registration and issue costs reduce the APIC, resulting in a net APIC of $1,460,000 ($1,500,000 − $40,000). (APIC adjustments can be made as one net amount or shown separately as illustrated below.) The legal and consulting fees are expensed.

Investment in Columbus Co	3,000,000	
APIC Common stock	40,000	
Expenses	110,000	
Common stock (C/S)(par)		1,500,000
APIC-C/S		1,500,000
Cash ($40,000 + $110,000)		150,000

Considering all the factors involved in recognizing a business combination and all the different measurements, it would be very unusual for the acquirer's entry recognizing the combination to balance.

If the amount necessary to balance the entry is a debit, it will be recognized as goodwill. Goodwill is an intangible asset resulting from the acquisition of a business. It represents the asset's fair value in excess of the identifiable net assets acquired less liabilities. The value is derived from the acquired business's unidentifiable benefits (eg, reputation, customer loyalty, brand identity).

An item must be capable of being objectively measured in monetary terms in order to be recognized; therefore, **goodwill** is **only recorded** on the balance sheet when a **purchase** of another entity occurs. A company may not capitalize the internal costs of developing or maintaining goodwill.

If the amount necessary to balance the entry is a credit, it will be recognized as gain on bargain purchase.

Business Combinations: Measuring Goodwill or Gain From a Bargain Purchase

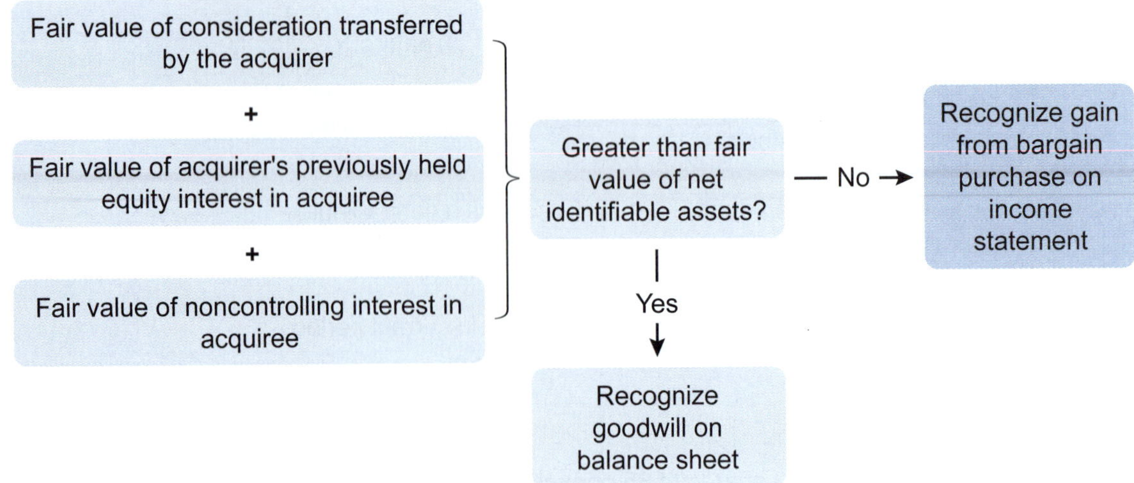

Example #1: Goodwill Calculation

On February 4, Year 6, Window, Inc. paid $860,000 for all the issued and outstanding common stock of Door Corp. On that date, the carrying amounts of Door's recorded assets and liabilities were $800,000 and $180,000, respectively. Door's recorded assets and liabilities had fair values of $840,000 and $140,000, respectively.

Determine the amount of goodwill that Window should report as of February 28, Year 6:

Goodwill is the difference between the amount of consideration that Window paid and the fair value of Door's net assets, as follows:

Purchase price	$860,000
Less:	
Assets (FV)	(840,000)
Liabilities (FV)	140,000
Goodwill	**$160,000**

Initial Value of Goodwill

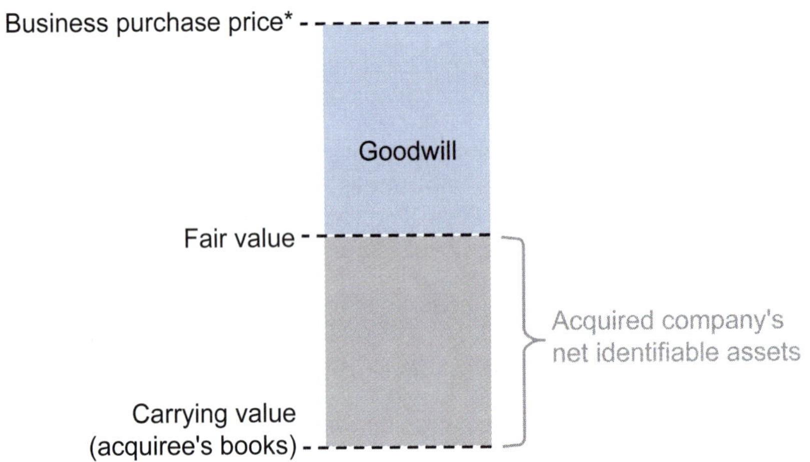

Goodwill is recognized only when business combination or purchase occurs.

Example #2: Recording Goodwill

Assume that P Co. acquired all (100%) of the stock of S Co. in an acquisition on December 31, Year 1, for a payment of $900,000 cash. At the time, the book value of S was $600,000, and all of the assets and liabilities had fair values equal to their book values, with the exception of equipment with a remaining life of five years and a fair value $100,000 higher than book value.

The accounts of the two companies at December 31, Year 1, are presented in a worksheet, along with the combining entry.

Everything acquired @ FMV of stock given or cash paid:

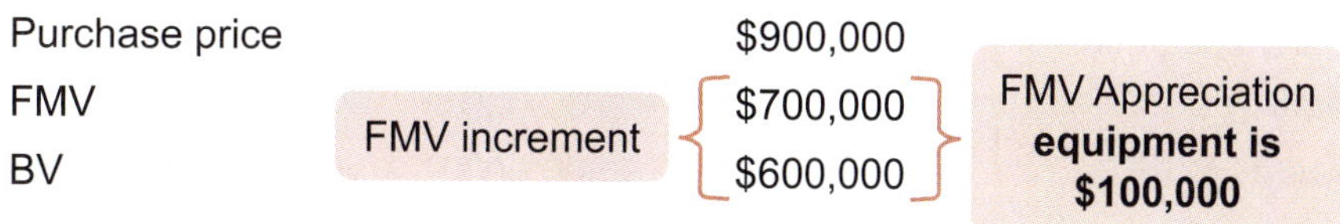

Purchase price	$900,000
FMV	$700,000
BV	$600,000

Accounts	P Co.	S Co.	Debits	Credits	Consolidated
(in thousands)					
Cash	100	100			200
Equipment	8,000	500	100		8,600
Investment in S	900			900	–
Goodwill			200		200
$1 C/S	(1,000)	(100)	100		(1,000)
APIC	(3,000)	(100)	100		(3,000)
R/E	(5,000)	(400)	400		(5,000)

To acquire investment (in books):

	Debit	Credit
Investment	900,000	
Cash		900,000

To consolidate (on worksheet):

	Debit	Credit
C/S	100,000	
APIC	100,000	
R/E	400,000	
Equipment	100,000	
Goodwill	200,000	
Investment		900,000

Goodwill is the balancing entry in the above: it represents the excess of the $900,000 investment over the $700,000 fair value of the net identifiable assets ($600,000 book value + $100,000 excess of fair value over book value of equipment = $700,000).

Example #3: Calculating and Recording Bargain Gain

Assume that P Co. acquired all (100%) of the stock of S Co. in an acquisition on December 31, Year 3, for $500,000 cash. At the time, the book value of S was $600,000, and all of the assets and liabilities had fair values equal to their book values, with the exception of equipment with a remaining life of five years and a fair value $100,000 higher than book value.

The accounts of the two companies at December 31, Year 3, are presented in a worksheet, along with the combining entry.

Everything acquired @ **FMV** of stock given or cash paid:

Purchase price		$500,000
FMV	FMV increment	$700,000
BV		$600,000

FMV Appreciation **equipment is $100**

Accounts	P Co.	S Co.	Debits	Credits	Consolidated
(in thousands)					
Cash	100	100			200
Equipment	8,000	500	100		8,600
Investment in S	(900)			900	–
Goodwill				200	(200)
$1 C/S	(1,000)	(100)	100		(1,000)
APIC	(3,000)	(100)	100		(3,000)
R/E	(5,000)	(400)	400		(5,000)

To acquire investment (in books):

Investment	500,000	
Cash		500,000

To consolidate (on worksheet):

C/S	100,000	
APIC	100,000	
R/E	400,000	
Equipment	100,000	
Bargain gain		200,000
Investment		500,000

Bargain gain is the balancing amount: it represents the excess of $700,000 fair value ($600,000 + $100,000) over the $500,000 purchase price.

Example #4: Calculating Bargain Gain with Contingent Consideration

Damon Co. purchased 100% of the outstanding common stock of Smith Co. in an acquisition by issuing 20,000 shares of its $1 par common stock that had a fair value of $10 per share and providing contingent consideration that had a fair value of $10,000 on the acquisition date. Damon also incurred $15,000 in acquisition costs. On the acquisition date, Smith had assets with a book value of $200,000, a fair value of $350,000, and related liabilities with a book and fair value of $70,000.

Determine the amount of **bargain gain** that Damon should report.

In this scenario, $200,000 FV of acquirer shares (20,000 shares × $10 FV per share) + $10,000 FV of contingent consideration = $210,000 total consideration. Acquisition-related costs of $15,000 are expensed. The calculation of the bargain gain is as follows:

FV of net identifiable assets	($350,000 assets - $70,000 liabilities)	$280,000
FV of acquirer shares	(20,000 shares × $10)	200,000
FV of contingent consideration	Given	10,000
Bargain gain		**$ 70,000**

Noncontrolling Interest

Representative Task (Application): Prepare journal entries to record the identifiable net assets acquired in a business combination that includes a noncontrolling interest.

The acquirer also recognizes any **noncontrolling interest** (NCI) in the acquiree at fair value. An NCI is the minority interest where the nonparent shareholders own **less than 50%** of the outstanding stock (ie, the parent **owns more than 50%** or the controlling interest).

For example, assume that a parent owns 80% of a subsidiary. The consolidated balance sheet would be as follows:

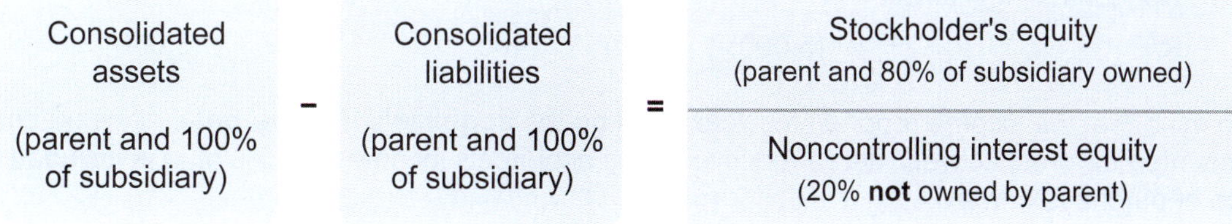

NCI is initially calculated by multiplying the NCI ownership percentage by the total FV of the subsidiary. At year end, the NCI is determined using the equity method.

Assume that P Co. acquired 90% (10% noncontrolling interest) of the stock of S Co. in an acquisition on December 31, Year 1, for a payment of $900,000 cash. At the date of acquisition, S had 100,000 shares of stock outstanding with an FMV of $8 per share.

The book value of S was $600,000, and all of the assets and liabilities had fair values equal to their book values, with the exception of equipment with a remaining life of five years and a fair value $100,000 higher than book value.

The accounts of the two companies at December 31, Year 1, are presented in a worksheet, along with the combining entry.

The consolidating worksheet would appear as follows:

Purchase price	$900,000	
FMV	$700,000	FMV increment
BV	$600,000	

The FMV of the **noncontrolling interest** at the date of acquisition is 100,000 × $8 = $800,000 × 10% = **$80,000**.

The calculation of goodwill or gain is as follows:

Fair value of consideration transferred (cost to the acquirer)	$900,000
+ Fair value of noncontrolling interest	80,000
(−) Fair value of net identifiable assets of acquiree	(700,000)
Goodwill	$280,000

Accounts	P Co.	S Co.	Debits	Credits	Consolidated
(in thousands)					
Cash	100	100			200
Equipment	8,000	500	100		8,600
Investment in S	900			900	–
Goodwill			280		280
$1 C/S	(1,000)	(100)	100		(1,000)
APIC	(3,000)	(100)	100		(3,000)
Noncontrolling interest				80	(80)
R/E	(5,000)	(400)	400		(5,000)

Keep in mind that the income reported for Year 1 will be the **acquirer's income only**, since purchases are accounted for prospectively, not retroactively. The acquiree's income (or 90% of it) is included from the date of purchase onward.

To record 90% acquisition:

Investment	900,000	
Cash		900,000

To consolidate (on worksheet):

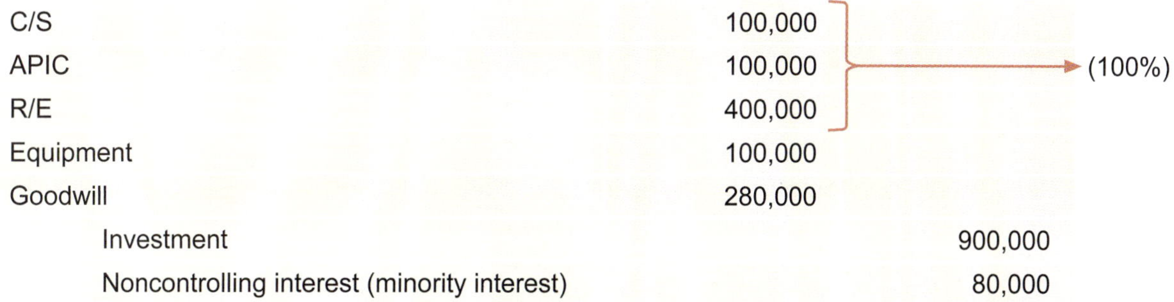

Account	Debit	Credit	
C/S	100,000		(100%)
APIC	100,000		(100%)
R/E	400,000		(100%)
Equipment	100,000		
Goodwill	280,000		
Investment		900,000	
Noncontrolling interest (minority interest)		80,000	

On a consolidated balance sheet, all assets and liabilities of the parent and subsidiary are combined, to show the resources under the parent company's control (ie, the resources to which it has access). However, the NCI is reported as part of *stockholders' equity*, so financial statement users understand that ownership of the subsidiary is less than 100%.

Noncontrolling Interest Disclosure

Stockholders' equity	
Contributed (paid-in) capital	
Preferred stock	$XXX
Common stock	XXX
Additional paid-in capital (from various sources)	XXX
Total paid-in capital	XXX
Noncontrolling interest in consolidated subsidiaries (if consolidated financial statements)	XXX
Retained earnings (appropriated and unappropriated)	$XXX
Accumulated other comprehensive income (loss)	XXX
Less: Treasury stock (cost method)	(XXX)
Total stockholders' equity	XXX

The NCI amount is periodically adjusted for its share of net income and other comprehensive income:

- Net income will include all revenues, expenses, gains, and losses of the parent and all subsidiaries, after adjusting for intercompany items
- Other comprehensive income will include all amounts recognized by the parent and all subsidiaries, after eliminating intercompany items

BAR 9
Consolidated Financial Statements

BAR 9: Consolidated Financial Statements

9.01 Consolidated Financial Statements

Consolidations

Representative Task (Remembering & Understanding): Recall basic consolidation concepts and terms (eg, controlling interest, noncontrolling interest, primary beneficiary, variable interest entity).

Consolidations (a type of business combination) are required whenever the acquirer (parent) acquires a **controlling financial interest** (ie, greater than 50%) in the acquiree (subsidiary). The assets and liabilities of the subsidiary are purchased at FV on the acquisition date.

The **economic entity concept** provided in ASC 805 is used for consolidation purposes. This represents a conceptually more consistent method of consolidation and improves financial reporting. Consolidated financial statements (F/S) present the financial position and operating results of entities under common control as if they were a single economic entity.

Transactions between a parent and subsidiary (eg, buying inventory from a subsidiary) are referred to as **intercompany transactions**. These items can distort the financial statements because the transactions are not at arm's length (ie, with a related party). As a result, related accounts (eg, accounts receivable, inventory) are grouped together (ie, consolidated) as one account, and intercompany transactions are eliminated.

The method will:

- Better reflect the investment made by the acquirer
- Enhance financial statement comparability between companies
- Provide more complete and relevant financial information.

Consolidated Group

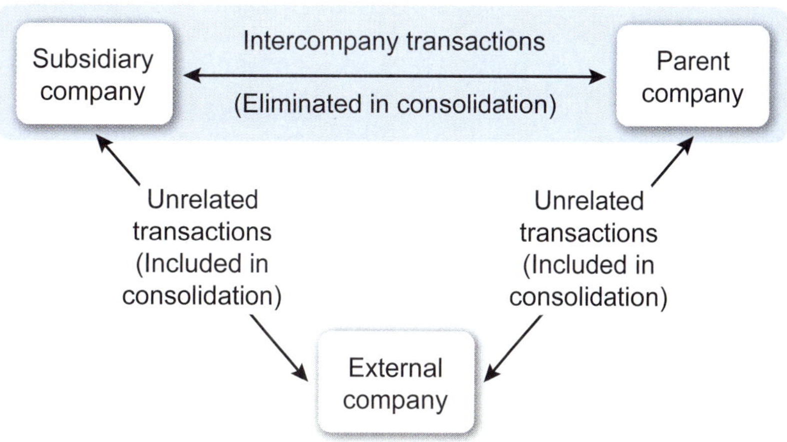

Controlling interest

Ownership interest in an entity determines the amount of *effective* control the investor has on the entity's decisions and financial benefits. A majority interest in an entity means that the investor (ie, the acquirer) has greater than 50% of the outstanding voting shares. As this is considered a "majority interest" (ie, controlling financial interest), **consolidated financial reporting** is required.

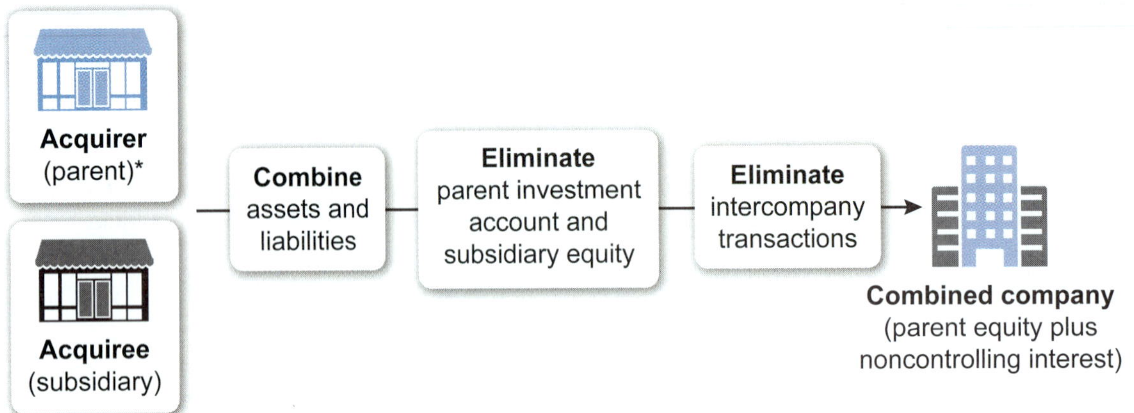

**Includes equity issued to purchase acquiree*

The ownership interest can be either *direct* or *indirect*. Direct ownership is when the voting shares of an entity are held directly by a person or another entity. Indirect ownership includes ownership held through another company.

For example, assume Lisa has a 25% direct ownership interest in Company A and a 28% indirect ownership interest in Company A through her ownership in Company B (40% of Company B × 70% of Company B's ownership of Company A). Her total ownership (53%) represents a majority interest in Company A.

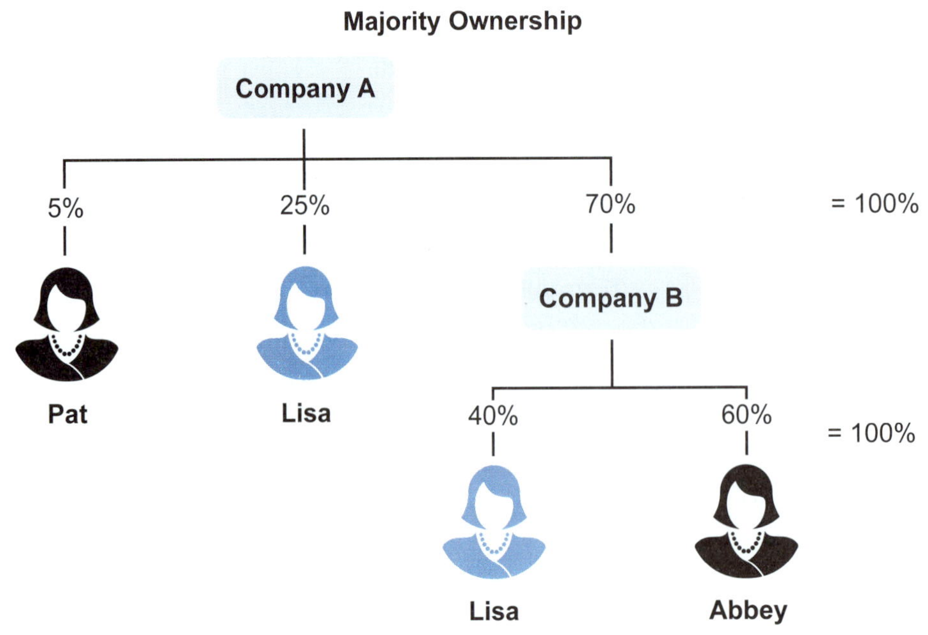

Noncontrolling Interest

When an entity (ie, an acquirer) purchases *more than 50%* of another entity, that acquiring company is said to have a **controlling interest**. The remaining part of the acquired entity, which is equal to or less than 50%, is said to be the **noncontrolling** interest (NCI).

On a consolidated balance sheet, all assets and liabilities of the parent and subsidiary are combined to show the resources under the parent company's control (ie, the resources to which it has access), even the portion retained by any NCI. The *noncontrolling interest* is reported as part of **stockholders' equity**, so financial statement users understand that ownership of the subsidiary is less than 100%.

Consolidated Balance Sheet

Assume parent owns 80% of subsidiary.

Consolidated assets (parent and 100% of subsidiary)	–	Consolidated liabilities (parent and 100% of subsidiary)	=	Stockholder's equity (parent and 80% of subsidiary owned) ――― Noncontrolling interest equity (20% **not** owned by parent)

NCI is initially recorded based on the FV of the subsidiary on the date of acquisition. The amount reported as the NCI is periodically adjusted for its share of net income and other comprehensive income:

- Net income will include all revenues, expenses, gains, and losses of the parent and all subsidiaries, after adjusting for intercompany items
    - An appropriate amount will be allocated to the NCI on the income statement (I/S) and will be closed to the noncontrolling interest account
    - The remainder will be allocated to the parent and will be closed to retained earnings
- Other comprehensive income will include all amounts recognized by the parent and all subsidiaries, after eliminating intercompany items
    - An appropriate amount will be allocated to the NCI on the statement of comprehensive income and will be closed to the noncontrolling interest account
    - The remainder will be allocated to the parent and will be closed to accumulated other comprehensive income

If the subsidiary issues additional stock to outside investors, NCI ownership increases and parent ownership decreases.

Assume that Sage Co. has 20,000 shares outstanding, with total equity of $500,000. Thyme, Inc. owns 80% (ie, 16,000 shares) of Sage. The remaining 20% ownership of Sage (ie, 4,000 shares) represents the NCI, with a total value of $100,000 (20% × $500,000 equity).

Sage issued 5,000 additional shares to outside investors for $200,000, increasing total equity to $700,000 ($500,000 + $200,000) and total shares to 25,000 (20,000 + 5,000). All 5,000 new shares were allocated to NCI, *increasing* NCI to 36% (9,000 / 25,000 shares) and *decreasing* Thyme's ownership percentage from 80% to 64% (16,000 / 25,000).

Variable Interest Entity (VIE) and Primary Beneficiary

A **variable interest entity (VIE)** exists when an investor has a *controlling* financial interest in another entity, but the amount of control in the VIE is **disproportionate** to its ownership. A VIE relationship often occurs as a result of one of two common circumstances:

- An entity forms a separate entity for the purpose of holding certain assets or incurring liabilities. This may be done to keep items off the balance sheet, referred to as "off balance sheet financing." It also may be done for legitimate business reasons, such as setting up a separate entity to acquire assets to be leased to the reporting entity while passing tax benefits to the owners
- An entity enters a relationship with another that occupies many of the other entity's resources and becomes the focus of its operations, making the other entity essentially a division of the reporting entity

US GAAP Criteria For Variable Interest Entity (VIE)

- Equity is insufficient to finance activities
- Equity investors lack:
  - Ability to make decisions
  - Obligation to absorb losses
  - Right to receive returns

A VIE's **primary beneficiary** has the power and authority to direct the VIE's operations and to participate in its gains and losses to a significant extent. If a reporting entity determines that it is the primary beneficiary of a VIE, it is required to prepare consolidated F/S, treating the VIE as a subsidiary.

- If the entities are **not related**, the creation of the relationship will be treated as comparable to an acquisition, and the same principles for recognizing the combination and for preparing consolidated F/S will be followed
  - Assets and liabilities of the VIE are reported at their fair values
  - The VIE's equity accounts are eliminated
  - The noncontrolling interest may represent 100% of the equity of the VIE
- If the entities are **related**, the combination and subsequent consolidated F/S will be prepared using book values

Variable Interest Entities (VIE)

Does entity have sufficient equity to sustain normal operations?
- No → Entity is a VIE
- Yes → Is its value independent of another entity's assets?
  - No → Entity is a VIE
  - Yes → Do investors participate in entity gains and losses?
    - No → Entity is a VIE
    - Yes → Entity is NOT a VIE

Entity is a VIE → Is investor the primary beneficiary to VIE?
- Yes → Consolidate
- No → Do not consolidate

Foreign Currency

Representative Task (Remembering & Understanding): Recall the basic functional currency concepts including the indicators to be considered when determining a subsidiary's functional currency.

Representative Task (Application): Calculate foreign currency translation adjustments (local currency to functional currency and/or functional currency to reporting currency) to prepare consolidated financial statements.

Overview of Foreign Currency

There are several ways in which an entity may be involved in foreign operations (ASC 830):

- They may enter into **foreign currency transactions** with an entity in a foreign country that involves a receipt or payment in a foreign currency. The entity must determine how that transaction will be reported in U.S. dollars
- An entity may have **financial instruments** denominated in a foreign currency (eg, a receivable or payable), meaning it will be settled by the receipt or payment of some amount of foreign currency. The amount of the receivable or payable must be converted into U.S. dollars for inclusion on the reporting entity's financial statements (F/S)
- An entity may get involved in foreign currency **exchange transactions**, such as forward exchange contracts. These transactions may be entered into for a variety of reasons but, regardless, often result in a net amount being paid or received to settle the contract, representing a liability or asset
- An entity may have a **foreign investee** (ie, a foreign division or subsidiary) that maintains books and records in a foreign currency but will be included in the reporting entity's consolidated F/S. The F/S must be converted into U.S. dollars to include them

Foreign Currency Transactions

When an entity enters into a transaction that will be settled through the payment or receipt of foreign currency, it is initially recognized in the functional currency of the entity. An entity's functional currency is the currency that has the greatest economic impact on the entity's financial performance.

For example, a company based in the northern part of Washington State may obtain all its raw materials from Canadian suppliers, assemble its product in the United States, and then sell all its output to Canadian customers. Even though the company might maintain its books and records in U.S. dollars, its functional currency would be the Canadian dollar.

Various factors will be considered when identifying the functional currency. Some may be more important than others, depending on the circumstances, and not all will necessarily apply. These factors may include which currency has the greatest influence on the following:

- Cash flows
- Sales prices
- Demand for the company's products or services
- Expense
- Financing and financing costs
- Intra-entity arrangements

In general, an entity's functional currency is its local currency. Usually, it is also the currency in which it maintains its books and records, but that is not always the case.

- When a transaction occurs in some currency other than the functional currency, it is remeasured as if the transaction had originally occurred at the functional currency
- When the functional currency is not the same as the currency used for reporting, amounts are translated from the functional currency into the reporting currency

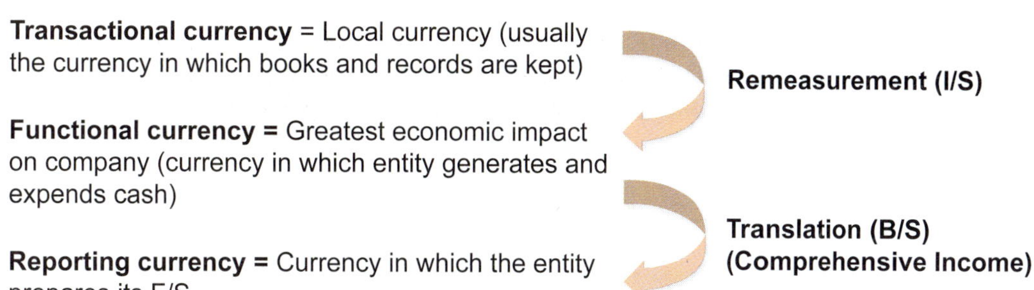

If the foreign subsidiary is *included* in the company's consolidated financial statements (F/S), it must *convert* the subsidiary's F/S from the local currency (ie, the currency in which the subsidiary's books and records are maintained) into the parent's reporting currency.

Remeasure vs. Translate

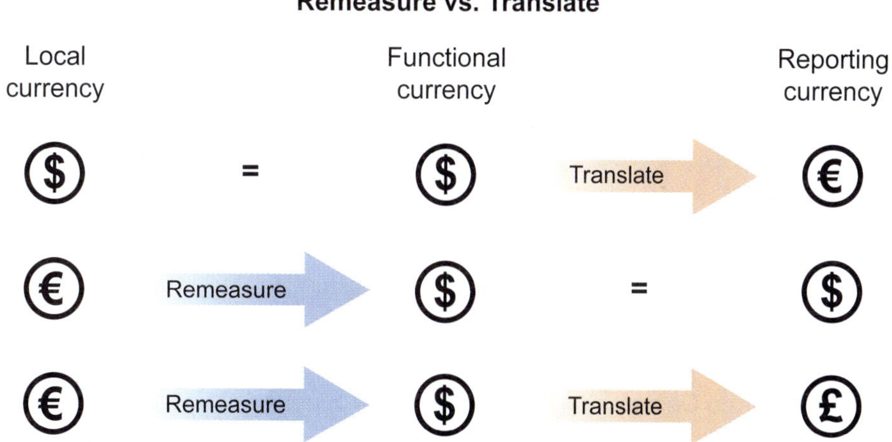

Remeasurement

When an entity enters into a transaction that will be settled in a foreign currency, it is initially recorded in the entity's functional currency using the transaction date exchange rate (ie, spot rate). If the transaction includes a nonmonetary asset (eg, equipment), it is remeasured at the historical exchange rate on each balance sheet date so that the carrying value does not change. This reporting reflects the asset's cost as if it had been purchased in the entity's functional currency.

Tally Co., a U.S. company, acquired equipment from a European manufacturer on November 2, Year 2, for €200,000. Payment was due in euros on February 2, Year 3. The spot rates to purchase one euro were as follows:

November 2, Year 2	$1.50
December 31, Year 2	1.35
February 2, Year 3	1.45

Determine the cost of the equipment and how much foreign currency transaction gain or loss Tally will recognize in Year 3.

In this scenario, Tally recorded the equipment purchase in its functional currency, U.S. dollars (USD), using the spot rate.

Purchase Equipment: €200,000 × $1.50(11/2 Yr 2 Spot Rate)		
Equipment (historical exchange rate)	300,000	
A/P		300,000

The spot rate used decreased from November 2 to December 31; therefore, a foreign currency gain is recorded in Year 2.

Remeasure A/P: ($1.50 − $1.35) × €200,000		
A/P	30,000	
Foreign currency gain		30,000

The spot rate increased from December 31 to February 2. A corresponding foreign currency loss is recorded in Year 3, reflecting the increased USD required to satisfy the A/P.

Remeasure A/P: ($1.35 − $1.45) × €200,000		
Foreign currency loss	20,000	
A/P		20,000

The **equipment's cost**, using the *transaction date* spot rate, is **$300,000**. The **Year 3 foreign currency loss is $20,000**.

Besides plant, property, and equipment, other nonmonetary items include the following:

- Marketable securities and inventory carried at cost
- Prepaid expenses
- Intangibles
- Deferred charges, credits, and deferred income
- Preferred stock carried at issuance price and common stock
- Revenues and expenses that are nonmonetary in nature, such as cost of sales, depreciation, and amortization

Monetary assets and liabilities (eg, A/P) are **remeasured using the exchange rate** at the balance sheet date and settlement date to match exchange rate changes with the transactional cash flows. **Foreign currency gains and losses** resulting from those changes are recognized in income.

Sparrow Co., a U.S. company, purchased merchandise from a vendor in England on November 12, Year 3, for £400,000. Payment was due in British pounds on January 12, Year 4. The spot rates to purchase one pound were as follows:

November 12, Year 3	$1.15
December 31, Year 3	1.11
January 12, Year 4	1.08

Determine the foreign currency transaction gain to be reported on Sparrow's financial statements at December 31, Year 3, and on the settlement date of January 12, Year 4.

Sparrow would recognize a foreign currency gain of $20,000 on December 31, Year 3, and a gain of $12,000 on January 12, Year 4, calculated as follows:

Date	Rate	Payable in functional currency	Foreign currency gain or loss
November 12, Year 3 (Transaction date)	$1.15	$460,000 (£400,000 × $1.15)	$0 (Initial amount)
December 31, Year 3 (Balance sheet date)	1.11	$444,000 (£400,000 × $1.11)	$16,000 Year 3 gain ($460,000 − $444,000)
January 12, Year 4 (Settlement date)	1.08	$432,000 (£400,000 × $1.08)	$12,000 Year 4 gain ($444,000 − $432,000)

Remeasurement of revenues, expense, gains, or losses (I/S) will be determined by their natures.

- Many revenues and expenses that are incurred throughout the period will be remeasured at the weighted average exchange rate
- Gains and losses will be remeasured using the rates in effect on the dates of the transactions generating the gains and losses
- Revenues and expenses that are nonmonetary in nature, such as cost of sales, depreciation, and amortization, are remeasured using historical rates
  - Depreciation and amortization are remeasured using the same rates that are applied to the items being depreciated and amortized
  - Cost of sales is remeasured by remeasuring beginning and ending inventory at their historical rates and purchases at the weighted average rate

The amount required to balance the entry is referred to as a **remeasurement adjustment**.

- The remeasurement adjustment occurs because items are being remeasured at different exchange rates and the result is not likely to balance
- The remeasurement adjustment is recognized in income (I/S)

Translation

When the local currency is the **functional currency**, the parent will need to translate the F/S of the subsidiary (ie, foreign investee) into the reporting currency.

Financial Statement Translation Process	
Step 1	Translate income statement items (provides translated net income): • Revenue and expenses: weighted average rate • Gains/losses on fixed assets: rate on transaction date
Step 2	Translate balance sheet (B/S) items: • Assets and liabilities: rate on B/S date • Contributed capital accounts and dividends: historical rates • Retained earnings (RE): rolled forward from translated net income and dividends
Step 3	Recognize translation adjustment in other comprehensive income (ie, the difference between RE calculated in Step 2 and unadjusted RE).

The normal translation process used in periods when there is not significant inflation involves applying exchange rates to F/S accounts as follows:

- Assets and liabilities are reported as of the F/S date; therefore, they are translated using the F/S date *exchange rate*
- The results of operations over a period are reported in the income statement; therefore, income statement items are translated using a *weighted average exchange rate* for that period
- Capital accounts and dividends are translated at *historical rates*
- Retained earnings are rolled forward with translated net income and dividends added to the prior ending balance

Pane had a wholly owned subsidiary in a foreign country that used the euro as its currency. At December 31, the exchange rate was $1 U.S. for €1.25. The weighted average exchange rate for the year was $1 U.S. for €1.50. At December 31, the subsidiary had assets of €1 million and revenue for the year of €2 million.

Determine what amounts of assets and revenue would translate for consolidation.

An appropriate exchange rate should be used based on the type of account being translated:

- Assets and liabilities use the current exchange rate as of the balance sheet date
- Revenues and expenses use a weighted average exchange rate (ie, average exchange rate for the entire period)

Here, Pane has a foreign subsidiary that operates in euros. To include the subsidiary's results in Pane's consolidated financial statements, the subsidiary's assets and revenue must be translated using the exchange rates provided, calculated as follows:

Item	Translation calculation	Translated amount
Assets	€1,000,000 / 1.25 (12/31 exchange rate)	$ 800,000
Revenue	€2,000,000 / 1.50 (weighted average rate)	$1,333,333

Note: Based on the exchange rates provided, it takes more than €1 to equal the spending power of $1. Because the rates were expressed as how many euros equal $1, the foreign subsidiary's items must be divided (not multiplied) by the exchange rate to be translated.

The translation adjustment is recognized in **other comprehensive income** on the parent's balance sheet. Generally, the cumulative translation adjustment remains in **accumulated other comprehensive income (AOCI)** until such time as the investment in the foreign investee is either disposed of or substantially liquidated.

Representative Task (Application): Determine the appropriate presentation of foreign currency translation adjustments in the consolidated statement of comprehensive income.

Comprehensive income is separated into two main categories on the income statement:

Net income + **Other comprehensive income** = Comprehensive income

- **D**erivative cash flow hedges
- **E**xcess adjustment on defined benefit pension plans
- **N**et unrealized holding gains and losses on available-for-sale debt securities
- **T**ranslation adjustments from foreign currency

Net income (loss) is closed annually to an entity's retained earnings. However, because OCI reports the *unrealized portion* of certain transactions that may not be realized in the future, it is closed to accumulated OCI (AOCI), a separate component of stockholders' equity.

Comprehensive Income

Retained earnings	
Dividends	Beg. bal.
Net loss	Net income
	Ending bal.

Accumulated other comprehensive income	
	Beg. bal.
Loss from OCI	Income from OCI
	Ending bal.

Comprehensive income = Net income (loss) + OCI or loss

OCI = other comprehensive income

The purpose of comprehensive income is to report all changes in equity from nonowner sources. Therefore, by including OCI, comprehensive income provides a more complete accounting of all *changes from nonowner sources*.

A *consolidated statement* of comprehensive income shows the details from both the income statement and OCI. It may be referred to as a "Statement of Earnings and Comprehensive Income." Due to the consolidation requirements, *noncontrolling interest* is explicitly listed on the statement.

ABC Inc.
Consolidated Statement of Comprehensive Income
For the Year Ended December 31, Year 1

Sales revenue	$20,000
Cost of goods sold	12,000
Gross profit	8,000
Net income including noncontrolling interest (s)	$12,000
Other comprehensive income (loss), net of tax	
Gain on an effective cash-flow hedge	1,200
Cumulative translation adjustments	(500)
Total other comprehensive income (loss), net of tax	700
Total comprehensive income including noncontrolling interests	$12,700
Less: Net income attributable to noncontrolling interests	1,682
Less: Cumulative translation adjustments attributable to noncontrolling interests	98
Total comprehensive income attributable to noncontrolling interests	1,780
Total comprehensive income attributable to ABC, Inc.	$10,920

BAR 10
Derivatives & Hedge Accounting

BAR 10: Derivatives & Hedge Accounting

10.01 Derivatives & Hedge Accounting

Derivatives

Representative Task (Remembering & Understanding): Identify the characteristics of a freestanding and/or embedded derivative financial instrument to be recognized in the financial statements.

Derivative Characteristics

Derivatives are financial instruments that derive their value from the performance of an underlying asset, such as a share of stock, a commodity, or a currency. Financial instruments are defined under ASC 815 to include the following:

- Cash
- Ownership interests in an entity (eg, stock)
- Contracts that create both:
  - An obligation to transfer one or more financial instruments by one entity; and
  - A right to receive one or more financial instruments by another entity (eg, derivatives, debt securities, accounts receivable/payable, loans, etc.).

Derivatives are commonly settled through transfers of cash or other liquid assets, taking into account how the prices of the underlying asset evolved relative to the terms set in the original derivative contract.

Examples of Derivatives	
Option Contract	Has *right but not obligation* to purchase/sell an underlying asset in the future • Call option: right to purchase underlying security • Put option: right to sell underlying security
Forward Contract	Negotiated contract in which two parties agree to purchase and sell an underlying asset at a prespecified price at a future date
Futures Contract	*Standardized versions* of forwards for standardized amounts (eg, X tons of grade Y steel) and dates (eg, the last day of the quarter) traded on an exchange
Interest Rate or Foreign Currency Swap	A forward base contract or agreement between two counterparties to exchange streams of cash flows over a specified period in the future

Derivatives have the following three characteristics (**NUNS**):

- **No net investment:** To be considered a derivative, there must either be no initial net investment or an initial net investment that is smaller than would normally be required for an instrument that would respond similarly in the market.

Derivatives with **no initial net investment** include interest rate swaps, futures, and forward exchange contracts.

Derivatives with initial net investments that are **smaller than normally required** include stock options.

- **An Underlying and a Notional amount:** The notional amount is basically the number of units (bushels, pounds), and the underlying is the factor that affects the derivative's value (specified price, interest rate, exchange rate).

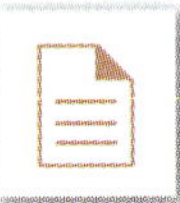

For example, in a forward exchange contract, the **notional** amount would be the number of foreign currency units (FCUs), and the **underlying** would be the future exchange rate.

- **Net Settlement:** The derivative can be settled in a net amount. In the case of a forward exchange contract, for example, the entity does not actually buy or sell the FCUs but, instead, receives or pays the difference between the agreed-upon exchange rate and the market rate.

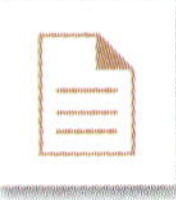

For example, in the case of an interest rate swap, the parties do not pay each other the contractual interest amounts. The difference between the rates is paid from one counterparty to the other on contractually set dates.

Derivative Instrument Characteristics (NUNS)

- No net investment
- An underlying and a notional amount
- Net settlement

Because one of the characteristics of a derivative is the requirement that it can be settled on a **net basis**, a derivative will always be settled by the **transfer of a financial instrument**. As a result, a derivative is always considered a financial instrument for financial reporting purposes.

- Derivatives may be assets or liabilities
- Derivatives are always reported at their *fair values*

- Unrealized gains and losses are generally *recognized in income*
  - Unrealized gains and losses on cash flow hedges are temporarily recognized in other comprehensive income (OCI) instead of income
  - Unrealized gains and losses on fair value hedges are recognized in income along with offsetting losses or gains on the hedged item
  - All other unrealized gains and losses on hedges are recognized in income in the period of the increase or decrease in value
- Derivatives can be *freestanding* or *embedded*
  - **Freestanding** financial instruments are entered into separately from other transactions or as part of some other transaction and are legally detachable and separately exercisable
  - **Embedded** derivatives do not stand alone but rather are a part of another host contract. Together, the host contract and embedded derivative create a hybrid instrument

For example, convertible bonds have an added feature in that they can be converted into common stock. As a result, increases in the stock price mitigate market risk as the bondholders can convert their bonds into shares of stock if the value of the stock exceeds that of the bonds. As a result, the value of the bonds will fluctuate as interest rates and the stock's value fluctuates.

- The convertible bond would be considered a **compound** or **hybrid instrument**
  - The bond is the **host instrument**
  - The conversion feature (ie, option) would be considered an **embedded derivative**

Risks Associated with Derivatives

Various business risks are associated with the use of derivatives.

- **Credit (or counterparty) risk:** The counterparty in a contract not honoring its obligations
- **Market risk:** Adverse changes in economy-wide conditions will affect the fair value of the derivative. This risk is only applicable to derivatives used for speculation
- **Legal risk:** Legislative or regulatory changes may alter or void the derivative's contracts
- **Basis risk:** Changes in the value of the derivative may not match exactly changes in the value of the asset (or flows) that is being hedged. In this case, the derivative will fail to hedge risks completely.

For example, a bank that lends only to farmers in a certain area has a concentration of credit risk associated with the possibility of weather-related crop failures or general declines in agricultural prices affecting all the bank's customers at once. In the event of a weather-related crop failure, the farmers will default on their loans.

Required Disclosures

Derivative instruments create **off-balance-sheet** risk (ie, risks that cannot be reflected on the F/S), due to the possible changes in amounts owed. The required disclosures for derivatives in the notes to the F/S include the following:

- Disclose the **credit risk** from counterparties and the maximum amount of losses from the derivatives
- Significant concentrations of risk (ie, multiple contracts with the same party)
- Activity, region, or economic characteristic of derivatives
- The entity's policy of requiring collateral or other security
- The entity's policy arrangements to mitigate the credit risk
- Optional to disclose **market risk**—that is, the risk that a loss may occur as a result of changes in the market value of financial instruments due to economic circumstances

In the specific case of the interest rate swap, there are two risks that cannot be reflected on the F/S but need to be disclosed in connection with such an agreement:

- The risk of exchanging a lower interest rate for a higher one
- The risk that the other bank might default on the agreement (credit risk)

Finally, an entity may hold investments whose fair value cannot be reasonably estimated. When this is true, any information that might assist the F/S user in determining the value of the investments must be disclosed. An explanation of the reason the value cannot be estimated is also needed.

Reasons for Acquiring Derivatives

Entities acquire derivatives for several reasons:

1. **Investments:** An entity may invest its excess working capital, or amounts set aside in sinking funds, in derivatives such as stock options to increase its return on investment

For example, when an entity's stock options are publicly traded, they generally sell for substantially less than the entity's stock. An increase in the stock's value results in a comparable increase in the stock option's value.

Based on a lower investment amount, the return is greater. However, if the value of the stock decreases, there is a comparably disproportionate decrease in the value of the derivative, making it a relatively high-risk investment.

2. **Arbitrage:** Arbitrage is the ability to take advantage of price differentials in separate markets, allowing the entity to enter transactions that are potentially profitable without significant risk of loss

For example, the six-month future price of a commodity was $1, and the entity may enter a futures contract requiring it to buy 100,000 units at $1 at the end of six months. In another market, the six-month future price may be $1.05, and the entity may enter into a futures contract requiring it to sell 100,000 units at $1.05 after six months. In reality, it will neither buy nor sell the commodity. Instead,

- If the market price is below $1, the entity will pay the difference between $1 and the market price to the counterparty in the buy contract. At the same time, the entity will receive the difference between $1.05 and the market price from the counterparty to the sell contract. As a result, the entity will earn the difference, $.05 per unit.
- If the market price is above $1.05, the entity will receive the difference between $1 and the market price from the counterparty in the buy contract. At the same time, the entity will pay the difference between $1.05 and the market price to the counterparty to the sell contract. As a result, the entity will earn the difference, $.05 per unit.
- If the market price is between $1 and $1.05, the entity will receive the difference between $1 and the market price from the counterparty in the buy contract. At the same time, the entity will receive the difference between $1.05 and the market price from the counterparty to the sell contract. As a result, the entity will earn the difference, $.05 per unit.

3. **Hedge:** A hedge is the use of a derivative to reduce or eliminate a risk that the entity is subject to either as a result of an asset or a liability recognized on its F/S or a future transaction. Hedges reduce or eliminate the risk of an adverse change in circumstances, but hedges can also reduce or eliminate the opportunity to take advantage of a favorable change

For example, an entity has a commitment for an asset being manufactured for it that is expected to be delivered in six months at a cost of 100,000 Foreign Currency Units, or FCU (such as euros or pesos), which has an exchange rate of $1.25. In other words, 1 FCU will cost $1.25, and the cost of the machine is $125,000.

If the exchange rate of the FCU increases to $1.30, the asset will cost the entity $130,000 instead of $125,000, which may be more than the entity has budgeted for the acquisition. The entity may enter into a derivative such as a forward exchange contract under which it is required to acquire 100,000 FCUs at the end of six months at the exchange rate of $1.25 per FCU.

- If the exchange rate increases above $1.25, the entity will pay more for the asset but will receive the difference from the counterparty
- If the exchange rate decreases below $1.25, the entity will pay less for the asset but will be required to pay the difference to the counterparty

4. **Speculation:** Entities may use derivatives to raise revenues by shouldering other parties' risks and placing trades based on educated guesses on where the entity believes the market is headed. Derivatives used for speculation are acquired to increase potential gains but may also produce losses

Someone who wants to make a large investment in the stock market can do so without buying any stocks through the use of **stock index futures** using the Standard and Poor's 500 index (S&P Index).

Assume that a company wants to make a $10,000,000 investment in the U.S. stock market on October 1 at a time the S&P Index is 1,000. The company can buy a stock index futures contract for 10,000 units of the S&P Index. With an underlying of 1,000 and a notional amount of 10,000, this is the equivalent of making an investment of $10,000,000 (1,000 × 10,000). The company does not, however, put up any cash.

Let's assume that the futures contract has a settlement date on January 2 of the following year and that the S&P Index has risen to 1,200 as of the end of the current year. The increase of 200 in the underlying multiplied by the 10,000 notional amount means that the company expects to receive a payment for $2,000,000 (200 × 10,000) from the party that took the other side of the futures contract.

There is no entry on October 1 since no exchange of cash took place. At the end of the year, the expectation of receiving a settlement of $2,000,000 on the January 2 settlement date is reported as follows:

12/31		
Receivable on derivative	2,000,000	
Gain on derivative		2,000,000

This is a gain on the speculative use of derivatives since the company acquired the derivative purely as an attempt to profit from stock market increases.

If, instead, the S&P Index dropped to 800 during that time period, the company would have to pay $2,000,000 to the other side. A payable and loss would be recorded for the cash expected to be paid at settlement. Notice that no actual stock needs to be involved: the derivative is settled by a transfer of cash from one side to the other.

Valuing Derivatives

As indicated, all derivatives are required to be reported at **fair value**. Derivatives that trade on **public markets** are reported at their **quoted prices**. For derivatives that do not trade on public markets, fair values are commonly estimated using various valuation models such as the following:

- Black-Scholes: used to estimate the value of stock options
- Monte Carlo simulations
- Binomial trees
- Zero-coupon method: used to estimate the value of interest rate swaps

The calculations used in these models are generally complex and require specialized knowledge or computer programs.

Options: When fair value is not readily determinable through one of the methods listed above, the *intrinsic value* of the instrument is often used.

- An option to purchase a share of stock for $30 (ie, strike price) when its market value is $30 has no intrinsic value because it provides no benefit to the holder
- A call option to purchase a share of stock at $30 when its market value is $35 has an intrinsic value of $5
- A put option to sell a share of stock at $30 when its market value is $25 has an intrinsic value of $5
- Depending on the length of the exercise period remaining, there may be a *time value*, which would be added to the intrinsic value in determining the value of the option

Option Relationships

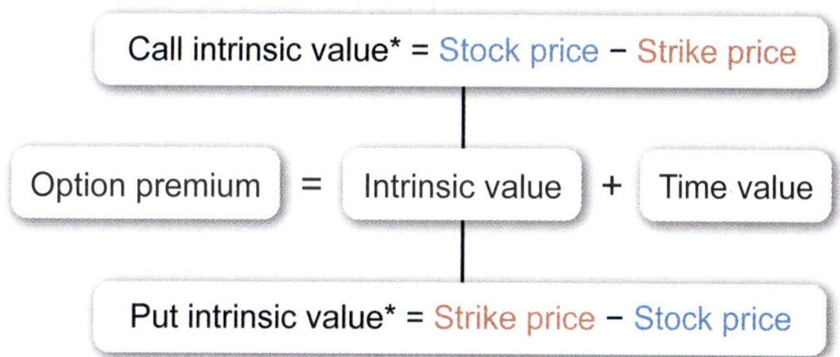

**Intrinsic value is the greater of the calculation, or zero. Intrinsic value cannot be negative.*

Forward exchange contracts: The fair value of a forward exchange contract is determined by the exchange rate that is used to value it. The types of exchange rates that might be used are the following:

- The **spot rate**, which is the actual exchange rate on a particular date
- The **forward rate**, which is what the exchange rate is expected to be at some point in the future
    - There might be, for example, 30-day, 60-day, or 90-day forward rates
    - A 60-day forward rate would indicate the exchange rate that is expected to be in effect 60 days from that date

A forward exchange contract is generally entered into at the appropriate forward rate as of the date of the contract.

For example, on June 1 of the current period, a company enters into a forward exchange contract in which it agrees to buy 100,000 euros 90 days in the future. It prepares quarterly financial statements, and as a result, its next financial statements will be prepared as of June 30. The contract will be settled with a net payment on August 29, at the end of 90 days.

Applicable exchange rates are the following:

	June 1	June 30	August 29
Spot rate	$1.30	$1.33	$1.29
60-day forward rate	1.35	1.39	1.28
90-day forward rate	1.37	1.42	1.30

On June 1, when the contract is entered into, it will be based on the 90-day forward rate, since that is the rate that is expected to apply when the contract will be settled at the end of 90 days. In essence, the company is agreeing to buy 100,000 euros for $137,000 ($1.37) on August 29, and the counterparty is agreeing to sell 100,000 euros for $137,000.

Since each party is basically required to exchange currencies that are expected to be equal in value, the forward exchange contract would have no value at that time. No entry would be recorded, although both parties would have disclosures to make.

On June 30, the forward exchange contract will be adjusted to its fair value for financial statement purposes. Although the actual fair value may differ due to the time value of money, volatility, and other factors, the fair value would approximate the difference between the expected values of the currencies that will be exchanged as of the balance sheet date.

As of June 30, the contract will now be settled at the end of 60 days. On June 30, the 60-day forward rate is 1.39, indicating the following:

- The buying party will be paying $137,000 for euros that are expected to be worth $139,000. The fair value of the forward exchange contract would be approximately $2,000
- The selling party will be receiving $137,000 for euros that are expected to be worth $139,000. The forward exchange contract represents an obligation to be reported as a liability for approximately $2,000

The buying party will recognize a gain, and the selling party will recognize a loss.

The buying party's entry may be the following:

Forward exchange contract	2,000	
Gain on forward exchange contract		2,000

The seller's entry may be the following:

Loss on forward exchange contract	2,000	
Forward exchange contract		2,000

The contract will be settled on August 29, when the spot rate is 1.29. The buyer would theoretically pay $137,000 to the seller for euros that are actually only worth $129,000. In reality, however, the buyer will pay the seller the difference of $8,000. Since the exchange rate has gone from 1.39 at June 30 to 1.29 at August 31, the buyer will incur a loss, and the seller will have a gain, of 100,000 × the difference of $0.10 or $10,000.

The buying party's entry may be the following:

Loss on forward exchange contract	10,000	
Forward exchange contract		2,000
Cash		8,000

The seller's entry may be the following:

Cash	8,000	
Forward exchange contract	2,000	
Gain on forward exchange contract		10,000

Hedging

Representative Task (Remembering & Understanding): Identify the criteria necessary to qualify for hedge accounting.

When a derivative contract is entered into for the purposes of mitigating or eliminating a risk, it is referred to as a **hedge**. In order to account for a derivative such as a forward exchange contract as a hedge, it must designate the derivative as a hedge and must meet certain requirements. This includes the following:

- Documenting the relationship between the hedge and the hedged risk
- Indicating that the hedge is expected to be highly effective
- Explaining how the entity measures the hedge's effectiveness

Assuming that the derivative contract does qualify as a hedge and that hedge reporting is elected, the entity will have to determine if it is a fair value hedge or a cash flow hedge.

Fair Value vs. Cash Flow Hedge

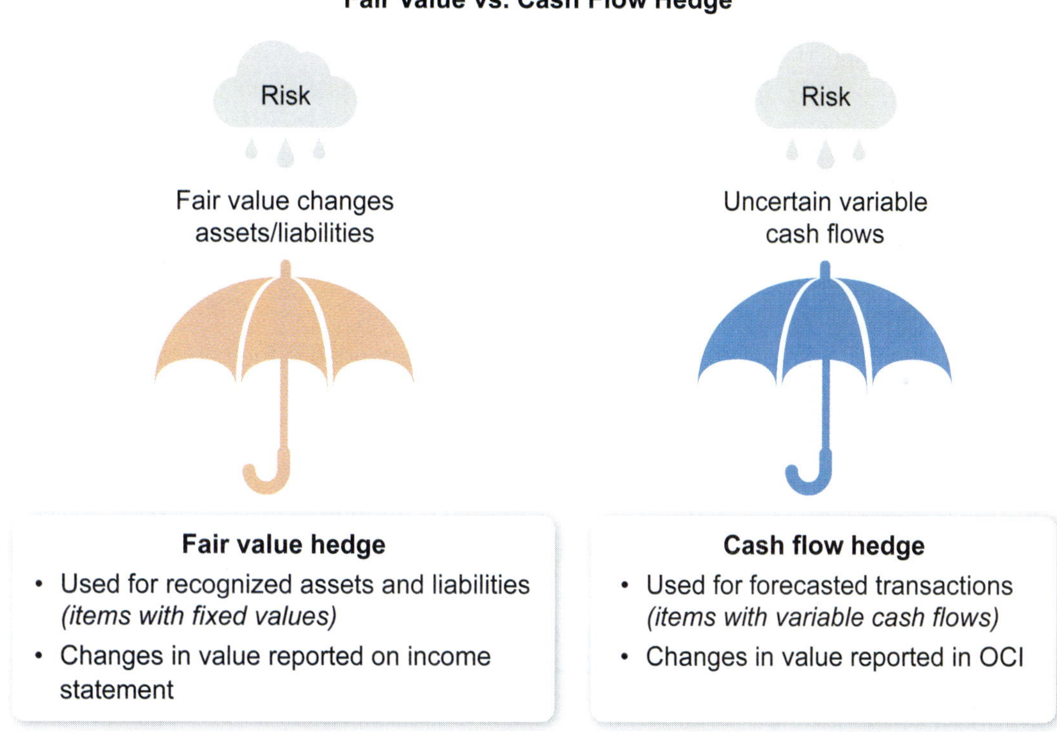

Fair Value Hedges

As the name implies, a fair value hedge protects a company against risks associated with changes in fair values, such as the fair value of a reported asset or liability (hedging against a **recognized asset** or liability on the balance sheet or a **firm purchase commitment**). Since all derivatives are required to be reported at fair value, on each balance sheet date, the carrying value would be increased or decreased, as appropriate.

- The increase or decrease will be recognized as a gain or loss in the income statement
- A corresponding loss or gain will be recognized on the hedged item in the same period

The corresponding loss or gain on the hedged item will be recognized regardless of the normal accounting for the item.

Assume your client is an oil distributor. On October 1, it purchased 1 million gallons of gasoline from its supplier (a refinery), paying $3.30 per gallon (a wholesale price). The client plans to sell oil to various airlines in early January but is concerned that, in the meantime, the price of oil might drop considerably from the current selling price of $3.50 (a retail price).

To protect from losses in the value of its inventory, the client sells a gasoline futures contract based on a wholesale gasoline price index per gallon (the underlying) times 1 million gallons (the notional amount), with a settlement date of January 2. Assume the price of the index drops $0.20 (or 20 cents) per gallon by the end of the year.

The purchase of the inventory by the distributor from the refinery is recorded as follows:

10/1		
Inventory	3,300,000	
Cash		3,300,000

When the futures contract is established, there is no entry, since no cash is involved. This is a fair value hedge since the distributor is hedging against an existing asset.

As of the end of the year, the decline of $0.20 per gallon in the price of oil results in a loss on the inventory of $200,000. The futures contract, however, is now expected to result in a collection of $200,000 upon settlement. The entries are the following:

12/31		
Loss on market decline in inventory (I/S)	200,000	
Inventory (B/S)		200,000
Receivable on derivative (B/S)	200,000	
Gain on fair value hedge (I/S)		200,000

Both the loss on inventory and gain on the fair value hedge are included in the computation of net income, so there is no net income effect. This, of course, was the goal of the hedge.

Cash Flow Hedges

As the name implies, a cash flow hedge protects an entity from fluctuations in cash flows. If an entity enters into a contract involving a receivable or payable that will be settled in a foreign currency at some point in the future (ie, a **forecasted transaction** or **anticipated transaction**), the entity may enter into a forward exchange contract to make certain that the number of dollars required to settle the contract does not fluctuate as the exchange rate changes.

When a derivative such as a forward exchange contract is accounted for as a cash flow hedge, it too, like all derivatives, must be adjusted to its fair value on each balance sheet date. The change in value, however, is not reported in profit or loss but, rather, is reported in **other comprehensive income (OCI)**. The amount in OCI is reversed when the effect is recognized on the hedged transaction.

Let's now go back to the prior example used for fair value hedges. On October 1, consider the issues from the point of view of the airline that is planning on purchasing the gasoline in early January. The airline might enter into a mirror image of the very same contract to hedge against a price increase. However, for the airline, it would be a **cash flow hedge** since there is no asset (like the inventory), liability, or fixed commitment for the purchase.

On October 1, the airline enters into a derivative based on the gasoline index with the same notional amount of 1 million gallons. There is **no entry** on that date.

On December 31, the price decline of $0.20 per gallon in the index means that the airline expects to have to pay $200,000 on the settlement date. The entry is the following:

12/31		
Other comprehensive income—loss on cash flow hedge	200,000	
Payable on derivative		200,000

Note that the loss is **not** included in the calculation of net income. The reason is that the decline in gasoline is expected to reduce the cost of inventory in the next period; this loss will be offset by a reduction in the cost of sales in the next period. Since the offsetting event is not yet reflected in net income, neither can the hedge.

Hedge Effectiveness

Some hedges do not entirely protect a company against the risk that the hedge is intended to mitigate. A fair value hedge, for example, may not offset all changes in the fair value of the hedged item. Likewise, a cash flow hedge may not offset all changes in the cash flows associated with the hedged item.

The degree to which a change in the value of a fair value hedge offsets the change in the value of the hedged item or the degree to which a change in the cash flows of a cash flow hedge offset changes in the cash flows of the hedged item is called the hedge's **effectiveness**.

- A hedge is **perfectly effective** if all changes in the fair value or cash flows of the hedged item are offset by corresponding changes in the hedge.
- A hedge is **highly effective** if most changes in the fair value or cash flows of the hedged item are offset by corresponding changes in the hedge. The portion not offset is the degree to which the hedge is ineffective.
- A hedge is considered **ineffective** if relatively few or none of the changes in the fair value or cash flows of the hedged item are offset by changes in the hedge.

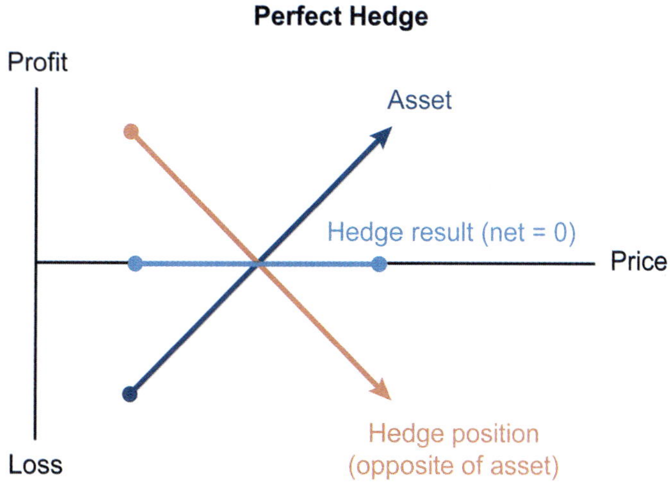

Changes in the fair value of a hedging instrument, including both the effective and ineffective portions, are reported as follows:

- **Fair value hedges:** Recognized in income on the same line as the corresponding gain or loss on the hedged item in the income statement
- **Cash flow hedges:** Recognized in OCI, to be taken into income in the same period in which changes to the hedged item affect income
- **Net investment hedges** (ie, a foreign currency cash flow hedge designed to mitigate foreign currency exposure due to a net investment in a foreign operation): Recognized in the *currency translation adjustment section of OCI*

Representative Task (Remembering & Understanding): Recall the appropriate presentation of gains and losses on derivative financial instruments (swaps, options, and forwards) in the financial statements.

To **summarize**, when derivatives (eg, swaps, options, forwards) are used as speculation or fair value hedges, gains and losses are reported in net income (in the case of a fair value hedge, there will be offsetting amounts on the asset or commitment being hedged). When derivatives are used as cash flow hedges, gains and losses are reported in OCI (they are transferred to net income when the expected events occur, and offsetting amounts are reported in net income).

Derivatives Summary

Speculation (nonhedge)

- Acquired to take on risk in the hopes of profit
- Gain or loss in income from continuing operations **(I/S)**

Fair value hedge

- Acquired to hedge against a recognized asset or liability or a firm purchase commitment
- Gain or loss in income from continuing operations **(I/S)** should be offset by loss or gain on hedged item

Cash flow hedge

- Acquired to hedge against a forecasted future transaction
- Gain/loss in OCI **(B/S)**
- Nothing included in net income until forecasted activity occurs

Net investment hedge—foreign currency hedge against an investment in foreign operations

- Acquired to hedge against currency risk from a major investment in a company with a functional currency (ie, the currency in which books are maintained) other than the U.S. dollar
- Gain/loss in OCI **(B/S)**
- Offsets translation losses or gains from investment in foreign operations

Interest Rate Swaps

Representative Task (Application): Use given inputs (interest rates, notional amounts, fair value measurements) to prepare the journal entries to record the net settlements and changes in fair value for an interest rate swap that qualifies for hedge accounting (fair value hedge, cash flow hedge).

An interest rate (IR) swap is a derivative contract that allows two parties to exchange payment streams based on interest rates. IR swaps allow entities to hedge exposure to changes in interest rates. If the entity believes that interest rates are likely to rise, it can hedge the exposure by exchanging its variable rate cash flows for fixed rate cash flows (or vice versa) to reduce risk.

Interest Rate Swap: Exchanging Interest Rate Risk

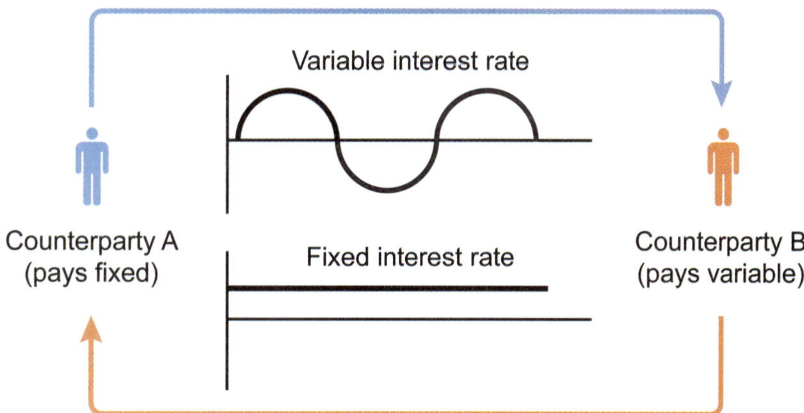

The swap counterparties exchange a **fixed payment stream** based on a single interest rate set at the swap's inception and a **floating payment stream** reflecting an interest rate that resets at regular intervals on the basis of a reference interest rate (eg, Fed funds rate, LIBOR).

The counterparties are not required to pay the full amount owed on the periodic payment dates, so *credit risk is reduced*. The **difference** between the two counterparties' payments for the period is the **cash due**, which is **paid** by the **counterparty** with the **greater payment obligation**.

Counterparty A owes: Notional principal × Fixed interest rate × Time period

and

Counterparty B owes: Notional principal × Variable interest rate × Time period

IR Swap Used as a Fair Value Hedge

When a recognized asset (eg, note receivable) or liability (eg, bond) has a stream of interest payments, an IR swap can be used as a fair value hedge. An IR swap can be established for an entity to receive fixed and pay variable interest payments, effectively changing the fixed interest payments into variable interest payments. The swap is recorded at fair value, with changes in fair value reported on the income statement.

For example, on July 1, Year 1, Company A issues a $1 million, 5.5% note payable at par due in three years, with semiannual interest payments due on January 1 and July 1 until maturity. The company would like to hedge the interest rate risk associated with the note.

The company enters into a $1 million notional IR swap to receive fixed interest payments of 5.5% and pay variable interest payments of Fed funds + 1%. The swap is entered into at market rates, and no cash was exchanged at inception. The company designates the swap as a fair value hedge.

Swap terms: receive fixed, pay variable

Notional: $1 million *(matches note payable)*

Company A receives 5.5% fixed payments and pay variable payments of Fed funds + 1% semiannually

Swap maturity: three years

July 1, Year 1: Company A issues the note payable. The IR swap fair value is zero.

Cash	1,000,000	
Note payable		1,000,000

January 1, Year 2: Company A pays semiannual interest. Fed funds rate is 5.0%

Interest expense (5.5% × $1 million × 6/12 months)	27,500	
Cash		27,500

Company A records the cash settlement of the semiannual swap receivable at 5.5% less the amount payable at Fed funds + 1%. The Fed funds rate is 5.0%; therefore, the rate used to determine the amount payable is 6.0% (5% + 1%). This results in an increase adjustment to the interest expense of $2,500 [(6.0% – 5.5%) × $1 million × 6/12 months].

Interest expense (swap settlement)	2,500	
Cash		2,500

Company A has not benefited from the swap because the swap's benchmark interest rate has increased. Company A has determined that the hedge provided from the swap is perfectly effective (ie, eliminated the interest rate risk associated with the note payable); therefore, the fair value decline on the note payable is offset by the fair value increase on the swap.

The swap's fair value has increased by $2,500, and the note's fair value has decreased by $2,500 as of January 1, Year 2. Company A records the following entries for the changes in fair value:

Note payable (B/S)	2,500	
Gain on hedge activity (I/S)		2,500
Loss on hedge activity (I/S)	2,500	
Swap contract (B/S)		2,500

IR Swap Used as a Cash Flow Hedge

Cash flow hedges are used to reduce the **risk of variable cash flows** from a recognized asset or liability or a forecasted transaction. An IR swap can be established for an entity to receive variable and pay fixed interest payments, protecting the entity against future cash flow uncertainty. The swap is recorded at fair value, with change in the swap's fair value recorded in other comprehensive income.

For example, on July 1, Year 1, Company B borrows $1 million from the bank at Fed funds + 2%, due in three years with semiannual interest payments due on January 1 and July 1 until maturity. The company would like to hedge the interest rate risk associated with the note.

The company enters into a $1 million notional IR swap to receive variable interest payments of Fed funds + 2% and pay fixed interest payments of 6%. The swap is entered into at market rates, and no cash was exchanged at inception. The company designates the swap as a cash flow hedge.

Swap terms: receive variable, pay fixed

Notional: $1 million

Company B receives variable payments of Fed funds + 2% and pays 6% fixed payments semiannually

Swap maturity: three years

July 1, Year 1: Company B borrows funds from the bank. The IR swap fair value is zero.

Cash	1,000,000	
Note payable		1,000,000

January 1, Year 2: Company B pays semiannual interest. Fed funds rate is 5%.

Interest expense ([5% + 2%] × $1 million × 6/12 months)	35,000	
Cash		35,000

Company B records the cash settlement of the semiannual swap payable at 6% less the amount receivable at Fed funds + 2%. The Fed funds rate on January 1, Year 2, is 5%; therefore, the rate used to determine the amount receivable is 7% (6% + 1%). This results in a reduction to the interest expense of $5,000 [(7% – 6%) × $1 million × 6/12 months].

Cash	5,000	
Interest expense (swap settlement)		5,000

The swap's fair value has increased by $5,000 due to the increased Fed funds rate. Company B records the following entries for the changes in fair value:

Interest rate swap (asset)	5,000	
Other comprehensive income		5,000

Alternative Accounting Approach for Nonpublic Entities (Interest Rate Swaps)

The Private Company Council of the FASB established an alternative accounting approach that is available to nonpublic entities when accounting for certain interest rate swaps, often referred to as "plain vanilla" interest rate swaps, and that have become very common among large and small entities.

This Simplified Hedge Accounting Approach gives nonpublic companies the option to use this simpler approach to account for certain types of interest rate swaps that are entered into for the purpose of economically converting variable rate interest payments to fixed rate payments.

An interest rate swap to which the alternative accounting approach applies is one related to the following circumstances:

- The entity has an obligation that bears interest at a variable rate
- The entity enters into a derivative contract known as an **interest rate swap** under which
  - the entity will receive payments from the other party at a variable rate; and
  - the entity will make payments to the other party at a fixed rate
- As a result of the swap, the net interest paid by the entity is equivalent to what would have been paid if the obligation had interest at a fixed rate

In order to qualify for the alternative treatment, the variable rate in the swap must vary according to changes in the same index that causes changes in the rate on the related obligation. In addition,

- The terms must be virtually identical such that they mirror the terms of the underlying obligation
- The settlement date on which payments are exchanged for the swap is very close to the dates on which payments are made on the underlying obligation.
- The initial fair value of the swap is zero, indicating that the interest rates are comparable on the date it is entered into and that the parties have different views on anticipated future changes in the index rate
- The notional amount of the swap, the amount on which the swapped interest rates are calculated, must be equal to or lower than the principal balance of the hedged instrument
- All interest payments must be designated as hedged, in proportion to the ratio of the notional amount of the hedge and the principal balance of the underlying obligation

If all conditions are met and the entity elects to apply the alternative accounting approach, there are several differences in the requirements. First, *documentation* and other elements are not required to be completed in advance. They may be completed any time until the first set of F/S on which the alternative accounting approach is applied are either issued or available to be issued, whichever is earlier.

The remaining differences are included in the *alternative accounting approach*, which will be applied as follows:

- It is assumed that the swap is perfectly effective and the debt obligation is accounted for as if it bore interest at a fixed rate
- The hedge, the interest rate swap, is reported at its settlement amount rather than its fair value
- Any difference between reported amounts and payments made or received are reported in *OCI*

The accounting for an interest rate swap under the alternative approach will result in the following:

- Interest expense will be debited for an amount calculated by applying the fixed rate to the principal balance, adjusted for the amount of time elapsed since the previous calculation
- Principal will be debited for the amount by which it is reduced as a result of applying the terms of the obligation to any payments made
- An asset or liability will be debited or credited to adjust the amount reported as the balance of the derivative to the settlement value of the interest rate swap
- Cash will be credited for the net amount paid, including the payment on the underlying obligation adjusted for the net amount received from the counterparty or paid to the counterparty to the swap, depending on whether the index rate has increased or decreased, respectively
- The amount required to balance the entry will be reported as a debit or credit to OCI.

BAR 11
Leases

BAR 11: Leases

11.01 Lease Accounting: Lessor

The AICPA Blueprint splits coverage of lease content between Financial Accounting and Reporting (FAR) and Business Analysis and Reporting (BAR). FAR focuses primarily on lessee activity, while BAR addresses lessor transactions.

BAR also includes a task to interpret agreements, contracts, and/or other supporting documentation to determine the appropriate accounting treatment of a leasing arrangement and prepare the journal entries that the lessee should record. Relevant FAR material has been included as an Appendix to this chapter.

Lease Basics

Representative Task (Remembering & Understanding): Identify the criteria for classifying a lease arrangement for a lessor.

Lease Definition

ASC 842 defines a **lease** as "a contract, or part of a contract, that conveys the right to control the use of identified property, plant, or equipment (an identified asset) for a period of time in exchange for consideration."

A **lessee** is the party that *pays rent* to the lessor for the right to use the lessor's property for a period of time. When a lease involves real property, the lessee is also called the *tenant*. A **lessor** owns the property and grants the lessee the right to use it for a period of time in exchange for paying rent. When a lease involves real property, the lessor is also called the *landlord*.

Lease Classification

From the perspective of a **lessor**, a lease may be classified as an operating lease or a finance lease. Use the mnemonic **Special-PO-T-75-90** to remember the steps required to determine the classification of a lease.

Finance leases are further subdivided for the lessor. When the payments' present value exceeds the lessor's carrying value at commencement, the lease is a **sales-type lease** (with or without profit). When the present value of all lease payments equals the asset's carrying value at the beginning of the lease, the lease is a **direct finance lease**.

Lessor Lease Types	
Operating Lease	Lease does not meet any of the criteria for a finance lease (similar to renting). Recognize lease payments as revenue on a straight-line basis.
Finance Lease: Sales-Type	Lease meets at least one of the five criteria shown in the image below.
Direct Financing Lease	Lease does not meet any of the criteria for a finance lease but is not an operating lease because the following conditions exist: • Collectability of lease payments is probable • Residual value guaranteed by a compensated third party (eg, insurance) • PV of payments plus PV of guaranteed residual value constitutes substantially all the leased asset's FV

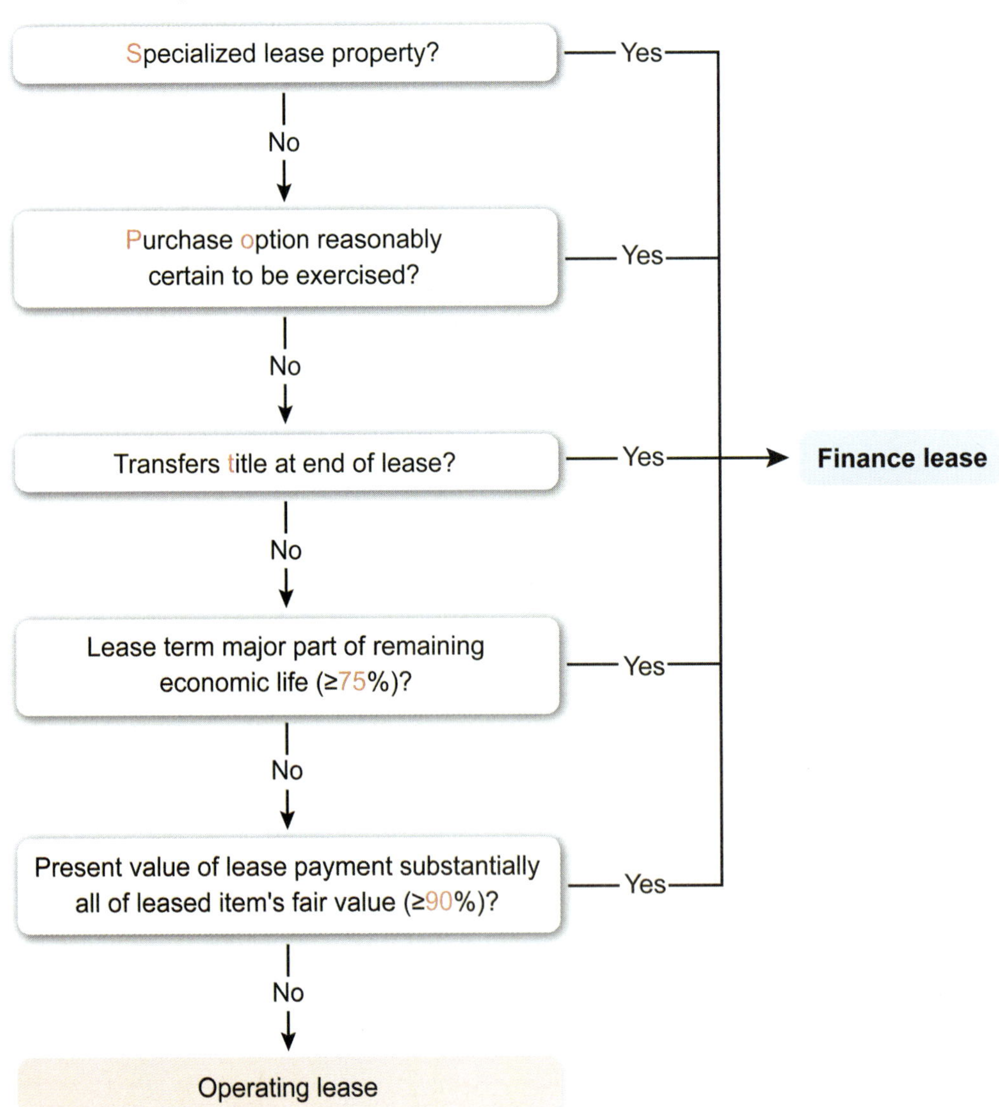

Lease Term

The lease term is the period of time during which the lease is expected to be in force. It begins at the commencement date and is the sum of the following:

- **Initial lease term:** This is the original noncancelable term of the lease that does not include any renewal periods
- **Periods for which a renewal option is likely to be exercised by the lessee**
- **Periods for which an option to terminate is unlikely to be exercised:** This might be the case when a lease contains a provision that requires the lessee to pay a significant penalty to the lessor for not renewing the lease.
- **Periods for which a renewal option** (or option not to terminate) is **controlled by the lessor**.

Lease Disclosure Requirements

Disclosures for leases by lessors are very comprehensive. The overarching requirement is to show disclosures that enable users of financial information to assess the amount, timing, and uncertainty of cash flows from leases. Disclosure requirements are both qualitative and quantitative.

Qualitative disclosures for lessors include a general description of the lease arrangement, variable lease payments, options, nonlease payments, and residual values.

Quantitative disclosures for lessors include the following:

- Explanation of assumptions and judgments
- Lease revenues received
- Lease sales (vs. regular sales)
- For each type of lease, future lease payments for each of the next five years and the total for all remaining years in the aggregate
- A reconciliation of sales-type lease receivables with total balance sheet receivables
- Gross investment and net investment in leases
- Description of assets under operating leases, risks associated with residual values, and important changes in unguaranteed residual values

Representative Task (Application): Calculate the carrying amount of lease-related assets and liabilities and prepare journal entries that a lessor should record.

Representative Task (Application): Calculate the amount of lease income that a lessor should recognize in the income statement.

Operating Lease

At the commencement date, the lessor must defer initial direct costs (eg, commissions or payments made to an existing tenant to get them to terminate their lease early). Note: Initial direct costs do *not* include costs that would have been incurred regardless of whether the lease was obtained (eg, advertising, certain legal fees, cost to evaluate a prospective lessee's financial condition).

After the commencement date, the following are generally recognized on a straight-line (S/L) basis over the lease term:

- **Fixed lease payments:** Amount paid by the lessee and included in income by the lessor. When there is a difference between the cash received and the amount to be recognized, it is recorded as either Rent Receivable or Deferred Rent, depending on whether the payment received is higher or lower than the lease income to be recognized. Total lease payments / years in lease term = Annual Rent Revenue.

Lessor Operating Lease Revenue: Straight-Line Lease Payments

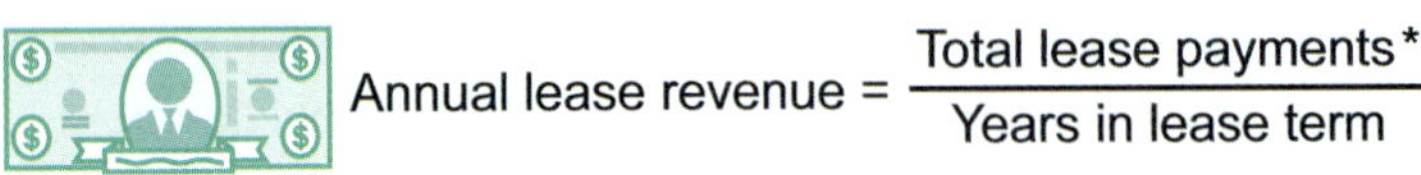

$$\text{Annual lease revenue} = \frac{\text{Total lease payments*}}{\text{Years in lease term}}$$

**Includes fixed payments and any nonrefundable lease bonus*

Variable lease payments: Amounts paid by the lessee that are included in the lessor's income as appropriate (eg, rent increases based on a change in an index, interest rate, or comparable external factor such as the federal funds rate)

- **Depreciation:** Lessor depreciates the actual asset (ie, even though the lessee records a right-of-use asset, the leased property itself remains on the lessor's balance sheet as an asset).
- **Rent received in advance:** Classified as unearned (deferred revenue)
- **Security deposits**
  - Nonrefundable: Unearned revenue until earned
  - Refundable: Liability until returned
- **Uneven rental payments** (eg, free rent): Recognized uniformly (evenly) over the lease term

Sales-Type Lease

If a lease meets one of the five criteria as a finance lease (ie, **Special-PO-T-75-90**), the lease is accounted for by the lessor as a sales-type lease, either with or without profit. A sales-type lease results in a **gain or loss** to the lessor at the time of the sale.

Recognition

At the commencement date, the lessor must:

Derecognize the leased asset (so long as collectability of lease payments is probable), and

Recognize:

- Net investment in the lease, which includes the following:
  - Lease Receivable, measured at PV of future lease payments and any amount expected from a residual value guarantee
  - Unguaranteed Residual Asset, measured at PV.

- Selling profit or loss =
  - Fair value of asset (or, if lower, Lease Receivable + Prepaid Lease Payments)
  - Less: Carrying amount of asset net of unguaranteed residual asset
  - Less: Deferred initial direct costs
- Initial direct costs, which are either:
  - Expensed immediately when the lease includes a selling profit, or
  - Deferred over the lease term as an increase in Lease Receivable and decrease in overall Interest Revenue when there is no selling profit.

Sales-Type Lease: Lessor Accounting		
Step 1	Record net investment in lease and derecognize (sell) leased asset	• Present value of lease payments, plus any residual value guarantee • Recognize profit or loss on leased asset immediately
Step 2	Record initial direct costs	• Recognize expenses immediately
Step 3	Record payment, interest revenue, and reduction in net investment in lease	• Debit cash for lease payment • Credit interest revenue • Credit net investment in lease for the difference

After the commencement date, the lessor must recognize the following:

- **Interest income** on the net investment in the lease
- **Variable lease payments** (that are not already included in the Lease Receivable) in the period in which the circumstances that fix the payments occur
- **Credit losses** on the net investment in the lease

Sales-Type Lease With Selling Profit

The five criteria that a lessor uses to identify a sales-type lease are the same criteria used by a lessee to identify a finance lease. The seller is usually a manufacturer or dealer of the asset and uses the lease as a way of selling the asset on an installment basis.

The fair value of the leased property differs from the cost, which creates a dealer's profit or loss. A sales-type lease results in both profit during the period of the sale and interest revenue earned over the lease term.

Profit on Sales-Type Lease

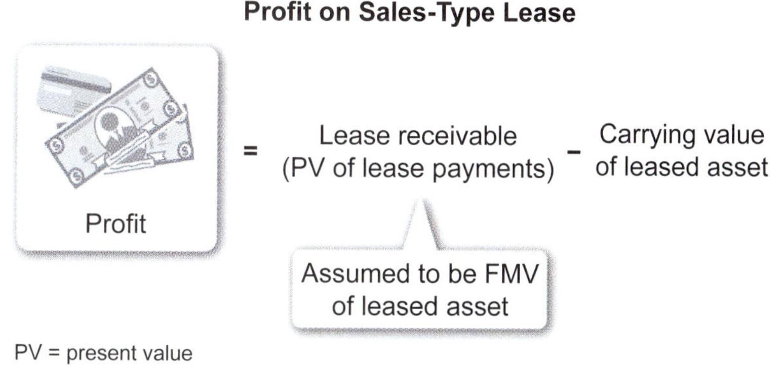

PV = present value

Recognition

At the commencement of the lease, the lessor recognizes the following:

- A leased asset, treated like a sale and removed (ie, derecognized)
- A net investment in the lease, which is the lease receivable (ie, present value [PV] of lease payments) plus any residual value guarantee
- Profit or loss: the FMV of the leased asset (ie, lease receivable) less the leased asset's carrying value
- Executory costs, which are expensed immediately

Assume that the lessor has leased equipment to a lessee with the following terms:

- Eight years with payments of $75,000 per year, due at the beginning of the year
- The estimated economic life of the equipment is 10 years
- Title to the equipment passes at the end of the lease
- There is no residual value
- The rate implicit in the lease is 11%
- The lessor's cost of the equipment is $300,000

Since the first payment of $75,000 is due on Day 1 (ie, annuity due), the PV of the eight lease payments at 11% (5.7122 PV factor) = $428,415.

Lease Receivable	Interest Rate	=	Interest Revenue	–	Lease Payment	=	Reduction In Lease Receivable
428,415					75,000		75,000
(75,000)							
353,415	11%	=	38,876	–	75,000	=	36,124
(36,124)							
317,291	11%	=	34,902	–	75,000	=	40,098
(40,098)							
277,193							

The **initial entry** to remove the asset from the books and record the lease receivable at PV of lease payments (note that there are no other payments, initial direct costs, or residual value in this example) is as follows:

Lease receivable	428,415	
Equipment		300,000
Gain on sale (plug)		128,415

First payment on January 1, Year 1:

Cash	75,000	
Lease receivable		75,000

On December 31, Year 1, interest income is recognized, but the payment hasn't been received yet:

Interest receivable	38,876	
Interest revenue [11% × ($428,415 − 75,000)]		38,876

Second payment on January 1, Year 2:

Cash	75,000	
Lease receivable		36,124
Interest receivable		38,876

Sales-Type Lease Without Selling Profit

Here the lessor is **financing** the **acquisition** of an asset by the lessee but is **not earning a profit**. This commonly happens when the lessor is a financial intermediary whose business model hinges on earning interest revenue.

The **PV** of the **lease payments** will be equal to the **fair value** of the property, and the lessor will earn only interest income. This makes our example a little simpler since there is no profit, COGS, or inventory to account for.

Assume the same facts as the last example, except that the lessor's cost of the equipment is $428,415 (ie, equal to the PV of the lease payments). Only the initial entry is different here, since there is no profit to recognize; the rest of the entries are the same.

Initial entry to remove the asset from the books and record the Lease Receivable at PV of lease payments:

Lease receivable	428,415	
Equipment		428,415

Direct Financing Lease

A direct financing lease occurs in **rare situations** in which none of the five criteria (ie, Special-PO-T-75-90) are met, but it's also not an operating lease. Collectability of the lease payments is probable, and there is a **residual value guaranteed by a compensated third party** (eg, an insurance company).

The combined PV of the following constitute *substantially* all the leased asset's fair value:

- The lessee's lease payments
- The lessee's guaranteed residual value
- The third party's guaranteed residual value

Recognition

The accounting for a direct financing lease is generally similar to a sales-type lease without selling profit, but in cases where there is a selling profit, the accounting varies a bit. Instead of immediately recognizing the selling profit, it is *deferred and recognized as interest income when payments are received*. Any initial direct costs incurred by the lessor are included in the net investment (ie, Lease Receivable) and amortized over the lease term.

Sale-Leaseback Transaction

Representative Task (Application): Prepare journal entries that the seller/lessee should record for a sale-leaseback transaction.

Note that the sale-leaseback material is from the perspective of the lessee, not the lessor; however, the AICPA Blueprint tests this topic in the BAR section.

Companies use **sale-leaseback** transactions as a **financing tool**. The property owner (seller-lessee) sells an asset, then immediately leases all or part of the asset back from the new owner (buyer-lessor). This provides cash to the seller-lessee that can be used for other projects.

The **seller-lessee** records a sale at the asset's fair value and *recognizes a gain or loss* from the transaction as part of net income. The seller-lessee then records an operating lease for the use of the asset. However, if the lease meets any of the finance lease criteria, there is no sale or leaseback on the property; the transaction is accounted for as a loan because there is no transfer of ownership.

In this situation, where the leaseback would qualify as a **finance lease**, the accounting is simple:

- The asset remains on the seller-lessee's books
- No sale or gain (loss) is recorded
- No lease accounting is applied
- The transaction is accounted for as a Note Payable

Sale-Leaseback Transaction

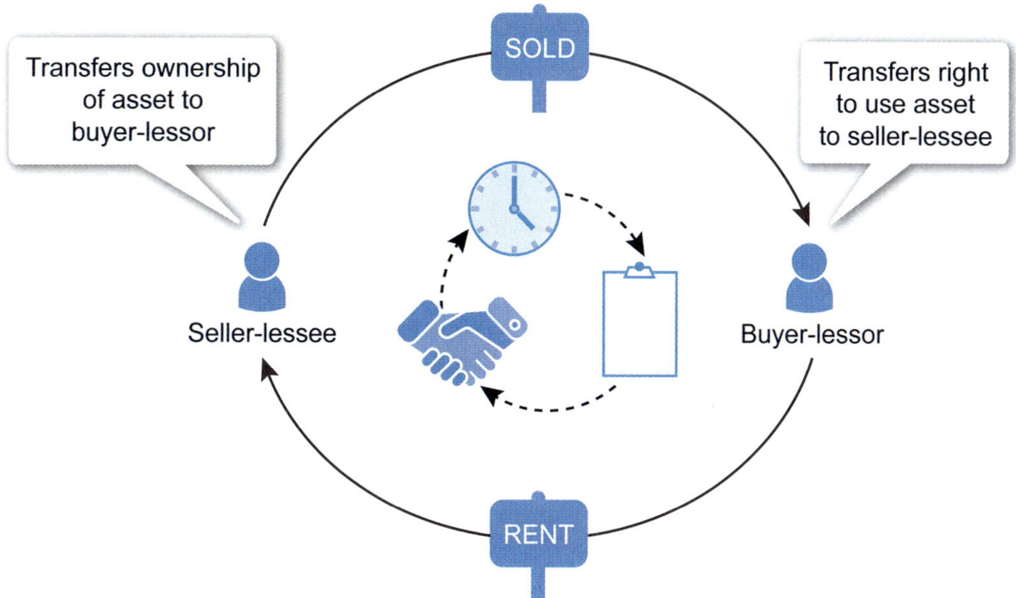

Fiona, Inc. needs cash. On December 31, Year 1, Fiona sells a building with an adjusted basis of $80,000 and a fair value of $100,000 to Kahuna Co. for $100,000 at a 10% interest rate, then immediately leases back the building from Kahuna Co. The PV of the lease payments totals $100,000, and the title transfers back to Fiona at the end of the lease term. The first lease payment is due December 31, Year 2.

In this situation, Fiona didn't really sell the building to Kahuna, because the leaseback terms (Special-PO-T-75-90) allow the seller-lessee, Fiona, to retain substantially all the rights and risks of ownership.

The transaction allowed Fiona to raise a lump sum of cash—the $100,000 selling price—in exchange for paying back the $100,000 over the course of the lease term. The transaction is, in substance, a **loan**.

Assuming a 10% interest rate and yearly payments of $20,000, Fiona's journal entries on the sale date and for the first payment would be as follows:

December 31, Year 1		
Cash	100,000	
Note payable		100,000

December 31, Year 2		
Interest expense (10% × $100,000)	10,000	
Note payable (difference)	10,000	
Cash		20,000

Now, let's see how the accounting changes for a sale-leaseback that *does not meet* any of the five criteria (ie, the leaseback is an **operating lease**).

On December 31, Year 1, Fiona Inc. sells equipment to Kahuna Co. for $10,000, then immediately leases it back. The equipment has an original cost of $12,000, a carrying value of $9,000, and a fair value of $10,000.

The lease term is 10 years and requires annual payments of $1,184, starting on the sale date. The estimated remaining useful life of the equipment is 15 years. With an implicit rate of 10%, known to both parties, the PV of the lease payments is $8,000.

None of the Special-PO-T-75-90 criteria are met, so the leaseback is an operating lease. The situation is therefore considered both a sale and an operating lease, resulting in the following seller-lessee journal entries for Fiona, Inc.:

December 31, Year 1 – To Record The Sale Of Asset		
Cash	10,000	
Accumulated depreciation	3,000	
Equipment (cost)		12,000
Gain on sale-leaseback		1,000

December 31, Year 1 – To Record The Operating Lease		
Right-of-use asset	8,000	
Lease payable		8,000

December 31, Year 1 – To Record The Initial Payment		
Lease payable	1,184	
Cash		1,184

This initial principal-only payment reduces the remaining lease liability to $8,000 − $1,184, or $6,816.

December 31, Year 2 – To Record Annual Lease Payment And Amortization Of The ROU Asset		
Lease expense*	1,184	
Lease payable**	502	
Cash		1,184
Right-of-use asset		502

**Lease expense = interest exp. ($6,816 × 10%) + amortization exp. ($1,184 − $682)*

***Lease payable reduction and ROU asset amortization = $1,184 payment − $682 interest exp.*

Representative Task (Analysis): Interpret agreements, contracts, and/or other supporting documentation to determine the appropriate accounting treatment of a leasing arrangement and prepare the journal entries that the lessee should record.

Below is an example of a simulation related to lessee accounting. Although the AICPA Blueprint includes lessee accounting in the FAR section, the simulation is included in the BAR area. The relevant lease documents will be presented first, and then the journal entries and explanations will follow.

Example 1: Exhibits

Present Value (PV) Factors	
PV of an ordinary annuity at 6%, 5 periods	4.212
PV of an annuity due at 6%, 5 periods	4.465
PV of a single sum at 6%, 5 periods	0.747
PV on an ordinary annuity at 8%, 5 periods	3.993
PV of an annuity due at 8%, 5 periods	4.312
PV of a single sum at 8%, 1 period	0.926
PV of an ordinary annuity at 6%, 4 periods	3.465
PV of an annuity due at 6%, 4 periods	3.673
PV of a single sum at 6%, 1 period	0.943

Email from PetCare, Inc. lease accountant

From: twilson@petcare.com
Sent: January 2, Year 1
To: ssvide@petcare.com

Subject: Decker Lease - Communication system

Per your request for additional information on the PetCare, Inc. communications system lease:

- Decker has indicated that the estimated economic life of the equipment is 10 years with a fair value of $50,000
- Our incremental borrowing rate is 6% (rate implicit in the lease is unknown)
- We have incurred $1,000 in initial direct costs
- Decker has agreed that the first 6 months will be rent-free
- Decker has agreed to a $1,000 signing bonus

The payment schedule will be as follows:

12/31/Y1	$5,000
12/31/Y2 - 12/31/Y5	$10,000

If you have any questions, please call me at ext. 919.

Tammy Wilson, Lease Accountant
twilson@petcare.com

Decker Leasing Company
Equipment Lease Agreement

THIS EQUIPMENT LEASE ("Lease") is made and effective on **January 2, Year 1,** by and **Decker Leasing Company** ("Lessor") and PetCare, Inc. ("Lessee"). NOW, THEREFORE, in consideration of the mutual covenants and promises hereinafter set forth, the parties here to agree as follows:

Lease. Lessor hereby leases to Lessee, and Lessee hereby leases from Lessor, the following described equipment ("the Equipment"): Model JT101 - Communication (Telephone) System.

Term. The term of this Lease is five years and shall commence on January 2, Year 1.

Lease Payment. The annual lease payment for equipment shall be paid in installments of $10,000 due at the end of each year, beginning on December 31, Year 1. Any installment payment not made by the tenth (10th) day of following month shall be considered overdue and a late payment charge equal to one percent (1%) per month on an overdue amount will be assessed. Lessor agrees to provide to lessee a $1,000 signing bonus.

Lease Incentive. Lessor agreed to a lease-signing bonus of $1,000

Lease Commission. Lessee agrees to pay a $1,000 commission to Lessor

Repairs. Lessee, at its own cost and expense, shall keep the Equipment in good repair, condition and working order and shall furnish all parts, mechanisms and devices required to keep the Equipment in good mechanical working order.

Surrender. Upon the expiration or earlier termination of this Lease, Lessee shall return the equipment to Lessor in good repair, condition, and working order, ordinary wear and tear resulting from proper use thereof alone excepted, by delivering the Equipment at Lessee's cost and expense to such place as Lessor shall specify within the city or county in which the same was delivered to Lessee.

Indemnity. Lessee shall indemnify Lessor against, and hold Lessor harmless from, all claims, actions, suits, proceedings, costs, expenses, damages, and liabilities, including reasonable attorney's fees and costs, arising out of, connected with, or resulting from Lessee's use of the Equipment, including without limitation the manufacture, selection, delivery, possession, use, operation, or return of the Equipment.

This instrument constitutes the entire agreement between the parties on the subject matter hereof.

IN WITNESS WHEREOF, the parties hereto have executed this Lease as of the day and year first above written.

Signed: *Susan Ehlers*, Decker Leasing Company

Cassandra Penny, President, PetCare, Inc.

PetCare, Inc. has signed a rental contract (with no renewal option) with Decker Leasing Company for telecommunications equipment on January 2, Year 1. **Refer to the lease documents above for additional information.**

Part 1: Review each of the finance lease criteria (Special-PO-T-75-90) and determine if the criteria is met to classify as a finance lease.

Finance Lease Criteria	Lease Terms	Criteria Met? (Solution)
Specialized lease property?	None indicated	**No**
Purchase option reasonably certain to be exercised?	No purchase option	**No**
Transfers title at end of lease?	Surrender equipment at end of term	**No**
Lease term major part (≥ 75%) of remaining economic life?	5-year lease term / 10-year useful life = 50%	**No (50% < 75%)**
PV of lease payments substantially all (≥ 90%) of leased item's FV?	PV = $37,405 (*calculated*) $37,405 PV / $50,000 FV = 75%	**No (75% < 90%)**

Since the lease fails to meet any of the finance lease criteria, it is an **operating lease**. The lessee journal entries are as follows.

Part 2: The lease was for 5 years. Record the initial entry on January 2, Year 1:

Right-of-use asset*	37,405	
Lease liability		37,405

*The right-of-use asset is **$37,405**, calculated as follows:

Lease liability at PV of lease payments ($37,405, see calculation below)
− Lease incentives (eg, lease-signing bonus) received (−$1,000)
+ Initial direct costs incurred (eg, commissions) (+$1,000)
Right-of-use asset ($37,405)

The PV of the lease payments is **$37,405**, calculated as follows:

- The PV of an ordinary annuity of $10,000 at 6% over five years ($10,000 × 4.212 = $42,120)
- The lump sum of $5,000 at 6% in Year 1 ($5,000 × 0.943 = $4,715)
- Total: $42,120 − $4,715 = $37,405

The total of the lease payments is $45,000 [($10,000 × 4 years) + ($5,000 for the first year)], Lease expense will be recognized on an straight line basis at $9,000 each year (ie, $45,000 / 5 years).

There are essentially two components of lease expense for a lessee in an operating lease: **accreted interest expense** and **amortization expense**. While these may be calculated separately, they are reported as a **single straight-line lease expense** each year on the income statement.

Record the entry on December 31, Year 1:

Lease expense	9,000	
Lease liability*		2,244
Right of use asset**		6,756
Lease liability	5,000	
Cash		5,000

**Lease liability is increased for accreted interest: 6% × $37,405, or $2,244.*

***Right-of-use asset is reduced for the amount amortized (ie, the difference between the lease expense and the accreted interest): $9,000 − $2,244, or $6,756.*

Again, notice that the total lease expense here is equal to the accreted interest expense of $2,244, plus amortization expense of $6,756, for a total of $9,000 lease expense.

Record the entry at December 31, Year 2:

Lease expense	9,000	
Lease liability*		2,079
Right of use asset**		6,921
Lease liability	10,000	
Cash		10,000

**Lease liability is increased for accreted interest on the Year 2 beginning lease liability amount of $34,649 (ie, $37,405 + $2,244 accreted interest − $5,000 payment): 6% × $34,649, or $2,079.*

***Right-of-use asset is reduced for the amount amortized: $9,000 − $2,079, or $6,921.*

Total lease expense will still be $9,000, consisting of accreted interest expense of $2,079 and amortization expense of $6,921.

The following table shows how the lease liability will change over the life of the lease under the effective interest method. Remember, the lessee uses the implicit rate if it is known; this is true even if the implicit rate is higher than the incremental borrowing rate. Here, the implicit rate is unknown, so the incremental rate is used.

Amortization table:

Lease Liability	Interest Rate	=	Accreted Interest Expense	−	Lease Payment	=	Net Reduction In Lease Liability
37,405	6%	=	2,244	−	5,000	=	2,756
(2,756)							
34,649	6%	=	2,079	−	10,000	=	7,921
(7,921)							
26,728	6%	=	1,604	−	10,000	=	8,396
(8,396)							
18,332	6%	=	1,100	−	10,000	=	8,900
(8,900)							
9,432	6%	=	566	−	10,000	=	9,434
(9,434)							
0*							

**Note that there is a $2 difference due to rounding for simplicity purposes.*

Example 2

Let's do another simulation to see how the *lessee* calculations and entries change when the first payment is made at the beginning of the lease term (ie, annuity due). In this case, the entire first payment reduces the lease liability.

Anita Gonzales
agonzales@remyco.com

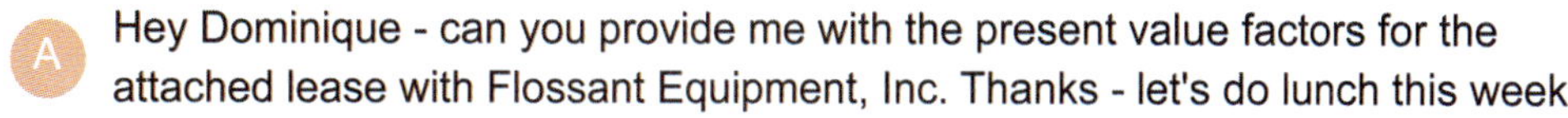

D Lunch sounds good. Here is the info you requested:

Present value of an ordinary annuity, 12%, 7 periods	4.5637
Present value of an annuity due, 11%, 8 periods	5.7122
Present value of a single sum, 11%, 1 period	0.9009
Present value of a single sum, 12%, 1 period	0.8929

Email from Remy Co. lease accountant

From: agonzales@remyco.com
Sent: January 2, Year 1
To: dsalido@remyco.com

Subject: Flossant Equipment Lease

Per your request for additional information on the equipment lease:

- Remy has indicated that the estimated economic life was 10 years (used for ROU amortization)
- Remy has informed us that the rate implicit in the lease is 11%
- Our incremental borrowing rate is 10%

I've requested the present value factors from Dominique. I'll forward them to you when I receive them.
If you have any questions, please call me at ext. 5206
Anita Gonzales, Lease Accountant

Flossant Equipment, Inc.
Equipment Lease Agreement

THIS EQUIPMENT LEASE ("Lease") is made and effective on **January 1, Year 1,** by and between **Flossant Equipment, Inc.** ("Lessor") and **Remy Co.** ("Lessee"). NOW, THEREFORE, in consideration of the mutual covenants and promises hereinafter set forth, the parties here to agree as follows:

Lease. Lessor hereby leases to Lessee, and Lessee hereby leases from Lessor, the following described equipment ("the Equipment"): Model SJC B872-02.

Term. The term of this Lease is ten years and shall commence on January 1, Year 1.

Lease Payment. The annual lease payment for the Equipment shall be paid in advance in installments of $75,000 due at the beginning of each year, beginning of each year, starting January 1, Year 1. Any installment payment not made by the fifth (5th) day of the month shall be considered overdue and a late payment charge equal to one percent (1%) per month on any overdue amount will be assessed.

Repairs. Lessee, at its own cost and expense, shall keep the Equipment in good repair, condition and working order and shall furnish any and all parts, mechanisms and devices required to keep the Equipment in good mechanical working order.

Surrender. Upon the expiration or earlier termination of this Lease, Lessee shall return the Equipment to Lessor in good repair, condition, and working order, ordinary wear and tear resulting from proper use thereof alone excepted, by delivering the Equipment at Lessee's cost and expense to such place as Lessor shall specify within the city or county in which the same was delivered to Lessee.

Indemnity. Lessee shall indemnify Lessor against, and hold Lessor harmless from, any and all claims, actions, suits, proceedings, costs, expenses, damages, and liabilities, including — reasonable attorney's fees and costs, arising out of, connected with, or resulting from Lessee's use of the Equipment, including without limitation the manufacture, selection, delivery, possession, use, operation, or return of the Equipment.

This instrument constitutes the entire agreement between the parties on the subject matter hereof and it shall not be amended, altered, or changed except by a further writing signed by the parties hereto.

IN WITNESS WHEREOF, the parties hereto have executed this Lease as of the day and year first above written.

Signed: *Jennifer Lin*, Flossant Equipment, Inc.

Jeremy Cook, President, Remy Co.

Remy Co. has signed an equipment lease with Flossant Equipment on January 1, Year 1. Refer to **the lease documents above for additional information.**

Part 1: Review each of the finance lease criteria (Special-PO-T-75-90) using the lease information and determine if the finance lease criteria was met:

Finance Lease Criteria	Lease Terms	Criteria Met? (Solution)
Specialized lease property?	None indicated	**No**
Purchase option reasonably certain to be exercised?	No purchase option	**No**
Transfers title at end of lease?	Title passes to lessee at end of lease	**Yes**
Lease term major part (≥ 75%) of remaining economic life?	8-year lease term / 10-year useful life = 80%	**Yes** **80% ≥ 75%**
PV of lease payments substantially all (≥ 90%) of leased item's FV?	Fair value unknown	**Unknown**

**Only one of the criteria need be "yes" for the lease to be a finance lease; therefore, it is irrelevant what the fair value is.*

Part 2: Record the initial entry and first payment at January 1, Year 1:

Since the first payment of **$75,000** is due on Day 1 (ie, annuity due), the PV of the eight lease payments at 11% is **$428,415** ($75,000 × 5.7122 PV factor).

Account	Debit	Credit
Right-of-use asset (ROU)	428,415	
Lease liability		428,415
Lease liability	75,000	
Cash		75,000

Record the entries at December 31, Year 1:

Account	Debit	Credit
Interest expense	38,876*	
Interest payable		38,876

**Accrued interest expense calculation: 11% × $353,415 liability (as of 12/31/Yr 1)*

Account	Debit	Credit
Amortization expense	42,842	
Right-of-use asset (ROU)		42,842

ROU asset amortization is a noncash lease-related expense recorded annually over the shorter of the leased asset's useful life or the lease term. If there is a purchase option likely to be exercised or title to the leased asset transfers to the lessee at the end of the lease term, the asset's useful life is used because the lessee will own the asset. In this lease, title passes at the end of the lease, so the ROU is amortized (on the straight-line basis) over the 10-year life of the asset. Amortization expense as of December 31, Year 1, is **$42,842** ($428,415 / 10 years).

Record the second payment at January 1, Year 2:

Lease liability	36,124	
Interest payable	38,876	
Cash		75,000

Amortization table:

Lease Liability	Interest Rate	=	Accreted Interest Expense	-	Lease Payment	=	Net Reduction In Lease Liability
428,415					75,000		75,000
(75,000)							
353,415	11%	=	38,876	-	75,000	=	36,124
(36,124)							
317,291	11%	=	34,902	-	75,000	=	40,098
(40,098)							
277,193							

**The implicit rate is used if known, even if it is greater than the lessee's incremental rate.*

Appendix: FAR Lessee Content

Content from the Financial Accounting and Recording text is provided below to assist with fully understanding the BAR content.

FAR – Lease Basics

Lease material relevant to FAR has been included as an Appendix to this chapter. Information relevant to both FAR and BAR (eg, definition of a lease) has been included above in the BAR discussion where appropriate.

Classification of a Lease

For a *lessee*, a lease is classified as either an **operating lease** (ie, a true rental) or a **finance lease**, which transfers substantially all the rights and risks of ownership (ie, more like a purchase/sale). Use the mnemonic **Special-PO-T-75-90** to remember the steps required to determine the classification of a lease.

A short-term lease is one that **does not exceed one year** and does not include an option to purchase the asset.

Lessee Disclosure Requirements

Required lease disclosures are designed to enable users of financial information to assess the amount, timing, and uncertainty of cash flows from leases. Disclosure requirements are both qualitative and quantitative.

Qualitative disclosures include a general description of lease arrangements, variable lease payments, options, nonlease payments, and residual values.

Quantitative disclosures include the following:

- Interest and amortization costs for finance leases
- Lease costs disclosed separately for operating and short-term leases
- Any variable lease costs
- Weighted average lease term
- Discount rate used in calculation of PV
- Reconciliation of beginning and ending balances of right-of-use asset
- Contractual obligations and options that the lessee is expected to exercise for each of the next five years and a total for the remaining years in the aggregate
- Future lease payments by type of lease for each of the next five years and a total for all remaining years, undiscounted
- Lease transactions with related parties

Initial Measurement of Lease Payments

Lease payments represent the amount that the lessee will probably pay for the use of the underlying asset (*not* including amounts allocated to nonlease components; see below) under the terms of the lease during the lease term, as defined above. Such payments may include the following:

- **Fixed payments:** This is the amount that the lessee is required to pay the lessor over the lease term, minus any lease incentives paid/payable to the lessee. Lease incentives may include the following:
  - Payments made to or on behalf of the lessee
  - Losses incurred by the lessor to assume the lessee's preexisting lease with another party
- **In substance fixed payments:** These are payments that the lessee is required to pay the lessor that appear to be variable, but they really aren't. For example, a clause is written in the lease to create variability of payments, but it has no economic substance
- **Certain variable lease payments:** These are rent increases based on a change in an index, interest rate, or comparable external factor (eg, CPI, federal funds rate). Note: Other types of variable lease payments are *not* included in "lease payments"
- **Exercise price of purchase option reasonably certain to be exercised:** Determining whether any option (eg, renewal, purchase, termination) is reasonably certain to be exercised is based on all relevant economic factors, such as the following:
  - Contractual terms/conditions compared with the market
  - Leasehold improvements that are expected to have significant economic value to the lessee
  - Costs relating to terminating the lease and obtaining a new lease
  - The importance of the underlying asset to the lessee's operations

For purposes of calculating present value (PV) of lease payments, a purchase option reasonably certain to be exercised will be treated as a lump sum paid at the end of the noncancelable lease term.

- **Penalties:** If the lease term reflects the lessee exercising an option to terminate the lease, then any penalties for such termination should be included in lease payments
- **Amounts likely to be owed under residual value guarantees (RVG):** In some cases, the lessee guarantees that the property will be worth at least a certain amount when it is returned to the lessor at the termination of the lease and, thus, must make up for certain deficiencies; this is referred to as a **residual value guarantee**
  - The RVG is included in the lease liability because the lessee has an obligation to return the leased asset's expected value to the lessor
  - To determine the probable amount included in the lease payments, the guaranteed value is compared with the leased asset's expected residual value at the end of the lease term
    - When the guaranteed value is *greater* than the leased asset's expected value, the difference is included in the total lease payments
    - When the guaranteed value is *less* than the leased asset's expected value, the guarantee is excluded from the total lease payments.
  - A lease provision that requires the lessee to make up for damage, extraordinary wear and tear, or excessive usage would *not* be considered a lessee guarantee of the residual value and would be treated similar to variable lease payments
  - Amounts paid by the lessee to obtain a third-party guarantee of residual value would *not* be included in lease payments

Lease Payments

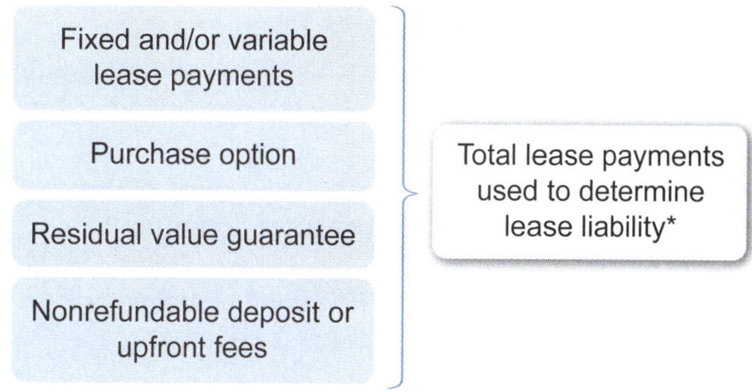

**Lease liability = present value of lease payments*

Components

An item in a contract is a **component** if it conveys some benefit (ie, a good/service) to the *lessee*. Components are classified as either *lease components* or *nonlease components*. Both types are accounted for separately, and lease payments are allocated to each of the separate components proportionately based on the stand-alone price of each lease and nonlease component.

For example, nonlease components such as maintenance service obligations (ie, the lessor is required to maintain the property) are separated from the lease components of a contract and are recognized as incurred, depending on the entity's accounting policy for maintenance.

Some items specified in a lease, however, are not considered components, and, thus, *no portion* of the lease payments are allocated to them. For example, any direct payment/reimbursement to the lessor of costs associated with ownership (eg, payment of taxes/insurance on the underlying asset) conveys a good/service to the lessee that is *separate* from the right to use the property. Noncomponent payments from the lessee are typically expensed as received by the lessor.

Lease Liability Components

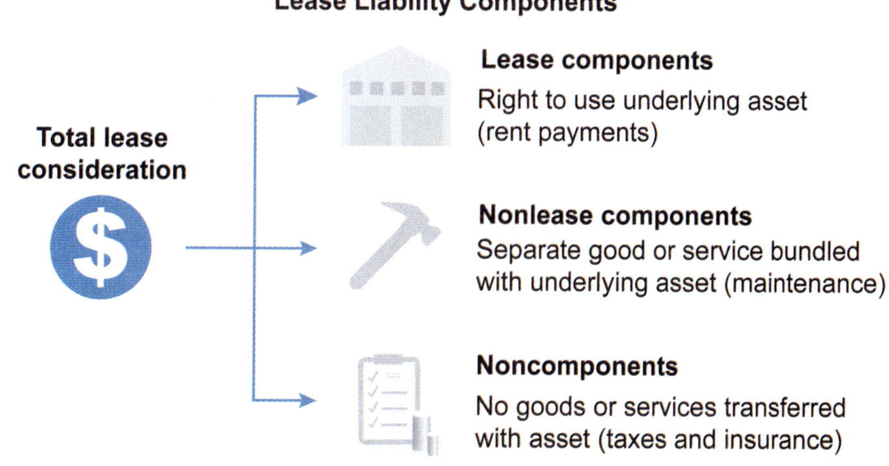

Operating Lease

An **operating lease** is similar to a *rental* because it does not involve transferring ownership of a leased asset from a lessor (ie, owner) to a lessee (ie, tenant). For lease terms longer than one year, at lease inception, the lessee records a **right-of-use (ROU)** asset and a corresponding **lease liability**.

Operating Lease: Lessee Accounting	
Right-of-use (ROU) asset and lease liability	Recorded at present value of lease payments
Prepaid rent	Prepaid asset until recognized as rent expense
Refundable security deposit	Long-term receivable
Leasehold improvements	Capitalized and amortized over shorter of remaining lease term or useful life
Lease (rent) expense	Expensed uniformly over lease term on straight-line basis

Right-of-Use (ROU) Asset

The **ROU** asset includes the following:

- The initial measurement of the lease liability (at PV of lease payments)
- Any lease payments made at or before the commencement date, less any lease incentives (eg, lease-signing bonus) received
- Any initial direct costs incurred (eg, commissions, certain legal fees)
  - Amortized over the term of the lease for the difference between the total lease expense and accreted interest for each period

ROU asset = Lease liability (present value of lease payments)
+ Initial direct costs
+ Prepaid lease payments
− Lease incentives received

Lease Liability

Lease liability is recorded at PV of lease payments.

- **Variable lease payments** are included in the lease liability in the period in which the obligation is incurred
- Likewise, **early termination penalties** are included in the lease liability as a lease payment at PV when it is reasonably certain that early termination will be exercised. This also shortens the lease term used
- To determine the **PV of the lease payments**, the lessee should use the rate implicit in the lease if it is known. If it is not readily determinable, the incremental borrowing rate is used
  - The incremental borrowing rate is the rate the lessee would otherwise pay to borrow the same amount of money over the same amount of time in a similar economic environment

Recognition: After the commencement date, lease payments are expensed over the lease term, generally on a straight-line basis. Total lease expense is composed of accreted interest expense and amortization of the ROU asset. While these may be calculated separately, they are reported as a single straight-line lease expense each year on the income statement.

Deposits: Refundable maintenance deposits, or security deposits, are assets (ie, receivables) if it is probable that they will be returned to the lessee. Maintenance expenses, however, should be expensed in the period incurred or capitalized in accordance with the lessee's maintenance accounting policy.

Leasehold Improvements

When a lessee pays for enhancements (eg, interior walls, electrical fixtures, plumbing) to a leased space, the changes are called **leasehold improvements**. Regardless of the type of lease (eg, operating, finance), leasehold improvements are **capitalized and amortize**d over the shorter of the lease term or the asset's useful life.

Operating Lease Examples

Example 1

A company signed an **operating lease** agreement to use office space for five years. The company took possession and began to use the building on January 1, Year 1. Annual rent of $24,000 is due on the first day of each year. Assuming an implicit interest rate in the lease of 6%, the present value of the lease payments at the inception of the lease is $107,163.

On December 31, Year 3, what amount should the company report as the lease liability balance on its balance sheet?

When the lease commences, the lessee recognizes an ROU asset. The lessee also recognizes a lease liability that is measured at the present value of the lease payments. Each period, the lease liability increases by the amount of effective interest expense (ie, the outstanding balance of the lease multiplied by the applicable interest rate) and decreases by the actual lease payments paid.

Because rent is due at the beginning of each period (ie, an annuity due), there is no interest due with the first payment because no time has passed since the lease commenced. The company should report a lease liability of $83,163 at Year 1, $64,153 at Year 2, and **$44,002 at Year 3**.

Beginning Lease Liability	+	Effective Interest Expense	−	Lease Payment	=	Ending Lease Liability
$107,163	+	($0 × 6%)	−	$24,000	=	$83,163 Yr 1 balance
$83,163	+	($83,163 × 6%)	−	$24,000	=	$64,153 Yr 2 balance
$64,153	+	($64,153 × 6%)	−	$24,000	=	**$44,002** Yr 3 balance

Recognition: After the commencement date, lease payments are expensed over the lease term, generally on an **S/L basis**. Total lease expense is composed of accreted interest expense and amortization of the ROU asset. While these may be calculated separately, they are reported as a single straight-line lease expense each year on the income statement.

Deposits are assets (ie, receivables) if it is probable that they will be returned to the lessee.

Maintenance expenses should be expensed in the period incurred or capitalized in accordance with the lessee's maintenance accounting policy.

Example 2

On January 1, a company enters into an operating lease for office space and receives control of the property to make leasehold improvements. The company begins alterations to the property on March 1, and the company's staff moves into the property on May 1. The monthly rental payments begin on July 1. The recognition of rental expense for the new offices should begin in which month?

An operating lease takes effect when the lessee takes control of the property at the commencement of the lease. The date when the lessee makes leasehold improvements to the space (ie, March) or moves into the space (ie, May) does not determine control. Rent payments can begin at a later date, but rent expense begins when the lessee has control of the property.

Here, the lessee enters into the lease agreement in January. At that point, the lessee has control over the space, so the rent expense begins in January.

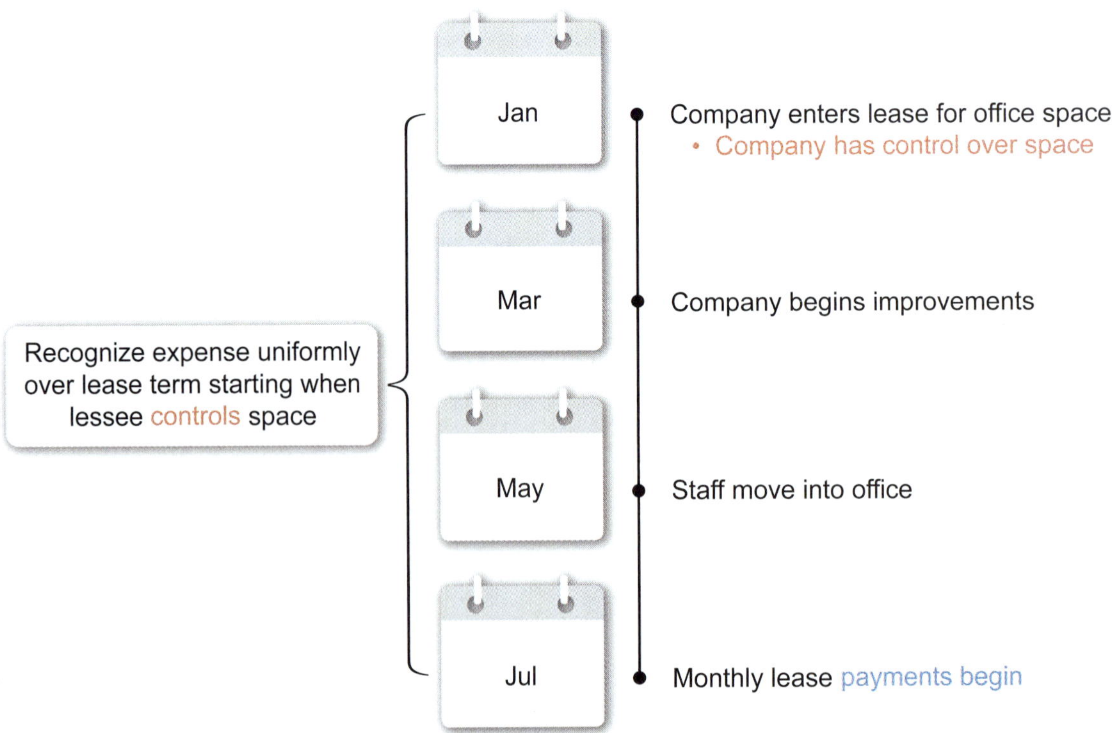

Example 3

Main, a pharmaceutical company, signed an operating lease agreement to use office space for five years. Main took possession and began to use the building on July 1, Year 1. Rent was due the first day of each month. Monthly lease payments escalated over the five-year period of the lease as follows:

Period	Lease Payment
July 1, Year 1–September 30, Year 1	$ 0*
October 1, Year 1–June 30, Year 2	$17,500
July 1 Year 2–June 30, Year 3	$19,000
July 1, Year 3–June 30, Year 4	$20,500
July 1, Year 4–June 30, Year 5	$23,000
July 1 Year 5–June 30, Year 6	$24,500

**rent abatement during move-in, construction*

Determine the amount that Main should report as lease expense in its income statement for the year ended June 30, Year 2.

Main took possession of the space on July 1, Year 1. Therefore, Main should report **$240,300 in lease expense** on its income statement for the year ended June 30, Year 2 ($20,025 × 12 months).

Lease payments are expensed uniformly over the lease term on a straight-line basis. Monthly lease expense equals the total lease payments divided by the months in the lease term. Here, Main has a 60-month operating lease with escalating lease payments each year. Monthly lease expense is $20,025, calculated as follows:

October 1, Year 1–June 30, Year 2 ($17,500 × 9 months)	$ 157,500
July 1, Year 2–June 30, Year 3 ($19,000 × 12 months)	228,000
July 1, Year 3–June 30, Year 4 ($20,500 × 12 months)	246,000
July 1, Year 4–June 30, Year 5 ($23,000 × 12 months)	276,000
July 1, Year 5–June 30, Year 6 ($24,500 × 12 months)	294,000
Total lease payments	$1,201,500
Monthly lease expense ($1,201,500 / 60 months)	$ 20,025

Finance Leases

Overview

A **finance lease** is generally one in which the rights and risks of ownership have essentially transferred from the lessor to the lessee. That is, in substance it's a purchase, although in form it's a lease. Just as with an operating lease, the lessee recognizes both a right-of-use asset and a liability at the PV of the lease payments.

While an operating lease liability would generally not be considered debt for purposes of ratios, debt covenants, etc., a finance lease liability is considered part of the lessee's total debt (ie, it is part of "Debt" in the Debt-to-Equity ratio). Another key difference is that the right-of-use asset will normally be amortized on an S/L basis, not unevenly as with an operating lease.

Criteria

If the lease meets one of the following five criteria (**Special-PO-T-75-90**), the lessee accounts for the lease as a finance lease, as if they *own* it. If not, it is considered an operating lease.

1. Due to its **Specialized nature**, the leased property has no foreseeable alternative use to the lessor at the end of the lease term
2. The lease contains a **"Purchase Option reasonably certain to be exercised"**
3. The lease **transfers Title**, *ie*, *ownership*, of the property to the lessee by the end of the lease term
4. The lease term is for the **"major part"** (75%) of the remaining economic life of the property. ASC 842 suggests 75% or more of the estimated economic life of the property at inception as meeting this "major part" criterion; however, this is no longer a bright-line test*
5. The PV of lease payments and any residual value guaranteed by the lessee that is not already reflected in the lease payments is equal to **"substantially all"** (90%) of the FMV of the property at inception. ASC 842 suggests 90% of FMV as meeting this "substantially all" criterion; however, this is no longer a bright-line test[1]

Recognition

After the commencement date, the lessee will report **interest expense** on the liability and **amortization of the ROU asset** (generally on an S/L basis unless another basis is more representative of the lessee's consumption pattern) in the income statement.

Finance Lease: Lessee Accounting		
Step 1	Record right-of-use (ROU) asset and lease liability	• Present value of lease payments
Step 2	Amortize ROU asset each lease period	• Straight-line method over shorter of lease term or useful life (used for purchase option or title transfer)
Step 3	Record payment, interest expense, and reduction in lease liability	• Debit interest expense • Credit cash for lease payment • Debit lease liability for the difference

1 *If the beginning of the lease term falls "at or near the end" of the estimated economic life of the leased property, criteria 4 and 5 cannot be used for purposes of classifying the lease. ASC 842 suggests within the last 25% of the economic life as a reasonable guideline for assessing the property to be "at or near the end" of its useful life.*

The lessee must amortize the ROU asset over the shorter of the useful life or the lease term, unless there is a purchase option that is reasonably certain to be exercised or the title (T) transfers at the end of the lease. When this is the case, the property is amortized over the useful life of the asset even if it is longer. This same rule applies to leasehold improvements under a finance lease.

Amortization of Right-of-Use Asset

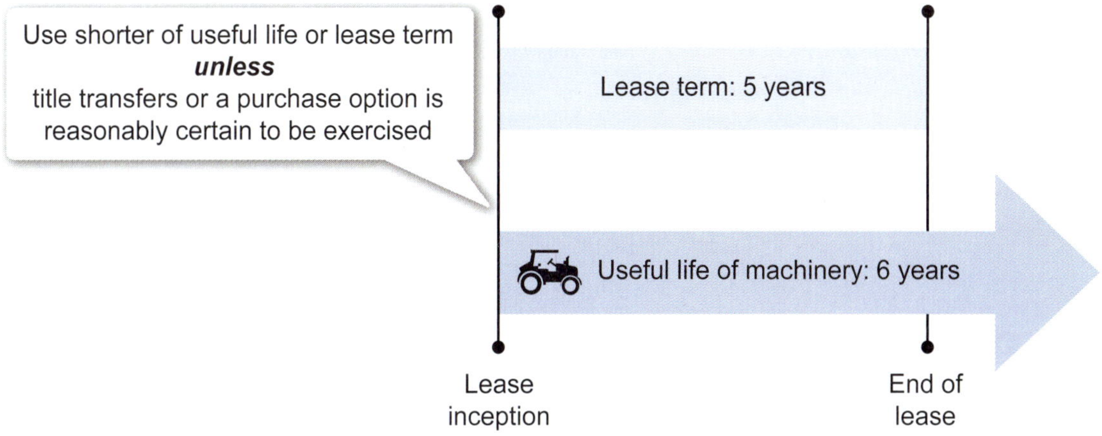

Use shorter of useful life or lease term ***unless*** title transfers or a purchase option is reasonably certain to be exercised

Lease term: 5 years

Useful life of machinery: 6 years

Lease inception

End of lease

For finance leases containing a **residual value guarantee**, the total lease payments include the probable amount that the lessee will owe at the end of the lease. It is included in the liability because the lessee has an obligation to pay the leased asset's guaranteed minimum value to the lessor.

- **Variable lease payments** that are not already included in the lease liability are expensed as incurred
- **Interest expense** on the lease liability is reported by the lessee for the time it has been outstanding during the year. If the first payment in a finance lease is made at *lease inception*, no time has passed for interest to accrue. Therefore, the payment consists entirely of a reduction in the lease liability.

Finance Lease Payments Over Time

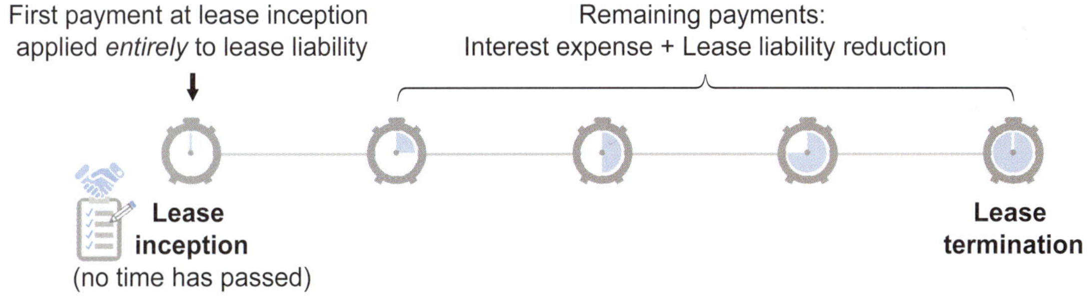

First payment at lease inception applied *entirely* to lease liability

Remaining payments: Interest expense + Lease liability reduction

Lease inception
(no time has passed)

Lease termination

BAR 12
Public Company Reporting

BAR 12: Public Company Reporting

12.01 Public Company Reporting

Regulations S-K and S-X

Representative Task (Remembering & Understanding): Recall public company reporting requirements of Regulation S-X and Regulation S-K.

Unless exempt by regulation, companies with $10+ million of assets, 2,000+ shareholders (500+ if nonaccredited investor shareholders), and securities that trade on a national securities exchange or an over-the-counter market must have their securities registered. This is governed by the 1933 Federal Securities Regulations Act. The ongoing reporting requirements are governed by the 1934 Act.

- **Regulation S-K regulates the disclosure of** *nonfinancial statement* **data**
- **Regulation S-X regulates the disclosure of** *financial statement* **(F/S) data**

SEC Presentation Requirements Example

Public offering registration statement: prospectus

Basic information:

- Company history
- Discussion of risks
- Directors, officers, and major stockholders
- Intended use of proceeds
- Company debt

→ Regulation S-K

Financial information:

- Audited balance sheet
- Audited income statement for the last 5 years

→ Regulation S-X

Filing requirements are as follows:

<table>
<tr><th>Type of Filer</th><th>Market Value of Outstanding Securities</th><th>Annual Revenues</th><th>10-K</th><th>10-Q</th></tr>
<tr><td>Large accelerated filer</td><td>$700M and up</td><td>N/A</td><td>60 days</td><td>40 days</td></tr>
<tr><td>Accelerated filer</td><td>$250M–$700M</td><td rowspan="2">$100M and up</td><td rowspan="2">75 days</td><td rowspan="2">40 days</td></tr>
<tr><td>Accelerated filer and SRC</td><td>$75M–$250M</td></tr>
<tr><td rowspan="2">Nonaccelerated filer and SRC</td><td>$75M–$700M</td><td>Under $100M</td><td rowspan="2">90 days</td><td rowspan="2">45 days</td></tr>
<tr><td>Under $75M</td><td>Unlimited</td></tr>
</table>

Note that Regulations S-K and S-X require fewer disclosures from smaller reporting companies (SRCs). A company qualifies as an SRC if it has:

- Less than $250 million in public float (ie, equity held by nonaffiliated investors), or
- Less than $700 million in public float and less than $100 million in annual revenues.

SEC Reports

Annual Report (Form S-1)

Form S-1 is filed prior to a company's initial public offering. It registers the company's shares on the national exchange.

Quarterly Report (Form 10-Q)

Form 10-Q requires F/S, Management Discussion and Analysis, quantitative and qualitative disclosures about market risk, and information about controls and procedures. Form 10-Q is required within:

- **40 days** of the end of each of the first three quarters for accelerated and large accelerated filers, or
- **45 days** for nonaccelerated filers.

F/S, which are **reviewed** (as opposed to audited), will include the following:

- Comparative balance sheets as of the end of the current quarter and the most recent preceding fiscal year end. These will include only major captions, and items representing less than 10% of total assets that have not changed by more than 25% may be combined with other items
- The income statement and statement of comprehensive income for the current quarter and corresponding quarterly period of the preceding year. For the second and third quarters, the year-to-date for both the current and the preceding years is presented. This includes only major captions. Items representing less than 15% of average net income for the three most recent fiscal years that have not changed by more than 20% when compared to the corresponding preceding fiscal period's statement of income may be combined with other items
- Cash flows for the end of the preceding fiscal year to the end of the most current quarter and the corresponding quarterly period of the preceding fiscal year. The statement is abbreviated and reports a single figure for net cash flows from operating activities and only reports individual changes from investing and financing activities if they exceed 10% of average net cash flows from operating activities for the preceding three years

- The statement of changes in equity may also be presented
- Disclosures are limited to those needed to avoid the financial information being misleading. Information included with the most recent annual financial statements that has not changed significantly may be omitted

The 10-Q must be filed for the first three quarters of the fiscal year (the fourth quarter requires the 10-K, not another 10-Q). While management provides its evaluation as to the effectiveness of internal controls on an annual basis, Form 10-Q requires information about changes in controls over financial reporting that are likely to have a material effect since the previous report.

SEC Reporting Requirements

Financial Statement	Interim Periods Presented
Balance Sheet	• Most recent quarter • End of the preceding fiscal year
Statements of Comprehensive Income	• Most recent quarter • End of the preceding fiscal year to the most recent quarter • Corresponding quarterly period of the preceding fiscal year
Statements of Cash Flows	• End of the preceding fiscal year to the end of the most recent quarter • Corresponding quarterly period of the preceding fiscal year

Annual Report (Form 10-K)

Form 10-K provides a comprehensive picture of a company's business, its risks, and its performance, including audited F/S.

- **Business:** Risk factors (not required for SRCs), unresolved SEC comments on reporting, human capital resources, legal proceedings, market for common equity, stockholder matters, and issuer purchases of equity securities
- **Management's discussion and analysis (MD&A):** Principal objectives of MD&A, financial condition and results of operations, quantitative and qualitative disclosures about market risk (not required for SRCs), liquidity and capital resources, and critical accounting estimates
- **Financial statements and supplementary data:** Two years of balance sheets, three years of income statements, statements of cash flows, and statements of comprehensive income
  - No supplementary data and only two years of F/S required for SRCs
- **Disclosures:** Changes in and disagreements with accountants on accounting and financial disclosures, controls, and procedures
  - Management's evaluation of effectiveness of disclosure controls and procedures
  - Management's annual report on internal control over financial reporting

The **deadline** for filing the Form 10-K is within:

- **60 days** after the close of the company's fiscal year for large, *accelerated* filers,
- **75 days** for *accelerated* filers, or
- **90 days** for *nonaccelerated* filers.

Information Statements (Form 8-K)

Form 8-K is required to be filed within **four business days** of an event of major significance, such as the following:

- Entering into or terminating a material agreement
- Bankruptcy
- Acquisition or disposal of assets
- Change in directors, CEO, or auditor
- Results of operations and financial condition

Common SEC Reports

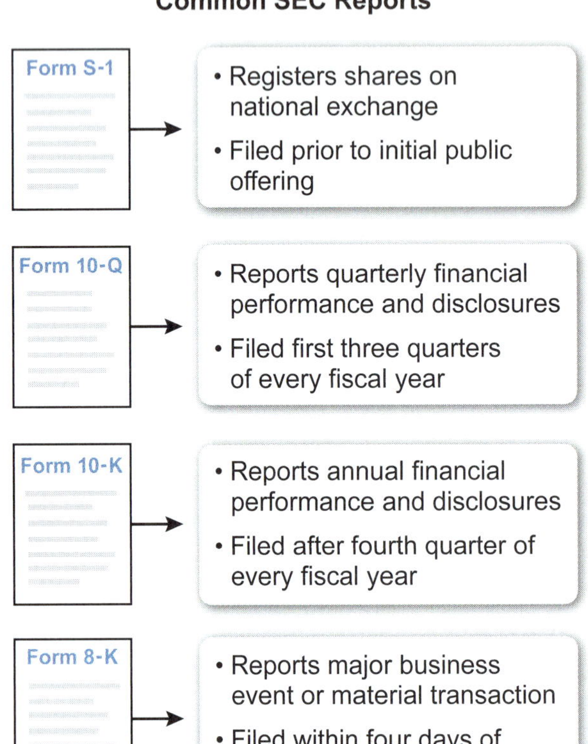

Interim Financial Reporting

Companies that issue annual financial statements typically issue interim reports on a **quarterly** basis as well. In general, the application of **generally accepted accounting principles** to a report covering three months will be no different than for a report covering one year because an interim period is an integral part of the overall year. Timeliness is emphasized over reliability. These statements should be marked "unaudited."

As a result **(ASC 270)** states:

- **Revenues** are recognized in each quarter as earned and realized. For example, estimates must be made each quarter when applying the percentage-of-completion (period of time) method of construction accounting to determine the profit in each period
- **Expenses** are matched to each quarter. For example, a property tax bill covering an entire year must be allocated equally to the four quarters
- **Accounting changes** made in an interim period are to be reported by retrospective application

For example, assume that a client received an annual rental payment of $300 from a client on 1/2/Year 1 and paid a $100 property tax bill covering all of calendar Year 1 on 3/15/Year 1. The effects of these items on the Year 1 interim reports are as follows:

Quarter	1st	2nd	3rd	4th
Rent income	75	75	75	75
Property tax	(25)	(25)	(25)	(25)

When computing income taxes at an interim date, the company estimates the **effective annual tax rate**. This should take into account estimates of total taxable income for the year and any tax-planning strategies the company plans to adopt during the year.

The estimated annual tax rate should be updated at each interim date, and the provision for income taxes in later quarters will be based on the current estimated rate applied to cumulative income reduced by provisions reported in early periods.

For example, if a client has income of $100 in the first quarter of Year 1 and expects the effective annual tax rate for all of Year 1 to be 25%, then the provision for income taxes in the first quarter will be $100 × 25% = $25.

If the client has an additional $150 of income in the second quarter and revises their estimate of the effective annual tax rate for all of Year 1 to 30%, then the provision for income taxes in the second quarter will be calculated as follows:

Income in second quarter of Year 1	$150
Plus: Income in first quarter of Year 1	100
Income for six months ended 6/30/Year 1	250
Expected effective annual tax rate	30%
Income taxes for six-month period	75
Less: Amount reported in first quarter	(25)
Income tax provision in second quarter	**$ 50**

Another item requiring special handling on interim reports is inventory. The use of **inventory** estimation techniques is permissible for interim reports. A special problem, however, involves fluctuations in inventory values at interim dates.

Because interim periods are integral parts of the entire year, they must be computed in a manner that will result in consistent presentations with the full year. A company sometimes experiences declines in inventory values at interim dates that are **expected to be recovered** by year end. In these cases, inventory should not be written down to market at the interim date. On the other hand, if a decline in value is not expected to be recovered before year end, then the inventory should be written down.

Assume that a client has suffered a substantial drop in the replacement cost of their inventory at the end of the first quarter but believes these values will recover before the end of the year. The decline in market will not be reported in the first quarter.

- If the client is incorrect, and values do not recover by the end of the year, the decline will be reported in the fourth quarter
- If the client does not believe prices will recover by year end, they will write down the inventory to market in the first quarter
- If the client is incorrect, and values recover in the third quarter of the year, the increase in market will have to be reported in the third quarter to offset the decline reported in the first quarter

Any increase in value in the third quarter that exceeds the decline reported in the first quarter is ignored; inventory is not valued at market when it is higher than cost.

Accounting Item	Treatment for Interim Reporting
Property taxes, bonuses, depreciation	Allocated to all quarters
Inventory losses	**Recognized** in that quarter
Major expenses	**Recognized** in that quarter, unless benefit future quarters, then allocated
Discontinued operations	**Recognized** in that quarter
Income tax expense	Estimated each quarter using estimated annual effective tax rate.

XBRL

Representative Task (Remembering & Understanding): Recall the purpose, objective, and key characteristics of XBRL business reporting.

The extensible Business Reporting Language (XBRL) is an open-source XML-based specification that labels financial data with standardized, computer-readable identifying tags. Instead of treating financial information as a block of text (eg, standard Internet page or Word document), XBRL provides a tag for each individual item of data. For example, "net income" has its own unique tag, which allows computers to generate a comparison of net income from multiple companies.

XBRL can handle data in different languages and accounting standards. By allowing computers to **select, analyze, store, and exchange financial data**, XBRL reduces the chance of errors when generating reports and improves the efficiency, accuracy, and timeliness of financial reporting.

In addition, XBRL has the following characteristics:

- It is built on Extensible Markup Language (XML)
- It is able to handle data in different languages and accounting standards
- It is required for use in all public companies' filed financial statements

XBRL

Reporting line items

- Cash and cash equivalents $25,000
- Accounts payable $10,000

Represented by

XBRL tags

```
<us-gaap:CashCashEquivalents
 decimals="0"contextRef="End2020"unitRef="USD">
 25000 </us-gaap:CashCashEquivalents>

<us-gaap:AccountsPayable
 decimals="0"contextRef="End2020"unitRef="USD">
 10000 </us-gaap:AccountsPayable>
```

Segment Reporting

Representative Task (Remembering & Understanding): Recall the criteria used to identify reportable segments

Representative Task (Remembering & Understanding): Recall the financial statement note disclosure requirements for reportable segments.

Publicly held companies are required to report certain key information about significant segments of their business, referred to as **reportable segments**. The definition of "segment" is based on a concept known as the **management approach**, in which a segment represents any group of activities with revenues and expenses that is regularly evaluated by management as a single unit.

According to ASC 280, a segment is a component of a public entity that has three characteristics:

- It is involved in business activities that may result in earning revenues and incurring expenses, whether external or internal
  - External activities involve transactions with other entities
  - Internal activities involve transactions with other components of the same public entity
- Its performance is evaluated by management for the purposes of resource allocation
- Financial information identifiable to the component is available

Different segments can be in the same line of operations, as long as management evaluates them separately for internal purposes. Segments may be identified by the following:

- **Activity:** Such as manufacturing components making up one segment and distribution centers making up another
- **Product:** Such as those components distributing heavy equipment making up one segment and those distributing software making up another
- **Customers:** Such as those components making sales domestically making up one segment and those selling internationally making up another

There are three different tests to identify a reportable segment. A segment is reportable if it contributes at least **10% of the total for all segments** of one or more of the following:

- Revenues
- Assets
- Profits

The **revenue** test is based on combined revenues of all segments, including those resulting from intersegment sales. This is the case even though consolidated revenues on the income statement will eliminate intersegment activity.

Segment Reporting Test*	
Revenue	Segment revenue ≥ 10% of company's total revenue
Assets	Segment assets ≥ 10% of company's identifiable assets
Profits	Segment profit or loss ≥ 10% of combined profit or loss of all segments

**Tests evaluated by company's management and/or chief operating decision makers*

Assume that the client has four industry segments with the following revenue information:

Segment	Sales to Unaffiliated Companies (Outside)	Intersegment Sales	Total Sales
A	$ 20	$ 25	$ 45
B	150	45	195
C	35	0	35
D	95	30	125
Total	**$300**	**$100**	**$400**

Although consolidated revenue on the income statement is reported at $300, the 10% test is applied to total sales of $400, so segments with total sales of at least $40 are reportable. Segments A, B, and D are reportable, and C is not.

There is also a 75% test, discussed below, that requires additional reportable segments to be included when the total external revenue reported by segments is less than 75% of total external revenues. That criterion is met in this case: 75% of $300 (the unaffiliated revenue) = $225. Reportable Segments A, B, and D = $265, which is at least 75%.

The 10% test applying to **profits** is the most complex. First, the calculated amount for each segment represents **operating income** only (sales reduced by cost of sales and selling, general, and administrative expenses). Furthermore, expenses incurred at the overall corporate level (such as the salaries of the company's top officers) are excluded from the computations. Common costs, however, must be included and allocated among the various segments, using an appropriate technique (always identified in exam questions).

Assume that the company had total sales of $1,000, of which $300 occurred in Segment C. Segment C had operating expenses of $90. The company as a whole had $200 of common expenses and allocates common costs based on sales. The operating profit of Segment C is computed as follows:

Sales	$300
Less: Operating expenses	(90)
Income before common costs	210
Less: Common costs [200 × (300 / 1,000)]	(60)
Operating profit	**$150**

All segments that have **operating profits** are combined, and all segments that have operating losses are combined. The **10% test** is applied to the **higher** (absolute value) of the combined profits or combined losses. This means that it does not matter if the larger total is the total of the segments with profits or losses. 10% of the number represented by the larger total is the threshold. In addition, it does not matter if the segment earned a profit or incurred a loss. If the amount of a component's profit or loss is at least equal to the threshold amount, it is a reportable segment.

Let's assume that the four industry segments of a business have the following operating income figures:

Segment	Operating Profit (loss)
A	$1,850
B	(190)
C	150
D	(310)

The combined operating profits are $1,850 + $150 = $2,000, and the combined operating losses are $190 + $310 = $500. Because $2,000 is higher, the 10% test requires a segment to have $200 or higher net profit or loss, so that segments A and D are the reportable segments.

The 10% test applied to **assets** includes identifiable assets only, not goodwill. There are no special complications, and this is rarely tested.

In addition to reporting significant segments based on the management approach, a public company should also report data for **foreign operations** (geographic areas) if such operations contributed at least 10% of total revenues or total identifiable assets. Reporting of revenues should separately identify sales to unaffiliated customers and intersegment sales.

Finally, a company should report revenues from **major customers**, referring to those that individually provided at least 10% of consolidated revenues.

Public Company Concentrated Business Reporting Requirements	
Information Disclosed	**Reporting Metric**
• Reportable segments (ie, management approach)	• At least 10% of company's revenues, assets, or profits
• Major geographic areas (ie, foreign operations, customers)	• At least 10% of company's revenues or identifiable assets
• Major customers (ie, existence, revenues provided)	• At least 10% of company's revenues

There must be enough segments separately reported so that at least *75% of unaffiliated revenues (to outsiders)* is shown by reportable segments. If the 75% test is not satisfied, additional segments must be designated as reportable (even if they don't meet the three tests) until the test is satisfied.

- Don't exceed 10 reported segments; combine the smaller segments. There is a practical limit to the number of segments reported (ie, reporting too many segments may make information needlessly detailed)
- Report aggregate information for all non-key segments
- It is not required to disclose allocated costs and expenses of reportable segments
- An enterprise may consider aggregating two or more operating segments if they have similar economic characteristics and if the segments are similar in each of the following areas:
  - Nature of products and services
  - Production process
  - Type of customers
  - Methods used to distribute their products or services
  - Nature of regulatory environment

Disclosure: An enterprise must disclose the following general information:

- General information, including how reportable segments are identified and the types of products and services from which each reportable segment derives its revenues
  - Title and position of the Chief Operating Decision Maker
  - How reported measures of segment profit or loss are used to assess segment performance and allocate resources
- Enterprise-wide disclosures (eg, external product and service revenue, major customers (≥10% revenue), geographic data on revenue and long-lived assets
- Certain info about the basis of measurement for reported segment profit or loss and segment assets:
  - Internal and external revenues
  - Interest income and expense
  - Depreciation, depletion, and amortization expense and other significant noncash items
  - Unusual items
  - Equity in net income of equity method investees
- Income tax reconciliations of the segment amounts to the enterprise amount, including revenues, profit or loss, and assets

- Additional breakdown of segment expenses
  - Significant segment expenses
    - Regularly provided to chief operating decision maker
    - Included within each reported measure of segment profit or loss
    - Identified as significant based on qualitative and quantitative factors
  - Other segment expenses (remaining expenses)
    - By reportable segment including qualitative description
- Reporting of multiple measures of segment profit or loss allowed
  - At least one must be measure most consistent with U.S. GAAP
  - Reconciliation of measures to consolidated income statement required
- All annual segment disclosures required for interim periods as well
  - Segment disclosures required even if only one reportable segment

Three Tests

1. **Revenue** = If segment's revenues ≥ 10% of company's total revenue (includes intercompany/intersegment sales & transfers)
2. **Profit/loss** = If segment's P/L ≥ 10% of combined operating profit/loss of all segments that had a profit/loss.
   - Includes allocated common costs
   - Excludes corporate-level expenses:
     - Interest
     - Income taxes
     - Gain/loss from discontinued operations
3. **Segments asset test** = If segment's assets ≥ 10% of company's identifiable assets

Reportable Segment ≥ 10%

A. **Operations in different industries** (tests 1, 2, 3) → Meet any of three tests, disclose *all* three

B. **Foreign operations** (geographic areas) (tests 1 & 3) → Meet any one, disclose *all* three

C. **Major customer or export sales** (test 1) → Meet, disclose *only* one

BAR 13
Financial Statements of Employee Benefit Plans

BAR 13: Financial Statements of Employee Benefit Plans

13.01 Financial Statements of Employee Benefit Plans

Types of Pension Plans

Representative Task (Remembering & Understanding): Identify the required financial statements for a defined benefit pension plan and a defined contribution pension plan.

A pension plan is an agreement between an employer and employee (the participant) to give the employee benefits once they retire. There are two main types of plans:

- **Defined benefit plan:** The employer guarantees certain benefits to be paid to retired employees and is responsible for setting aside sufficient amounts to fulfill these promises. This type of plan is far less common than a defined contribution plan, and accounting for one is much more complicated due to the following:
  - **Matching:** Pension expense must be recognized at the time of employee service, not when benefits are paid to retired employees
  - **Estimation:** Costs are difficult to determine as they depend on the life span of employees, changes in wage rates, and the rates of return earned on investments. To compute pension expense, an actuary must first compute the present value (ie, actuarial present value) of the pension obligation three ways (ie, based on vested benefits, current wage rates, and future wage rates). Each computation represents the amount needed in a plan today to pay benefits to employees for service to date

Overview of a Pension Plan

- **Defined contribution plan:** The employer and employee contribute specific amounts during the time of service, and the retired employee receives whatever sum these contributions and earnings produce (eg, 401k plan). Accounting for this type of plan is straightforward:
  - The company accrues the required contributions at the time services are rendered by employees and reports pension expense
  - Contributions are normally required by law to be paid before the due date of the tax return for the contribution to be deductible, so companies generally fund liabilities quickly

There are **two required financial statements** (F/S) for defined contribution and defined benefit retirement plans. The purpose of these F/S is to provide information to users about the plan's ability to pay benefits.

- A statement of changes in net assets available for benefits (for the fiscal year)
- A statement of net assets available for benefits (as of fiscal year end)

Statement of Changes in Net Assets Available for Benefits

Representative Task (Application): Prepare a statement of changes in net assets available for benefits for a defined benefit pension plan and a defined contribution pension plan.

A **statement of *changes* in net assets available for benefits** reconciles the beginning balance of the plan assets to the ending balance of the plan assets. The ending balance equals the net assets available for benefits reported on the statement of net assets available for benefits. This statement can be thought of as the equivalent to an **income statement**.

ABC Company 401(k) Plan
Statement of Changes In Net Assets Available for Benefits
Year Ended December 31, Year 1

Additions:	
Investment income:	
Interest and dividends	$ 150,000
Net appreciation in fair value	200,000
	350,000
Interest income on notes receivable from participants	10,000
Contributions from:	
Employer	300,000
Participants	600,000
Rollovers	100,000
	1,000,000
Total additions	**$ 1,360,000**
Deductions:	
Benefits paid	350,000
Administrative expenses	7,500
Total deductions	**357,500**
Net increase (decrease) in assets	**$ 1,002,500**
Net assets available for benefits:	
Beginning of year	5,000,000
End of year	**$6,002,500**

Remember that changes in fair value include the following:

- **Unrealized gains/losses** on investments acquired during the period or held for the entire period
- **Realized gains/losses** on sales of investments, net of unrealized gains/losses previously recognized

Statement of Net Assets Available for Benefits

Representative Task (Application): Prepare a statement of net assets available for benefits for a defined benefit pension plan and a defined contribution pension plan.

To have funds to satisfy future retirement obligations, a benefit plan must have sufficient plan assets (eg, securities, real estate). A **statement of net assets available for benefits** reports the net assets actually available to be used in the future to satisfy pension plan obligations.

This statement can be thought of as the equivalent of the **balance sheet**. It has two sections:

- **Plan assets** (includes any receivables related to plan assets)
  - The plan assets are generally reported at **fair value**
  - Any investments considered to be **fully benefit-responsive**, however, are measured at **contract value**. "Fully benefit-responsive" means that the investment guarantees a certain value (ie, the contract value) to be paid to plan participants
- **Plan liabilities** (excluding future obligations to employees)
  - Examples of liabilities include refunds for excess contributions or accrued amounts owed related to the assets

Comparing net assets available for benefits to benefit obligations will provide the financial funding status of the plan (ie, over- or underfunded).

ABC Company 401(k) Plan Statement of Net Assets Available for Benefits *Year Ended December 31, Year 1*	
Assets:	
Investments:	
Investments at fair value	$4,424,500
Investments at contract value	1,300,000
Total investments	$5,724,500
Receivables:	
Receivable for employer contribution	$ 10,000
Receivables for participant contribution	43,000
Notes receivable from participants	250,000
Total receivables	$ 303,000
Total assets	**$6,027,500**
Liabilities:	
Accrued expenses	$ 7,500
Excess contributions payable	17,500
Total liabilities	**$ 25,000**
Net assets available for benefits	**$6,002,500**

Required Disclosures

Representative Task (Remembering & Understanding): Recall the disclosure requirements for the notes to the financial statements of a defined benefit pension plan and a defined contribution pension plan.

ASC 715 requires the following disclosures for a **defined benefit pension plan:**

Current amounts	Reconciliations	• Projected benefit obligation • Fair value of plan assets
	Amounts related to statement of net assets available for benefits	• Assets and liabilities recognized in statement of net assets available for benefits • Accumulated benefit obligation • Funded status
	Net benefit cost and other comprehensive income	• Amount of net benefit cost recognized • Net gain/loss and prior service cost recognized in OCI • AOCI amounts not yet recognized as part of net benefit cost
Future amounts & assumptions	Future amounts for employer and plan	• Benefits expected to be paid in each of the next five fiscal years and in total for the following five fiscal years • Estimate of contributions to be paid by the plan during the next fiscal year
	Assumed rates (weighted average)	• Discount rate, expected long-term rate of return on plan assets • Rate of compensation increase, interest crediting rate • Healthcare cost trend rate
Descriptions	Explanations and additional information	• Explanations of changes in benefit obligation and plan assets • Information on plan assets (investment policies, asset classes, etc.) • Description of the plan

Disclosures for a **defined contribution pension plan** include the following:

Disclosures	• Amount of cost recognized for the defined contribution plans, separate from any defined benefit plans • Description of nature and effect of any significant changes during the period affecting comparability

BAR

Area III: State and Local Governments

BAR 14
State & Local Governments

BAR 14: State & Local Governments

14.01 Overview of Governmental Accounting

BAR Coverage

The AICPA Blueprint splits coverage of state and local government concepts between Financial Accounting and Reporting (FAR) and Business Analysis and Reporting (BAR). FAR focuses primarily on the:

- Measurement focus and basis of accounting
- Purpose of funds.

BAR addresses the remaining governmental topics, including the:

- Format and content of the financial section of the annual comprehensive financial report
- Derivation of government-wide financial statements and reconciliation requirements
- Typical items and specific types of transactions and events (measurement, valuation, calculation and presentation in governmental entity financial statements).

The AICPA Blueprint has a significant number of representative tasks requiring the preparation of both journal entries and financial statements via examination of sample documents (ie, like a simulation but it is an application task rather than an analysis task).

Rather than have an enormous text, the editors have decided to present the governmental content in smaller, more manageable and understandable segments. We have provided many examples similar to multiple choice questions you will find on the exam.

As a result, only Proprietary funds address the statement preparation tasks because this fund requires a statement of cash flows in addition to the other mandatory statements.

Additional questions related to journal entry and statement preparation can be found in the question bank. We believe this is the optimum approach to passing the governmental section of the CPA Exam.

Annual Comprehensive Financial Report (ACFR)

An important determination in the presentation of government financial statements is the appropriate financial reporting entity. In other words, the government needs to determine which entities' financial results will be presented in the statements and how they will be presented.

- The **primary government** of the reporting entity refers to a general-purpose government unit that has a separately elected governing body and is independent of other government units (eg, city government).
- **Component units** refer to organizations within that government that operate with separate budgets and management but may be fiscally or legally dependent (ie, semi-autonomous) on the primary government (eg, city school district).

Example of Government Financial Reporting Entity

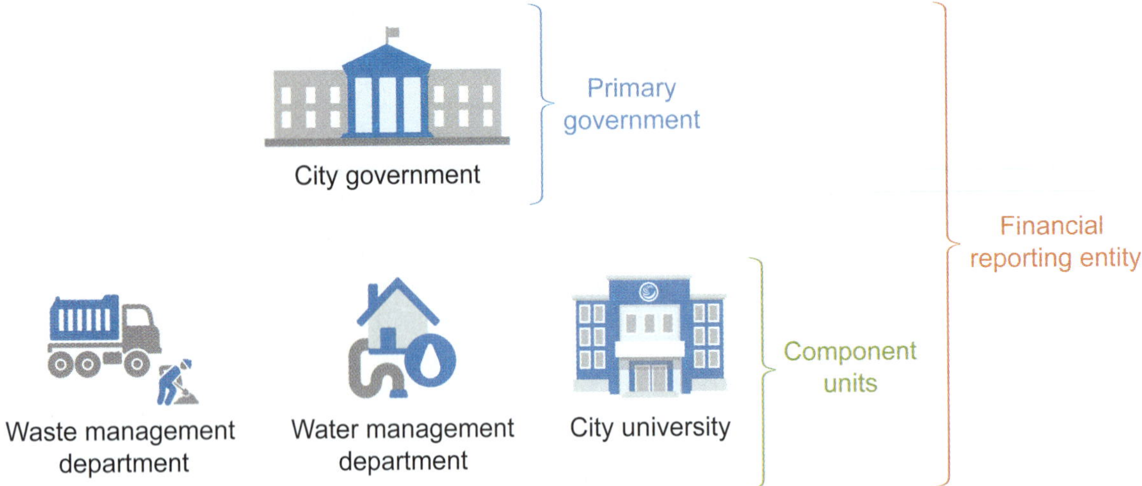

The Governmental Accounting Standards Board (GASB) establishes financial reporting standards for state and local governments in the U.S. Government entities file an annual comprehensive financial report (ACFR).

The ACFR consists of **three sections**:

- **Introductory:** includes a transmittal letter and general information about the entity (eg, officers' names)
- **Financial:** contains basic financial statements, management's discussion and analysis (MD&A), and required supplementary information on only the current fiscal year
- **Statistical:** contains financial trends as well as economic and demographic information (eg, employee headcount, median age, number of capital assets), typically in the form of statistical tables and schedules covering 10 fiscal years.

Sections of the Annual Comprehensive Financial Report (ACFR)

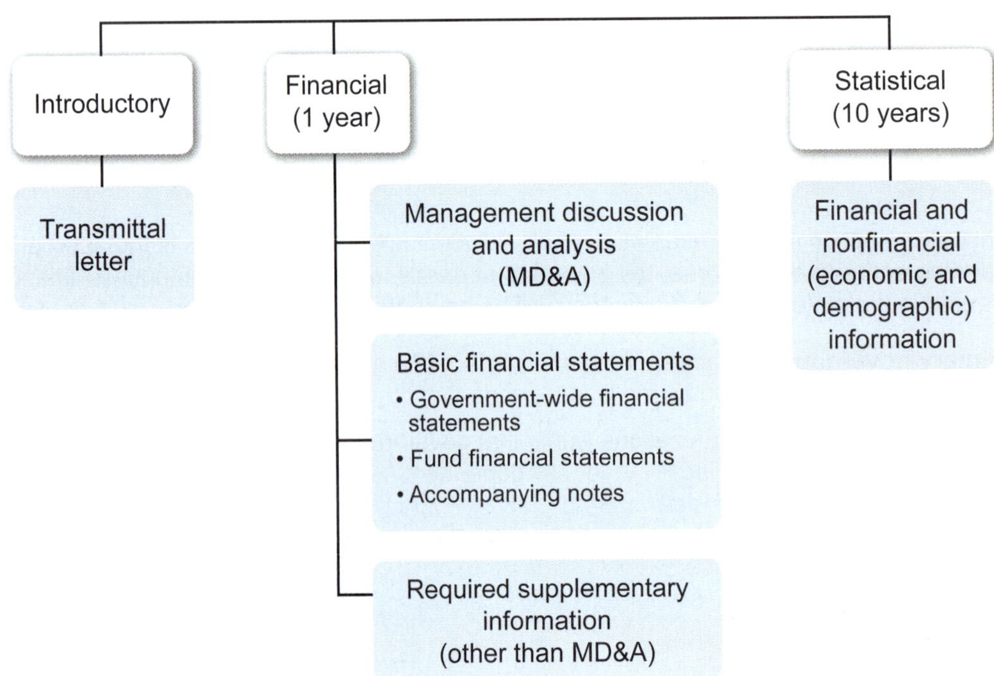

The **BAR section** of the CPA exam focuses on the **financial section**, which consists of five components:

- **Management Discussion & Analysis (MD&A):** The first section of the financial report is a discussion by management of the **significant activities** of the government as a whole during the reporting period and for the future. It also provides an overview of the government's **financial activities**. MD&A is considered to be Required Supplementary Information (RSI).
- **Government-wide Financial Statements:** All activities of the primary government are included, except for fiduciary activities. This section also includes discretely presented component units. These statements are designed to provide information about operational accountability, which shows how effective and efficient the organization has been at using its resources, and the resources available to meet its future obligations.
- **Fund Financial Statements:** The third section of the report includes information about individual funds and component units. Fund accounting uses **modified accrual accounting** (see detailed information below).
- **Notes to the Financial Statements:** The fourth section of the general purpose F/S is the Notes to the F/S. These are a *required part* of the basic F/S and should provide information that is not displayed on the face of the F/S and is essential to their fair presentation. Notes should distinguish whether they pertain to the primary government or its discretely presented component units.
- **Required Supplementary Information (RSI) other than MD&A:** The fifth and final section of the financial report includes other information required by various GASB pronouncements. The most important is a Statement of Revenues, Expenditures, and Changes in Fund Balance – Budget & Actual, called a Budgetary Comparison Schedule. This schedule is required for every governmental fund that prepared annual budgets (typically the general fund and special revenue funds, but also sometimes including others).

Management's Discussion and Analysis (MD&A)

Representative Task (Remembering & Understanding): Recall the objectives and components of management's discussion and analysis in the annual comprehensive financial report for state and local governments.

The first section of the ACFR contains Management's Discussion and Analysis (MD&A), a summary by management of the significant activities of the government that occurred during the reporting period and other items that are anticipated for the future.

Components of the Financial Section of the Annual Comprehensive Financial Report (ACFR)

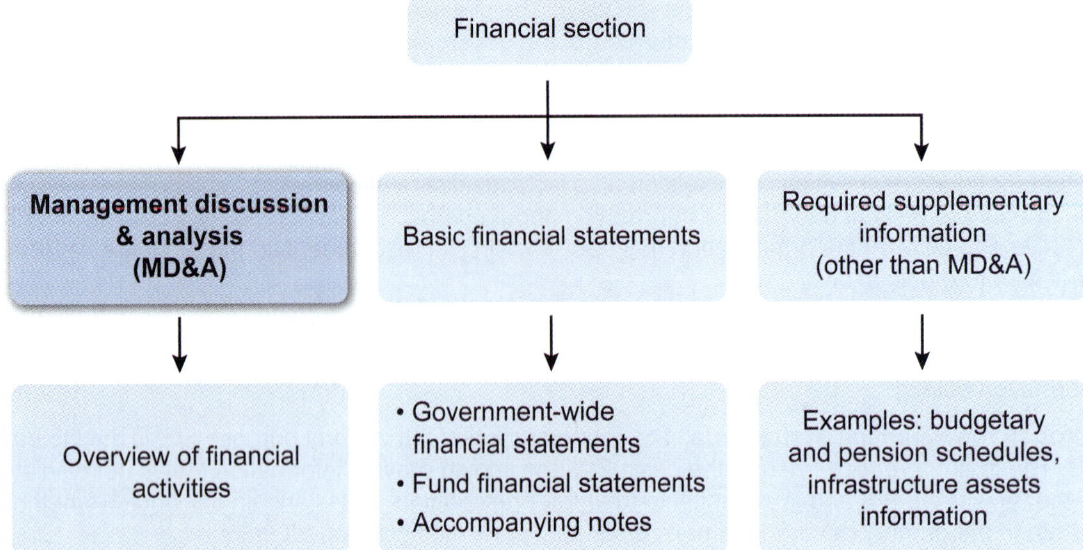

The MD&A section also provides an overview of the government's **financial activities**. MD&A is considered to be Required Supplementary Information (RSI). Items to be included include:

- **Comparison with prior year** – A brief discussion of the F/S with an analysis of amounts that changed considerably from the preceding year.
- **Overall F/S** – Condensed information from the government-wide F/S
- **Individual fund statements** – Key account information from the individual fund statements to follow with analysis of individually significant accounts.
- **Variance analysis** – Discussion of major differences between the original and final budgets for the year and actual results for the year.
- **Long-term activities** – Discussion of significant capital asset and long-term debt activity for the year, and the condition of infrastructure assets.
- **Expected events** – Descriptions of known facts, decisions, and conditions that may have a significant effect on future financial position and results of operations.

Required Financial Statements

Basic financial statements include (see F/S examples in Section 14-11):

- Government-wide Financial Statements
  - Statement of Net Position
  - Statement of Activities
- Governmental Funds Financial Statements
  - Balance Sheet
  - Statement of Revenues, Expenditures, and Changes in Fund Balances

- Proprietary Funds Financial Statements
  - Statement of Net Position
  - Statement of Revenues, Expenses, and Changes in Fund Net Position
  - Statement of Cash Flows (direct method)
- Fiduciary Funds Financial Statements
  - Statement of Fiduciary Net Position
  - Statement of Changes in Fiduciary Net Position

Comparison Of Types Of Financial Statements Issued

For-Profit Entities (GAAP)	Government Entities (GASB)			
	Government-wide Statements	Fund Statements		
		Governmental Funds	Proprietary Funds	Fiduciary Funds
Balance sheet	Statement of net position	Balance sheet	Statement of net position	Statement of fiduciary net position
Income statement	Statement of activities	Statement of revenues, expenditures, and changes in fund balances	Statement of revenues, expenses, and changes in fund net position	Statement of changes in fiduciary net position
Statement of cash flows	N/A	N/A	Statement of cash flows	N/A
Full accrual	**Full accrual**	**Modified accrual**	**Full accrual**	**Full accrual**

The method of accounting and measurement focus for each category listed above is as follows:

State And Local Government Fund Characteristics

Entity	Accounting System	Measurement Focus
Governmental funds	Modified accrual	Current financial resources
Proprietary funds	Full accrual	Economic resources
Fiduciary funds	Full accrual	Economic resources
Government-wide	Full accrual	Economic resources

Fund Accounting

A government unit's principles of accounting are different from those of a private business. A private business prepares financial statements (F/S) for use in lending and investing decisions, but government F/S are used to **provide accountability** for the **use of resources** and to make social and political decisions.

Because government F/S are prepared for distinct purposes, governments use unique required accounting methods (eg, fund accounting, budgetary accounting) to help achieve those purposes.

Government Accounting Methods

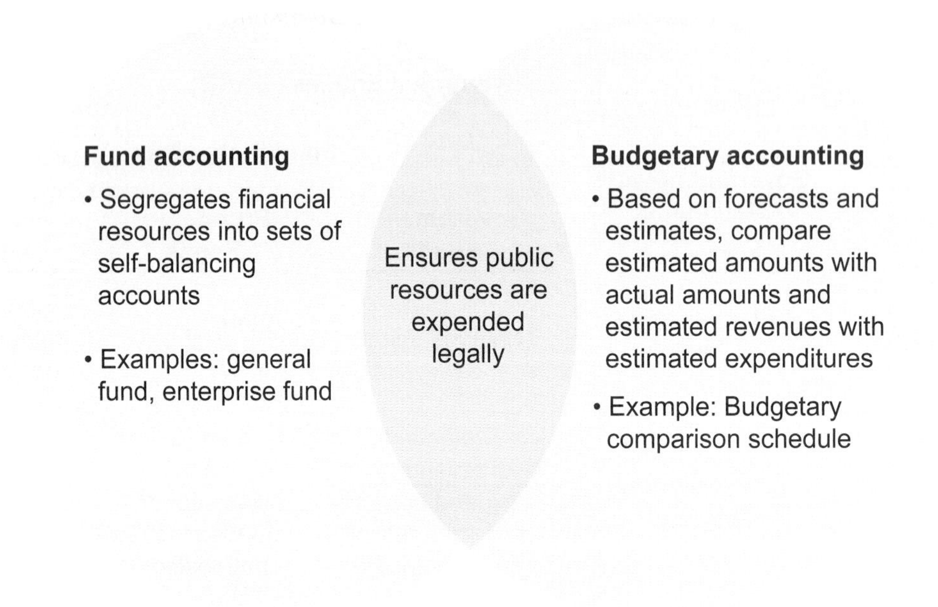

Fund accounting
- Segregates financial resources into sets of self-balancing accounts
- Examples: general fund, enterprise fund

Ensures public resources are expended legally

Budgetary accounting
- Based on forecasts and estimates, compare estimated amounts with actual amounts and estimated revenues with estimated expenditures
- Example: Budgetary comparison schedule

- **Fund accounting** segregates financial resources into sets of self-balancing accounts (eg, general fund, enterprise fund), with each set controlled by a government entity with a specific mission and legal restrictions on the use of the resources.
- Budgetary accounting is based on forecasts and estimates and enables the planning, preparation, and tracking of a balanced budget. Budgeting compares estimated expenditures with estimated revenues and actual revenues/expenditures with estimated revenues/expenditures. This tracking helps to ensure legal restrictions on use of funds are followed.

Most governments use **fund accounting** internally and prepare the government-wide statements with worksheet adjustments from this fund accounting base. Governmental accounting consists of 3 broad categories of funds - governmental funds, proprietary funds, and fiduciary funds.

- **Governmental Funds** – Generally have a budgetary focus and the main emphasis of reporting is the sources, uses, and balances of current financial resources. These are for activities that are primarily funded by taxation or other mandatory payments and are virtually unique to government. *Modified accrual accounting* is used.
- **Proprietary Funds** – Generally have an operations orientation and the main emphasis of reporting is determining income, financial position, changes in financial position, and cash flows using the economic resources approach. These are for activities that are primarily funded by voluntary payments for goods and services by users, and that resemble businesses. *Accrual accounting* is used, in a virtually identical fashion to private businesses.
- **Fiduciary Funds** – Generally are oriented toward the accounting for assets and the main emphasis of reporting is net position and changes to net position using the economic resources approach. These are for activities that most closely resemble not-for-profit organizations, including trusts and agency activities. The trust and custodial funds use accrual accounting.

Fund Categories and Types

Governmental* (serving the public)	**Proprietary*** (business-like)	**Fiduciary** (resources held for others)
1. Permanent (assets with restricted principal)	1. Internal service (goods and services to other funds)	1. Pension trust (employee pensions and retirement benefits)
2. Debt service (interest and principal payment)	2. Enterprise (goods and services to users for fees)	2. Investment trust (resources invested on behalf of multiple agencies)
3. Capital projects (major acquisitions)		3. Private purpose trust (unclaimed tax refund)
4. Special revenue (earmarked source)		4. Custodial (assets equal liabilities)
5. General fund (all other activities)		

State and local government units must have at least 1 fund, the general fund.

**Included in government-wide financial statement.*

Major Funds

On the fund F/S, we report by major fund category as opposed to by fund type. A major fund is:

- General fund
- Other funds representing *both:*
  - **10% or more** of total category assets, liabilities, revenues, or expenditures/expenses of either Governmental or Enterprise category; and
  - **5% or more** of total entity (Governmental & Enterprise) assets, liabilities, revenues, or expenditures/expenses.
- Any other funds that management believes are **useful** to present separately.

Modified Accrual

Representative Task (Application): Calculate the amount of nonexchange revenue to be recognized by state and local governments using the modified accrual basis of accounting and prepare journal entries.

Representative Task (Application): Calculate expenditures to be recognized under the modified accrual basis of accounting (paid from available fund financial resources) for state and local governments and prepare journal entries.

Governmental funds use **modified accrual accounting** rather than accrual accounting. The modified accrual method combines cash accounting with accrual accounting:

- Revenues are recorded only when cash is received, but expenses are recorded when incurred.
- Capital assets acquired are reported as expenditures because they are considered current use of funds. Therefore, there is neither a depreciation nor an amortization expense.

Modified accrual accounting is easiest to understand if the **interperiod equity concept** focus on one period at a time is kept in mind. The interperiod equity concept keeps the focus on a single period, with the revenues of the period intended to cover the spending of that period.

This is consistent with the idea of trying to maintain a **balanced budget** so that costs in the current period aren't paid by future taxpayers. At the same time, this focus on evaluating government activity one period at a time means that future periods are essentially ignored.

In measuring the transactions under modified accrual accounting, the following **measurement principles** are used:

- **Revenues** – These are recognized in the period they are **available to spend**, which means collectible in the current period to pay liabilities, or **within 60 days** after year end. Revenues billed or collected in advance are deferred until the appropriate future period. Revenues that are not measurable are treated as available to spend once they are collected.
- **Costs** – These are recognized using the expenditure principle. Costs are recorded in the period that the obligation to pay them arises, whether this is before or after the period in which the government is actually using the assets or services. Costs are generally recorded when the related fund liability is incurred, except as it relates to unmatured interest on long term debt, as this is only recorded when it becomes legally due.
- **Reporting** – The F/S that are prepared include a balance sheet to present the financial position and a statement of revenues, expenditures, and changes in fund balance to present the flow of financial resources during the year. There is no equivalent in modified accrual reporting to a statement of cash flows.
- **Accountability** – Budgets are typically developed at the beginning of each year, and the focus of governmental financial reporting is on determination of compliance with budgets and accountability for resources. Any fund utilizing annual budgets must prepare a reconciliation of budget to actual amounts to be presented as supplementary information in the F/S. Elected officials are accountable to their constituents.

Gripp County levied property taxes of $2,000,000 in Year 6, of which 1% is expected to be uncollectible. The county has a calendar year end and provides the following additional information with regard to collections:

- $120,000 of taxes levied in Year 5 will be collected on March 31, Year 6.
- $50,000 of taxes levied in Year 6 will be collected on January 31, Year 7.
- $80,000 of taxes levied in Year 6 will be collected on March 31, Year 7.

Determine the amount of property tax revenue Gripp County should report in its Year 6 general fund and prepare the related journal entries.

Under the modified accrual approach, revenues are recognized in a government unit's general fund when they are measurable and available to spend. For property taxes, this occurs in the year the tax levy takes place (ie, in advance of collection). Revenue recognized is directly reduced from the levied amount due to:

- Amounts expected to be collected more than 60 days after year end (ie, deferred revenue).
- Amounts that are estimated to be uncollectible.

To determine Gripp County's Year 6 property tax revenue, the levy must be reduced by uncollectible taxes and any deferred amounts (those not collected within 60 days of December 31, Year 6). The revenue is calculated as follows:

Gross property tax levied	$2,000,000
Less: Estimated uncollectible ($2,000,000 × 1%)	(20,000)
Less: Year 6 taxes collected on March 31, Year 7	(80,000)
Plus Year 5 taxes collected on March 31, Year 6)	120,000
Total general fund Year 6 property tax revenue	**$2,020,000**

Property tax receivable	2,000,000	
Property tax revenue		1,900,000
Deferred revenue (Year 6)		80,000
Allowance for uncollectible property taxes		20,000

For the taxes levied in Year 5 but collected more than 60 days after year end, the following journal entry is required:

Deferred revenue (Year 5)	120,000	
Property tax revenue		120,000

ABC City acquired a fire truck at the beginning of January, Year 2, at a total cost of $50,000. The truck is expected to last for 5 years and have a $5,000 residual value. ABC reported the acquisition in the general fund and is preparing the December 31, Year 2, balance sheet for the governmental funds. Prepare the journal entry for the acquisition of the truck.

Expenditure	50,000	
Cash		50,000

The purchase of a long-lived asset for a governmental fund (ie, modified accrual accounting) requires recording a one-time outflow called an expenditure for the asset's full amount. The truck is not capitalized nor depreciated over time (ie, no matching principle). In other words, the carrying amount on the balance sheet would be $0.

Budgetary Accounting

Representative Task (Remembering & Understanding): Recall and explain the types of budgets used by state and local governments.

Representative Task (Application): Prepare journal entries to record budgets (original and final) of state and local governments.

Representative Task (Application): Prepare journal entries to record encumbrances of state and local governments.

When annual budgets are utilized in the accounting for a government department, *expected sources and uses* may include:

- **Estimated revenues** – Revenues that are expected to be available to spend in the period.
- **Estimated other financing sources** – Expected proceeds from issuance of long-term debt and operating transfers from other government departments.
- **Appropriations** – Expenditures that are expected to occur in the period.
- **Estimated other financing uses** – Expected operating transfers to other government departments.

Operating Budgets

- Regularly occurring activities
  - Personnel costs
  - Public works
  - Community programs

Capital Budgets

- Long-lived assets
- Associated financing sources
  - Road maintenance
  - Building construction

Budgetary entries are made at the beginning of the year and closed out (reversed) at the end of the year. These *estimated accounts* are used to control expenditures, account for taxes that are being levied, estimate transfers in and out, and for planning purposes. If a balanced budget has been prepared, the sum of the estimated revenues and estimated other financial sources will equal the sum of the appropriations and estimated other financial uses.

If a *budgetary surplus or deficit* is expected, it will be reported as an *increase or decrease in the equity*. The equity section of a government department using modified accrual accounting consists of **fund balances**, and the budgetary account used is **budgetary fund balance – unreserved**. It is identified as unreserved because it represents anticipated activity, but no actual legal commitments.

The budget for the City of Goodville for the year ending December 31 was adopted and recorded on January 2 of the same year. After recording the budget, the accounting records showed a debit balance of $50,000 in the budgetary fund balance account. This indicates that appropriations are $50,000 greater than estimated revenues.

Deficit		
Estimated revenues	250,000	
Budgetary fund balance - unreserved	**50,000**	
Appropriations (estimated expenditure)		300,000

On the other hand, if the accounting records showed a credit balance of $50,000 in the budgetary fund balance account, this indicates that appropriations are $50,000 less than estimated revenues.

Surplus		
Estimated revenues	250,000	
Budgetary fund balance - unreserved		**50,000**
Appropriations (estimated expenditure)		200,000

- Net amount reported (retained earnings equivalent)
- Projected budget **deficit** reported as a **debit**
- Projected budget **surplus** reported as a **credit**

The legislative budget for a department using modified accrual accounting includes expected revenues of $700, bond proceeds of $200, expenditures of $500, and operating transfers to assist other departments of $250. Here, estimated revenues exceed appropriates, creating a budget surplus (credit to fund balance).

Prepare the appropriate journal entry at the beginning of the fiscal year:

Account	Debit	Credit
Estimated revenues	700	
Estimated other financial sources	200	
Budgetary fund balance – unreserved		**150**
Appropriations		500
Estimated other financial uses		250

Revenues

When using the **modified accrual approach**, revenues are recognized when they are both measurable and available to spend. The **financial resources** approach is used, which measures only the current financial resources available to the government.

- The requirement that taxes be available to spend in the current period does not mean the taxes must be collected during the current period. Revenue expected to be collected in the **first 60 days** of the following fiscal year may be considered available to spend in the current year.

Revenues and inflows of resources include both **exchange and nonexchange** transactions:

Governmental Revenue: Exchange vs. Nonexchange Transactions

Exchange

- Goods/services/cash of **equal** value are exchanged between government and another entity
- Example: government performing garbage removal services for a fee

Nonexchange

- Government gives/receives something of value **without** directly receiving/giving **equal value** in return
- Example: government assessing a local sales tax on consumers who make retail purchases

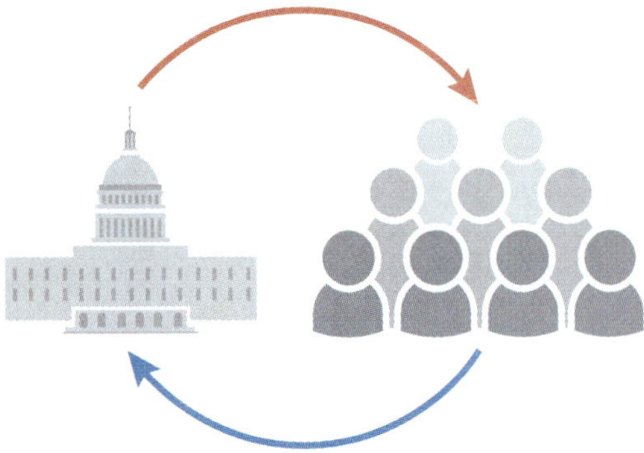

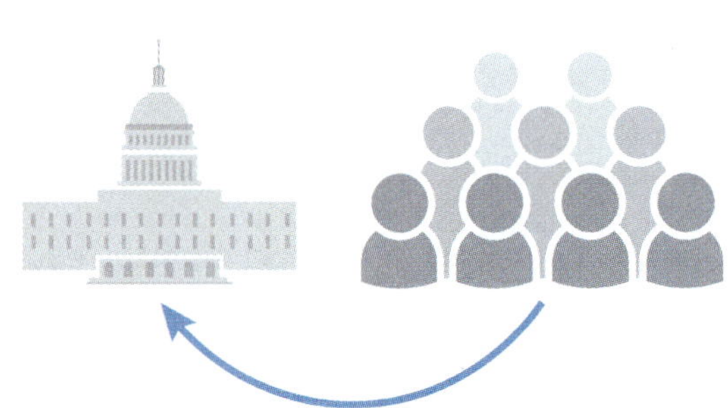

Exchange transactions consist of goods or services and cash (of equal value) that are exchanged between a government entity and another entity. For example, if a government provides garbage removal services to its citizens for a fee, the citizens and the government exchange cash and a service of equivalent value.

Nonexchange transactions occur when the government gives/receives without directly receiving/giving equal value in exchange. For example, a government that charges a sales tax to consumers derives tax revenue without directly providing anything in exchange.

There are four types of nonexchange transactions:

Government Revenue: Nonexchange Transactions

Revenue Type	Description	Examples
Derived tax revenue	Taxes assessed on the exchange transactions of others	Sales tax, income tax
Imposed nonexchange revenue	Taxes and fees assessed on assets or rights	Property taxes, fines, permits
Government-mandated nonexchange revenue	Funds provided to another governmental unit for a specific purpose	Federal grants
Voluntary nonexchange revenue	Transactions entered willingly by parties to support a specific program	Unrestricted grants

Assume a calendar-year government levies $2,200 in property taxes on 11/1/Year 1. It expects to collect as follows:

November Year 1	$400
December Year 1	900
January Year 2	300
February Year 2	250
March Year 2	225
Estimated uncollectibles	125

The entry to record the **billing** is **as follows**:

11/1/Year 1		
Property Taxes receivable - current	2,200	
Revenues		1,850
Deferred revenues		225
Allowance for uncollectibles		125

The amounts expected during Year 1 and the first two months (approximately 60 days) of Year 2 are considered available to spend in Year 1.

The deferred revenues are **reclassified** at the beginning of Year 2 when they represent the current year (ie, after 60 days):

1/1/Year 2		
Deferred revenues	2,200	
Revenues		2,200

In addition to taxes, grants provide revenue. Assume our client is a local government and the state government authorizes a $900 **unrestricted grant** that will be paid to the local government later in the current year, the entry at the time the grant is *approved* is:

Receivable from state grant	900	
Revenues		900

The *collection* of the grant is straightforward:

Cash	900	
Receivable from state grant		900

If the state grant is **restricted**, then it is not considered available until the local government has acted in accordance with the restriction. For example, if the $900 state grant is paid to the local entity immediately, but stipulates that the money must be spent on the purchase of new equipment, the receipt of the money (assuming no prior accrual occurred) is recorded as follows:

Cash	900	
Deferred revenues		900

When $600 of the money is *spent* on appropriate equipment, an expenditure of $600 is reported and a simultaneous entry is made to show that this portion of the grant is now available:

Deferred revenues	600	
Revenues		600

If the remainder of the grant money is not spent, it may have to be returned to the state government:

Deferred revenues	300	
Cash		300

Expenditures

Under modified accrual accounting, costs are reported in accordance with the **expenditure principle**, which means that the focus is on the **outflow of financial resources** to pay for the good or service rather than on the benefits resulting from the cost. Thus, there is no parallel to the matching principle, and no attempt to amortize costs that benefit multiple periods.

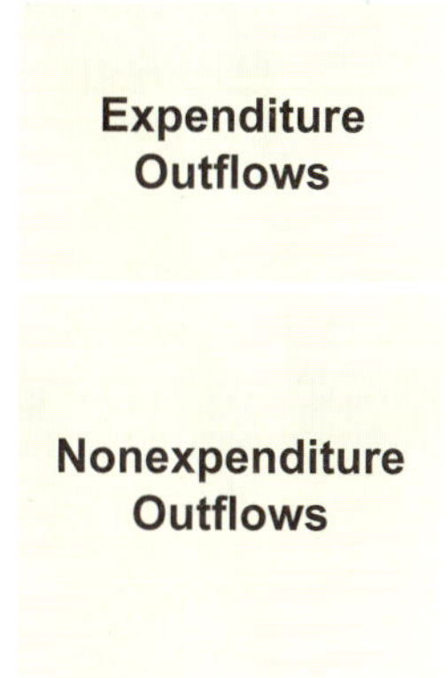

Expenditure Outflows

- Operating
- Capital
- Debt service

Nonexpenditure Outflows

- Other financing uses (nonoperating)
- Special items (infrequent or unusual and under control of entity)
- Extraordinary items (infrequent and unusual and not under control of entity)

Because of the importance of adhering to budgets in the governmental process, the initial entry in connection with the acquisition of an asset or service is made when the **order is placed** with the vendor. An open order is known as an **encumbrance** and can be considered a form of estimated expenditure. Unlike an appropriation, however, this represents an actual legal commitment, and requires that a portion of the fund balance be reserved.

For example, if an **order to purchase supplies is placed**, and the governmental entity estimates that the invoice for the supplies will be $900 when received, the following entry is made:

Encumbrances	900	
Reserved for Encumbrances		900

When an **order has been filled**, two entries need to be made. The first is to cancel the encumbrance since it is no longer an open order. This just involves reversing the entry made when the order was placed:

Reserved for Encumbrances	900	
Encumbrances		900

The actual invoice from the vendor is also recorded. Keep in mind that it might not be for the exact same amount as was estimated in the encumbrance. If the supplies ordered earlier are billed to the government department for $890, the entry to record the approval for payment is:

Expenditures	890	
Vouchers payable		890

The actual **payment** of the voucher later is recorded as follows:

Vouchers payable	890	
Cash		890

Notice that the purchase of the supplies is recorded as an expenditure, even though the supplies may not have been used yet. This is known as the **purchases** method. It contrasts with the approach used by private businesses to record supplies as expenses only once they are used, known as the **consumption** method.

To avoid exceeding budgetary limits placed on the department, the sum of the expenditures recorded to date and the open encumbrances should not exceed the **appropriations**. For example, if appropriations for supplies were recorded in the initial budgetary entry for $1,500, and expenditures to date are $890, open encumbrances for additional orders should not exceed $610. If it appears the budget for the year will be exceeded, the department should usually request a supplementary appropriation or other modification to the legislative budget.

Keep in mind that purchases of fixed assets are recorded as expenditures at the time of delivery of the assets to the government. Also note that the government may bypass the recording of encumbrances for repetitive expenditures, such as **salaries and wages** of employees.

Note: At the end of any reporting period, the remaining balance of funds that are available for use for a city would be = **Appropriations − Encumbrances − Expenditures = funds available**.

Expenditures may be *categorized* in detail in several different ways:

- **Function or Program** – The category identifies the purpose or objectives of the expenditure. Examples are highways and streets, health and welfare, education, general government, **public safety**, disaster relief, and defense. Program includes drug addiction, education, and elderly. (**WHY - Purpose**)
- **Organizational Unit (department)** – This category groups expenditures based on the government's organizational structure. Examples include **police and fire departments**, city clerk, personnel department, parks, and recreational departments. These can be combined to form a Function category, such as public safety.
- **Activity** – This category classifies expenditures by activity, which allows the ability to measure economy and efficiency of operations (eg, **police protection**).
- **Character** – This category identifies the fiscal period that the benefits are expected. Examples are *debt service-past* (matured interest and principal), *current services-present* (salaries and supplies), and *capital outlay-future* (police car and construction expenditures) (**WHEN**).
- **Object** – This category identifies the types of items purchased or services obtained. Examples are personnel services, salaries, rent, utilities, depreciation, and supplies. (**WHAT - Type**)
  - The statement of Revenues, Expenditures, and Changes in Fund Balance generally reports expenditures by function within character classifications. Budgets often report expenditures by object class.
  - Function must be presented in either statement or footnotes.

Closing Entries

At the end of the fiscal year, several closing entries are required under modified accrual accounting. One is to close the entry that was made at the beginning of the year to record the budget.

For example, if the legislative budget included expected revenues of $700, bond proceeds of $200, expenditures of $500, and operating transfers to assist other departments of $250, the journal entry made at the **beginning of the fiscal year** would have been:

Estimated revenues	700	
Estimated other financial sources	200	
Budgetary fund balance – unreserved		150
Appropriations		500
Estimated other financial uses		250

At the **end of the year**, the closing entry for the budgetary is:

Budgetary fund balance – unreserved	150	
Appropriations	500	
Estimated other financial uses	250	
Estimated revenues		700
Estimated other financial sources		200

This is simply a reversal of the opening entry and is unaffected by the actual revenues and costs during the year.

The **second closing entry** that is needed is comparable to private businesses, and involves the *nominal accounts* created during the year for inflows and outflows related to revenues, other financing sources, expenditures, and other financing uses.

For example, if revenues recorded during the year totaled $710, other financial sources $190, expenditures $490, and other financial uses $230, the closing entry at the end of the year is:

Revenues	710	
Other financial sources 190	190	
Fund balance – unreserved 180		180
Expenditures		490
Other financial uses 230		230

Notice that the excess of inflows over outflows of $180 is closed into fund balance – unreserved, which is the modified accrual accounting equivalent to retained earnings (or retained earnings – unappropriated) of a private business.

A third closing entry is needed for **open encumbrances**, that is, orders that were placed during the year but not fulfilled as of the end of the year. Since an encumbrance represents a legal commitment to purchase, it reduces the unreserved fund balance.

Assume that during the year, orders totaling $500 were placed, and $470 of those were fulfilled, with the remaining $30 still open at year end. As a result, there is a debit balance of $30 in Encumbrances and a credit balance of $30 in Reserved for encumbrances prior to the closing entries. The closing entry to zero out these accounts is:

	Debit	Credit
Fund Balance – unreserved	30	
Encumbrances		30

The unreserved fund balance is reduced because of the commitment, and a separate fund balance – Reserved for Encumbrances – now identifies the outstanding orders on the balance sheet.

If this represents the first year of operations for the specific government department, the **equity (fund balance) section** of the balance sheet will report the following amounts:

Fund balance – Unreserved	150
Fund balance – Reserved for encumbrances	30
Fund balance – Reserved for inventories	80

14.02 Government-wide Financial Statements

Overview

Representative Task (Remembering & Understanding): Identify and recall basic concepts and principles associated with government-wide financial statements (eg, required activities, financial statements, financial statement components).

Components of the Financial Section of the Annual Comprehensive Financial Report (ACFR)

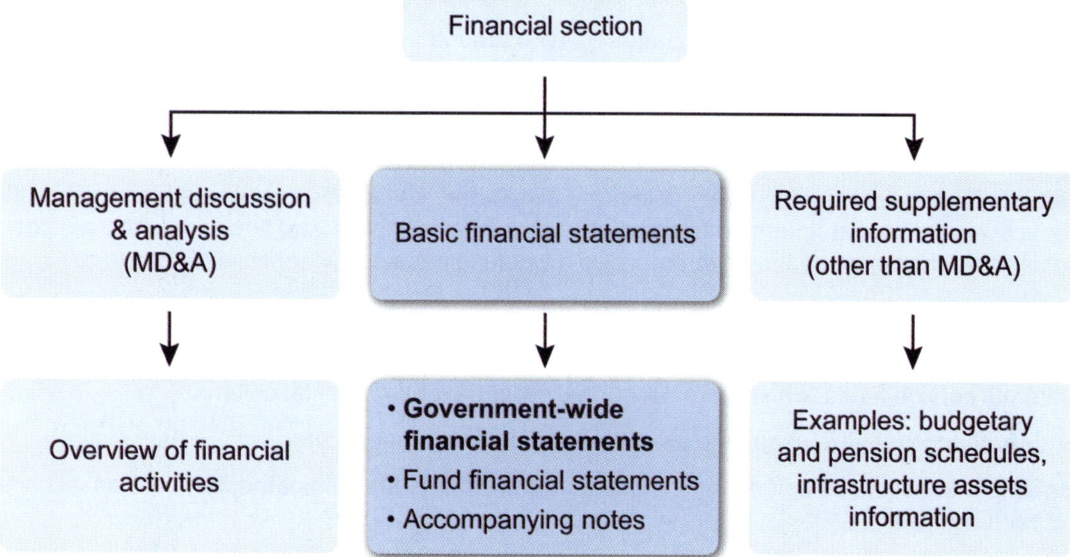

These statements are designed to provide information about **operational accountability**, which shows how effective and efficient the organization has been at using its resources, and the resources available to meet its future obligations. The statements reflect activities such as providing a judicial system, police and fire protection, etc.

Government-wide F/S consist of:

- Statement of Net Position
- Statement of Activities

Statement of Net Position

Representative Task (Application): Prepare the government-wide statement of net position for a state or local government from trial balances and supporting documentation.

Representative Task (Application): Calculate the net position balances (unrestricted, restricted, and net investment in capital assets) for state and local governments and prepare journal entries.

There are **four columns** on the **Statement of Net Position:**

- **Governmental activities** – Activities that are financed primarily through taxes and other nonexchange transactions.
  - This column reports the consolidated results of all **governmental and internal service** funds.
  - The presentation uses **accrual** accounting, even though the government funds are all modified accrual funds.
  - Capital assets are reported and depreciated in the asset section, and long-term debt is included in the liability section.
  - Interfund transactions within this column are eliminated, so that the internal service fund is often effectively eliminated. Interfund transactions within the enterprise and fiduciary funds are not eliminated, however, so the government as a whole is not actually consolidated.
- **Business-type activities** – Activities that are normally financed through user charges.
  - This reports the consolidated results of all the **enterprise funds**. Note that it does not include internal service funds, which were accounted for in the governmental column.
  - **Accrual** accounting is used here as in the individual fund accounting.
  - Interfund transactions among the various enterprise funds are eliminated, but not transactions with other fund types.
- **Total** – This column simply adds together the amounts from the two primary government columns for governmental and business-type activities. Note that fiduciary activities were not reported in either of the two previous columns, so this total doesn't actually reflect all of the net assets held by the government.
- **Component units** – Legally separate organizations for which the elected officials of a primary government are financially accountable.
  - This column reports the combined results of all the component units for which separate reporting was selected (those receiving blended treatment were already included in one of the first two columns of this statement).
  - No eliminations are made.

Sample City
Statement of Net Position
December 31, Year 1

	Primary government			
Assets	**Governmental activities**	**Business-type activities**	**Total**	**Component units**
Cash and cash equivalents	$13,597,899	$10,279,143	$23,877,042	$ 303,935
Investments	27,365,221	-	27,365,221	7,428,952
Receivables (net)	12,833,132	3,609,615	16,442,747	4,042,290

The Statement of Net Position is a type of balance sheet, except that the form is:

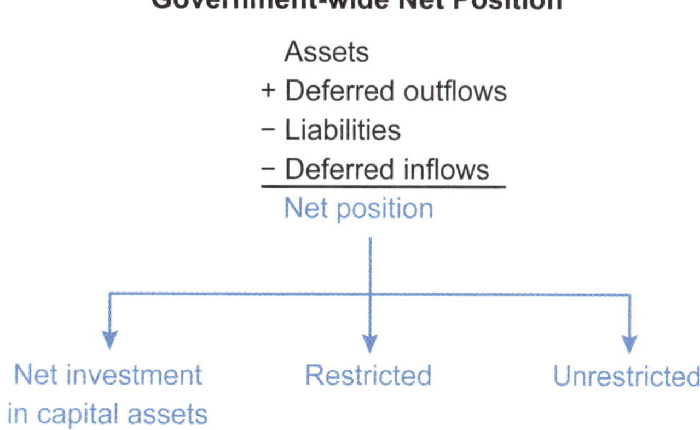

- This format is called the **Net Position Format**, which is encouraged, although a *balance sheet format* is also permitted (assets + deferred outflows of resources = liabilities + deferred inflows of resources + net position). Regardless of which format is used, however, the statement of net position will report the residual amount as the **net position**, consisting of **three components:**
  - **Net investment in capital assets:** the excess of existing capital assets less accumulated depreciation and associated debt
  - **Restricted net position:** funds that are restricted by constitution, external resource providers, or legislation
  - **Unrestricted net position:** the residual amount with no restrictions
- Terms like net assets, fund balance, or equity should not be used.
- It is preferred to present assets and liabilities in order of liquidity.

The City of Arvida compiled the following information for its capital assets, exclusive of infrastructure assets, as of December 31, Year 5:

Cost of capital assets	$4,700,000
Accumulated depreciation	925,000
Debt related to capital assets	1,040,000

Determine the amount that Arvida should report for net investment in capital assets on the December 31, Year 5, government-wide statement of net position.

A government-wide statement of net position presents total net position as three categories to provide additional transparency to financial statement users: net investment in capital assets, restricted net position, and unrestricted net position.

Net investment in capital assets is calculated by taking the cost of capital assets and subtracting accumulated depreciation as well as any debt associated with the assets.

Here, the City of Arvida's net investment in capital assets is $2,735,000, calculated as follows:

Cost of capital assets	$4,700,000
Less accumulated depreciation	925,000
Less debt related to capital assets	1,040,000
Net investment in capital assets	**$2,735,000**

A city council designates funds for future equipment replacement. In which of the following should the city report the designation?

- Restricted component of net position
- Net investment in capital assets
- Nonspendable fund balance
- Unrestricted component of net position

Restricted net position represents funds that are restricted by constitution, external resource providers, or legislation. Unrestricted net position is the residual amount with no restrictions.

Here, the city council designates funds for *future* equipment replacement. This is an **internal designation** indicating how the government intends to spend the funds. The funds are not restricted by law or an external resource provider. Therefore, in the city's statement of net position, the funds are an **unrestricted component of net position**.

Deferred Outflows and Deferred Inflows of Resources

When the government consumes net assets, it is considered an outflow of resources if it is applicable to the current reporting period. **Deferred outflows** of resources represent the consumption of net assets that are applicable to a future reporting period. Deferred outflows of resources are not assets but are similar in that they have a positive effect on net position.

- Prepaid rent would *not* be an example of a deferred outflow. This is because the outflow of resources, cash, is matched by the inflow of resources, prepaid rent and, as a result, net position has not decreased.

- *Grant expenditures made in advance* of the grantee meeting timing requirements on the other hand, is a deferred outflow. The outflow of resources, cash, is not matched by an inflow of resources and, as a result, net position has decreased.

Similarly, inflows of resources are acquisitions of net assets that are applicable to the current reporting period. **Deferred inflows** of resources are basically the opposite of deferred outflows of resources. They are acquisitions of net assets that are applicable to a future reporting period. Deferred inflows are not liabilities, but they are similar in that they have a negative effect on net position.

- Deferred revenue, for example, would not be an example of a deferred inflow. This is because the inflow of resources, cash, is matched by incurring an obligation to perform, a liability and, as a result, net position has not increased.
- *Grant funds received in advance* of the grantee meeting timing requirements, on the other hand, is a deferred inflow. The inflow of resources, cash, is not matched by an obligation as the grant funds would have been received with the passage of time and, as a result, net position has increased.

Many items that result from government activities may be considered deferred outflows of resources or deferred inflows of resources, depending on which side of the transaction the governmental entity is on. Some of the items that are addressed include:

- Current and advanced debt refunding
- Nonexchange revenue transactions
- Sales of future revenues
- Sale and leaseback transactions
- Grants
- Qualified hedging derivatives

If deferred outflows or deferred inflows are disclosed in the aggregate, the notes to the F/S should describe the details of what is included in the net amounts.

Capital Assets

Representative Task (Remembering & Understanding): Identify capital assets reported in the government-wide financial statements of state and local governments.

Representative Task (Application): Calculate the net general capital assets balance for state and local governments and prepare journal entries (initial measurement and subsequent depreciation and amortization).

Government entities must have a **General Capital Assets (GCA)** account and a **General Long-Term Liabilities (GLTL)** account, which are included in the government-wide F/S. These accounts are designed to capture inflows and outflows to/from funds.

GCA are usually recorded at purchase or construction cost and are reported in three areas:

- The government activities column of the government-wide statement of net position
- The proprietary fund (and roll-up to the government-wide F/S)
- The fiduciary fund (and do not roll up to the government-wide F/S)

The general fund of Divide City acquired three police cars at the beginning of January, Year 2, at a total cost of $75,000. The cars are expected to last for five years and have a $15,000 salvage value. Straight-line depreciation is used. Calculate the amount that the police cars will be reported at on the December 31, Year 3, government-wide statement of net position.

Government-wide F/S present the governmental unit's net position over time; therefore, they are prepared using the **accrual basis** of accounting. As a result, **fixed assets are capitalized** and **depreciated** over their useful lives in a manner similar to for-profit entities.

On the acquisition date, the cars are reported at their cost of $75,000. On December 31, Year 3, the carrying value (CV) of the police cars must reflect two years of depreciation expense, calculated as follows:

($75,000 cost − $15,000 salvage value) / 5 year useful life × 2 years = $24,000

The **CV** of the police cars in December, Year 3, is therefore $51,000, calculated as follows:

$75,000 cost − $24,000 depreciation = $51,000

Donated assets are recorded at fair market value on the date of donation. GCA are increased/decreased by:

- Acquisition or construction
- Depreciation (also see Infrastructure section below)
- Disposal and/or impairment

Donation Or Works Of Art, Historical Treasures, And Similar Assets To A Government Unit	
General Rule	The government unit capitalizes the donation at its historical cost or fair value on the date of donation if items are held as a collection
Exception	Capitalization is not required if the following conditions apply: • Donation is held for public exhibition, education, or research • Donation is cared for, protected, and preserved • Proceeds from the sale of donated items would only be used to buy similar assets (eg, artwork) for the collection

Intangible assets that are identifiable should be recognized in the statement of net position at historical cost.

Infrastructure assets (eg, streets, sidewalks, highways) are accounted for in the governmental activities column of the government-wide F/S. Generally, these assets are recorded at historical cost and depreciation.

Costs for repairs, maintenance, and improvements for such assets can be difficult to gauge, and these assets are, in a sense, indefinite in duration. Therefore, a modified approach to depreciation has been developed.

Governments may **omit depreciation** on infrastructure assets if they can demonstrate that the regular costs incurred to maintain them give them an indefinite life. This approach may be used if the government:

- Uses an asset management system to manage the infrastructure and
- Documents how the assets are being preserved at a minimum level established by the government.

If these conditions are met, infrastructure assets are recorded as capital expenditures and are not depreciated; however, additions and improvements are still capitalized. Two schedules related to this option are included in the required supplementary information:

- A schedule reflecting the condition of the government's infrastructure
- A schedule comparing needed and actual expenditures of maintaining the infrastructure

General and Proprietary Long-Term Liabilities

Representative Task (Remembering & Understanding): Identify general and proprietary long-term liabilities reported in the government-wide financial statements of state and local governments.

Representative Task (Application): Calculate the total indebtedness to be reported in the government-wide financial statements of a state or local government.

Representative Task (Application): Calculate the net general long-term debt balance for state and local governments and prepare journal entries (eg, debt issuance, interest payments, issue premiums, issue discounts).

General and long-term liabilities are reported only in the government-wide F/S (similar to capital assets presentation). A **general long-term liability (GLTL)** is one that is not included in either the proprietary or fiduciary funds. **Specific long-term debt** is so called as the debt will be repaid from a specific proprietary or fiduciary fund.

Remember that the proprietary F/S will roll up into the government-wide F/S; however, the fiduciary F/S do not roll up. GLTL are affected by the following types of transactions:

- Amortization of bond premiums/discounts
- Issuance and retirement of debt
- Changes in liabilities associated with compensated absences, pensions, claims/judgments, etc.

GTLT are reported at *net present value* (ie, face value adjusted for any premium or discount), using the effective interest rate on the transaction date. Bond-related expenses, such as premium/discount amortization, amortization of bond issuance costs, and accrued interest expense, are reported in the government-wide statement of activities.

The issuance of GLTL is generally recorded as Other Financing Sources in either the Capital Projects fund or the Debt Service fund. Related expenditures (such as issuance costs) are also recorded in the same fund. The valuation and liability accounts are reflected in the government-wide statement of net position.

A government has the following liabilities at the end of the year:

General obligation bonds	$4,500,000
Compensated absences	375,000
Salaries payable	140,000

Calculate the amount of liabilities that should be reported in the governmental activities column of the government-wide statement of net position.

Remember the primary government's net position is presented in two different categories on this statement:

1. **Governmental activities** include the government's general administration, taxes, nonexchange transactions, and intragovernmental transfers. Governmental activities aggregate the financial position of the governmental funds and the internal service funds.
2. **Business-type activities** include transactions involving charges and fees to external users in exchange for providing goods and services. Business-type activities aggregate the financial position of the enterprise funds.

Here, the government reports long-term debt (general obligation bonds of $4,500,000) and current liabilities (compensated absences of $375,000 and salaries payable of $140,000). There is no information provided indicating that these amounts relate to enterprise funds or the government's component units. Therefore, all liabilities should be reported in the governmental activities column of the statement of net position, for a total of **$5,015,000** ($4,500,000 + $375,000 + $140,000).

Pension and Post-Retirement Liabilities

Representative Task (Remembering & Understanding): Recall the recognition and measurement requirements for a net pension liability for a defined benefit pension plan for state and local governments.

Pensions include retirement income and other post-employment benefits provided through a pension plan, such as death and disability benefits or life insurance. **Other post-employment benefits (OPEB)** include post-employment healthcare (eg, medical, dental, vision, or hearing) and other post-employment benefits provided separately from a pension plan. Pensions and OPEB are accounted for similarly in the financial statements.

Defined benefit pension plans provide recipients with a **guaranteed level of income** upon retirement. The amount is typically based on the employee's salary, years of service, and age at retirement, and the employer bears the investment risk.

Government entity pension plans are **fiduciary funds** and are reported on the statement of fiduciary net position and statement of changes in fiduciary net position. Additionally, any net pension liability or net OPEB liability is also reported on the governmental funds balance sheet.

Required financial statements include:

- The statement of fiduciary net position
- The statement of changes in fiduciary net position
- Required Notes to Financial Statements

Net pension liability (NPL) is the total pension liability (TPL) less the plan's fiduciary net position (ie, pension plan assets; in other words, it is simply the *net liability* of the pension plan).

There must be an **actuarial evaluation** of the pension liability at least every two years. The prior year valuation can be rolled forward, but only for one year. All actuarial assumptions must be in alignment with assumptions provided in the Actuarial Standards of Practice issued by the Actuarial Standards Board.

Projected benefit payments:

- Are based upon the benefit terms existing at the plan's fiscal year end
- Include the effects of projected salary changes and service credits
- Include the effects of projected automatic post-employment benefit changes (including COLAs)
- After discounting, are attributed to plan member service periods using the entry age actuarial cost method with each period's service cost determined as a level percentage of pay
- Are attributed individually to each plan member, from the time the member begins to accrue pension benefits through the member's retirement.

Sample Disclosure - Net Pension Liability *(in millions)*

	Fund 1	Fund 2	Fund 3	Totals
Fund Status	Closed* Yr 3	Open	Open	
Total Pension Liability (TPL)	$35,710	$125,750	$224,080	$385,540
Fiduciary Net Position (FNP)	26,780	70,975	236,450	334,205
Net Pension Liability Or (Asset)	$8,930	$54,775	$(12.370)	$51,335
FNP as a Percentage Of TPL	75.0%	56.4%	105.5%	
Discount Rate	6.75	5.40	3.26	

**Payments are no longer made to the fund; however, the liability remains until all past participants have fully received their pension payments.*

Representative Task (Application): Recall the recognition and measurement requirements for a net other post-employment benefit (OPEB) liability for an OPEB plan for state and local governments.

Other post-employment benefits (OPEB) provided by employers include health care coverage, life insurance, disability coverage, and other services such as access to legal advice. These benefits are provided separately from pension benefits. Governments are not mandated to provide OPEB.

Similar to pension obligations, the standards for OPEB address recognizing and measuring:

- Plan liabilities
- Deferred outflows and inflows of resources
- Plan expenses
- Note disclosures and required supplemental information

The GASB standards only address *how to measure* the long-term liability and annual cost of OPEB for the purpose of reporting the amount in the financial statements. The GASB standards do not address how the government entity measures OPEB benefits in determining *how much to set aside* to fund those future OEPB disbursements.

Employer and nonemployer OPEB obligations are determined as a portion of the present value of projected plan payments (for current and inactive employees) that is attributed to past periods of service *less* the OPEB's fiduciary net position amount.

The total OPEB liability is generally determined through an **actuarial valuation**. As with pension obligations, an **actuarial evaluation** of the OPEB liability must be completed at least every two years.

For OPEB plans with less than 100 plan members (ie, smaller government entities), a specified alternative measurement method is available that replaces the actuarial valuation method requirement. The alternative method uses the same measurement steps that an actuarial valuation method would use but allows for simplification of certain assumptions.

Benefit payment projections must be based on claims cost (or age-adjusted premiums that approximate claims cost) and the benefits and legal agreements valid at the measurement date. Projected benefit calculations must reflect projected salary changes and service credits and projected automatic post-employment benefit changes (including COLAs). Projections must also include taxes or assessments that are expected to be imposed on benefit payments.

If these benefits are provided through a defined benefit OPEB plan administered through a trust, the liability shown is the net OPEB liability; otherwise, the liability shown is the total OPEB liability.

	Pensions	Other Post-Employment Benefits (OPEB)
Inclusions	• Retirement income • Other benefits provided through a pension plan	• Healthcare • Other benefits provided separately from a pension plan
Reporting	• Statement of fiduciary net position • Statement of changes in fiduciary net position • Governmental funds balance sheet (net liability)	
Net Liability Calculation	• Actuarial present value of projected benefit payments that is attributed to past periods of employee service − plan's fiduciary net position = net liability	
Net Liability Recognized	• To the extent expected to be liquidated with current financial resources	

Since the governmental fund financial statements are prepared using *modified accrual accounting*, it is important to note that the net liability is only recognized to the extent that the net liability will be liquidated with current financial resources. Therefore, the net liability reported on the governmental funds balance sheet is very likely just a portion of the government entity's total net pension or OPEB liability. The rest will be the responsibility of future taxpayers and is not reported on the balance sheet.

Statement of Activities

Representative Task (Application): Prepare the government-wide statement of activities for a state or local government from trial balances and supporting documentation.

Representative Task (Application): Calculate the amount of nonexchange revenue to be recognized by state and local governments using the accrual basis of accounting and prepare journal entries.

Representative Task (Application): Calculate expenses to be recognized under the accrual basis of accounting for state and local governments and prepare journal entries.

The government-wide **statement of activities** is similar to an income statement and presents the revenues and expenses of a governmental unit on the **full accrual basis**. (As a reminder, full accrual basis of accounting recognizes revenue (or expenses) when they are earned (or consumed), regardless of cash received or paid.)

Expenses are shown in the first column and reported in separate rows by function (eg, public safety, water, and sewer). **Program revenues** are presented in the next column and are reported in separate rows by function and also in separate columns by program type (eg, charges for services, operating grants, capital grants).

Statement of Activities

		Program revenues		
	Expenses	Charges for services	Operating grants and contribution	Capital grants and contribution
Primary government				
General government	200	3	11	6
Public safety	100	8	22	7
Total government activities	**300**	**11**	**33**	**13**
Business-type activities				
Water and sewer	50	9	5	13
Municipal airports	20	15	19	16
Total business-type activities	**70**	**24**	**24**	**29**
Total primary government	370	35	57	42
Component units	**10**			

The right-most section of the government-wide statement of activities shows **net (expense) revenue** in separate columns by government activities, business-type activities, and discretely presented component unit activities. If the component units are not shown, then the statement is representing the *primary government* only and will be so labeled.

Statement of Activities

	Net (expense) revenue and changes in net position			
	Primary government			
	Governmental activities	Business-type activities	Total	Component units
Primary government				
General government	(220)		(220)	
Public safety	(137)		(137)	
Total government activities	**(357)**		**(357)**	
Business-type activities				
Water and sewer		(81)	(81)	
Municipal airports		(70)	(70)	
Total business-type activities		**(151)**	**(151)**	
Total primary government	(357)	(151)	(508)	
Component units				**10**

The columns provide detailed information about how the entity has **used its resources** on the various types of activities. Government activities are financed mainly through taxes, business-type activities through user fees, and discretely presented component units that are fiscally independent.

Revenues

All revenues and expenses are reported on the statement of activities. Revenues (ie, inflow of resources) are classified as either **program revenues** or **general revenues** depending on their purpose. Although program revenues are directly associated with a specific program, general revenues are not.

Program revenues are reported in three categories.

- **Charges for services:** payments from private individuals for services received (eg, garbage collection).
- **Operating grants and contributions:** revenues received mostly from other government agencies for administrative purposes (eg, contributions received from the state to pay salaries of faculty members).
- **Capital grants and contributions:** revenues obtained specifically for capital projects (eg, grants received from a city for a school to purchase a vehicle).

General revenues include all taxes levied and other nontax revenues that are not restricted to a specific program. Because general revenues are not restricted, they are not reported in categories.

The **net (expense) or revenue** is broken out between governmental activities, business-type activities, and component units, the same as in the Statement of Net Position.

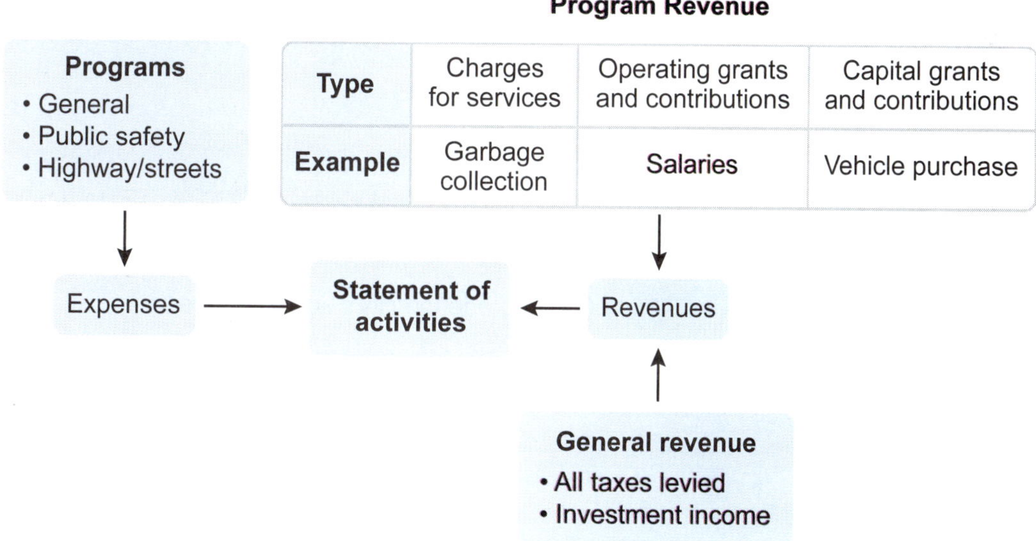

Note: Expenses are reported first and general revenues are reported at the bottom right section

After that, separate additions or deductions are made for **special items, extraordinary items, and transfers** (between categories). If a government had contributions to term and permanent endowments and contributions to permanent fund principal, these would also be shown after general revenues.

Finally, the **net position** at the beginning and end of the year are reconciled.

A government's public safety function charged its customers $10 million for current year services and received cash payments of $8 million for those services. It also received cash payments of $1 million for prior year services.

To prepare the journal entry to record the charges for services, credit $10 million to revenue (it is all recognized under full accrual), debit $8 million to cash for those services, and then debit the balance of $2 million to accounts receivable:

Cash	8,000,000	
Accounts receivable	2,000,000	
Revenue		10,000,000

The $1 million in cash received for prior year services is not credited to revenue in the current year (it was already recognized during the prior year):

Cash	1,000,000	
Accounts receivable		1,000,000

During the same year, it incurred personnel expenses of $7 million for public safety personnel, made debt interest payments of $4.2 million, and had other public safety operating expenses of $2 million. The journal entry is as follows:

Expenses—public safety ($7M + $2M)	9,000,000	
Interest expense	4,200,000	
Cash		13,200,000

The entity received a capital grant of $486,000 to upgrade the city's sewer facilities.

Cash	486,000	
Capital grant - sewer		486,000

14.03 Governmental Funds Financial Statements

Overview

Representative Task (Remembering & Understanding): Identify and recall basic concepts and principles associated with governmental fund financial statements (eg, required funds, financial statements, financial statement components).

Governmental fund financial statements include the general fund, special revenue, capital projects, debt service fund, and permanent fund. A balance sheet and statement of revenues, expenditures, and changes in fund balance will be prepared with columns for each major fund and a total for all minor funds. The Balance Sheet also includes deferred outflows of resources and deferred inflows of resources, like the government-wide statement of net position.

Government Entities: Funds and Basis of Accounting

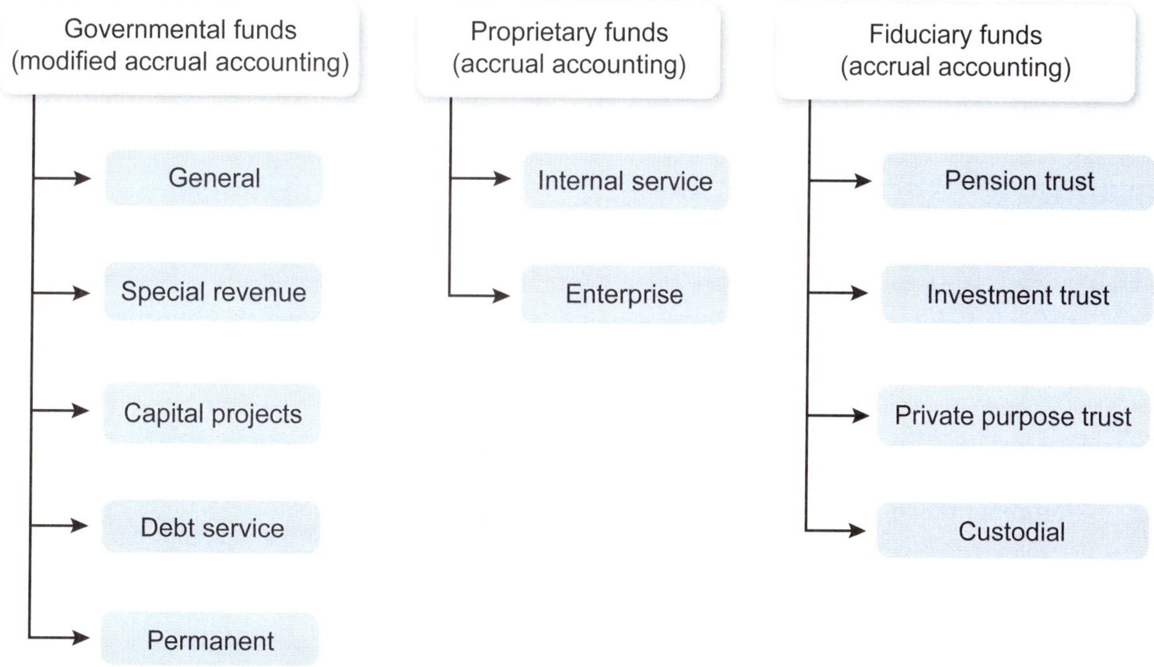

Required Funds

A government unit must have one general fund, but can establish as many special revenue, capital projects, and permanent funds as needed to account for the various activities that fit these categories. A debt service fund is only needed if the entity issues general obligation debts.

- **General** – This fund accounts for and reports any activity or function by the government unit that is not being accounted for in another fund, such as general operations, public safety, public works, culture and recreation. Revenue sources include income, sales and property taxes, fees, fines, licenses, permits, and grants. Unassigned fund balance.
- **Special Revenue** – These funds are used to account for and report specific revenues from *earmarked* sources that are restricted or committed to be used to finance designated activities other than Capital Projects and Debt Service. An example is a gas tax that finances repairs and maintenance of the roads. Revenue sources include fees, grants, specific taxes, and other earmarked revenue sources. Restricted or committed fund balance.
- **Capital Projects** – These funds account for major acquisition or construction activities of capital assets, other than those financed by proprietary or trust funds. This fund accounts for and reports the financial resources that are restricted, committed, or assigned for these types of capital outlay. An example is the construction of a city hall, convention center, or a county courthouse. Revenue sources include special tax revenues, proceeds from bonds, transfers, or capital grants.
- **Debt Service** – This fund is responsible for accumulating and making interest and principal payments on the tax-supported debts of the governmental funds. The DSF accounts for and reports the resources that are restricted, committed, or assigned for this long-term debt purpose. The expenditures may also include premiums on issuance of bonds. Revenue sources include portions of property taxes and transfers.
- **Permanent** – These funds account for and report assets whose principal is restricted and may not be spent (nonexpendable fund) but must be invested permanently (the income is, however, spendable/expendable—endowment fund). Investments are reported at their fair values, with a few minor exceptions as per GASB 72. Revenue sources are usually from the investment earnings of the trust.

Required Financial Statements

Representative Task (Application): Prepare the balance sheet for the governmental funds of a state or local government from trial balances and supporting documentation.

Representative Task (Application): Calculate the fund balances (assigned, unassigned, nonspendable, committed, and restricted) for state and local governments and prepare journal entries.

Representative Task (Application): Prepare the statement of revenues, expenditures, and changes in fund balances for the governmental funds of a state or local government from trial balances and supporting documentation.

Balance Sheet

Governmental Fund F/S use modified accrual basis and the current financial resources approach. Only current assets and current liabilities are shown (ie, no fixed assets or long-term debt).

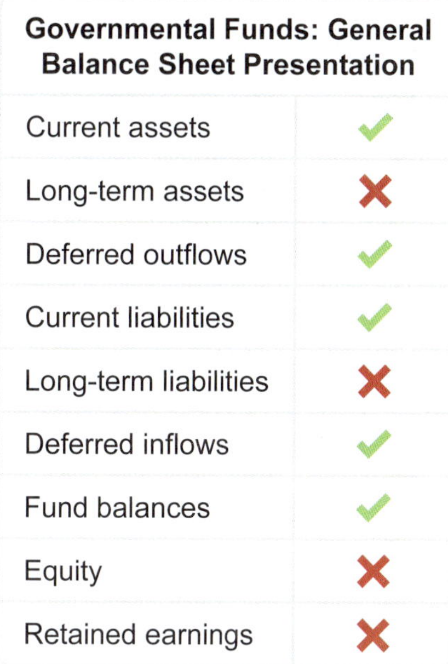

Governmental Funds: General Balance Sheet Presentation	
Current assets	✓
Long-term assets	✗
Deferred outflows	✓
Current liabilities	✓
Long-term liabilities	✗
Deferred inflows	✓
Fund balances	✓
Equity	✗
Retained earnings	✗

As a reminder, under modified accrual accounting:

- Governmental fund assets are recognized to the extent that they are currently available (eg, cash accounts receivable due within 60 days of year end)
  - The purchase of a long-lived asset for a governmental fund requires recording a one-time outflow called an expenditure for the asset's full amount.
- Governmental fund liabilities are recognized to the extent that they use currently available resources.
  - This means that most current liabilities are accrued because they are due within the next year (or 60 days after year end) and generally paid for with current resources.
  - Conversely, long-term liabilities are likely paid using future, unavailable resources and therefore generally are not accrued.

Balance Sheet

	General	Capital projects	Debt service	Other governmental	Total governmental
Assets:					
Cash and cash equivalents	420	550	–	17	987
Account receivable	239	8	–	2	249
Total assets	659	558	–	19	1,236
Liabilities, deferred inflows, and fund balance:					
Liabilities:					
Accounts payable	377	125	–	14	516
Deferred inflows:					
Unavailable revenue	42	25	–	–	67

Balance Sheet

	General	Capital projects	Debt service	Other governmental	Total governmental
Fund balance:					
Nonspendable	9	–	–	–	9
Restricted	200	360	–	–	560
Assigned	10	48	–	–	58
Unassigned	21	–	–	5	26
Total liabilities, deferred inflows, and fund balance	659	558	–	19	1,236

There are five **fund balance categories** that are classified in a hierarchy that is designed to indicate the extent to which government is bound to honor those constraints.

The classifications, ranging from the *most restrictive to the least restrictive*, are:

- A **nonspendable** fund balance includes funds that cannot be spent for one of two reasons:
  - They are not in spendable form, such as assets like inventories or prepaid expenses that are not expected to be converted into cash; and long-term loans or notes receivable and property held for resale, unless they are restricted, committed, or assigned.
  - They are legally or contractually required to be maintained, such as the principal balance of a permanent fund.
- A **restricted** fund balance includes funds that are restricted for a specific purpose. Restrictions may be:
  - Imposed externally, such as by creditors, grantors, contributors, or the laws or regulations of others
  - Imposed by law
- A **committed** fund balance includes funds that are required to be used for a specific purpose as a result of constraints imposed by the highest level of decision-making authority.

- An **assigned** fund balance includes funds that the government INTENDS to spend for a specific purpose but are not restricted or committed and do not require assignment by the highest level of decision-making authority.
- The **unassigned** fund balance includes all General funds that do not belong in another classification, such as not being restricted, committed, or assigned to a specific purpose.

Statement of Revenues, Expenditures, and Changes in Fund Balances

The governmental funds statement of revenues, expenditures, and changes in fund balances is similar to an **income statement** but presents the revenues and expenditures of a governmental unit on the modified accrual basis.

Remember, under modified accrual accounting, governmental fund revenues are recognized when they are **measurable and available** to spend. Measurable means quantifiable in monetary terms and available to spend means collectible in the current period or within 60 days of year end (unless otherwise stated). Virtually all outflows are recorded as expenditures.

Dayne County's general fund had the following disbursements during the year:

Payment of principal on long-term debt	$100,000
Payments to vendors	500,000
Purchase of a computer	300,000

Determine the amount should Dayne County report as expenditures in its governmental funds statement of revenues, expenditures, and changes in fund balances.

A governmental fund financial statement is prepared on the modified accrual basis and therefore utilizes the **expenditure principle**, where most costs (ie outflows) are reported as expenditures, for a total of **$900,000** (100,000 + 500,000 + 300,000 = 900,000).

Statement of Revenues, Expenditures, and Changes in Fund Balances

	General	Capital projects	Debt service	Other governmental	Total governmental
Revenues:					
Property taxes	2,020	–	–	–	2,020
Licenses and permits	230	–	–	380	610
Total revenues	2,250	–	–	380	2,630
Expenditures:					
General government	2,050	–	–	120	2,170
Public safety	3,370	–	–	–	3,370
Debt service	–	–	3,450	–	3,450
Capital outlay	–	2,240	–	–	2,240
Total expenditures	5,420	2,240	3,450	120	11,230

Statement of Revenues, Expenditures, and Changes in Fund Balances

	General	Capital projects	Debt service	Other governmental	Total governmental
Excess (deficiency) of revenues over expenditures	(3,170)	(2,240)	(3,450)	260	(8,600)
Other financing sources (uses)					
Transfers in	1,360	1,750	3,450	–	6,560
Transfers out	(1,280)	–	–	–	(1,280)
Total other financing sources (uses)	80	1,750	3,450	–	5,280
Net change in fund balance	(3,090)	(490)	–	260	(3,320)
Fund balance, beginning of year	3,460	820	–	1,410	5,870
Fund balance, end of year	550	330	–	1,670	2,550

Reconciliation

Representative Task (Application): Prepare worksheets to convert the governmental fund financial statements to the governmental activities reported in the government-wide financial statements.

Representative Task (Application): Prepare the schedule to reconcile the total fund balances and the net change in fund balances reported in the governmental fund financial statements to the net position and change in net position reported in the government-wide financial statements

To fairly present the government-wide F/S, the **governmental funds' activities** must be **reconciled from modified accrual to accrual accounting** at year end. To reconcile the governmental fund Balance Sheet to the government-wide Statement of Net Position generally includes:

- Adding capital assets (reported at historical cost and depreciated)
- Adding long-term liabilities
- Reducing unearned revenue
- Adding internal service fund net position balances.

A simplified reconciliation would appear as follows:

Alexes City
Reconciliation of Governmental Fund Balances to Net Position of Governmental Activities
December 31, Year 1

Total governmental fund balances	$10,000,000
Long-term assets used by governmental funds	61,000,000
Internal service fund balances	1,000,000
Long-term liabilities incurred by governmental funds	(30,000,000)
Net Position of governmental activities	**$42,000,000**

In reconciling the governmental fund Statement of Revenues, Expenditures and Changes in Fund Balances to the government-wide Statement of Activities, adjustments include:

- Reporting revenues and Other Expenses on the accrual basis
- Reporting depreciation as an expense (rather than as an expenditure)
- Reporting long-term debt as a liability (instead of Other Financing Sources); debt principal repayments are reported as a reduction of that liability (rather than as an expenditure)
- Adding in internal service fund net revenues

In preparing Chase City's reconciliation of the statement of revenues, expenditures, and changes in fund balances to the government-wide statement of activities, which of the following items should be subtracted from changes in fund balances:

- Capital asset purchases
- Payment of long-term debt principal
- Internal service fund increase in net assets
- Book value of capital assets sold during the year

The **book value of capital assets sold** during the year would need to be subtracted from the reconciliation because a government-wide statement of activities would report only the gain while the fund statement would report the total proceeds from the sale. Capital asset purchases and payment of long-term debt principal would be included at the same amount in both statements. An internal service fund is a proprietary fund and would be presented in a statement of revenues, expenses, and changes in fund balance. Therefore, since there is no statement of revenues, expenditures, and changes in fund balance, no reconciliation would be necessary.

14.04 Proprietary Funds Financial Statements

Concepts and Principles

Representative Task (Remembering & Understanding): Identify and recall basic concepts and principles associated with proprietary fund financial statements (eg, required funds, financial statements, financial statement components).

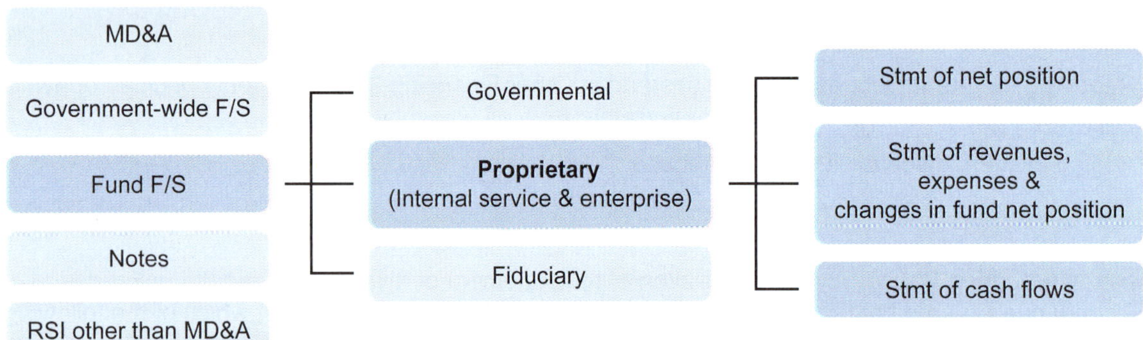

Proprietary funds are used to account for the **business-like activities** of a government entity. These funds most closely resemble private businesses and use an **economic resources focus** along with **full accrual accounting**.

A government will establish as many enterprise and internal service funds as needed to account for activities that fit these descriptions. They are funded primarily by voluntary payments from users for goods and services provided.

- **Internal Service** – These funds render services or provide goods to other funds within the government entity, charging the other funds directly for those services. An example is a maintenance department, IT dept, janitorial department, or a motor pool. Revenue sources include billings for services, grants, and interest earnings.
- **Enterprise** – These funds account for activities financed by voluntary payments for goods and services rendered to the payers. Often a user fee is paid. Examples include city-operated water utilities, airports, transit systems, public hospitals, public universities, public housing, lotteries, or post offices. Revenue sources include charges for services, interest and investment income, shared revenues (property or gas tax), and transfers in.

Required Financial Statements

Representative Task (Application): Prepare the statement of net position for the proprietary funds of a state or local government from trial balances and supporting documentation.

Representative Task (Application): Prepare the statement of revenues, expenses, and changes in fund net position for the proprietary funds of a state or local government from trial balances and supporting documentation.

Representative Task (Application): Prepare the statement of cash flows for the proprietary funds of a state or local government.

There are three proprietary fund financial statements: the statement of net position (balance sheet equivalent), the statement of revenues, expenses, and changes in fund net position (income statement equivalent), and the statement of cash flows.

The statement of net position (Balance Sheet), statement of revenues, expenses, and changes in fund net position, and statement of cash flows will be prepared with columns for each major enterprise fund and a total for all minor enterprise funds. The internal service funds are reported in a separate column in these statements (note their inclusion here and not with the governmental funds, where they were grouped in the government-wide F/S).

Statement of Net Position

A proprietary funds **statement of net position** is similar to a balance sheet and presents the assets, liabilities, and net position of a governmental unit on the **full accrual** basis, just like for-profit entities. However, the difference between assets (plus deferred outflows) and liabilities (plus deferred inflows) is called **net position** because governments are not profit-earning entities and do not have owners or equity interests.

Major enterprise funds are shown in separate columns along with a total column for all enterprise funds and a column for all internal service funds. Additionally, assets and liabilities are distinguished between current (available or due within one year) and noncurrent.

Just like in the government-wide statement of net position, proprietary funds total net position is classified into three categories:

- **Net investment in capital assets:** the excess of existing capital assets less accumulated depreciation and associated debt
- **Restricted net position:** funds that are restricted by constitution, external resource providers, or legislation
- **Unrestricted net position:** the residual amount with no restrictions

Statement of Net Position
Proprietary Funds

	Municipal Water Utility	Other Enterprise Funds	Total Enterprise Funds	Internal Service Fund
Assets				
Current assets				
Cash	42	17	59	55
Accounts receivable	3	11	14	14
Total current assets	45	28	73	69
Noncurrent assets				
Capital assets	20	7	27	24
Less accumulated depreciation	(5)	(6)	(11)	(6)
Total noncurrent assets	15	1	16	18
Total assets	60	29	89	87
Liabilities				
Current liabilities				
Accounts payable	7	5	12	10
Total current liabilities	7	5	12	10
Noncurrent liabilities				
Bonds payable	5	-	5	4
Total noncurrent liabilities	5	-	5	4
Total liabilities	12	5	17	14
Net Position				
Net investment in capital assets	10	1	11	14
Restricted	3	23	26	10
Unrestricted	35	-	35	49
Total Net Position	48	24	72	73

Statement of Revenues, Expenses, and Changes in Fund Net Position

This statement is the income statement equivalent (ie, operating statement) for proprietary funds. On this statement, a governmental unit is required to distinguish between **operating and nonoperating activities** based on whether inflows or outflows from its proprietary fund are derived from sources within the regular course of the fund's activities.

Capital contributions and **transfers** are also shown separately. Capital contributions include inflows from contributed capital assets, grants, and contributions restricted for capital purposes, and fees and charges restricted to capital assets acquisition.

Proprietary Funds: Components Of The Statement Of Revenues, Expenses, And Changes In Fund Net Position	
Operating Revenues And Expenses	Related to the fund's normal, day-to-day activities
Nonoperating Revenues And Expenses	Outside the fund's normal, day-to-day activities
Capital Contributions	Inflows for contributed capital assets
Transfers In And Out	Resources received from and provided to other funds

Statement of Revenue, Expenses, and Changes in Fund Net Position
Proprietary Funds

	Municipal Water Utility	Other Enterprise Funds	Total Enterprise Funds	Internal Service Fund
Operating revenues				
Charges for services	15	12	27	20
Miscellaneous	2	8	10	10
Total operating revenues	17	20	37	30
Operating expenses				
Personnel	11	6	17	17
Depreciation	1	2	3	1
Total operating expenses	12	8	20	18
Nonoperating revenues (expenses)				
Interest revenue	1	8	9	2
Interest expense	(2)	(5)	(7)	(3)
Total nonoperating revenues (expenses)	(1)	3	2	(1)
Change in net position	4	15	19	11
Net position, beginning of year	44	9	53	62
Net position, end of year	48	24	72	73

Statement of Cash Flows

The statement of **cash flows**, with a few adjustments, is similar to that of a private entity, except that there are four sections and a reconciliation (**OINCR**):

- **Operating**
  - Must be prepared under the direct method with a reconciliation (indirect) also presented
  - Does not include interest or dividends
- **Investing**
  - Includes interest/dividend income
  - No capital asset acquisition/disposal
  - Loans made
- **Noncapital Financing**
  - Includes interest expense on unsecured loans
  - Transfers, grants, subsidies, and property taxes received
- **Capital & Related Financing**
  - Includes interest expense on secured loans for capital assets
  - Includes financed purchases and sales of capital assets (normally investing)

Of the following choices, which format must a proprietary fund use on the statement of cash flows (SCF) to report operating activities?

- Indirect method, beginning with operating income
- Direct method
- Indirect method, beginning with change in net assets
- Either direct or indirect method

The SCF provides detailed information about an entity's cash receipts and payments during a reporting period. To enhance transparency and meet the unique needs of users of government financial statements, GASB has several requirements of proprietary fund SCFs that are distinct from an SCF of a private business:

The operating activities section must be prepared using the **direct method**.

The statement has four sections (instead of three): operating activities, noncapital financing activities, capital and related financing activities, and investing activities.

A **reconciliation** of operating income (not net income) to net cash from operating activities must be provided at the bottom of the statement.

ABC City
Statement of Cash Flows
Proprietary Funds
For the Year Ended December 31, Year 1

	Business-type activities: enterprise funds			
Cash flows from operating activities	**Water and sewer**	**Parking facilities**	**Total**	**Governmental activities: internal service funds**
Receipts from customers	$11,400,200	$1,345,292	$12,745,492	$15,326,343
Payments to suppliers	(2,725,349)	(365,137)	(3,090,486)	(2,812,238)
Payments to employees	(3,360,055)	(750,828)	(4,110,883)	(4,209,688)
Internal activity: payments to other funds	(1,296,768)	-	(1,296,768)	-
Claims paid	-	-	-	(8,482,451)
Other receipts (payments)	(2,325,483)	-	(2,325,483)	1,061,118
Net cash provided by operating activities	$1,692,545	$229,327	$1,921,872	$883,084

GASB requires operating activities section be prepared using the **direct method**

14.05 Fiduciary Funds Financial Statements

Concepts and Principles

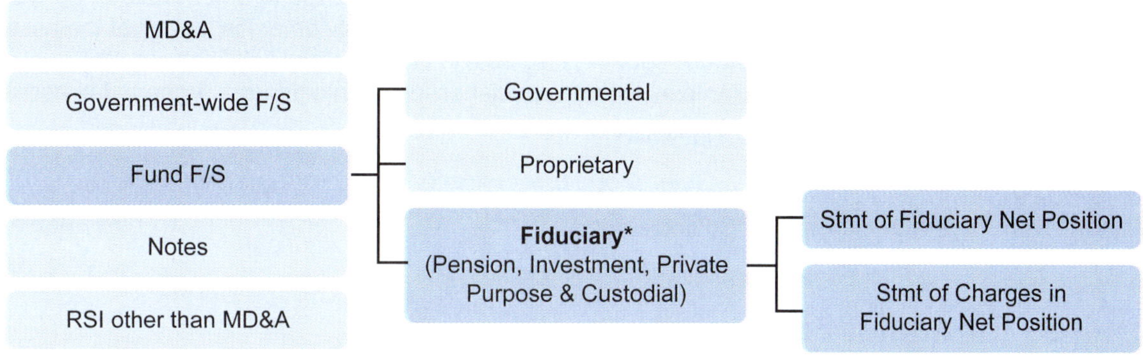

Accrual basis, Current economic resources approach

Representative Task (Remembering & Understanding): Identify and recall basic concepts and principles associated with fiduciary fund financial statements (eg, required funds, financial statements, financial statement components).

Representative Task (Application): Prepare the statement of net position for the fiduciary funds of a state or local government from trial balances and supporting documentation.

Representative Task (Application): Prepare the statement of changes in fiduciary net position for the fiduciary funds of a state or local government from trial balances and supporting documentation.

Fiduciary funds account for resources held by a government in a **trustee or custodial capacity** for other entities.

- All **trust funds** make use of the **economic resources measurement focus** and the **accrual** basis of accounting in the same way as proprietary funds.
- **Custodial funds**, however, are a bit atypical in that they only report assets and liabilities. Accordingly, custodial funds do not report equity and do not utilize measurement focus but do employ the **accrual** basis of accounting to recognize assets and liabilities.

There are four types of fiduciary funds:

- **Investment trust** – These account for pooled resources that are being invested on behalf of multiple government entities for which this specific government entity is trustee.
- **Pension trust** (and other employee benefits) – These account for government employee pensions and other post-retirement benefits for which the government is trustee. Two RSI schedules are required: Funding progress and employer contributions.
- **Private purpose trust** – These account for resources that are being held for the benefit of private persons or organizations or other governments. Examples include a fund to hold cash for unclaimed tax refunds or escheat property as well as a scholarship fund. Could be expendable or nonexpendable.
- **Custodial** – These account for collected amounts that must be transferred to other funds or outsiders. An odd characteristic of custodial funds (formerly referred to as *agency funds*) is that all of the assets held belong to others (held in a custodial capacity), so assets always equal liabilities, and the custodial fund has no equity section at all. Examples include special assessments and the property tax assessor.
    - Special assessment (streetlights, sidewalk)
        - Government obligated – capital projects or debt service fund
        - Government NOT obligated – Custodial fund

Required Financial Statements

Statement of Fiduciary Net Position

A **Statement of Fiduciary Net Position** is prepared with columns for each major fiduciary fund and a total for all minor fiduciary funds. The trust and custodial funds use the **accrual basis** and the **economic resources approach**.

- Remember that none of these funds were included in the government-wide F/S.
- Since custodial funds always have a net asset balance of zero (all assets are owed to outsiders and, therefore, have equal liabilities), they will not be included in the statement of changes in fiduciary net position, only on the Statement of Fiduciary Net Position.

Statement of Fiduciary Net Position
Fiduciary Funds

	Pension Funds	Custodial Funds
Assets		
Cash	2	44
Interest receivable	51	18
Investments	65	-
Total assets	118	62
Liabilities		
Accounts payable	-	-
Bonds payable	13	62
Total liabilities	13	62
Net Position		
Restricted	105	-
Total Net Position	105	-

Statement of Changes in Fiduciary Net Position

The Statement of Changes in Fiduciary Net Position lists the changes to each fiduciary fund type to illustrate significant year-to-year changes in net position.

Statement of Changes in Fiduciary Net Position
Fiduciary Funds

	Pension Funds	Custodial Funds
Assets		
Contributions	41	74
Miscellaneous	7	6
Total additions	48	80
Deductions		
Administrative expense	8	58
Payments to others	24	22
Total deductions	32	80
Change in net position	16	-
Net position, beginning of year	89	-
Net position, end of year	105	-

14.06 Notes to the Financial Statements

Notes to the Financial Statements

Representative Task (Remembering & Understanding): Recall the disclosure requirements for significant accounting policies, infrastructure and capital assets, and long-term liabilities in the notes to the basic financial statements of state and local governments.

Notes to the F/S are a required part of the basic F/S and should provide information that is not displayed on the face of the F/S and is **essential** to their fair presentation. Notes should distinguish whether they pertain to the *primary government or its discretely presented component units.*

Components of the Financial Section of the Annual Comprehensive Financial Report (ACFR)

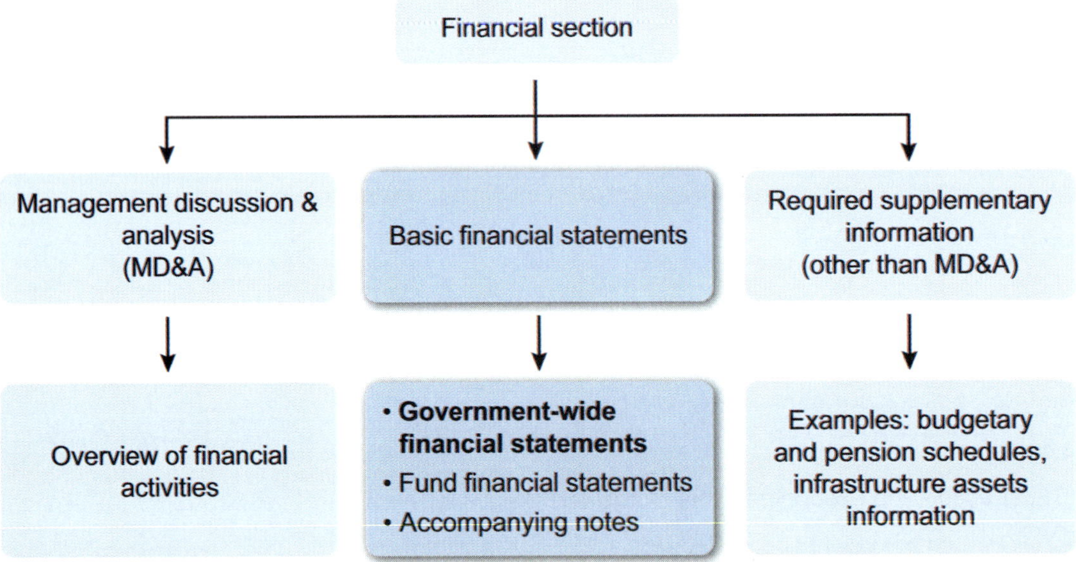

Some notes presented by governments are identical to notes presented in business financial statements. It is acceptable to present notes in a very extensive format.

Annual Comprehensive Financial Report (ACFR): Notes to Financial Statements

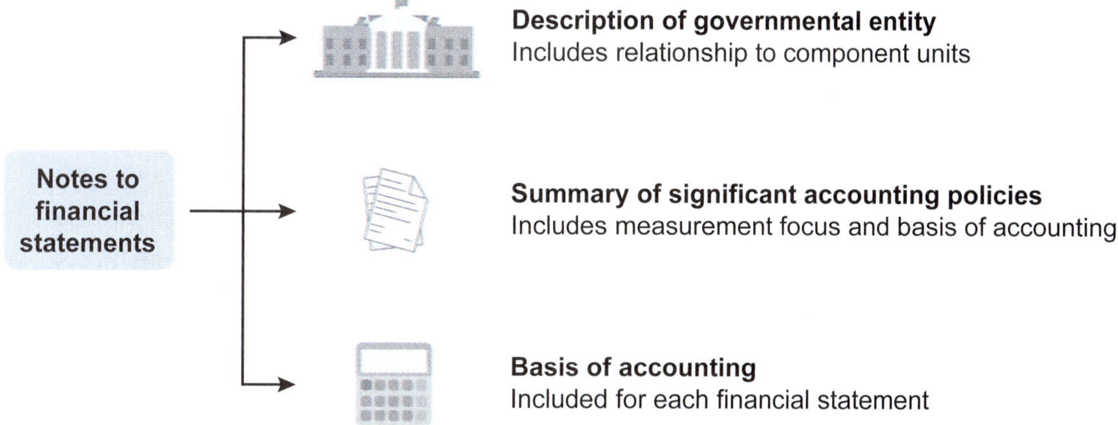

The Notes essential to fair presentation include:

- **Summary of accounting policies**, including:
  - A description of the government-wide F/S
  - The basis of accounting applied, such as accrual for government-wide F/S and proprietary and fiduciary fund statements, and modified accrual for government fund F/S
  - Policies regarding cash and cash equivalents; capitalization and determining useful lives; and infrastructure
- **Disclosures** related to:
  - Cash
  - Investments
  - Significant contingent liabilities
  - Significant effects of subsequent events
  - Pensions and other post-employment benefits
  - Significant violations of legal or contractual provisions
  - Debt service requirements
  - Leases
  - Construction and other significant commitments
  - Capital assets
  - Long-term liabilities
  - Deficit in fund balance or net position
  - Interfund balances and transfers
  - Donor-restricted endowments
- **Related party transactions**
- A **description** of the **reporting entity**
- **Segment information** for enterprise funds

Flower City uses the modified approach for reporting eligible infrastructure assets. In which of the following components of its basic financial statements, if any, would Flower report this information?

- Letter of transmittal
- Statement of activities
- Notes to the financial statements
- Not required to report.

The **financial section** of the ACFR includes the **notes to the financial statements (F/S)**. One required note is a **summary of the entity's significant accounting policies**. The summary contains a wealth of information, including discussion of accounting policies selected when more than one permitted policy is available.

For example, governments have the *option* to omit depreciation on infrastructure assets if they can demonstrate that the regular costs incurred to maintain those assets result in an indefinite life. This modified approach is permissible though not required. Because more than one acceptable approach exists, the summary of significant accounting policies must report whether the modified approach is used or not.

In addition, GASB 42 requires disclosures about *capital asset impairment* if both (a) the decline in service utility of the asset is large in magnitude, and (b) the event or change in circumstance is outside the normal life cycle of the capital asset (unexpected). If the asset is no longer to be used, it should be reported at the lower of carrying value or fair value.

GASB 102 requires state and local governments to provide F/S users with information regarding certain risks. These risks are related to concentrations or constraints that could impact the entity's level of service or ability to meet obligations as they come due or increased risk of loss.

A **concentration** occurs as a result of a *lack of diversity* related to an aspect of a significant inflow/outflow of resources (eg, reliance on only one primary revenue source).

A **constraint** is a *limitation* imposed by either an external party or by formal action of the entity's decision-making authority (eg, a state-imposed debt limit).

The governmental entity must determine whether a concentration or constraint makes the reporting unit(s) vulnerable to the risk of a "substantial impact." If an event has occurred, has begun to occur, or is more than likely to occur, then the entity must make the following disclosures in the notes to the financial statements:

The concentration or constraint

Each event associated with the concentration or constraint

Actions taken by the entity prior to the issuance of the F/S to mitigate the risk

14.07 Required Supplementary Information (RSI) Other Than MD&A

Required Supplementary Information (RSI)

Representative Task (Remembering & Understanding): Recall the objectives and components of required supplementary information other than management's discussion and analysis in the annual comprehensive financial report for state and local governments.

Representative Task (Remembering & Understanding): Recall the objectives and components of budgetary comparison reporting in the annual comprehensive financial report for state and local governments.

There are **four types of RSI**, other than MD&A, that are **required** under GASB:

- Budgetary Comparison Schedule (BCS)
  - This schedule is required for **governmental funds** that have legally adopted annual budgets, including the **general fund** and major **special revenue funds**.
  - GASB 34 states that the minimum budgetary information required to be reported in BCSs includes the original budget, the final appropriations budget, and actual inflows/outflows and balances on a budgetary basis.
- **Information about Infrastructure Assets** (for Entities Reported Using the Modified Approach)
  - A schedule reflecting the condition of the government's infrastructure,
  - A comparison of the needed and actual expenditures to maintain the government's infrastructure.
- **Claims Development Information** When the Government Sponsors a Public Entity Risk Pool
- **Pension schedules:**
  - Schedule of Funding Progress (for Entities Reporting Pension Trust Funds)
  - Schedule of Employer Contributions (for Entities Reporting Pension Trust Funds)

Budgetary Comparison

Identify which of the following items is needed to prepare the budgetary comparison schedule for a local government:

- Explanation of variances
- Original budget
- Description of government entity's budgeting process
- Computation of variances from budget to actual

City of UWorld
Budgetary Comparison Schedule
General Fund (Non-GAAP Budgetary Basis)
For the Year Ended December 31, Year 3

	Budgeted amounts			
	Original	**Final**	**Actual amounts (Budgetary basis)**	**Variance with final budget Positive (Negative)**
Revenues:				
Taxes	$312,000	$315,000	$321,000	$6,000
Licenses and permits	103,000	103,000	94,000	(9,000)
Charges for services	189,000	189,000	197,000	8,000
Fines	55,000	53,000	53,000	–

The BCS provides valuable information to taxpayers, such as whether the government took in less revenue than planned or made unreasonable expenditures that did not adhere to the budget.

The budget-to-actual inputs are needed *before* calculations and explanations of budget-to-actual variances can be prepared. The calculations and explanations themselves do not provide the inputs necessary to prepare the BCS. A description of a government's budgeting process is helpful information; however, it too will not provide information that is directly useful in preparing the BCS.

14.08 Financial Reporting Entity, Including Blended and Discrete Component Units

Component Units

Representative Task (Remembering & Understanding): Recall the criteria for classifying an entity as a component unit of a state or local government and the financial statement presentation requirements (discrete or blended).

A component unit is an autonomous organization (eg, a school district) that operates with separate budgets and management but is included in the financial statements of the primary government where:

- The primary government controls a **voting majority** of the autonomous organization's governing board. In the absence of a governing board, this criterion is considered to be met if the primary government performs the duties a governing board would normally perform.
- The autonomous organization is **fiscally dependent** on the primary government. In this context, dependence means the primary government:
  - Establishes and approves the organization's budget. Determines the organization's tax rates or amounts charged for services
  - Provides approval before the organization can issue debt
- The autonomous organization is a **financial benefit or burden** to the primary government.

Accounting

The accounting for component units may be either:

- **Discretely presented** (ie, separately stated) – Separate accounting for the activities of the component unit in separate columns is the presumed method (ie, most component units are discretely presented). This is usually appropriate when:
  - Management consists of separately elected officials,
  - Budgets are developed separately from the primary government, and
  - The services provided are not primarily to the government itself.

- **Blended** – When the component unit serves other parts of the primary government, or is dependent on the overall government legislative body for funding or budgeting, it may be more appropriate to account for the activities of the component unit along with the remaining funds of the government.
  - Where it serves the other departments and is paid by those departments, an **internal service fund** may be appropriate.
  - Where funding is received from services to outsiders, an **enterprise fund** may be appropriate.
  - Blending is also required for a component unit that was incorporated as a **not-for-profit** corporation with the government as the only corporate member.
  - Generally shown in the **Governmental Activities column**.

Acceptable Presentation Methods Of A Component Unit In Government Financial Statements	
Discrete Presentation	Results presented in a distinct column on the face of the government-wide financial statements
Blended Presentation	Results combined with primary government and presented as an additional fund of the government

An entity that raises and holds economic resources for the direct benefit of a government (eg, a library society that raises money, which will go to the government operating the library) is required to be reported as a component unit.

14.09 Interfund Transactions

Interfund Transactions

Representative Task (Application): Prepare journal entries to recognize interfund activity within state and local governments.

Representative Task (Application): Prepare eliminations of interfund activity in the government-wide financial statements of state and local governments.

It is common for various funds within a government unit to **transfer or exchange resources**. For example, operating transfers are movements of cash from one fund to finance current period activities in another fund (eg, general fund providing tax revenue to capital projects fund).

There are **four** different **types** of **cash transfers** that may take place between different funds:

- Operating transfers
- Quasi-external transactions
- Reimbursements
- Loans

To distinguish these transfers from ordinary revenues and expenditures/expenses, they are classified as **other inflows/outflows** (eg, other financing uses). When an operating transfer to/from another fund is recorded, the account used depends on the type of fund recording the transaction.

Interfund Transaction: Operating Transfers

	Modified Accrual Accounting (Governmental Funds)	Full Accrual Accounting (Proprietary And Fiduciary Funds)
Transfer In	Other financing sources	Other revenues
Transfer Out	Other financing uses	Other expenses

Operating Transfers

Operating transfers, also called **interfund transfers**, are the most common, and represent movements of cash from one fund to finance current period activities in another fund. They also can establish or close a fund. To distinguish them from ordinary revenues and expenditures/expenses, they are classified as follows:

- The transferee reports the amount received as:
  - Other financing sources if using modified accrual accounting
  - Other revenues if using accrual accounting
- The transferor reports the amount paid as:
  - Other financing uses if using modified accrual accounting
  - Other expenses if using accrual accounting.

If $100 is sent from the general fund to the debt service fund to help finance interest payments that must be made that year, the entry in the **general fund** is:

Other financing uses	100	
Cash		100

The entry in the **debt service fund** is:

Cash	100	
Other financing sources		100

Quasi-External Transactions

Quasi-external transactions are payments from one fund to another for services or goods that are being provided. These are reciprocal transactions, involving an earnings process, unlike the previous examples of operating and residual equity transfers, in which a transfer is made without any benefit received by the transferor.

- The transferee is receiving money that represents earned revenue.
- The transferor reports the payment as an:
  - Expenditure if it uses modified accrual accounting
  - Expense if it uses accrual accounting

Assume the town has a water utility enterprise fund whose customers include, along with the citizens of the town, the other departments of the government. If a bill of $300 is paid by the capital projects fund for water used in the current year, the entry in the **capital projects fund** is:

Expenditures – utilities	300	
Cash		300

The entry in the **enterprise fund** is:

Cash	300	
Revenues		300

Notice that this type of transaction could easily have taken place between unrelated entities in a normal supplier/customer relationship, and that is the reason for identifying these as quasi-external transactions.

Reimbursements

Reimbursements are repayments from one fund to another for costs paid earlier on its behalf.

- The transferee will record the receipt of money as either a settlement of a **receivable** it recorded when making the payment or as a reduction of an earlier **expenditure** or **expense** it recorded.
- The transferor records the payment of money as the settlement of a **payable** it recorded when the other fund paid costs on its behalf or as its own **expenditure** or **expense**.

Assume the general fund paid $900 for 9 government employees to attend a conference, including 4 employees of the general fund itself and 5 employees of the internal service fund. The internal service fund later reimbursed the general fund $500 for its employees.

At the time of payment for the conference, the **general fund**, if it was **not** aware it was going to later be reimbursed, would have recorded:

Expenditures – conference	900	
Cash		900

When the **internal service fund** later reimbursed the general fund, it would then have recorded:

Expenses – conference	500	
Cash		500

This would have reduced the net expenditure of the **general fund**:

Cash	500	
Expenditures – conference		500

On the other hand, if both funds knew at the time of the conference that the general fund would later be reimbursed, the entry in the **general fund** for its payment would have been:

Expenditures - conference	400	
Due from internal service fund	500	
Cash		900

At the same time, the **internal service fund** would have recorded:

Expenses – conference	500	
Due to general fund		500

The later reimbursement would settle the due to/due from accounts.

Loans

Loans are temporary transfers between funds that are to be repaid later. They are handled through interfund **receivable** and **payable** accounts.

For example, if the enterprise fund lends $400 to the special revenue fund, the entry in the **enterprise fund** is:

Due from special revenue fund	400	
Cash		400

The entry in the **special revenue** fund is:

Cash	400	
Due to enterprise fund		400

Of course, the later repayment involves both funds making the exact opposite entries from the original loan entries.

Transfers are reported on the government-wide statement of activities. For transfers to be reported, they must be between governmental activities and business-type activities. Two kinds of transfers that are reported include:

- Permanent transfers
- Recurring transfers from either governmental activities to business-type activities, or vice versa

Permanent transfers are made once, while the recurring transfers are typically made annually.
A reimbursement would not be included, but a quasi-external would.

14.10 Sample Statement Preparation

TBS for Proprietary Funds Financial Statements

Representative Task (Application): Prepare the statement of revenues, expenses and changes in fund net position for the proprietary funds of a state or local government from trial balances and supporting documentation.

Representative Task (Application): Prepare the statement of net position for the proprietary funds of a state or local government from trial balances and supporting documentation.

Representative Task (Application): Prepare the statement of cash flows for the proprietary funds of a state or local government.

As discussed at the beginning of the Government section in the BAR text, the AICPA Blueprint has a significant number of representative tasks requiring the **preparation of financial statements** from examining trial balances and supporting documentation. Note that these are **application tasks**, not analysis (which typically requires critical thinking skills).

Since these are application tasks, the simulation below focuses on testing statement preparation only. Governmental funds, fiduciary funds, and government-wide financial statements are prepared in a similar fashion.

The key to preparing multiple financial statements is to understand the interrelationships between the statements (ie, how amounts roll up to another statement). Identification of key pieces of information from documents (eg, a trial balance) is also necessary.

The example provided below focuses on the proprietary funds as the equivalents of a balance sheet, income statement, and statement of cash flows are all required. Additional questions related to statement preparation for the other funds and governmental-wide F/S can be found in the question bank.

Exhibits – Source Documents

Interoffice Memo

To: Accounting manager December 20, Year 3
From: Treasurer
RE: Commodities

The district received $1,685 of food commodities from the U.S. Department of Agriculture. This should be reflected on the statement of cash flows as a noncash noncapital financing activity.

Woodland School District – Enterprise Funds
Post-closing Trial Balance
As of June 30, Year 2

Accounts payable and accruals	(661)
Cash and cash equivalents	5,892
Due from other funds	2,124
Due to other funds	(616)
Furniture and equipment	1,992
Investments	125
Net investment in capital assets	(1,914)
Supplies and materials	2,354
Unrestricted net position	(9,218)

Woodland School District
Cash Analysis
For the Year Ended June 30, Year 3

Beginning balance		5,892
Sources:		
Collections from user charges	5,904	
Non-operating grant	16,473	
Capital contribution	750	
Investment interest income	295	
Proceeds from sale of investments (including gain)	130	23,552
Uses:		
Furniture and equipment acquisition	(1,523)	
Investment acquisition	(152)	
Payroll disbursements	(11,384)	
Payments to suppliers	(7,891)	
Payments for other operating expenses	(829)	(21,779)
Ending balance		7,665

Town of Woodland
Pre-closing Trial Balance
As of June 30, Year 3

Accounts payable and accruals	(1,303)
Capital contributions	(750)
Cash and cash investments	7,665
Contractor services	343
Depreciation expense	982
Due from other funds	1,907
Due to other funds	(616)
Furniture and equipment, net	2,533
Gain from sale of investments	(17)
Grants	(16,952)
Investment earnings	(295)
Investments	164
Net position capital assets, beginning	(1,914)
Operating revenues	(5,687)
Other operating costs	884
Payroll costs	11,384
Supplies and materials inventory	2,049
Supplies and materials cost	8,841
Unrestricted net position, beginning	(9,218)

Required Financial Statements

Required: Prepare the financial statements below by reference to the source documents provided above under the Exhibits section. Round all amounts to the nearest whole dollar.

Woodland School District – Enterprise Fund
Statement of Revenues, Expenses, and Changes in Fund Net Position
For the Year Ended June 30, Year 3

Operating revenues	
Operating expenses:	
Depreciation expense	
Payroll costs	
Contractor services	
Supplies and material cost	
Other operating costs	
Total operating expenses	
Operating income (loss)	
Nonoperating revenues (expenses)	
Investment earnings	
Gain on sale of investments	
Grants	
Total nonoperating revenues (expenses)	
Income (loss) before capital contributions	
Capital contributions	
Change in net position	
Net position - July 1, Year 2	
Net position - June 30, Year 3	

Woodland School District – Enterprise Fund
Statement of Net Position
As of June 30, Year 3

Assets

Current assets:

Cash and cash equivalents

Investments

Due from other funds

Supplies and materials

Total current assets

Noncurrent assets:

Furniture and equipment, net

Total assets

Liabilities

Current liabilities:

Accounts payable and accruals

Due to other funds

Total current liabilities

Net position

Net investment in capital assets

Unrestricted

Total net position

Woodland School District – Enterprise Fund
Statement of Cash Flows
For the Year Ended June 30, Year 3

Cash flows from operating activities
Cash received from user charges
Cash payments for payroll costs
Cash payments to suppliers
Cash payments for other operating expenses
Net cash used for operating activities

Cash flows from noncapital financing activities
Nonoperating grants received

Cash flows from capital and related financing activities
Capital contributions
Acquisition of capital assets
Net cash used for capital and related activities

Cash flows from investing activities
Purchase of investments
Proceeds from investment maturities
Investment interest income
Net cash provided by investing activities
Net increase in cash and cash equivalents
Cash and cash equivalents - beginning
Cash and cash equivalents - ending

Reconciliation of operating income (loss) to net
Cash provided (used) by operating activities
Operating income (loss)
Adjustments:
Depreciation expense
Commodities used
Change in due from other governments
Change is supplies and materials
Change in accounts payable and accruals
Net cash provided by operations

Statement of Revenues, Expenses, and Changes in Fund Net Position with Explanations

Woodland School District – Enterprise Fund
Statement of Revenues, Expenses, and Changes in Fund Net Position
For the Year Ended June 30, Year 3

Operating revenues	5,687
Provided on the pre-closing trial balance as of June 30, Year 3	
Operating expenses:	
Depreciation expense	982
Provided on the pre-closing trial balance as of June 30, Year 3	
Payroll costs	11,384
Provided on the pre-closing trial balance as of June 30, Year 3	
Contractor services	343
Provided on the pre-closing trial balance as of June 30, Year 3	
Supplies and material	8,841
Provided on the pre-closing trial balance as of June 30, Year 3	
Other operating costs	884
Provided on the pre-closing trial balance as of June 30, Year 3	
Total operating expenses	22,434
Operating expenses = 982 + 11,384 + 343 + 8,841 + 884 = 22,434	
Operating income (loss)	16,747
Operating revenue − operating loss = 5,687 − 22,434 = (16,747)	
Nonoperating revenues (expenses)	
Investment earnings	295
Provided on the pre-closing trial balance as of June 30, Year 3	
Gain on sale of investments	17
Provided on the pre-closing trial balance as of June 30, Year 3	
Grants	16,952
Provided on the pre-closing trial balance as of June 30, Year 3	
Total nonoperating revenues (expenses)	17,264
Nonoperating revenues = 295 + 17 + 16,952 = 17,264	
Income (loss) before capital contributions	517
Operating loss plus nonoperating revenue = (16,747) + 17,264 = 517	
Capital contributions	750
Provided on the pre-closing trial balance as of June 30, Year 3	
Change in net position	1,267
Income before contributions + contributions = 517 + 750 + 1,267	
Net position - July 1, Year 2	11,132
Post closing trial balance: net investment in capital assets + unrestricted net position = 1,914 + 9,218	
Net position - June 30, Year 3	12,399
Change in net position + beginning net position = 1,267 + 11,132 = 12,399	

Statement of Net Position with Explanations

Woodland School District – Enterprise Fund
Statement of Net Position
As of June 30, Year 3

Assets	
Current assets:	
Cash and cash equivalents	7,665
Provided on the pre-closing trial balance as of June 30, Year 3	
Investments	164
Provided on the pre-closing trial balance as of June 30, Year 3	
Due from other funds	1,907
Provided on the pre-closing trial balance as of June 30, Year 3	
Supplies and materials	2,049
Provided on the pre-closing trial balance as of June 30, Year 3	
Total current assets	11,785
Sum of current assets: 7,665 + 164 + 1,907 + 2,049	
Noncurrent assets:	
Furniture and equipment, net	2,533
Provided on the pre-closing trial balance as of June 30, Year 3 OR Beginning balance + Acquisitions − Depreciation = 1,992 + 1,523 − 982	
Total assets	14,318
Current assets + Noncurrent assets = 11,785 + 2,533	
Liabilities	
Current liabilities:	
Accounts payable and accruals	1,303
Provided on the pre-closing trial balance as of June 30, Year 3	
Due to other funds	616
Provided on the pre-closing trial balance as of June 30, Year 3	
Total current liabilities (ie, total liabilities)	1,919
Sum of 1,303 + 616	
Net position	
Net investment in capital assets	2,455
Beginning balance + Additions − Depreciation expense = 1,914 + 1,523 − 982	
Unrestricted	9,944
Plug: Total net position − Net investment in capital assets = 12,399 − 2,455	
Total net position	12,399
Total assets − Total liabilities = $14,318 − $1,919	

Statement of Cash Flows – Part 1

Woodland School District – Enterprise Fund
Statement of Cash Flows
For the Year Ended June 30, Year 3

Cash flows from operating activities:	
Cash received from user charges	5,904
Cash payments for payroll costs	(11,384)
Cash payments to suppliers	(7,891)
Cash payments for other operating expenses	(829)
Net cash used for operating activities	(14,200)
Cash flows from noncapital financing activities	
Nonoperating grants received	16,473
Cash flows from capital and related financing activities	
Capital contributions	750
Acquisition of capital assets	(1,523)
Net cash used for capital and related activities	(773)
Cash flows from investing activities	
Purchase of investments	(152)
Proceeds from investment maturities	130
Investment interest income	295
Net cash provided by investing activities	273
Net increase in cash and cash equivalents	1,773
Cash and cash equivalents - beginning	5,892
Cash and cash equivalents - ending	7,665

All amounts listed above, excluding subtotals and totals, are provided on the cash analysis schedule for the Year ended June 30, Year 3

Statement of Cash Flows – Part 2

Reconcilation of operating income (loss) to net cash provided (used) by operating activities	
Operating income (loss)	(16,747)
Provided on the statement of revenues, expenses and changes in fund net balance	
Adjustments:	
Depreciation expense	982
Provided on the statement of revenues, expenses and changes in fund net balance	
Commodities used	1,685
Provided on interoffice memo exhibit	
Change in due from other funds	217
Difference between post closing trial balance as of June 30, Year 2 and pre-closing trial balance as of June 30, Year 3 ($2,124 − $1,907)	
Change in supplies and materials	305
Difference between post closing trial balance as of June 30, Year 2 and pre-closing trial balance as of June 30, Year 3 ($2,354 − $2,049)	
Change in accounts payable and accruals	(642)
Difference between post closing trial balance as of June 30, Year 2 and pre-closing trial balance as of June 30, Year 3 ($661 − $1,303)	
Net cash provided by operations	(14,200)
Sum of all amounts *Must agree with net cash used for operating activities as shown in first section*	

14.11 Sample Financial Statements

Sample City
Statement of Net Position
December 31, 20X1

	Primary Government			
	Governmental Activities	**Business-Type Activities**	**Total**	**Component Units**
Assets				
Cash and cash equivalents	$ 13,597,899	$10,279,143	$ 23,877,042	$ 303,935
Investments	27,365,221	–	27,365,221	7,428,952
Receivables (net)	12,833,132	3,609,615	16,442,747	4,042,290
Internal balances	175,000	(175,000)	–	–
Inventories	322,149	126,674	448,823	83,697
Capital assets, net of Acct. Dept. (**Infrastructure**)	170,022,760	151,388,751	321,411,511	37,744,786
Total assets	224,316,161	165,229,183	389,545,344	49,603,660
Deferred Outflows				
Grant expenditures paid in advance of meeting timing requirements				
Deferred loss from sale/leaseback				
Payment to acquire rights to future parking revenue				
Liabilities				
Accounts payable	6,783,310	751,430	7,534,740	1,803,332
Deferred revenue	1,435,599	–	1,435,599	38,911
Noncurrent liabilities:				
Due within one year	9,236,000	4,426,286	113,662,286	1,426,639
Due in more than one year	83,302,378	74,482,273	157,784,651	27,106,151
Total liabilities	100,757,287	79,659,989	180,417,276	30,375,033
Deferred Inflows				
Grant amounts received in advance of meeting timing requirements				
Deferred *gain* from sale/leaseback				
Net Position				
Net investment in capital assets	103,711,386	73,088,574	176,799,960	15,906,392
Restricted for:				
Capital projects	11,705,864	–	11,705,864	492,445
Debt service	3,020,708	1,451,996	4,472,704	–
Community development projects	4,811,043	–	4,811,043	–
Other purposes	3,214,302	–	3,214,302	–
Unrestricted (deficit)	(2,904,429)	11,028,624	8,124,195	2,829,790
Total net position	**$123,558,874**	**$85,569,194**	**$ 209,128,068**	**$19,228,627**

Sample City
Statement Of Activities
For the Year Ended December 31, 20X1

		Program Revenues			Net (Expense) Revenue And Changes In Net Position			
					Primary Government			
Functions/Programs	Expenses	Charges For Service	Operating Grants And Contributions	Capital Grants And Contributions	Governmental Activities	Business-Type Activities	Total	Component Units
Primary Government								
Governmental Activities:								
General government	$ 9,571,410	$ 3,146,915	$ 843,617	$ –	$ (5,580,878)	$ –	$ (5,580,878)	$ –
Public safety	34,844,749	1,198,855	1,307,693	62,300	(32,275,901)	–	(32,275,901)	–
Public works	10,128,538	850,000	–	2,252,615	(7,025,923)	–	(7,025,923)	–
Engineering services	1,299,645	704,793	–	–	(594,852)	–	(594,852)	–
Health and sanitation	6,738,672	5,612,267	575,000	–	(551,405)	–	(551,405)	–
Cemetery	735,866	212,496	–	–	(523,370)	–	(523,370)	–
Culture and recreation	11,532,350	3,995,199	2,450,000	–	(5,087,151)	–	(5,087,151)	–
Community development	2,994,389	–	–	2,580,000	(414,389)	–	(414,389)	–
Education (payment to school district)	21,893,273	–	–	–	(21,893,273)	–	(21,893,273)	–
Interest on long-term debt	6,068,121	–	–	–	(6,068,121)	–	(6,068,121)	–
Total governmental activities	105,807,013	15,720,525	5,176,310	4,894,915	(80,015,263)	–	(80,015,263)	–
Business-Type Activities:								
Water	3,595,733	4,159,350	–	1,159,909	–	1,723,526	1,723,526	–
Sewer	4,912,853	7,170,533	–	486,010	–	2,743,690	2,743,690	–
Parking facilities	2,796,283	1,344,087	–	–	–	(1,452,196)	(1,452,196)	–
Total business-type activities	11,304,869	12,673,970	–	1,645,919	–	3,015,020	3,015,020	–
Total Primary Government	$117,111,882	$28,394,495	$5,176,310	$6,540,834	$ (80,015,263)	$ 3,015,020	$ (77,000,243)	$ –
Component units								
Landfill	$ 3,382,157	$ 3,857,858	–	$ 11,397	–	–	–	$ 487,098
Public school system	31,186,498	705,765	3,937,083	–	–	–	–	(26,543,650)
Total component units	$ 34,568,655	$ 4,563,623	$3,937,083	$ 11,397	–	–	–	$(26,056,552)
	General Revenues:							
	Taxes:							
	Property taxes, levied for general purposes				$ 51,693,573	$ –	$ 51,693,573	$ –
	Property taxes, levied for debt service				4,726,244	–	4,726,244	–
	Franchise taxes				4,055,505	–	4,055,505	–
	Public service taxes				8,969,887	–	8,969,887	–
	Payment from Sample City				–	–	–	21,893,273
	Grants and contributions not restricted to specific programs				1,457,820	–	1,457,820	6,461,708
	Investment earnings				1,958,144	601,349	2,559,493	881,763
	Miscellaneous				884,907	104,925	989,832	22,464
	Special item—gain on sale of park land				2,653,488	–	2,653,488	–
	Transfers				501,409	(501,409)	–	–
	Total General Revenues, Special Items, And Transfers				76,900,977	204,865	77,105,842	29,259,208
	Change in net position				(3,114,286)	3,219,885	105,599	3,202,656
	Net position—beginning				126,673,160	82,376,829	209,033,689	16,025,971
	Net position—ending				**$123,558,874**	**$85,596,714**	**$209,139,288**	**$ 19,228,627**

Sample City
Balance Sheet (GASB 54 Classifications) Governmental Funds
December 31, 20X1

Assets	General	HUD Programs	Community Redevelopment	Route 7 Construction	Other Governmental Funds	Total Governmental Funds
Cash and cash equivalents	$3,418,485	$1,236,523	$ –	$ –	$ 5,606,792	$ 10,261,800
Investments	–	–	13,262,695	10,467,037	3,485,252	27,214,984
Receivables, net	3,644,561	2,953,438	353,340	11,000	10,221	6,972,560
Due from other funds	1,370,757	–	–	–	–	1,370,757
Receivables from other governments	–	119,059	–	–	1,596,038	1,715,097
Liens receivable	791,926	3,195,745	–	–	–	3,987,671
Inventories	182,821	–	–	–	–	182,821
Total assets	$9,408,550	$7,504,765	$13,616,035	$10,478,037	$10,698,303	$ 51,705,690
Deferred Outflow						
Deferred loss on sale and leaseback of building						
Grant expenditures paid in advance of meeting timing requirements						
Liabilities and Fund Balances						
Liabilities						
Accounts payable	$3,408,680	$ 129,975	$ 190,548	$ 1,104,632	$ 1,074,831	$ 5,908,666
Due to other funds	–	25,369	–	–	–	25,369
Payable to other governments	94,074	–	–	–	–	94,074
Deferred revenue	4,250,430	6,273,045	250,000	11,000	–	10,784,475
Total liabilities	$7,753,184	$6,428,389	$ 440,548	$ 1,115,632	$ 1,074,831	$ 16,812,584
Deferred Inflows						
Deferred gain on sale and leaseback of building						
Grant amounts paid in advance of meeting timing requirements						
Fund Balances						
Nonspendable	$ 974,747	$ –	$ –	$ –	$ –	974,747
Restricted			100,000			100,000
Committed	40,292	41,034	19,314	5,792,587	1,814,122	7,707,349
Assigned		1,035,342	13,056,173	3,569,818	7,809,350	25,470,683
Unassigned	640,327					640,327
Total fund balances	**$1,655,366**	**$1,076,376**	**$13,175,487**	**$ 9,362,405**	**$ 9,623,472**	**$ 34,893,106**

Amounts reported for governmental activities in the Statement of Net Position are different because:	
Capital assets used in governmental activities are not financial resources and therefore are not reported in the funds.	$161,082,708
Other long-term assets are not available to pay for current-period expenditures and therefore are deferred in the funds.	9,348,876
Internal service funds are used by management to charge the costs of certain activities, such as insurance and telecommunications, to individual funds. The assets and liabilities of the internal service funds are included in governmental activities in the Statement of Net Position.	2,994,691
Long-term liabilities, including bonds payable, are not due and payable in the current period and therefore are not reported in the funds.	(84,760,507)
Net Position of governmental activities	**$123,558,874**

Sample City
Statement of Revenues, Expenditures, and Changes in Fund Balances Governmental Funds
December 31, 20X1

Revenues	General	HUD Programs	Community Redevelopment	Route 7 Construction	Other Governmental Funds	Total Governmental Funds
Property taxes	$51,173,436	$ –	$ –	$ –	$ 4,680,192	$ 55,853,628
Franchise taxes	4,055,505	–	–	–	–	4,055,505
Public service taxes	8,969,887	–	–	–	–	8,969,887
Fees and fines	606,946	–	–	–	–	606,946
Licenses and permits	2,287,794	–	–	–	–	2,287,794
Intergovernmental	6,119,938	2,578,19	–	–	2,830,916	11,529,045
Charges for services	11,374,460	–	–	–	30,708	11,405,168
Investment earnings	552,325	87,106	549,489	270,161	364,330	1,823,411
Miscellaneous	881,874	66,176	–	2,939	94	951,083
Total assets	$86,022,165	$2,731,473	$13,616,035	$ 273,100	$10,698,303	$ 97,482,467
Expenditures Current						
General government	$ 8,630,835	$ –	$ 417,814	$ 16,700	$ 121,052	$ 9,186,401
Public safety	33,729,623	–	–	–	–	33,729,623
Public works	4,975,775	–	–	–	3,721,542	8,697,317
Engineering services	1,299,645	–	–	–	–	1,299,645
Health and sanitation	6,070,032	–	–	–	–	6,070,032
Cemetery	706,305	–	–	–	–	706,305
Culture and recreation	11,411,685	–	–	–	–	11,411,685
Community development		2,954,389	–	–	–	2,954,389
Education—payment to school district	21,893,273	–	–	–	–	21,893,273
Debt Service						
Principal	$ –	$ –	$ –	$ –	$ 3,450,000	$ 3,450,000
Interest and other charges	–	–	–	–	5,215,151	5,215,151
Capital Outlay	–	–	2,246,671	11,281,769	3,190,209	16,718,649
Total expenditures	**88,717,173**	**2,954,389**	**2,664,485**	**11,298,469**	**15,697,954**	**121,332,470**
Excess (deficiency) of revenues over expenditures	$ (2,695,008)	$ (222,916)	$ (2,114,996)	$(11,298,469)	$ (7,791,714)	$(23,850,003)
Other Financing Sources (Uses)						
Proceeds of refunding *bonds*	$ –	$ –	$ –	$ –	$38,045,000	$ 38,045,000
Proceeds of long-term capital-related debt	–	–	–	–	1,300,000	18,829,560
Payment to bond refunding escrow agent	–	–	–	–	(37,284,144)	(37,284,144)
Transfers in	129,323	–	–	–	5,551,187	5,680,510
Transfers out	(2,163,759)	(348,046)	(2,273,187)	–	(219,076)	(5,004,068)
Total other financing sources and uses	$ (2,034,436)	$ (348,046)	$25,256,373	$ –	$ 7,392,967	$ 20,266,858
Special Item						
Proceeds from sale of park land	3,476,488	–	–	–	–	3,476,488
Net change in fund balances	(1,252,956)	(570,962)	13,141,377	(11,025,369)	(398,747)	(106,657)
Fund balances—beginning	2,908,322	1,647,338	34,110	20,387,774	10,022,219	34,999,763
Fund balances—ending	$ 1,655,366	$1,076,376	$13,175,487	$ 9,362,405	$ 9,623,472	$ 34,893,106

Sample City
Statement of Net Position Proprietary Funds
December 31, 20X1

	Business-Type Activities—Enterprise Funds			
	Water and Sewer	**Parking Facilities**	**Total**	**Governmental Activities—Internal Service Fund**
Assets				
Current assets:				
Cash and cash equivalents	$ 8,416,653	$ 369,168	$ 8,785,821	$ 3,336,099
Investments	–	–	–	150,237
Receivables, net	3,564,586	3,535	3,568,121	157,804
Due from other governments	41,494	–	41,494	–
Inventories	126,674	–	126,674	139,328
Total current assets	12,149,407	372,703	12,522,110	3,783,468
Noncurrent assets:				
Restricted cash and cash equivalents	–	1,493,322	1,493,322	–
Capital assets:				
Land	813,513	3,021,637	3,835,150	–
Distribution and collection systems	39,504,183	–	39,504,183	–
Buildings and equipment	106,135,666	23,029,166	129,164,832	$14,721,786
Less accumulated depreciation	(15,328,911)	(5,786,503)	(21,115,414)	(5,781,734)
Total noncurrent assets	131,124,451	21,757,622	152,882,073	8,940,052
Total assets	$143,273,858	$22,130,325	$165,404,183	$12,723,520
Deferred Outflows				
Payment to receive rights to future parking Revenue				
Liabilities				
Current liabilities:				
Accounts payable	$ 447,427	$ 304,003	$ 751,430	$ 780,570
Due to other funds	175,000	–	175,000	1,170,388
Compensated absences	112,850	8,827	121,677	237,690
Claims and judgments	–	–	–	1,687,975
Bonds, notes, and loans payable	3,944,609	360,000	4,304,609	249,306
Total current liabilities	4,679,886	672,830	5,352,716	4,125,929
Noncurrent liabilities:				
Compensated absences	451,399	35,306	486,705	-
Claims and judgments	–	–	–	5,602,900
Bonds, notes, and loans payable	54,451,549	19,544,019	73,995,568	–
Total noncurrent liabilities	54,902,948	19,579,325	74,482,273	5,602,900
Total liabilities	$ 59,582,834	$20,252,155	$ 79,834,989	$ 9,728,829
Deferred Inflows				
Net Position				
Net investment in capital assets	$ 72,728,293	$ 360,281	$ 73,088,574	$ 8,690,746
Restricted for debt service	–	1,451,996	1,451,996	–
Unrestricted	10,962,731	65,893	11,028,624	(5,696,055)
Total net position	$ 83,691,024	$ 1,878,170	$ 85,569,194	$ 2,994,691

Sample City
Statement of Revenues, Expenses, and Changes In Fund Net Position Proprietary Funds
For the Year Ended December 31, 20X1

	Business-Type Activities—Enterprise Funds			
	Water and Sewer	**Parking Facilities**	**Total**	**Governmental Activities—Internal Service Fund**
Operating Revenues				
Charges for service	$11,329,883	$1,340,261	$12,670,144	$15,256,164
Miscellaneous	–	3,826	3,826	1,066,761
Total operating revenues	11,329,883	1,344,087	12,673,970	16,322,925
Operating Expenses				
Personal services	3,400,559	762,348	4,162,907	4,157,156
Contractual services	344,422	96,032	440,454	584,396
Utilities	754,107	100,726	854,833	214,812
Repairs and maintenance	747,315	64,617	811,932	1,960,490
Other supplies and expenses	498,213	17,119	515,332	234,445
Insurance claims and expenses	–	–	–	8,004,286
Depreciation	1,163,140	542,049	1,705,189	1,707,872
Total operating expenses	6,907,756	1,582,891	8,490,647	16,863,457
Operating income (loss)	4,422,127	(238,804)	4,183,323	(540,532)
Nonoperating Revenues (Expenses)				
Interest and investment revenue	454,793	146,556	601,349	134,733
Gain on disposal of capital assets	–	104,925	104,925	20,855
Interest expense	(1,600,830)	(1,166,546)	(2,767,376)	(41,616)
Miscellaneous expense	–	(46,846)	(46,846)	(176,003)
Total nonoperating revenues (expenses)	(1,146,037)	(961,911)	(2,107,948)	(62,031)
Income (loss) before contributions and transfers	3,276,090	(1,200,715)	2,075,375	(602,563)
Capital contributions	1,645,919	–	1,645,919	18,788
Transfers out	(290,000)	(211,409)	(501,409)	(175,033)
Change in net position	4,632,009	(1,412,124)	3,219,885	(758,808)
Total net position—beginning	79,059,015	3,290,294	82,349,309	3,753,499
Total net position—ending	**$83,691,024**	**$1,878,170**	**$85,569,194**	**$ 2,994,691**

Sample City
Statement of Cash Flows Proprietary Funds
For the Year Ended December 31, 20X1

	Business-Type Activities—Enterprise Funds			
	Water and Sewer	**Parking Facilities**	**Total**	**Governmental Activities—Internal Service Fund**
Cash Flows from Operating Activities				
Receipts from customers	$11,400,200	$1,345,292	$12,745,492	$15,326,343
Payments to suppliers	(2,725,349)	(365,137)	(3,090,486)	(2,812,238)
Payments to employees	(3,360,055)	(750,828)	(4,110,883)	(4,209,688)
Internal activity—payments to other funds	(1,296,768)	–	(1,296,768)	–
Claims paid	–	–	–	(8,482,451)
Other receipts (payments)	(2,325,483)	–	(2,325,483)	1,061,118
Net cash provided by operating activities	1,692,545	229,327	1,921,872	883,084
Cash Flows from Noncapital Financing Activities				
Operating subsidies and transfers to other funds	290,000)	(211,409)	(501,409)	(175,033)
Cash Flows from Capital and Related Financing Activities				
Proceeds from capital debt	4,041,322	8,660,778	12,702,100	–
Capital contributions	1,645,919	–	1,645,919	–
Purchases of capital assets	(4,194,035)	(144,716)	(4,338,751)	(400,086)
Principal paid on capital debt	(2,178,491)	(8,895,000)	(11,073,491)	(954,137)
Interest paid on capital debt	(1,479,708)	(1,166,546)	(2,646,254)	41,616
Other receipts (payments)	–	19,174	19,174	131,416
Net cash (used) by capital and related financing activities	(2,164,993)	(1,526,310)	(3,691,303)	(1,264,423)
Cash Flows from Investing Activities				
Proceeds from sales and maturities of investments	–	–	–	15,684
Interest and dividends	454,793	143,747	598,540	129,550
Net cash provided by investing activities	454,793	143,747	598,540	145,234
Net (decrease) in cash and cash equivalents	(307,655)	(1,364,645)	(1,672,300)	(411,138)
Balances—beginning of the year	8,724,308	3,227,135	11,951,443	3,747,237
Balances—end of the year	**$ 8,416,653**	**$1,862,490**	**$10,279,143**	**$ 3,336,099**
Reconciliation of Operating Income (Loss) to Net Cash Provided (Used) by Operating Activities				
Operating income (loss)	$ 4,422,127	$ (238,804)	$ 4,183,323	$ (540,532)
Adjustments to reconcile operating income to net cash provided (used) by operating activities:				
Depreciation expense	1,163,140	542,049	1,705,189	1,707,872
Change in assets and liabilities:				
Receivables, net	653,264	1,205	654,469	31,941
Inventories	2,829	–	2,829	39,790
Accounts and other payables	(297,446)	(86,643)	(384,089)	475,212
Accrued expenses	(4,251,369)	(11,520)	(4,239,849)	(831,199)
Net cash provided by operating activities	$ 1,692,545	$ 1229,327	$ 1,921,872	$ 883,084

Sample City
Statement of Fiduciary Net Position Fiduciary Funds
December 31, 20x1

	Employee Retirement Plan	Private-Purpose Trusts	Custodial Funds
Assets			
Cash and cash equivalents	$ 1,973	$ 1,250	$ 44,889
Receivables:			
Interest and dividends	508,475	760	–
Other receivables	6,826	–	183,161
Total receivables	515,301	760	183,161
Investments, at fair value:			
U.S. government obligations	13,056,037	80,000	–
Municipal bonds	6,528,019	–	–
Corporate bonds	16,320,047	–	–
Corporate stocks	26,112,075	–	–
Other investments	3,264,009	–	–
Total investments	65,280,187	80,000	–
Total assets	65,797,461	82,010	$228,050
Liabilities			
Accounts payable	–	1,234	–
Refunds payable and others	1,358	–	228,050
Total liabilities	1,358	1,234	$228,050
Net Position			
Held in trust for pension benefits and other purposes	$65,796,103	$80,776	

Sample City
Statement of Changes in Fiduciary Net Position Fiduciary Funds
For the Year Ended December 31, 20X1

	Employee Retirement Plan	Private-Purpose Trusts
Additions		
Contributions		
Employer	$ 2,721,341	$ –
Plan members	1,421,233	–
Total contributions	4,142,574	–
Investment earnings:		
Net (decrease) in fair value of investments	(272,522)	–
Interest	2,460,871	4,560
Dividends	1,445,273	–
Total investment earnings	3,633,622	4,560
Less investment expense	216,428	–
Net investment earnings	3,417,194	4,560
Total additions	7,559,768	4,560
Deductions		
Benefits	2,453,047	3,800
Refunds of contributions	464,691	–
Administrative expenses	87,532	678
Total deductions	3,005,270	4,478
Change in net position	4,554,498	82
Net position—beginning of the year	61,241,605	80,694
Net position—end of the year	$65,796,103	$80,776

Sample City
Statement of Revenues, Expenditures, and Changes In Fund Balances—Budget and Actual (BCS) General Fund
For the Year Ended December 31, 20X1

	Budgeted Amounts		Actual Amounts (Budgetary Basis)
	Original	Final	
Revenues			
Property taxes	$52,017,833	$51,853,018	$51,173,436
Other taxes—franchise and public service	12,841,209	12,836,024	13,025,392
Fees and fines	718,800	718,800	606,946
Licenses and permits	2,126,600	2,126,600	2,287,794
Intergovernmental	6,905,898	6,571,360	6,119,938
Charges for services	12,392,972	11,202,150	11,374,460
Interest	1,501,945	550,000	552,325
Miscellaneous	3,024,292	1,220,991	881,874
Total revenues	91,043,549	87,078,943	86,022,165
Expenditures			
Current			
General government (including contingencies and miscellaneous)	11,837,534	9,468,155	8,621,500
Public safety	33,050,966	33,983,706	33,799,709
Public works	5,215,630	5,025,848	4,993,187
Engineering services	1,296,275	1,296,990	1,296,990
Health and sanitation	5,756,250	6,174,653	6,174,653
Cemetery	724,500	724,500	706,305
Culture and recreation	11,059,140	11,368,070	11,289,146
Education—payment to school district	22,000,000	22,000,000	21,893,273
Total expenditures	90,940,295	90,041,922	88,774,763
Excess (deficiency) of revenues over expenditures	103,254	(2,962,979)	(2,752,598)
Other Financing Sources (Uses)			
Transfers in	939,525	130,000	129,323
Transfers out	(2,970,256)	(2,163,759)	(2,163,759)
Total other financing sources and uses	(2,030,731)	(2,030,759)	(2,034,436)
Special Item			
Proceeds from sale of park land	1,355,250	3,500,000	3,476,488
Net change in fund balance	(572,227)	(1,496,738)	(1,310,546)
Fund balances—beginning	3,528,750	2,742,799	2,742,799
Fund balances—ending	**$ 2,956,523**	**$ 1,246,061**	**$1,432,253**